INVENTING THE NATION

General Editor: Keith Robbins

Already published in the Inventing the Nation series:

India and Pakistan	Ian Talbot
Russia	Vera Tolz
Italy	Nick Doumanis
China	Henrietta Harrison
Ireland	R. V. Comerford
Germany	Stefan Berger

Titles in preparation include:

France	Tim Baycroft
The United States of America	Richard Carwardine

Germany

Stefan Berger
Professor of Modern and Contemporary History,
University of Glamorgan, UK

A member of the Hodder Headline Group
LONDON
Distributed in the United States of America by
Oxford University Press Inc., New York

First published in Great Britain in 2004 by
Hodder Arnold, a member of the Hodder Headline Group,
338 Euston Road, London NW1 3BH

http://www.arnoldpublishers.com

Distributed in the United States of America by
Oxford University Press Inc.
198 Madison Avenue, New York, NY10016

British Library Cataloguing in Publication Data
A catalogue record for this book is available from the British Library

Library of Congress Cataloging-in-Publication Data
A catalog record for this book is available from the Library of Congress

ISBN 0 340 70585 X (hb)
ISBN 0 340 70584 1 (pb)

1 2 3 4 5 6 7 8 9 10

Typeset in 10pt Sabon by Charon Tec Pvt. Ltd, Chennai, India
Printed and bound in Great Britain by The Bath Press, Bath

For Jutta, Kristina and Vanessa

Contents

List of maps

List of illustrations

General editor's preface

The contemporary world is both repelled and attracted by the existence of the nation. Talk of globalization sometimes presumes that the nation will fade away as organizations and individuals build for themselves new networks which by-pass the commonalities and loyalties expressed in the idea of the nation. Nationalism, too, whenever it is that various writers have supposed it to have 'risen', has been held to have been an unmitigated disaster, at least when it has been accompanied, as it not infrequently has been, by virulent xenophobia and intolerance. In the twentieth century there were significant attempts to restrain or circumvent the influence of nationalism by creating international or supranational structures and agencies.

On the other hand, it is apparent that the nation has not in fact faded away and, despite the surge of new nations, or at least new states, in the second half of that century, there remain across the contemporary world communities which feel themselves to be nations, or are in the process of becoming nations, and who see in the attainment of statehood a legitimate, desirable and beneficial goal. In other contexts, too, old nations reaffirm themselves as necessary carriers of individuality and distinctiveness in a world threatened by homogeneity. It is asserted that the nation remains the essential building block in the structure of the contemporary world. Nationalism need not be vicious. Nations can and do speak peace unto nations.

It becomes clear, however, reading references of 'narrow nationalism' on the one hand or 'national liberation' on the other, that how particular nations come to exist or be defined remains obscure and contentious. This series revisits these issues in the light of extensive debates about national identity which have been conducted over recent decades by historians, anthropologists, political scientists and sociologists in particular. To speak of 'Inventing the Nation' picks up one of the interpretations which has gained favour, or at least excited interest. Influential writers have seen 'invention' taking place in Europe in the 'springtime of the nations' at the dawn of 'modern' history, though their explanations have varied. Others, however, have regarded 'invention' with some suspicion and identify a medieval if not primordial 'nation'. Problems of definition and location clearly abound.

In such a context, a volume on Germany presents particular challenges and difficulties. Stefan Berger is not one to avoid them. He presents his own interpretation with vigour and conviction. He is fully aware that he cannot simply write a simple narrative which traces, in linear fashion, following some preordained path, the emergence of the Federal Republic of the twenty-first century from the jumble of units which constituted the 'Germany' of the early nineteenth century. The concept of 'the German nation' brings with it, in full, the complexities of definition which have already been alluded to. Both its constitutional embodiments and its territorial limits have clearly been problematical and require special attention and explanation. 'Blood and iron', of course, is not absent from the story. Germany as the 'home of the Reformation' has brought additional division. The geographical position, size and power, or potential power of 'Germany' has inevitably meant that its national evolution and the ideologies that have, at times, underpinned the making of a German nation are of central importance in understanding the course of European history over the last two centuries.

Keith Robbins
University of Wales, Lampeter

Acknowledgements

A nation is a group of people united by a common mistake about their ancestry and a common dislike of their neighbours. As we shall see in this volume there is more than a kernel of truth in this witticism. Dislikes of neighbours and those deemed national 'others' have frequently been murderous. In the first half of the twentieth century inventions of Germany have arguably been far more murderous than the inventions of other nations in Europe. Hence the German case underlines, above all, the dangers involved in the propagation of nationalism. Eric Hobsbawm, in a speech marking his acceptance of the Prize for European Understanding in Leipzig in 1999, has provided a clarion call to his fellow historians to be a 'danger to national myths' and work against the grain of nationalist propaganda which is still seeking to set nations against each other.[1] In writing this book I hope to have played a very small part in the process of exploding nationalist myths and demonstrating the sometimes extremely brutal and gruesome consequences of those myths when they come to dominate identity politics.

In the process of thinking about and writing this book I have, as usual, amassed a debt of gratitude to many individuals and institutions. They are too numerous to be listed all. But I would like to mention in particular Peter Alter, John Breuilly, Chris Clark, Christoph Conrad, Jörg Echternkamp, Geoff Eley, Richard Evans, Robert Evans, Heiko Feldner, Hugo Frey, Karen Hagemann, Mark Hewittson, Henning Hoff, Miroslav Hroch, David Jackson, Peter Lambert, Jie-Hyun Lim, Chris Lorenz, Jörn Leonhard, Guy Marchal, Damian Mac Con Uladh, Jan Palmowski, Kevin Passmore, Matthew Stibbe, Benedikt Stuchtey, Klaus Tenfelde, Maiken Umbach, Eric Weitz, Thomas Welskopp and Oliver Zimmer, who have, at various occasions, discussed the topics of nationalism and national identity with me over the past years. Chris Clark, Karen Hagemann and Paul Holtom also helped with the illustrations for which I am very grateful. The series editor, Keith Robbins, has read the entire manuscript with great attention to detail and has made a number of very helpful suggestions. I also wish to thank my colleagues at Glamorgan who continue to provide an

[1] Eric Hobsbawm, 'Eine Gefahr für nationale Mythen sein', *Frankfurter Rundschau*, Easter 1999.

intellectually stimulating and friendly atmosphere. It is great to work in a history department which is free of the strife and petty arguments which often make life in academia so uncomfortable. The students who have been taking my comparative courses on national identities in Britain and Germany over the years will recognise many of the arguments contained in this book. Thanks to them for listening, engaging with the issues and discussing national identity issues with me. Finally, I would like to thank Christopher Wheeler, Michael Strang and Tiara Misquitta at Hodder Arnold for their patience and their help with preparing the manuscript. My greatest debt is, as always, to Jutta, Kristina and Vanessa and this book is, once again, dedicated to them.

Introduction: Constructing Germany

At the beginning there was no Germany. At the beginning? What is the beginning? Most national histories of Germany still start in the Middle Ages. Many chose the crowning of the Saxon duke, Heinrich I, in 919 as starting point for a German national history. For others the division of the Franconian empire of Charlemagne under his successors served as a convenient opening. As Chlovis and Western Franconia symbolized the origins of modern-day France, thus Otto and Eastern Franconia have been declared the birth of modern Germany. Myths of origins have been of crucial importance for the construction of national narratives all over Europe.[1] But such search for origins is deeply problematical. During the Middle Ages it was, after all, only a tiny elite of learned clerics and noblemen who occasionally talked about 'nation'. When this discourse began to influence a broader stream of people between 1750 and 1850, those who thought about Germany were confronted with one major problem: they could trace the German nation back in history, but they did not have a strong German state. Germany was not a stateless nation, like many of those which were part of the multinational states and empires that dominated Europe before 1914. Britain and Spain in the West were multinational as were the Ottoman, Habsburg and Romanov empires in central and eastern Europe. The so-called Holy Roman Empire of the German Nation was a motley collection of hundreds of largely autonomous dukedoms, principalities, free cities and clerical fiefdoms which lacked any strong central authority. It incorporated many territories where the majority of people did not speak a German dialect. And yet the Empire, from the late fifteenth century onwards, was a kind of weak German proto-state.[2]

1 Stefan Berger, Mark Donovan and Kevin Passmore, eds, *Writing National Histories: Western Europe since 1800* (London, 1999). I am currently directing a five-year European Science Foundation project (2003–8) on the theme of 'Representations of the Past: The Writing of National Histories in Europe' which is exploring the construction of European national histories in comparative perspective. For details see www.uni-leipzig.de/zhs/esf-nhist.

2 G. Schmidt, *Geschichte des Alten Reiches: Staat und Nation in der frühen Neuzeit 1495–1806* (Munich, 1999). For a good introduction in English to the history of the Holy Roman Empire see P. H. Wilson, *The Holy Roman Empire 1495–1806* (London, 1999).

The absence of a clearly defined geographical territory for the German nation up until 1871 was not problematic for the majority of the people inhabiting what was most often referred to as 'the German lands'. Many who lived in the Holy Roman Empire of the German Nation were entirely happy with a system that engendered a great deal of loyalty. When it was removed from the map of Europe in 1806 it left many people feeling rather mournful. Only its nationalist opponents rejoiced. They wanted to give the German nation firmer contours as a state. Their nationalism was focussed on improving the existing state structures or replacing them with something altogether different. Many wanted to make, first the Holy Roman Empire, and later, the German Confederation, into a more unified state. They had ridiculed the Empire as an abnormality and bemoaned the absence of state-building processes in medieval and early modern times. They compared the developments in the Holy Roman Empire with developments in Britain or in France, where a succession of strong monarchs had initiated successful state-building nationalisms. In the nineteenth century a 'greater-German' (*großdeutsch*) solution to the German question stood diametrically opposed to a 'small-German' (*kleindeutsch*) solution. The former incorporated the German-speaking parts of the Habsburg Empire; the latter excluded them and envisaged a Germany under Prussian leadership. In the so-called 'third Germany', the territories outside Prussia and the Habsburg Empire, plans for a German nation state which sought to evade Prussian dominance were popular. These territories often sought to maintain as much of their autonomy as possible under whichever shape the German nation was ultimately going to take. In many respects the very vagueness of territorial definitions of Germany throughout much of the modern period was itself a defining characteristic of 'Germanness'. Strong federal traditions characterized the German nation-building process right from the start.[3] That the small-Germans ultimately won the day in 1871 was by no means a foregone conclusion, as we shall see in Chapters 1 and 2.

Much of this book will nevertheless focus on the 'small Germany' that came into being in 1871 and underwent crucial transformations in 1918, 1938–40, 1949 and 1989. This in itself is a strong indication of how much the contemporary understanding of Germany is taking its cue, for better or worse, from the Bismarckian creation. We will have to take note of developments in Austria–Hungary, because its German-speaking territories were regarded as an integral part of the German cultural nation (*Kulturnation*) well into the twentieth century. A separate Austrian national consciousness only developed fully after 1945.

It was precisely the absence of firm geographical definitions of the nation which gave rise to a strong inclination among German nationalists to define Germany in cultural and linguistic terms. German was a language spoken in many areas of central Europe. It would perhaps be more accurate to speak of German languages, as German grammarians only came to agree on the basic rules of German usage in the course of the eighteenth and nineteenth centuries. The unification of the German language was a long-drawn-out process. It was by no means complete even at the time of the creation of the German Empire in 1871. Yet, for the most part, those speaking and writing in a German language

[3] Maiken Umbach, ed., *German Federalism: Past, Present, Future* (London, 2002).

could (sometimes with difficulty) understand each other. They did not have to learn a foreign language. A variety of cultural texts were produced in a language recognizable as German.

The celebrated national poets of Germany, Friedrich Schiller and Johann Wolfgang von Goethe wrote in the 1790s: 'Germans – you hope in vain to become a nation. Therefore, you can do it, educate yourselves to become a freer people!'[4] Goethe and Schiller were doubtful about a state-building process propagated by some intellectuals and opinion-formers in the early nineteenth century. They called on their countrymen to accept the absence of a nation state and instead to concentrate on culture and what, in German, has come to mean *Bildung* – a term almost impossible to translate into English.[5] National identity, then, meant many things to many people in the early nineteenth century. It meant little to the overwhelming majority of people living in the German lands and was propagated as a key focus for identity only by a small minority.[6]

Germany was, in other words, under construction. Traditional national narratives tend to hide the constructed nature of national identity. The national story has been portrayed as the organic evolution from a 'natural' sense of togetherness. Within the last two decades, however, a range of historians and social scientists have successfully challenged such naturalization of national identity discourses.[7] From Eric Hobsbawm's and Terence Ranger's *Invention of Tradition* collection to Benedict Anderson's hugely influential *Imagined Communities* and Homi Bhaba's *Nation and Narration*, those writing on national identity today are increasingly starting from the assumption that national identities are 'inventions'.[8] The overarching title for the current series puts itself squarely in this tradition. The term 'invention', however, might well be misleading. While there are no objective factors, such as ethnicity, religion, culture or geography which will explain the success or failure of nation-building processes, we can point to a number of elements which facilitate such processes. Rarely was something imagined from nothing. Imagination and invention is part of the story, but often nation-building is easier where the imagination can build on material remnants of the past. It has already been mentioned, for example, how important it is to give historical depth to claims of being a nation.

4 Friedrich Schiller and Johann Wolfgang von Goethe, *Xenien*, cited in Hans-J. Weitz, ed., *Goethe über die Deutschen* (Frankfurt/Main, 1978), p. 17.

5 'Perfection of the human character through the process of continuous (self-)education' would be a very imperfect and clumsy shorthand for describing a highly complex phenomenon. For a good introduction to the German idea of *Bildung* see Aleida Assmann, *Arbeit am nationalen Gedächtnis: Eine kurze Geschichte der deutschen Bildungsidee* (Frankfurt/Main, 1993).

6 The identity discourse itself was not yet 'invented'. As Lutz Niethammer has shown, it was very much a twentieth-century concept. Furthermore he compellingly shows that 'identity' has dubious value as an analytical concept. See Lutz Niethammer, *Kollektive Identität: Heimliche Quellen einer unheimlichen Konjunktur* (Reinbek, 2000).

7 For a good brief introduction to the historiography and the debates surrounding national identity see Anthony D. Smith, *The Nation in History: Historiographical Debates about Ethnicity and Nationalism* (Cambridge, 2000).

8 Eric Hobsbawm and Terence Ranger, eds, *The Invention of Tradition* (Cambridge, 1983); Benedict Anderson, *Imagined Communities: Reflections on the Origins and Spread of Nationalism* (London, 1991); Homi Bhaba, ed., *Nation and Narration* (London, 1990).

Finding historical antecedents and myths of origin has been a favourite pastime for nation-builders. Shared customs and memories also play an influential role in nation-building, as do notions of a common language and culture, of 'natural' geographical borders and of integrated economic and social systems.

Nations, however, do not display inert characteristics. Unchanging attributes and qualities are not rooted in the biological make-up of a people. Orderliness, cleanliness, resilience and efficiency are not permanent features of an unchanging national character of the Germans. Rather they are culturally produced ways of thinking about and performing the nation. The intellectual discourses and the accompanying social actions have always been highly contested. They can be understood as forever changing socio-cultural constructions of community and commonality. Those constructions and the accompanying apparent desire to feel national are, what is more, relatively recent mass phenomena. Some nationalists have thought of nations as always having existed. They might have been 'sleeping' and nationalists were, of course, forever ready to awaken the sleeping beauties of national identity, but the notion of an *a priori* national identity has been utterly rejected by theorists of national identity more recently.

Some medievalists have claimed that national identity debates have medieval origins.[9] They can point to the medieval *nationes* theories and the diverse myths of national origins which were around as early as the eleventh century. National stereotypes, xenophobia and the idea of the nation having external and internal enemies have all been traced back to medieval times. From the thirteenth century onwards national and linguistic borders were structuring universal Christian thoughts and ideas. Thus, for example, the popes called on the Christian *nationes*, and specifically on the *natio Germanica*, to fight the heathens in the Crusades. Later on the struggle against the Turks bolstered national discourses across Europe. Within medieval Europe references to the 'sacred territory' of the nation could justify territorial expansion.

The second half of the fifteenth century in particular witnessed a proliferation of written texts about the German nation. In early modern Europe a 'proto-nationalism'[10] emerged which developed the arsenal of medieval ideas about the nation, but the entire discourse still remained restricted to a tiny elite of educated people who communicated across the European continent – thanks largely to the invention of the printing press. In the eighteenth century, the age of the Enlightenment, national identity discourses spread as nation became a powerful tool to challenge the existing feudalism and dissolve the traditional social order.[11] But it was only in the second half of the nineteenth century that nationalism became the most important set of ideas for masses of Europeans. For about a century, between 1850 and 1950, the nation became the prime focus of loyalty for the majority of people. However, the ideas of the nation that were popularized

[9] For Germany see in particular Joachim Ehlers, *Die Entstehung des deutschen Reiches* (Munich, 1994). More generally Simon Forde, Lesley Johnson and Alan Murray, eds, *Concepts of National Identity in the Middle Ages* (Leeds, 1995).

[10] Herfried Münkler, 'Nation als politische Idee im frühneuzeitlichen Europa', in K. Garber, *Nation und Literatur im Europa der frühen Neuzeit* (Tübingen, 1989), pp. 56–86.

[11] Ernest Gellner, *Nations and Nationalism* (Oxford, 1983).

in the nineteenth century had often already been around for a very long time. National identity was not a *deus ex machina*, suddenly appearing from nowhere to occupy collective dispositions. This is why, in Chapter 1, we need to look back in time at some ideas of the German nation which preceded their employment by nineteenth-century nationalists.

By the second half of the eighteenth century, the emerging middle classes often felt excluded and alienated from the structures and moral values of feudalism. As traditional social structures melted away under the impact of industrialization and the emergence of capitalist social relations, the idea of the nation was central to the efforts of an elite group of middle-class opinion-leaders to think and perform a different social and political order. Apart from paying close attention to intellectual debates about the nation, this book will also discuss popular expressions of national identity. The success of this elite project of nationalism can, after all, only be measured in the repercussions these ideas had at the level of social, cultural and political action.[12]

With secularization religion did not lose its central role in popular identity creation, but nationalism became a powerful rival which took on religious connotations.[13] Images of a chosen people, a holy land and a historical mission as well as the idea of the nation as a brotherly community were all directly related to images familiar to anyone who knew the Bible. The religion of nationalism frequently integrated religion into its world-view and claimed a particular relationship between nation and religion. Thus, as we shall see below, in the northern, Protestant, parts of Germany Protestantism and nationalism often entered a symbiotic relationship. It would, however, be too easy to say that religion was relegated to second place and that nationalism took the place of religion. Identities, and this is another important point to keep in mind in all our discussions below, are flexible and situational. They depend on contexts. Religion and a range of other identities, for that matter, retained their fundamental importance and might have been more meaningful than nationalism for many people in specific contexts. What cannot be denied, however, is the phenomenal rise of nationalism as a mass ideology and a key focus for identity in the nineteenth century.

When we say that nationalism arose because it helped to dissolve the glue holding together traditional feudal societies, we are already alluding to another important point: nationalism never existed without a purpose. Hence, with any discussion of national identity it will be crucial to ask: what were national identities supposed to do? What was their function? National identity has been constructed to serve and to empower specific interests. And access to power, in turn, has frequently been crucial in ensuring the success or failure of particular constructions of national identity. As John Breuilly reminds us, nationalism has been primarily about gaining and retaining state power.[14] As an ideology, it has been particularly appropriate for modern states. Nation-building often followed the creation of institutional power centres, notably states. But nationalism across east-central Europe

12 On the power of nationalism on the popular level see generally Michael Billig, *Banal Nationalism* (London, 1995).

13 Hans-Ulrich Wehler, *Nationalismus: Geschichte, Formen, Folgen* (Munich, 2001), pp. 27–35.

14 John Breuilly, *Nationalism and the State*, 2nd edn (Manchester, 1993), p. 2.

preceded the formation of nation states. Hence nationalism contributed to the formation of nations. The invention of Germany started in the midst of civil society and was often directed against existing state structures. Improved processes of communication facilitated the work of nationalists, who proved themselves increasingly capable of mobilizing masses behind their ideas.[15] Given the absence of a strong state, German nationalists sought to create institutional structures, such as national associations, parliaments and academies, which would ultimately bring about a more unified German state. However, after the formation of a unified central state in 1871 the making of Germans became the central objective of the state. State- and civil society-driven efforts to foster a sense of national cohesion mutually re-enforced each other. The educational system and the army became known as 'schools of the nation', in which the young citizens of the future learnt how to feel German. Citizenship was interlinked with national identity, and the unification of the law played a crucial role in the formation of the national community, as the law defines national belonging and the rights and duties of those who do belong.

The law, of course, also excluded those who did not belong. Notions of 'the other' have played a major role for constituting 'self' in all nation-building processes. That 'other' could be internal or external. Emphasis on the other did not necessarily mean rejection. It could also lead to admiration, emulation and adaptation. Over recent years cultural transfer studies have pointed out that national identity discourses have not been formed in isolation from each other.[16] Ideas flowed between nations and often took on a life of their own in different national contexts. In discussing inventions of the German nation we will have to be aware of national cultures being constructed on the basis of a dialectical process through which indigenous and foreign elements are selectively appropriated. National identity thus becomes a process of cultural appropriation and mediation. What has been imagined as 'one's own' is shown to be bound up with what has been conceived of as 'other'. Research on cultural transfers thus has contributed to exposing the conceptual absurdity of notions of homogenous national characters and of national cultures comprised of national essences.

The state's desire for a more homogeneous nation, however, often produced intolerance and penalized differences. Internal and external borders were strengthened and exclusionary practices implemented. Nationalism has, however, always been Janus-faced: it has promised participation and exclusion.[17] Certainly the state's hold over nationalism was never exclusive. Official state nationalism was always contested by a wide variety of alternative and often oppositional nationalisms. Different national symbols and texts could be presented

[15] Karl W. Deutsch, *Nationalism and Social Communication*, 2nd edn (Cambridge, Mass., 1966).

[16] See, for example, Michel Espagne and Michael Werner, eds, *Transferts: les relations interculturelles dans l'espace Franco-Allemand* (Paris, 1988); Rudolf Muhs, Johannes Paulmann and Willibald Steinmetz, eds, *Aneignung und Abwehr: Interkultureller Transfer zwischen Deutschland und Großbritannien im 19. Jahrhundert* (Bodenheim, 1998).

[17] Wolfgang Hardtwig, *Nationalismus und Bürgerkultur in Deutschland 1500–1914* (Göttingen, 1994), p. 12; Dieter Langewiesche, *Nation, Nationalismus, Nationalstaat in Deutschland und Europa* (Munich, 2000), pp. 192, 195. Still a good overview in English is Michael Hughes, *Nationalism and Society: Germany 1800–1945* (London, 1988).

or the same national symbols and texts could be read and interpreted differently. Overall, national identity has acquired a range of meanings in diverse social and cultural contexts.[18]

Highlighting the contested nature of national identity has thus been a crucial concern of this volume. It needs to be recognized that the invention of the nation cannot be written as one overarching story. The multitude of possible inventions needs to be recovered and we will seek to provide tentative answers to why some inventions proved more successful and enduring than others. Contestation always took place on the basis of multiple meanings. National identity may have always aimed at homogeneity, but its extraordinary power and durability has been closely related to its flexibility and adaptability. Its diverse ingredients could be mixed and re-mixed and appear in a variety of different guises and under different banners.

The emphasis here is on the plurality of contested national identities in the German lands and on how diverse national symbols and signs have been translated into social action and demands for power, usually legitimizing or delegitimizing existing political and social orders. We will, however, be also looking at socio-cultural processes of nation-building under specific political and economic contexts.[19] How has the German nation been ritualized, symbolized and medialized over the last centuries? How has the collective memory of the nation been shaped? Collective memory is an important part of all imagined communities and is being produced through rituals and the symbolic enactment of the past in narrative and non-narrative forms.[20] Pierre Nora has pointed out the curious way in which collective memories and their specific sites function: in different contexts each memory appears in a different guise of national meanings, but it remains linked to the original site of memory.[21] If we take, for example, the Napoleonic wars as a major European site of memory, we find that they produced a wide variety of memories which were activated and interpreted in diverse ways for different political, social and cultural groups at various points in time during the nineteenth and twentieth centuries. In other words, collective memory is kaleidoscopic: twist the prism only a little, and the pieces fall into place producing an entirely different pattern. Memory landscapes result from diverse and often conflictual cultural acts creating and performing the past on the basis of physical and mental traces of the national idea.[22]

Nation becomes a discursive field, an arena in which many players negotiate and struggle over the diverse meanings attached to national identities. These

18 Katherine Verdery, 'Whither "Nation" and "Nationalism"?', in Gopal Balakrishnan, ed., *Mapping the Nation* (London, 1996), p. 228.

19 I am following here John Breuilly, 'Nationalismus als kulturelle Konstruktion: einige Überlegungen', in Jörg Echternkamp and Sven Oliver Müller, eds, *Die Politik der Nation: Deutscher Nationalismus in Krieg und Krisen 1760–1960* (Munich, 2002), p. 252.

20 Maurice Halbwachs, *The Collective Memory* (New York, 1980); Jan Assmann, *Das kulturelle Gedächtnis: Schrift, Erinnerung und politische Identität in frühen Hochkulturen* (Munich, 1992); David F. Crew, 'Remembering German Pasts: Memory in German History 1871–1989', *Central European History*, 33 (2000), pp. 217–34; Alon Confino and Peter Fritzsche, eds, *Work of Memory: New Directions in the Study of German Society and Culture* (Urbana, 2002).

21 Pierre Nora, *Zwischen Geschichte und Gedächtnis* (Berlin, 1990), p. 28.

22 Rudy Koshar, *From Monuments to Traces: Artifacts of German Memory, 1870–1990* (Berkeley, 2000), p. 9.

negotiations often involve strong emotions. Hence the nation as an imagined community is also always an emotional community.[23] In nineteenth- and twentieth-century Germany the prism was turned frequently, resulting in many different contextualizations of collective memory.

The structure of the book closely follows the major political ruptures resulting in reconstructions of national identity discourses. The first chapter will take us to the aftermath of the 1806 dissolution of the Holy Roman Empire. It will, first, review the full arsenal of ideas about Germany from the Middle Ages to the eighteenth century and subsequently analyse in depth the impact of the French revolutionary wars and the struggle against Napoleon on the development of these ideas between the 1790s and the 1810s. Chapter 2 will trace the growth of the national movement in Germany from the 1810s to 1871. It will discuss how diverse social groups used nationalism as a vehicle to demand greater participation in the affairs of the state. It will also analyse the disappointments of German nationalists in 1848 and seek to explain the eventual victory of 'small-German' inventions of the nation. The third chapter will comment on nationalization processes in Imperial Germany between 1871 and 1914. It will focus in particular on the construction of national enemies and the continued conflict between very different ideas of national identity.

Chapter 4 will take our story from the eve of the First World War to the coming to power of the Nazis in 1933. The impact of the war on nation-building in Germany cannot be emphasized strongly enough, which is why the chapter discusses in detail the implications of wartime nationalism, defeat and revolution on the construction of diverse national identities by different political groupings in the Weimar Republic. The rise of the idea of an ethnicized *Volksnation* and *Volksgemeinschaft*, emerging from the trenches of the First World War, proved the most powerful reconfiguration of the national idea and paved the way for the Nazis.

In Chapter 5 we will look at the National Socialist construction of the nation between 1933 and 1945 and discuss the extensive racialization of the nation. Chapter 6 will then investigate the reconstruction of German identities in the Federal Republic of Germany (FRG), while Chapter 7 will examine the GDR. How did the two Germanies come to terms with the National Socialist past, and how did their perception of the 'other' Germany contribute to the shaping of their respective national identity discourses? We will also look in both cases at the importance of economic identities and reflect, for West Germany, on the gradual Westernization of the national discourse.

Finally the last chapter will ask how reunification in 1990 impacted on national identity debates. How successful has the quest for a 'normal' national identity been and how are the debates about the National Socialist and the Communist pasts continuing to influence national identities in Germany today?

In contrast to other books in this series, this volume does not have an annotated guide to further reading at the end of the volume. Instead, I decided to point to the most important relevant literature in the footnotes to the individual chapters.

[23] Etienne François, Hannes Siegrist and Jakob Vogel, eds, *Nation und Emotion: Deutschland und Frankreich im Vergleich; 19. und 20. Jahrhundert* (Göttingen, 1995).

Overall, six themes will be pursued throughout all eight chapters of the book. First, we will pay special attention to the struggles between civic and ethnic inventions of the nation. Germany has often been described as a classic case of ethnic nationalism.[24] Following Hans Kohn's influential book,[25] many scholars have argued that nationalism changed its meaning significantly when it travelled from West to East in the course of the nineteenth century. The Western idea of the nation was perceived as predominantly voluntarist, culturally inclusive and founded on liberal political principles. Eastern Europe, by contrast, was haunted by ethnic nationalisms, culturally exclusive and politically authoritarian. Germany, geographically situated in the centre of Europe, occupied a middling position. Most commentators, however, have emphasized that it was already tainted by the ethnic nationalist virus, defining national identity primarily in terms of blood, common traditions, language and religion rather than in terms of politics.

The whole distinction between civic and ethnic forms of national identity has recently been questioned by Oliver Zimmer, who has put forward compelling arguments to replace it with a distinction between 'mechanisms which social actors use as they reconstruct the boundaries of national identity at a particular point in time' and 'the symbolic resources upon which they draw when they reconstruct these boundaries'.[26] Such a process-oriented approach seems indeed much better suited to understanding the workings of national identity formation, and gets away from the neat delineation between a good liberal, cosmopolitan, civic and political nationalism and a bad antiliberal, xenophobic, ethnic and cultural nationalism. Throughout this book we will present much evidence to underline the falseness of the latter constructions.

The second theme will be an exploration of the strength of economic national identities throughout the modern period.[27] In the first half of the nineteenth century visitors to the German lands commented frequently on the provincialism and the rural idylls they encountered. Much of Germany was an industrial backwater. After 1850, however, the Prussian economy was the most successful and dynamic in Europe. Imperial Germany overtook Britain as first industrial nation in Europe on the eve of the First World War. The continuing strength of the German economy throughout the twentieth century left a deep mark on inventions of German national identity. From the debates surrounding 'made in Germany' at the end of the nineteenth century to 'Deutschmark nationalism' at the end of the twentieth century, the economy has often been central to constructions of Germany. Similarly a succession of economic crises, some of them disastrous in their consequences, shaped the self-understanding of Germany.

24 Stefan Berger, 'Ethnic Nationalism *par excellence*? Germany 1789–1914', in Timothy Baycroft and Mark Hewittson, eds, *National Identities in Nineteenth Century Europe* (Oxford, forthcoming).

25 Hans Kohn, *Nationalism: Its Meaning and History* (New York, 1955).

26 Oliver Zimmer, 'Boundary Mechanisms and Symbolic Resources: Towards a Process-Oriented Approach to National Identity', *Nations and Nationalism*, 9 (2003), pp. 173–93.

27 See the interesting analysis by Harold James, *A German Identity 1770–1990*, rev. edn (London, 1990), who has foregrounded what he believes has been 'an excessive focus on economics in national life' (p. 2).

The economic crisis after 1873 gave nationalist politics a much sharper edge in Imperial Germany. Hyperinflation and the collapse of the currency in 1923, as well as the economic slump after 1929 etched themselves into German collective memory to such a degree as to determine economic policy-making even at the beginning of the twenty-first century.

The third theme is that of exclusion from the nation. We will investigate the treatment of foreigners in Germany and analyse the perception of foreign lands in the construction of German national identity. Furthermore, we shall explore the making of 'internal enemies' of the nation, such as Catholics, Jews and Socialists and ask how these groups attempted to come to terms with their 'othering'. Religion, class and race are important non-spatial forms of identity which have entered diverse alliances with forms of national identity throughout the last three centuries. From the Reformation onwards Protestantism remained closely connected to nationalism. Assimilated German Jews in the nineteenth century often vigorously defended their belonging to the nation, but were faced, time and again, with an antisemitism keen to exclude them from the nation. To trace the interrelationships and the antagonisms between nation and other sources for collective identity will be an important task of this book.

Fourth, we will analyse the gendering of the German nation. Constructions of nation and gender were closely intertwined.[28] Nationalism all too often depended on a motley collection of mostly male fantasies. They included the idea of 'separate spheres' for women and men. Whereas women were supposed to occupy the 'private sphere' of the home, men imagined themselves masters over the public sphere. But nationalism could also be a vehicle for women to express their desire for greater participation in the public sphere. Even where women expressly endorsed the dominant separate spheres ideology, their activities proved that they were not in fact completely excluded from the public sphere. Hence, throughout this book, I have tried to ask how women contributed to the various inventions of Germany. The nation was often conceived of as a community of fathers and brothers, but, as more recent research has emphasized, sisters and mothers have been equally important. Women participated in diverse national movements, and nationalist discourses impacted on male and female gender identities. Ideas of the German family as the nucleus of the German nation have been widespread, and the gender order has been closely intertwined with national and imperial symbolism. The decline of bourgeois family values in the twentieth century has often brought in its wake anxieties about the decline of the nation.

Fifth, we will pay special attention to the strength of federal inventions of the nation in Germany. As James Sheehan has pointed out, it is deeply problematic to speak about one German nation state before 1871.[29] It is far more appropriate to refer to the German-speaking lands. The relatively late unification of Germany strengthened regional identities and encouraged state-building processes below the level of a German nation state. When German-speakers wanted to give expression

28 Tamar Mayer, ed., *Gender Ironies of Nationalism: Sexing the Nation* (London, 2000).

29 James Sheehan, 'What is German History? Reflections on the Role of the Nation in German History and Historiography', *Journal of Modern History*, 53 (1981), pp. 1–23.

to their feelings of local and regional belonging, they used the term *Heimat*.[30] The *Heimat* discourse could be opposed to the nation and encourage particularism, but it also often worked towards the nation. The nation in Germany was more often than not imagined through the regions and the localities.

Finally, no one looking at German history even perfunctorily will be able to deny the huge influence of wars on inventions of national identity. The Thirty Years' War in the seventeenth century, the Seven Years' War in the eighteenth century, the wars of liberty against Napoleon and the wars of unification in the nineteenth century, and, of course, the First and the Second World Wars in the twentieth century all encouraged a fundamental rethinking of categories of Germanness. Furthermore, a variety of civil wars and revolutions, from 1848 to 1918 and beyond to 1953 and 1989, deeply impacted on understanding and defining the German nation.

Inventing Germany, as this book will demonstrate, was never a straightforward or easy exercise in a country 'that remained constitutionally unstable, territorially unsettled, and socially fractured'.[31] Germany was, of course, also at the hub of the most horrific nightmare of the twentieth century – the systematic industrial murder of European Jewry. The Holocaust, as Norbert Elias observed, was the most powerful sign that something had gone fundamentally wrong with Germany. The civilizing process, he concluded, had not worked in Germany.[32] Many writers have sought to explain why this should have been the case. The National Socialist past in general and the Holocaust in particular are still hotly debated in today's Germany. Most Germans, including virtually the entire political and intellectual class, want to learn the lessons of this past and get away from the *incertitudes allemands* that have haunted Europe for much of the nineteenth and twentieth centuries. As we shall argue in the final chapter, there are good reasons to be optimistic about the future.

30 There is no exact English equivalent for this word, which means 'the place where one feels at home'. It is often but not necessarily synonymous with the place where one was born and grew up.

31 Konrad H. Jarausch and Michael Geyer, *Shattered Past: Reconstructing German Histories* (Princeton, 2003), p. 29.

32 Norbert Elias, *The Germans: Power Struggles and the Development of Habitus in the Nineteenth and Twentieth Centuries* (New York, 1996).

1

A movement of 'marginal men': the national idea until 1819

Location: Berlin, a banquet at the palace of Prince Hardenberg; time: around 1810. Everyone who is someone has an invitation. People come dressed in the latest French 'Beau Monde' fashion; many of them speak French. In their midst one finds a man who stands out a mile: Friedrich Ludwig Jahn wears an incredibly unfashionable beard and (unheard of) long hair; he has come in an attire which he calls 'German garb' (*altdeutsche Tracht*): it consists of a long loose black jacket (double row of buttons and wide collar), black barret and simple trousers of grey. His dirty shoes look as though he has deliberately stained them, so as to mark him out from his polished surroundings. Whoever dares to talk to him soon turns away with the feeling that Jahn is intent to demonstrate one thing and one thing only: that he has no manners whatsoever [Figure 1.1].

Jahn was clearly a crank; he was also a nationalist. Born in 1778, the son of a Lutheran minister, he had studied theology. An ardent Prussian nationalist to begin with, he switched his allegiance to Germany in the 1800s. He spent the years after Prussia's defeat by Napoleon in 1806 as an itinerant propagandist attempting to stir up German nationalism and anti-French feeling. In 1811 he founded the nationalist gymnastics movement (*Turnerschaft*), and in 1815 he encouraged the formation of the first nationalist student association (*Burschenschaft*). But his ideas and his actions were those of an outsider.

Now that twentieth-century history has demonstrated the incredible power of mass nationalism, it is as well to start our journey into the making and remaking of Germany with this vignette, showing how marginal a phenomenon nationalism was at the beginning of the nineteenth century. Nationalists were, in Elie Kedourie's memorable phrase, 'marginal men',[1] on the fringes of society, but they were also men (and women) with a mission. If there was very little nationalism of any kind in the German-speaking lands during the early nineteenth century, people had been talking about the nation for a very long time.

The first half of this chapter will trace ideas about the German nation back to medieval times – to the Holy Roman Empire, the humanist discourses around

[1] Elie Kedourie, *Nationalism* (London, 1960).

Figure 1.1 Friedrich Ludwig Jahn in German garb.

1500 and early modern concepts of national identity. An arsenal of specific notions about Germany was already in place at the time when the very idea of the nation was revolutionized in the late eighteenth century through events in North America and in France. The second half of this chapter will explore the impact of the period between the 1790s and the 1810s on German nationalism. The French revolutionary wars and the struggle against Napoleon witnessed a complex mixture of responses from within the diverse German territories. Nationalist discourses flourished during this period and the men and women with a mission made themselves famous (many at the time would have said infamous) – so much so that the authorities decided to crush the small national movement in 1819.

Speaking the nation: German nationhood from the Middle Ages to the eighteenth century

The origins of the word 'German' can be traced back to late Latin. In the eighth century 'theodiscus' referred to all the various dialects spoken by Germanic tribes in central and western Europe (including Old English). In the ninth century, also in connection with the language, the word 'teutonicus' can be found. German designated a vague linguistic community (members of which were not necessarily able to understand each other!) more than a specific territory or ethnic community. The few educated people in medieval Europe, mainly clerics and members of the nobility, wrote about nations, *nationes* in Latin, from about the eleventh century onwards. References to a *natio Germanica* could be found in connection with medieval universities, church councils, noble orders, trade associations and *Reich* parliaments, but overall there were few references to a German nation.

Those nobles and clerics who spoke a German dialect preferred to see themselves as belonging to the successor state of the Christian Carolingian empire. The Frankish-Carolingian tradition and the emperor became key elements in the self-understanding of medieval German nation-building.[2] But unlike in the West, where French nation-building successfully nationalized the Carolingian tradition, the East Frankish *Reich* did not undergo a similar nationalization process. For a long time the different tribes (*gens*) making up the empire avoided calling it 'German', as they continued to cling to strong national–ethnic identities of their own. Saxons, Bavarians, Thuringians, Franks, Alemannen, Slavs, Danes and Bohemians were all described as nations (*gentium nationes*), yet they all were part of the Holy Roman Empire. Was the Empire primarily Saxon or primarily Frankish? How much of a feeling of commonality was there between the different East Frankish tribes? And was that common identity, where it existed at all, not primarily based on the Empire rather than on any notion of a *regnum teutonicum*? German was arguably less a term of self-description in the Middle Ages than a term popularized by the popes, especially Pope Gregory VII, to restrict the universal claims of the Holy Roman emperors. A German 'king' (*regnum teutonicum*) could be put on the same level as other kings in Europe; a Holy Roman emperor could and did claim superiority over all rulers, including the Pope.

The term 'Holy Roman Empire of the *German Nation*' (my emphasis) therefore made its first appearance rather late. It can only be found in fifteenth century

2 Joachim Ehlers, *Die Entstehung des deutschen Reiches* (Munich, 1994); also Wilfried Hartmann, *Ludwig der Deutsche* (Darmstadt, 2002). In English see also Josef Fleckenstein, *Early Medieval Germany* (Amsterdam, 1978).

documents – with the earliest mentioning having been traced back to 1409. It connected linguistically German nationhood with pride in the Empire and its Christian legitimation. The emperors attempted to use their universal claims and appeals to national pride in specific policy contexts, for example in their struggles with the Roman church, their struggle against invading Turks and Hungarians in the east, and their squabbles over territory with France and Burgundy in the west. But how much of a nation state was the fifteenth-century Empire? Many historians have been sceptical, pointing to the extreme weakness of central government within its constitutional structures and to the fact that the Empire remained essentially a Roman one to its dissolution in 1806. Its basic law, the Golden Bull of 1356, confirmed the wide-reaching sovereignty of the territorial powers within the Empire. Georg Schmidt, however, has made a compelling case for describing the reforms introduced by Emperor Maximilian I between 1495 and 1500 as the beginning of German statehood.[3] Schmidt has argued that the Empire fulfilled crucial state roles in that it mediated disputes, guaranteed rights, established the rule of law and implemented decisions. It had important central institutions, above all the law court (*Reichkammergericht*) in Wetzlar and the parliament (*Reichstag*) in Regensburg. It guaranteed peace and protected its members against external foes. Especially its developed legal culture was without parallel elsewhere in Europe. The system of law within the Empire (*Reichsstaatsrechtslehre*) remained the most important discipline at German universities until 1806. A collective and consensual system of decision-making guaranteed stability and prosperity for almost three centuries.

The system could break down, as happened in the Thirty Years' War between 1618 and 1648 and again in the Seven Years' War between 1756 and 1763, but overall the constitutional framework, brought up to date in the Peace of Westphalia of 1648, adapted well to historical change. Schmidt concedes that central government was much weaker than in other nation states at the time but argues that different functions of the state were carried out at different levels. The territorial states within the Empire were to develop, over time, their own systems of administration, finance and tax. They took charge of schooling, the law, the army and communication systems (especially travel). But the emperor retained an important and powerful position within the constitutional system. He had the power to wage war; the territorial rulers owed him allegiance, and he developed his own administrative and legal system. Hence state-building processes were under way both in the territorial states making up the Holy Roman Empire and also at the centre of government. If we are willing to see in the Holy Roman Empire a first German nation state (and for many historians that still is a big 'if'), then we can also say that right from the beginnings in the late fifteenth and early sixteenth centuries, the German nation state was a federal one and federal concepts of nationalism dominated the understanding of Germany.[4]

3 G. Schmidt, *Geschichte des Alten Reiches: Staat und Nation in der frühen Neuzeit 1495–1806* (Munich, 1999). On early modern German history in English see Michael Hughes, *Early Modern Germany 1477–1806* (Basingstoke, 1992).

4 Dieter Langewiesche and Georg Schmidt, eds, *Föderative Nation: Deutschlandkonzepte von der Reformation bis zum ersten Weltkrieg* (Munich, 2000).

Such a view of the Holy Roman Empire as proto-nation state finds further confirmation when one looks at the significant national discourses in the Empire around 1500.[5] German humanist scholars created a pool of common memories, values, symbols and myths which all were to have a major impact on later reinventions of the German nation. They developed a new genre of writing: historical–geographical descriptions of the German nation, the *Germania illustrata*.[6] The aim was to develop concepts of Germany, its geography, territory and history, which could underpin a stronger sense of nationhood. Humanists were a small university-trained and urban-based cosmopolitan elite outside the church. Some of them were in the pay of Maximilian I and they constructed the nation around the state-building attempts of the emperor. The invention of the printing press allowed them to reproduce the written word and exchange information and arguments more easily. The age of humanism therefore sees the emergence of a public sphere in which ideas about the nation were being discussed. Yet this public was still very small: we are talking about a few hundred people across the European continent.

In describing the virtues and values of those people living in *Germania*, most humanists fell back on the text produced by a classical Roman author, Tacitus, who wrote about the Germanic tribes in AD 98. Tacitus's text had been rediscovered by Italian humanist scholars in the fifteenth century. They used it as evidence to demonstrate that the Germanic tribes (*barbari*) had lacked the sophisticated culture and civilization of the Roman Empire. Their colleagues in the Holy Roman Empire, who were following closely what was happening in Italian humanist circles, responded by presenting a different reading of Tacitus's text. The Germanic tribes were described as a natural warrior people who were characterized by honesty, openness, decency, love of liberty and the purity of their morality which predestined them to a life of virtue. Humanists such as Jakob Wimpfeling, Conrad Celtis and Ulrich von Hutten formulated a catalogue of virtues for a people perceived as a linguistic, cultural and historical community. They hunted for and catalogued past German cultural achievements and celebrated every find as a contribution to enhancing Germany's greatness. They dug up and collected sources for a 'German' history in classical and medieval times.

Humanists not only defined what it meant to be German; they also constructed the mythical origins of Germans, who were all supposed to have descended from a certain Tuisco, the oldest adopted son of the biblical Noah. Furthermore it was also within this humanist discourse that national heroes were created. Charlemagne

[5] Caspar Hirschli, 'Das humanistische Nationskonstrukt vor dem Hintergrund modernistischer Nationalismustheorien', *Historisches Jahrbuch*, 122 (2002), pp. 355–96; R. Stauber, 'Nationalismus vor dem Nationalismus? Eine Bestandsaufnahme der Forschung zu "Nation" und "Nationalismus" in der frühen Neuzeit', *Geschichte in Wissenschaft und Unterricht*, 47 (1996), pp. 139–65.

[6] Ulrich Muhlack, 'Das Projekt der Germania Illustrata: Ein Paradigma der Diffusion des Humanismus?' and Reinhard Stauber, 'Hartmann Schedel, der Nürnberger Humanistenkreis und die "Erweiterung der deutschen Nation" ', both in Johannes Helmrath, Ulrich Muhlack and Gerrit Walther, eds, *Diffusion des Humanismus: Studien zur nationalen Geschichtsschreibung europäischer Humanisten* (Göttingen, 2002), pp. 142–85. See also Andrew C. Fix and Andrew Cooper, *Germania Illustrata: Essays on Early Modern Germany Presented to Gerald Strauss* (Kirksville, 1992).

appeared as a model nationalist who upheld all things German and rejected all things foreign. The legendary Arminius had fought for the liberty of the German tribes and the purity of German *mores* by defeating the Roman legions in the Teutoburg forest in AD 9. This battle between the Roman army and the 'freedom-loving' Germanic tribes became a crucial focus for national identity creation for the next 450 years. From the beginning, violence and war were thus closely connected to definitions of the German nation. Similarly, the idea of the Germans being morally superior to their neighbours was already present around 1500. Especially the over-civilized, corrupt and arrogant French and Italians, living a life of luxury and laziness, were regularly the object of German humanists' ridicule and condescension. In the latter part of the seventeenth century the expansionist policies of Louis XIV re-enforced anti-French feelings. The image of France as 'hereditary enemy' (*Erbfeind*) of Germany derives from this period.[7] Furthermore Russia was frequently constructed as not really belonging to Europe but to Asia, which meant that a whole string of unpalatable national stereotypes could be attached to Russians.[8] The humanists attributed roots and enemies to the nation. They also perceived the nation as demanding absolute obedience and subservience. Love for the nation was depicted as preceding love even for wife and children.

The Reformation of the sixteenth century made use of and developed further this humanist discourse about the nation. Within Protestantism 'nation' was used as an anti-universalist oppositional term against emperor and pope.[9] Medieval theories of translation[10] had legitimated the power of the pope and the emperor; the Protestant territories (*Reichsstände*) now constructed a Germanic past which was separate from and opposed to Rome. The Protestant *Landesfürsten* were in search of an idea which could legitimate their power and delegitimate the ideas of *sacerdotium* and *imperium* which formed the basis of the emperor's powers. Nationalism was a useful tool to defeat the militant universalism of the Counter-Reformation and to legitimate the setting up of separate territorial entities with their own constitutions. The Reformation was depicted as the moment when the German nation found itself. The nation became the counter-image to the universalist aspirations of the Holy Roman

7 Franz Bosbach, 'Der französische Erbfeind: Zu einem deutschen Feindbild im Zeitalter Ludwig XIV', in *idem*, ed., *Feindbilder: Die Darstellung des Gegners in der politischen Publizistik des Mittelalters und der Neuzeit* (Cologne, 1992), pp. 117–39.

8 Ekkehard Klug, 'Das "asiatische" Rußland: Über die Entstehung eines europäischen Vorurteils', *Historische Zeitschrift*, 245 (1987), pp. 265–89; see more generally Peter Brandt, 'German Perceptions of Russia and the Russians in Modern History', *Debatte*, 11 (2003), pp. 39–59.

9 'Volk, Nation, Nationalismus, Masse', in Otto Brunner, Werner Conze and Reinhart Koselleck, eds, *Geschichtliche Grundbegriffe: Historisches Lexikon zur politisch-sozialen Sprache in Deutschland*, Vol. 7 (Stuttgart, 1992), p. 287.

10 Medieval theories of translation argued that empires followed each other and that the legitimation of one was rooted in its being the heir to another. Hence the Holy Roman Empire was perceived as the direct heir of the classical Roman Empire and had inherited its self-understanding to represent the whole civilized world in its entirety. The Roman church had grown up within this framework and its missionary zeal had merged with the classical Roman heritage. The pope and the emperor represented the whole of Latin Christianity. In the twelfth century theories of translation were used extensively by the pope to justify his right to decide who should become German emperor.

Empire.[11] This early link between Protestantism and the national idea foreshadowed the close alliance between German nationalism and Protestantism in the nineteenth century.[12] The German nation had become, according to the prominent nineteenth-century theologian Friedrich Schleiermacher, the chosen instrument of God. This was to become a major problem for German Catholics.

It was a (partly) religious war, the Thirty Years' War, which introduced a new note into the national discourse in the first half of the seventeenth century: the German fatherland was now increasingly described as a community of suffering. The emphasis was on a powerless Germany which had become the 'playing field' for foreign armies. Books such as Jakob Grimmelshausen's *Der abenteuerliche Simplicissimus Teutsch*, first published in 1669, depicted the grim lawlessness and moral degeneration of the war against the background of German virtues. The national self was defined against the dark foil of national enemies. At the end of the Thirty Years' War it looked as though the Empire had been torn apart for good. To some, like Samuel Pufendorf, it appeared as a monstrosity, hopelessly outdated in its internal divisions and its weakness of central government. The future seemed to belong to a more centralized German nation rather than to a reconstitution of the Empire. Yet the Peace of Westphalia in 1648 recreated a patchwork of 299 sovereign territorial units under the *Reich* (Empire): 1475 knights (*Reichsritterschaften*) were directly responsible to the emperor.

Throughout the seventeenth and eighteenth centuries, however, the national idea was not necessarily defined against the *Reich*; many writers did not condemn but celebrated the diversity of regions and states within it. The absence of one capital city was seen as a particular strength, not a weakness, even if provincialism became a byword for Germanness outside the borders of the German lands. An Imperial Reform movement in the late eighteenth century wanted specifically to retain diversity and federalism but gain efficiency in government.[13] Centralization along French lines was rejected, as it would violate the much heralded freedoms of the 'German tribes'. In the 'third Germany', outside of Prussia and Austria, many were keen to avoid domination by either of those two hegemonic powers within the Empire.[14] The strong attachment to the idea of 'empire' also explains why, even after the dissolution of the Empire in 1806, the desire for national unity found expression in calls for a new empire, a new *Reich*. Many writers continued to stress its achievements rather than its shortcomings and failures.

[11] Heinz Schilling, 'Nationale Identität und Konfession in der europäischen Neuzeit', in Bernhard Giesen, ed., *Nationale und kulturelle Identität: Studien zur Entwicklung des kollektiven Bewußtseins in der Neuzeit* (Frankfurt/Main, 1991), pp. 192–252.

[12] See below, pp. 54 and 84.

[13] Michael Hughes, 'Fiat justitia, pereat Germania? The Imperial Supreme Jurisdiction and Imperial Reform in the Later Holy Roman Empire', in John Breuilly, ed., *The State of Germany: The National Idea in the Making, Unmaking and Remaking of a Modern Nation State* (London, 1992), pp. 29–46.

[14] Wolfgang Burgdorf, *Reichskonstitution und Nation: Verfassungsreformkonzeptionen und das Heilige Römische Reich Deutscher Nation im politischen Schrifttum von 1648–1806* (Mainz, 1998); Joachim Whaley, 'Thinking about Germany, 1750–1815: the Birth of a Nation?', *Transactions of the English Goethe Society*, new series 66 (1997), pp. 53–72.

The national discourse allowed for the construction of very different fatherlands. It could help glorify the history of individual territories, cement the confessional divide in Germany, and legitimate regionalist discourses. But it could equally be portrayed as underpinning the Holy Roman Empire as successor to the Roman Empire. In the hands of an increasingly self-confident, urban-educated bourgeois elite it could become a critique of absolutism, but it could also be used to stabilize dynastic loyalties. Backwards-oriented projections of a Germanic past stood next to projections of a future society of equal citizens under the rule of law. Aggressive xenophobia went hand in hand with calls for freedom and emancipation. Sometimes the egalitarianism of all members of the nation could be stressed; at other times the nation seemed to consist of a strictly hierarchical community of warriors. It was this openness of discursive constructions of nationhood which made nationalism so adaptable and flexible as an ideology: it could be used in different contexts and with different intentions.

Becoming national on the verge of modernity: the national discourse in the eighteenth century

In the second half of the eighteenth century a good deal of the force behind the national idea came from a new middle class which rose to prominence as a result of state modernization processes. The modern state was in need of a new class of people who could work for that state and fulfil its increasingly diverse and ambitious roles: civil servants, professors, medical doctors, lawyers, journalists and literati were all prominent members of a new social grouping which came to define itself through education. The extension of the bureaucratic state and its ambition to regulate and influence more areas of life needed a new ideology to legitimate the state in the eyes of its subjects or citizens. Identifying this new form of state as a nation was a promising idea in that respect. The emergence of the modern state and its functional elites coincided with the rise of an industrial society characterized by the decline of traditional hierarchical orders (*Ständegesellschaft*), a new division of labour, and greater regional and social mobility. The German *Bildungsbürgertum* rose in parallel to an economic middle class (*Wirtschaftsbürgertum*) who benefited from the growing economic freedoms. They were the main supporters of the emerging capitalist economic order. These middle classes developed a new morality and code of conduct which marked them out from both the aristocracy above them and the 'rabble' below. Nationalism was to become part and parcel of that morality. Claiming to speak for the nation, they demanded greater involvement in the processes of government. Overall, the period between 1750 and 1850 has been described by Otto Brunner as 'bridge period' (*Sattelzeit*) in which the modern age came fully into its own.[15] The fortunes of nationalism were going to be closely linked to the rise of modernity in Europe.

15 On the origins of the term *Sattelzeit* see Pim den Boer, 'The Historiography of German *Begriffsgeschichte* and the Dutch Project of Conceptual History', in Iain Hampsher-Monk, Karin Tilmans and Frank van Vree, eds, *History of Concepts: Comparative Perspectives* (Amsterdam, 1998), p. 18.

A veritable revolution of the literary market extended the middle-class public sphere. In the 1770s, 35,000 books were produced in the German language every year. At the same time the educated public could choose from 200 to 250 different journals which had, on average, a circulation of 600 to 700 copies. Reading societies were established in all major cities. The number of bookshops increased by 25 per cent between 1790 and 1800. Poets, novelists, philosophers and historians were in the vanguard of those constructing the discourse of Germanness in the eighteenth century.[16]

Arminius, already a favourite topic with the humanists, was rediscovered in literary texts around 1740 and several attempts were made to create a national epic around this historical figure.[17] Germanic myths and the Germanic past were to remain one of the most important quarries for nationalist ideas in modern Germany.[18] A famous poem by Johann Peter Uz, for example, glorified the Germanic past and juxtaposed it with a shameful German present:

O Shame! Are we related to you, You Germans of better times, Who feared the iron ring of cowardly bondage More than the most terrible death in the arms of freedom?	O Schande! Sind wir Euch verwandt, Ihr Deutschen jener bessern Zeiten, Die feiger Knechtschaft eisern Band Mehr, als den härtesten Tod im Arm Der Freiheit scheuten?
Us, who have dedicated ourselves to sick lust, Weakened from the poison of gentle customs, We want to be their descendants Who fought for their forests in a rough but terribly free manner?	Wir, die uns kranker Wollust weihn, Geschwächt vom Gifte weicher Sitten; Wir wollen deren Enkel sein, Die rauh, doch furchtbarfrei, für Ihre Wälder stritten?
The forests, where their fame still lingers around the mossy oaks, Where, when their steel flashed in unity Their iron arm was victorious, and Rome trembled?	Die Wälder, wo ihr Ruhm noch itzt Um die bemoosten Eichen schwebet, Wo, als ihr Stahl vereint geblitzt, Ihr ehrner Arm gesiegt und Latium Gebebet?
We sleep, as long as disunity wakes And swings her pale torch And, since she brought war to us, She constantly creeps around him, surrounded by the Furies.	Wir schlafen, da die Zwietracht wacht Und ihre bleiche Fackel schwinget, Und seit sie uns den Krieg gebracht, Ihm stets zur Seite schleicht, von Furien umringet.

16 Hans-Martin Blitz, *Aus Liebe zum Vaterland: Die deutsche Nation im 18. Jahrhundert* (Hamburg, 2000), whose magisterial treatment of eighteenth-century German nationalism influenced my own story considerably. See also Joseph Canning and Hermann Wellenreuther, eds, *Britain and Germany Compared: Nationality, Society and Nobility in the Eighteenth Century* (Göttingen, 2001).

17 Richard Kuehnemund, *Arminius or the Rise of a National Symbol in Literature (from Hutten to Grabbe)* (New York, 1966).

18 Klaus von See, *Deutsche Germanenideologie vom Humanismus bis zur Gegenwart* (Frankfurt/Main, 1970).

Her army of snakes hisses into our ear	Ihr Natternheer zischt uns ums Ohr,
To poison German hearts	Die deutschen Herzen zu vergiften
And if there will be no Hermann,	Und wird, kommt ihr kein Hermann vor
She will take a terrible revenge on Hermann's fatherland.	An Hermanns Vaterland ein schmählig Denkmal stiften.[19]

Characteristic of many patriotic texts of the eighteenth century was the close connection between notions of manliness and the national idea. In Uz's text the feminized descendants of the Germanic tribes, given over to a sickening sensuality, cannot be the true heirs of the tough and manly Germans who defended their freedom against the Romans in the Germanic forests. Men fought, killed and died whereas women stayed at home and raised a new generation of warriors.

Why did some writers turn to the nation in the eighteenth century and portray Germanic forests and singing bards as symbols of an imaginary German fatherland? Their panegyrics to the nation were a reaction to the massive political, social and economic change. The emergence of agrarian capitalism went hand in hand with a population boom, a transport revolution, the slow emergence of a market economy and, more generally, the capitalization of all social relationships to produce a sense of general crisis. The old order was dissolving everywhere and it was unclear what was going to take its place. Nationalism was an answer which suited the aspirations and values of the new middle classes. Hence the national topic had a high market value. Many young writers saw it as a way to gain recognition and establish themselves. Their social and economic position was often precarious. Their future was insecure if they could not establish themselves in what was increasingly resembling a national market for literature. Picking up the national theme and attempting to produce national literature was one way of doing that. Members of Friedrich Gottlieb Klopstock's (1724–1803) circle in Göttingen, the Göttinger Hain, were young men on the make, and nationalism seemed a promising vehicle for furthering their careers. If writers and intellectuals increasingly portrayed themselves as educators of the nation, then this was also a claim to greater social status and more economic security.[20] National education was a rallying cry directed in particular at lower social strata. The common people had to be educated to honour and value the people's culture (*Volkskultur*). Instead of singing vulgar and obscene songs, they should be taught to sing *Volkslieder*. The people, in other words, had not yet come to their true selves; they needed direction on the path to salvation, and the new class of writers and intellectuals were their self-styled leaders.

Such a posture was particularly evident around the time of the Seven Years' War, between 1756 and 1763, when literati became propagandists for the war efforts of all the states involved in the conflict. On the Prussian side a specifically German (as opposed to Prussian) national discourse was only introduced after the victory at Roßbach in November 1757, when the Prussian army defeated a

[19] Johann Peter Uz, 'Das bedrängte Deutschland' (1755), stanzas 7–11, in *idem, Sämtliche Poetische Werke* (Darmstadt, 1964), p. 39f.

[20] Wolfgang Hardtwig, *Genossenschaft, Sekte, Verein in Deutschland*, Vol. 1: *Vom Spätmittelalter zur Französischen Revolution* (Munich, 1999), pp. 285–303; Bernard Giesen, *Die Intellektuellen und die Nation: Eine deutsche Achsenzeit* (Frankfurt/Main, 1993), pp. 102–29.

combined French and *Reich* army.[21] Subsequently Prussian propagandists portrayed Frederick II as national rebel who wanted to defeat the Empire in order to build the nation. Prussia was seen as Germany's future. It had to be supported against an almighty coalition of European great powers. Such reasoning, of course, only existed in the realm of fantasy. Frederick waged war to make Prussia more powerful, not because he had any sympathies for German nationalism. Foremost on his mind was what benefited the dynasty and the state. A cult surrounding his person emerged and was celebrated in Protestant thanksgiving services, patriotic church services and sermons. Catholic Austria and France were portrayed as the main enemies of the nation. But Prussian propaganda also attempted to mobilize anti-French sentiments in the Catholic southern states of the German Empire by downplaying the Protestant element of the Hohenzollern's vocation. Incidentally, Austrian war propaganda also used nationalism as a vehicle to justify its own war efforts: Prussia, Austrian supporters claimed, had violated the peace within the German Empire and Austria was fighting to preserve the integrity and peacefulness of the whole nation, i.e. the Empire.

Once again, nationalism as an ideology could serve many masters, but everyone who used nationalist rhetoric for their own purposes had a major problem in defining the nation territorially. It was precisely because the borders of that imagined Germany had to remain so vague that self-definition through an 'other', a national enemy, became all the more important. To fight against that, often feminized, enemy and die for the fatherland was portrayed as the highest virtue:

I die a hero; even in death The sabre in my hand is threatening! Immortality brings the hero's death, The death for the fatherland!	*Ein Held fall ich; noch sterbend droht* *Mein Säbel in der Hand!* *Unsterblich macht der Helden Tod,* *Der Tod fürs Vaterland!*
Also one goes from this world Quicker than lightning; And who dies a hero, receives as reward, A high seat in heaven![22]	*Auch kömmt man aus der Welt davon,* *Geschwinder wie der Blitz;* *Und wer ihn stirbt, bekömmt zum Lohn* *Im Himmel hohen Sitz!*

Thomas Abbt, who devoted a whole pamphlet to the topic of dying for the fatherland in 1761, drew a parallel between fatherland and family: both required utmost devotion but the fatherland ultimately stood above the family. In the last instance the nation had to be a man's only lover. It had to be loved with religious devotion as the holiest object in one's life.[23] Much of the nationalist literature

[21] Klaus Bohnen, 'Von den Anfängen des Nationalsinns: Zur literarischen Patriotismusdebatte im Umfeld des Siebenjährigen Kriegs', in Helmut Scheuer, ed., *Dichter und ihre Nation* (Frankfurt/Main, 1993), pp. 121–37; also Eckhart Hellmuth, 'Die "Wiedergeburt" Friedrichs des Großen und der "Tod fürs Vaterland": Zum patriotischen Selbstverständnis in Preußen in der zweiten Hälfte des 18. Jahrhunderts', *Aufklärung*, 10:2 (1995), pp. 23–53

[22] Johann Wilhelm Ludwig Gleim, 'Bei Eröffnung des Feldzuges 1756, Lied no. 1, ll. 16–23, in *idem*, *Preußische Kriegslieder in den Feldzügen 1756 und 1757 von einem Grenadier* (Heilbronn, 1882), p. 7.

[23] Thomas Abbt, 'Vom Thod für das Vaterland', in Johannes Kunisch, ed., *Aufklärung und Kriegserfahrung: Klassische Zeitzeugen zum Siebenjährigen Krieg* (Frankfurt/Main, 1996), pp. 589–650.

produced in the Seven Years' War included violent fantasies of purging and annihilating national enemies who were devoid of all human qualities and could be compared to animals or worse, vermin. Yet the nationalists were to be bitterly disappointed at the end of the war. Frederick II had no interest in German nationalism as such. He abhorred the 'barbaric' German language and did not see any future for a German national literature. His preference was for French literature and the French language, which was, after all, the language of the European nobility. German nationalists could be useful at times of war, but otherwise they remained, not only in the eyes of Frederick, cranks.

The propagandists for the nation were, however, nothing if not persistent. Only a few years after the end of the Seven Years' War many German writers found themselves embroiled in what was dubbed the 'national spirit debate' (*Nationalgeistdebatte*).[24] Influenced by Montesquieu's discussion of collective national identities and their influence on the institutionalization of political rule, Friedrich Carl von Moser published a pamphlet in 1765 entitled *Of the German National Spirit*, in which he lamented the division of the nation. Such division, he argued, went hand in hand with the prevalence of despotism in the German lands. Moser was paid by the Habsburgs, and the anti-Prussian tendency of his booklet was rather obvious. The increasing powers of the territories within the Empire, especially Prussia, threatened the separation of the fatherland. A new nationalism, focussed on the Habsburg emperor was to unite the *Reich* and overcome separatism as well as religious division. Moser's ideal was a medieval society organized in estates which would rule through parliaments bound by the constitution of the Empire.

Unsurprisingly, representatives of the territorial states within the Empire contradicted Moser most energetically. They portrayed the nation as a community of tribes speaking a common language. As the *Reich* incorporated many non-Germanic tribes and people who did not speak a Germanic language, the idea of the *Reich*, they argued, could not be squared with the idea of the nation. Even more important than debates about territorial definitions of the nation in the 'national spirit debate' were arguments about the link between the national spirit and political rule.

Although Moser was no friend of either republicanism or modern constitutionalism, he found that he could not discuss a particular nation without reference to the political constitution of that nation. Soon others entered the fray with more radical ideas of reorganizing the nation. The Swiss authors and Enlightenment thinkers Isaak Iselin and Johann Georg Zimmermann argued that true nationalism could only be found within republics. (Zimmermann later was to modify his position and accepted the possibility of monarchical nationalism.) Several writers now used nationalism to put forward calls for participation of the new and highly educated middle classes in the affairs of the state. This, the second half of the eighteenth century, is precisely the time when early liberal ideas forged a strong alliance with the national idea. Champions of liberal ideas, who were often civil servants, used the national idea in their various schemes to reform the dynastic order and demand political participation for the propertied and educated.

24 Nicholas Vazsonyi, 'Montesquieu, Friedrich Carl von Moser, and the "National Spirit Debate" in Germany 1765–1767', *German Studies Review*, 22:2 (1999), pp. 225–46.

A representative, parliamentary and constitutional state and a levelled middle-class society – these were the twin aims of the aspiring liberal national movement.[25]

A fair number of Jews advocated liberal and national ideas in the late eighteenth and early nineteenth centuries. Educated middle-class Jews in the German lands perceived themselves by and large as belonging to the German cultural nation. Moses Mendelssohn, for example, criticized Frederick II for preferring French to German culture. Mendelssohn was a key member of the Berlin Enlightenment and a close friend of Gotthold Ephraim Lessing. According to Heinrich Heine, he was the Jewish Luther, achieving a renewal of Judaism and attempting to integrate the Jews into the German cultural nation. Mendelssohn's hopes were indeed for a dual identity, where Judaism could be combined with Germanness. This was essentially to remain the hope of large sections of the educated German-Jewish middle classes throughout the nineteenth century. But antisemitic sentiments remained widespread even among the *crème de la crème* of German intellectuals.[26] Jewishness was often perceived as a rival national rather than as a religious identity, and non-Jewish writers continued to exclude Jews from their definitions of Germanness. Despite the progress of Jewish emancipation (introduced in Prussia in 1812) and the recurrent pleas for religious toleration (most powerful in Lessing's ring parable in his drama about *Nathan the Wise*), and despite the generosity of Jewish associations in the wars of liberty against Napoleonic occupation in the early nineteenth century, Rahel Varnhagen still felt the prejudices directed against her: 'What nastiness to have to legitimate oneself again and again! That is the only reason why it is so revolting to be a Jewess!'[27] Nationalism was attractive to her because it promised inclusion in the German cultural nation. But even following a Christian marriage and conversion in 1814, she still found herself the object of smug antisemitic remarks. Antisemitism was to remain a characteristic of German nationalism and the hopes of educated German Jews of belonging fully to the German nation were not to be realized.[28]

If the 'national spirit debate' had focussed attention on the political constitution of the nation the German movement of the 1770s linked the national discourse firmly to language and literature. Johann Gottfried Herder's edited collection

[25] It should be noted here that these early representatives of liberal ideas did not yet go under the label 'liberal'. It was only around 1830 that 'liberalism' becomes more widely used as a term denoting a particular political movement demanding the rule of law and a constitutional state. Yet many key ideas of this 'liberalism' can be found in the thinkers of the Enlightenment in the second half of the eighteenth century. An excellent review of the more recent literature on liberalism and nation-building in Germany is Jan Palmowski, 'Mediating the Nation: Liberalism and the Polity in Nineteenth-Century Germany', *German History*, 19 (2001), pp. 573–98.

[26] Micha Brumlik, *Deutscher Geist und Judenhass: Das Verhältnis des philosophischen Idealismus zum Judentum* (Munich, 2000), traces antisemitic ideas in the writings of Kant, Fichte, Schleiermacher, Hegel, Schelling and Marx. See also Peter Pulzer, *The Rise of Political Anti-Semitism in Germany and Austria* (Cambridge, Mass., 1988).

[27] Quoted in Ulrike Landfester, 'Vom auserwählten Volk zur erlesenen Nation: Rahel Levin Varnhagens "Uremigrantenthum"', in Ute Planert, ed., *Nation, Politik und Geschlecht: Frauenbewegungen und Nationalismus in der Moderne* (Frankfurt/Main, 2000), p. 73.

[28] Antisemitism was, however, not specific to German national discourses and can be found, to varying degrees, across European nationalisms.

Of German Character and Art (1773) became a key programmatic text for the movement. It dealt with a culture and a history which was described as German and demarcated sharply towards French culture. Language, religion and literature had, he argued, shaped the German people (*Volk*). They also described the key elements of a dream of national unity constituted in the realm of culture.[29] Hölderlin's famous phrase that the Germans were 'poor in deeds but rich in thought' emanated from such a belief in the cultural mission of Germany. Members of the German movement founded national associations, academies and theatres. They developed their own historical semantics.[30] The Enlightenment belief that human nature was the same at all times and in all places was giving way to the assumption of the historicity of all cultures. Each people, in so far as they had a culture, had a history which developed in accordance with this people's national character.

In the absence of a unified German state and in the face of massive lack of interest in nationalism among the political and social elites in the German lands, culture and history, and not politics, seemed to many writers more promising areas in which to locate national identity. Germany, after all, had a reputation abroad as the nation of poets and philosophers. Inwardness and idealism were widely regarded as bywords for Germanness. Yet there were problems, too, about cultural definitions of the nation. In particular the notion of a national language did not fit well with the huge diversity of German languages throughout much of the eighteenth and nineteenth centuries.[31] It was no coincidence that people tended to talk about the language as they did about the country, in the plural: 'the German languages in the German lands'.

Attempts to standardize and unify the German languages had been ongoing for centuries. Luther's sixteenth-century translation of the Bible into German was an important starting point. In the seventeenth and eighteenth centuries a string of grammarians attempted to codify rules for the usage of a standardized German language. The Holy Roman Empire boosted attempts to come to a more unified German language, whilst the territorial states within it tended to be satisfied with regional variations. Linguistic societies were founded and individuals such as Johann Christoph Gottsched (1700–66), Christian Fürchtegott Gellert (1715–69) and Johann Christoph Adelung (1732–1806) furthered the codification of a single German language. Adelung in fact published the first comprehensive dictionary of High German and the first grammar book to be used in schools. Klopstock's attempt to create a German national literature meant developing a German language on which this could be based. Keeping German free of foreign influences and dialect forms was a favourite preoccupation of linguists. It was not just xenophobia, but also the desire to use a language which could be understood by all citizens which drove attempts to purify the German language. Baroque poets

[29] Otto W. Johnston, *Der deutsche Nationalmythos: Ursprung eines politischen Programms* (Stuttgart, 1990). See also *idem*, *The Myth of a Nation: Literature and Politics in Prussia under Napoleon* (Columbia, 1989).

[30] Matthias Dümpelmann, *Zeitordnung: Aufklärung, Geschichte und die Konstruktion nationaler Semantik in Deutschland 1770–1815* (Berlin, 1997).

[31] Martin Durell, 'Political Unity and Linguistic Diversity in Nineteenth-Century Germany', in Maiken Umbach, ed., *German Federalism: Past, Present and Future* (London, 2002), pp. 91–112.

had attempted to raise a literary standard. From the late seventeenth century onwards, German rapidly replaced Latin as the foremost academic language in the German lands. Theories about the special characteristics of the German language(s) abounded: it was supposed to be especially old or especially pure and superior to others in clarity and sound. All of these efforts produced, around 1800, a codified and accepted set of rules for written German (*Schriftdeutsch*), which was actually spoken by hardly anyone. The aim of greater linguistic unity of the nation was meant as an indictment of the continued division of the country by the selfish interests of petty princes. The rules for using that language were only acquired by a small intellectual elite, but as it was the same elite which became the main protagonists of nationalism, language continued to be constructed as a major constituent of nationhood.[32]

Nationalists tended to decry the alleged German disease of aping other nations: they wanted to replace Italian, French or English things with authentic German products. Thus a German national literature, they argued, would only be developed once French models in drama theory and poetry were thoroughly rejected. But what were authentic German models on which to base a national literature? It is revealing that nationalists fell back on Shakespeare as a model. He could be made into a Germanic writer, as the English were supposed to derive from German tribes, the Anglo-Saxons. Shakespeare and an English national literature had already contributed towards forming the English national character. The Anglo-Saxon bard was particularly commendable as his texts had helped to overcome both territorial as well as social divisions within the English nation. That was precisely what, according to his German-speaking admirers, was needed in the German lands too.

The lack of authentic Germanic models led nationalist authors such as Herder to complain that there was a dearth of authentic German heroes on which to base a national movement. By the second half of the eighteenth century sustained efforts were undertaken to make Martin Luther into such a German hero. Against the pope of the French Enlightenment, Voltaire, who had portrayed Luther as a fanatic monk opposed to the progress of reason, authors such as Justus Möser, Lessing, Goethe and Schiller reinterpreted Luther as a national integration figure. In Luther's case, though, the problem for nationalists was rather obvious: he had divided Germany confessionally, and Catholic Germans would hardly be able to see in him a national hero.

The nationalists' concern for authentic Germanness was much criticized and belittled by many leading intellectuals in the late eighteenth century. Cosmopolitanism, they argued, knew no national boundaries but sought to learn from other nations' achievements. Germans should take note of them rather than ignore them in the name of an illusory authenticity. According to Christoph Martin Wieland (1733–1813), most Germans identified with their regions rather than with an illusory nation. They were first and foremost Bavarians, Saxons, Badenese, Hamburgers and Prussians: 'But German patriots who love the whole German *Reich* as their fatherland, above everything else and are willing to bring considerable sacrifices for it; where are they? Who shows them to us, who calls them

[32] Michael Townson, *Mother-tongue and Fatherland: Language and Politics in Germany* (Manchester, 1992), pp. 81–97.

by their names? What have they achieved to date? And what can one expect of them in the future?'[33] Others, including the philosopher Georg Wilhelm Friedrich Hegel and the writer Johann Wolfgang von Goethe, were frequently taken aback by the narrowness of nationalist sentiments. Goethe's famous aphorism that Germans were 'admirable as individuals but miserable as a group' described his reservations about collective national mass hysteria.

But, of course, many nationalists equally subscribed to cosmopolitanism and warned against national hubris. Thus, for example, Herder argued that diverse people had different national characters but all of them had one mission, namely the perfection of mankind. National languages, connected to national characters, were all interesting in themselves. Hebrew, Greek and Latin could not necessarily claim to be more important than any other national languages. Hence an egalitarian, universal, Enlightenment vision underpinned Herder's cultural nationalism. If the Germans were portrayed as the Greeks of the contemporary age by writers such as August Wilhelm Schlegel (1767–1845) or Schiller, their mission, like that of the Greeks of old, was to contribute to the cultural progress of the entire world.

Language and literature were key debating points for early nationalists in Germany. Another major issue was the impact of the climate on the national character. This was an old idea going back to classical philosophy: put somewhat crudely, it argued that the colder climates of the north resulted in producing honest, courageous and strong peoples who loved their liberty, whereas the warmer climates of the south produced people who suffered from sensuality, slackness and slyness. The notion that the natural environment in its entirety had a major influence on the national character became important again in the late eighteenth century and was connected, again by Herder, among others, to the idea of authenticity. The national character was supposed to be purest where a people could be traced back to one lineage and where they had been able to stay in their original natural environments. Of course, given the migratory movements of the early Middle Ages, this was more or less impossible for any of the European peoples.

Much of our attention so far has been focussed on a small, extremely literate, intelligentsia and their importance for defining Germanness. According to Miroslav Hroch, members of such an elite were instrumental in producing a 'learned patriotism' across the European nations. Their influence was crucial in paving the way for the 'national awakening' which sought to produce mass support for nationalist programmes.[34] They were often in close contact with each other, they wrote (increasingly) the same language, they read the same texts and they thought of themselves as a community which transgressed the innumerable territorial divisions which characterized the Holy Roman Empire. The cosmopolitan literary patriotism of Klopstock's *Hermanns Schlacht* (1769), Herder's *Fragmente über die neuere deutsche Literatur* (1767/8) were attempting to make a specific morality rather than a specific politics or a specific territory the basis of German identity.

[33] Christoph Martin Wieland, 'Über deutschen Patriotismus' [1795], in *idem, Sämtliche Werke* (Nördlingen, 1984), Vol. 9, pp. 480–2.

[34] Miroslav Hroch, *Social Preconditions of National Revival in Europe: A Comparative Analysis of the Social Composition of Patriotic Groups among the Smaller European Nations* (Cambridge, 1985).

The impact of the French Revolution on the development of the German national discourse

The political reconstitution of the French nation around 1789 had major repercussions on the German thinking about national identity.[35] Between 1770 and 1815, close to 200 translations from French into German carried the words 'nation' and 'national' in the title.[36] After 1792 recurrent military conflicts involving the Empire and French armies heightened a sense of general crisis among the new middle classes in the German lands. The gradual erosion of the very foundations of the Holy Roman Empire led to its eventual dissolution in 1806. The subsequent attempt by Napoleon to create a new European order mobilized and politicized national discourses across Europe and carried them into broader sections of the population than ever before. The disciples of the nation could hark back to the earlier patterns established since the eleventh century. In the longer run the rejection of what were perceived as alien French revolutionary ideas became a key ingredient in many variants of German nationalism.

But in 1789 the French Revolution embodied the hopes and desires of most liberals and democrats across the German lands. Even before, many had expressed considerable sympathies for the Americans in their war of independence against Britain. Around 1775 most educated and liberal-minded Germans were convinced that America was fighting for the middle-class ideals that they themselves adhered to – above all, freedom and participation in the affairs of the state.[37] Under the impact of the French Revolution, German Jacobins, who could look back on a strong indigenous tradition of democratic ideas ranging back to the 1720s (especially in the south-western states of Germany),[38] debated issues such as people's sovereignty, political rights and the welfare state. Constitutions were being written by liberal democrats across Germany, and in some places attempts were made to establish new political orders – most famously in the case of the short-lived Mainz Republic in 1794. But Jacobin republicans were a minority among the minority of German liberals and at no point did they manage to mobilize mass opinion. Early supporters of the French Revolution rarely made use of nationalist ideas. Much more prevalent was the idea that the French were paving the way for the general progress of mankind. If anything, the community of the French and German people was emphasized: they both allegedly desired an end to despotic rule and the dynastic principle.

[35] The best introduction to the rise of early German nationalism can be found in: Jörg Echternkamp, *Der Aufstieg des deutschen Nationalismus (1770–1840)* (Frankfurt/Main, 1998).

[36] On the transfer of national concepts from France to Germany around the time of the French Revolution see Hans-Jürgen Lüsebrink, 'Conceptual History and Conceptual Transfer: the Case of "Nation" in Revolutionary France and Germany', in Hampsher-Monk, Tilmans and van Vree, eds, *History of Concepts*, pp. 115–28 (see note 16).

[37] Horst Dippel, *Germany and the American Revolution 1770–1800: A Sociohistorical Investigation of Late Eighteenth-Century Political Thinking* (Wiesbaden, 1978).

[38] Jürgen Riethmüller, *Die Anfänge der Demokratie in Deutschland* (Erfurt, 2002); Oliver Lamprecht, *Das Streben nach Demokratie, Volkssouveränität und Menschenrechten in Deutschland am Ende des 18. Jahrhunderts* (Berlin, 2001).

However, the more the ideals of the French Revolution drowned in streams of blood, the more disappointed the majority of German liberals became. Early enthusiasm gave way to disillusionment. Only a hardcore of democrats and republicans continued to support the French Revolution. The great majority of German liberals now turned towards the nation in an attempt to save the very same ideals that had led them to welcome the French Revolution. The latter had justified the demand for the freedom and equality of human beings by taking recourse to the idea of natural law. Human rights were derived from the notion of abstract freedom. They were non-historical and valid at all times and places. Instead, German liberals now reclaimed German history and invented a thousand-year-old German tradition of freedom. The Germanic tribes and their fight for 'freedom' against the Romans as well as the *Reich* and its constitution could be mobilized to criticize dynastic despotism and demand political reform and participation in the affairs of the state. A German past could be juxtaposed to the alleged excesses of rationalism in the French Revolution and to 'Asian', i.e. Russian, despotism. The Germanic past now became a fundamental strategy for justifying diverse concepts of German nationhood.[39]

Nationalism became the basis for liberalism, as liberals came to demand freedom and participation on the grounds of an alleged German national character. The nation, they argued, could only be properly established once basic freedoms and rights had been granted. It could not flourish under despotic rule. True nationalism was only possible where everyone was protected by the rule of law, by constitutional (and parliamentary) government and by the freedom of the press. This was very different from conservative ideas of nationalism at the time, which linked national commitment with loyalty towards the dynasty and the head of state. Conservative nationalists defended an estates-based idea of the nation. Liberal nationalists broadened the concept of the nation by introducing the idea of the people who, as citizens of the nation, demanded participation in the affairs of the state. Liberal nationalist thinkers such as Johann Gottlieb Fichte (1762–1813), but also key popularizers of nationalist thought, such as Ernst Moritz Arndt (1769–1860) and Jahn, remained deeply indebted to the universalist discourse of the Enlightenment and to rationalist, liberal individualist ideas which they took largely from British and French political thought. Their great theme remained the progress of humanity, and, importantly, the role of Germany within such a history of progress. Their writings were often characterized by apparently contradictory sentiments, and they suffered subsequently from a selective appropriation of their texts. They were at once ardent nationalists and pro-Europeans, convinced antirevolutionaries and fighters against servitude and despotism.

The disillusionment of liberal nationalists with the course of the French Revolution was as nothing to the steadfast opposition of the dynastic houses of Europe, which sought to extinguish the flame of revolution by means of war. They were in for a big surprise. The conscript armies of the Revolution proved themselves on the battlefield. By 1794 the French revolutionary armies had

[39] Jost Hermand and Michael Niedermeier, *Revolutio Germanica: Die Sehnsucht nach der 'alten Freiheit' der Germanen, 1750–1820* (Frankfurt/Main, 2002).

occupied the territories on the left bank of the Rhine, starting a twenty-year rule over these territories.[40] The peace of Lunéville in 1801 began the redrawing of the map of the German lands. Between 1803 and 1806 many territories in the Holy Roman Empire lost their sovereign status and were annexed by or amalgamated into larger states. In 1806 the Empire itself was dissolved.

In the same year, sixteen German princes formed the Confederation of the Rhine (*Rheinbund*) under the protection of the French emperor [Map 1]. Later nationalist mythology denounced the *Rheinbund* as a vicious form of treacherous particularism betraying the national idea. And contemporary anti-French propaganda sought to mobilize Germanic myths and heroes such as Hermann and Widukind to rally the German lands against Napoleon.[41] Yet the *Rheinbund* was characterized by its own pro-French nationalism.[42] Napoleon was depicted as the reborn Charlemagne creating a federal Germany within a federal Europe. He was not a French despot colonizing Europe, but a cosmopolitan citizen of the world freeing the European nations from despotism. The Code Napoleon was celebrated as realizing the ideal of the rule of law and as achieving reforms that had been championed by liberal nationalists ever since the eighteenth century. *Rheinbund* nationalism thus can serve as a reminder of how fluid ideas of the German nation were at the beginning of the nineteenth century.

The same year the *Rheinbund* was founded, Prussia suffered a crushing military defeat at the hands of Napoleon's armies in October 1806. It had to sign a harsh peace treaty at Tilsit in 1807. Prussia lost half of its territories and almost half of its population. Huge reparations payments led to an immediate crisis of Prussian finances. The monarch lacked authority and Prussian nationalism was at an all-time low. In this situation reform-minded civil servants around Freiherr Karl vom und zum Stein and Karl August von Hardenberg created a 'revolution from above' which sought to harness the powers of an 'enlightened nationalism'[43] to strengthen a more centralized and efficiently organized Prussian state.[44] A more rational socio-economic and political order, inspired by the philosophical writings of Immanuel von Kant, would produce the kind of harmony between king and citizens which would be the precondition for any revival of Prussia's fortunes. These reforming civil servants stood in between radical liberal and democratic ideas and aristocratic notions which idealized a harmonious community of subjects led by the king. Their primary concern was with Prussia, but their national rhetoric studiously avoided the question whether their commitment was to a Prussian

[40] T.C.W. Blanning, *The French Revolution in Germany: Occupation and Resistance in the Rhineland, 1792–1802* (Oxford, 1983).

[41] Wolfgang Burgdorf, *'Chimäre Europa': Antieuropäische Diskurse in Deutschland (1648–1999)* (Bochum, 1999), Chapters 5–8.

[42] Robert D. Billinger, 'Good and True Germans: The "Nationalism" of the Rheinbund Princes, 1806–1814', in Heinz Duchhardt and Andreas Kunz, eds, *Reich oder Nation? Mitteleuropa 1780–1815* (Mainz, 1998), pp. 105–39.

[43] Matthew Levinger, *Enlightened Nationalism: The Transformation of Prussian Political Culture, 1806–1848* (Oxford, 2000).

[44] On the series of reforms implemented in the German lands in the 1800s and 1810s see Hans-Ulrich Wehler, *Deutsche Gesellschaftsgeschichte*, Vol. 1: *1700–1815* (Munich, 1987), pp. 363–485. Also Jonathan Sperber, *Germany 1800–1871* (Oxford, 2004).

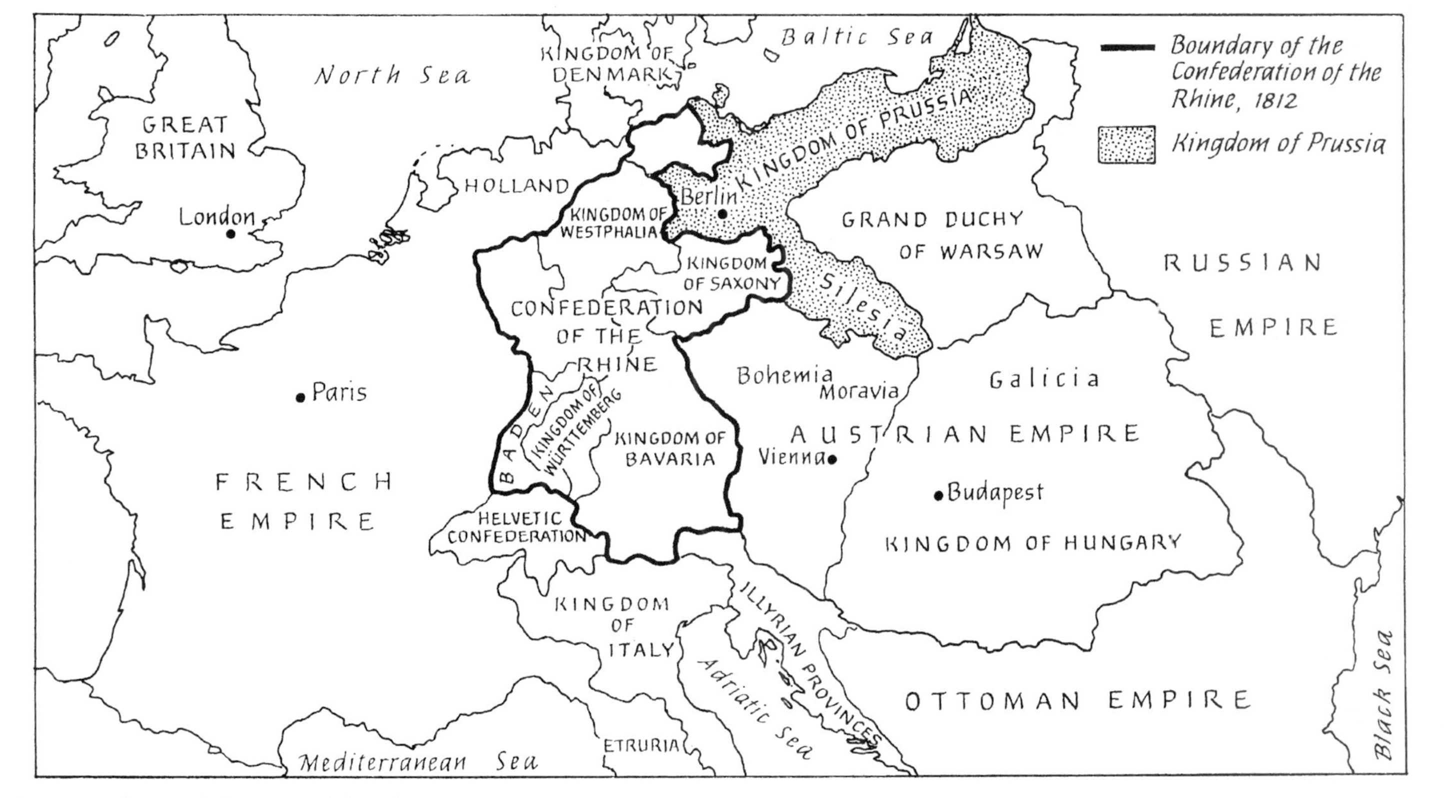

Map 1 The Confederation of the Rhine, 1812.

or to a German nation. The appeal to a German rather than a Prussian nation was perceived by many as more organic and compelling, especially as Prussia incorporated Polish- and Lithuanian-speaking territories. Precisely this multinational character of Prussia rendered German nationalism double-edged and, in turn, made the territorial aspect of the reformers' nationalism diffuse and vague.

Their primary concern with greater efficiency was particularly obvious in the long debates surrounding military reform. The military reformers, including August Neithardt von Gneisenau and Gerhard von Scharnhorst, argued strongly for conscription as the basis of a new army. The conscript armies of the French Revolution had convinced them of the power of nationalism in rallying the nation to arms. Against much aristocratic opposition they opened the officer caste to members from the middle classes. And against much middle-class opposition they pushed through conscription laws which made military service a national duty for everyone. The citizen had to be a national warrior.[45]

Contrary to later nationalist mythology, military service was not popular among the middle classes in the early nineteenth century. The soldier was not yet a role model for manly behaviour, and few people would have been willing to describe the army as school of the nation. Immediate reactions to the conscription law of 1813 were entirely negative. Young men fled their homes, desertions were common and doctors' notes abounded declaring the physical unfitness of the offspring of the Prussian middle classes. When national service was introduced in peacetime Prussia through Hermann von Boyen's army service law of 1814, the legislators sought to placate middle-class sentiments by reducing the period of active service for educated members of the middle classes from three years to one. Even then it proved unpopular.

The Prussian military reformers propagated their ideas of a new conscript army within a wider public relations campaign, which sought to combine ferocious anti-French feeling with loyalty to the Hohenzollern dynasty and the Prussian state. Academics and literary authors were in the vanguard of this campaign. Heinrich von Kleist's *Die Hermannsschlacht* of 1808 is only one example among many of how authors endorsed a sickening rhetorical violence in their attempts to rally Germans to the struggle against Napoleon. They embedded the idea of the French as 'hereditary enemy' more deeply in German national discourses,[46] and decried the lack of mass nationalism as a deplorable result of a misguided education system. A proper national education was identified as the key to release the potential of Germanness, which was already awaiting its awakening in every German. Germans, they argued, had to be made in school. A 'national school' was the precondition for a unified German nation state. As humanity was naturally organized into nations, people had to be taught national adherence as an expression of their specific form of humanity.

45 On the connection between conscription and nation-building generally see Ute Frevert, *Die kasernierte Nation: Militärdienst und Zivilgesellschaft in Deutschland* (Munich, 2001). Frevert's book is to be published in English: *A Nation in Barracks: Modern Germany, Military Conscription and Civil Society* (Oxford, 2004).

46 Michael Jeismann, *Das Vaterland der Feinde: Studien zum nationalen Feindbegriff und Selbstverständnis in Deutschland und Frankreich, 1792–1918* (Stuttgart, 1992).

German language and literature were regarded as the most important subject areas to develop the national character. Linguistics became an intensely nationalist subject area with attempts to produce a hierarchy of languages and to find the original language (*Ursprache*). Threats to the language were regarded as direct threats to national well-being. Purists such as Arndt and Jahn wanted to return to an illusory Germanic language of old and to cleanse the language of all 'foreign' elements. Their motivation was not just xenophobia; they also aimed to return to a language which would be accessible to all social classes and thereby able to overcome social differences and democratize public life. But many educated Germans, including Goethe, had nothing but scorn and derision for such attempts at dogmatic purification. What was more generally supported was a further push towards the unification and codification of the German language. So, for example, Joachim Heinrich Campe published his *Dictionary of the German Language* to general acclaim between 1807 and 1811, and a second edition was already in print in 1813. In literary studies a process of canon-building of what should be regarded as German national literature was taking shape. It was by no means obvious what should and should not be part of the canon. Thus, early nineteenth-century nationalists argued that the *Nibelungenlied* (later to become one of the key foci of German nationalist mythology) could not possibly be regarded as a piece of German national literature. It did not take place in Germany (its location is Burgundy), and its main protagonists all had major character flaws.

Apart from German language and literature, history took centre stage for those seeking to propagate a German national education. The national character of a people revealed itself most clearly in its past. That past, historians such as Heinrich Luden (1778–1847) emphasized, should not any longer be written as the story of dynastic houses but as history of the people. German values such as honesty, a developed sense of justice, seriousness, diligence, loyalty and thoroughness were, they argued, rooted in a historical ethnographic concept of the people. But German history could not be the history of a people; it had to be the history of peoples. Many subsequent historians viewed Germany as consisting of several distinct tribes who were all perceived, in a typical nature metaphor, as branches from one stem. Fichte's famous 'Speeches to the German Nation' at the Berlin Academy in 1807/8 emphasized the German nation as a product of history.[47] Historical societies spread rapidly in the first half of the nineteenth century. In 1850, of 190 scholarly societies in the German lands, about one-third were historical societies. Yet the majority of these studied the local and regional history of their particular territories (*Landesgeschichte*). National history was at best perceived as the sum total of those *Landesgeschichten*. Regional historical societies often formed close political ties with their respective territorial states. They legitimated the existence of these states more than they aspired to a non-existent unified German nation state.

[47] It should be noted that Fichte, of course, also emphasized the notion of Germany as a linguistic, cultural and political community. Arguably Fichte's speeches were so successful because they drew on all the diverse sources which made up German national consciousness in the early nineteenth century.

Language, literature and history were the foundation stones of a national movement. The same can be said for geography.[48] The idea of natural geographical borders was instrumentalized by the French revolutionary armies in the 1790s to legitimate their expansionist ambitions. German geographers responded in kind by constructing natural geographical borders for a German nation state of the future. The national character of the people became closely associated with the geographical characteristics of the country. A nation could only exist as such if it was in line with geographical logic and the 'will of nature'. For many nationalists, despairing about the indeterminacy of Germany's geographical borders, language was, however, more powerful than geography. This is evident from one of the most popular nationalist poems of the nineteenth century, Arndt's 'What is the German's fatherland?'

What is the German's fatherland?	Was is des Deutschen Vaterland?
So tell me the big country!	So nenne mir das große Land!
As far as the German tongue is spoken	So weit die deutsche Zunge klingt
And God in heaven sings songs	Und Gott im Himmel Lieder singt,
That shall be it!	Das soll es sein!
That, trusty German, call your own![49]	Das, wackrer Deutscher, nenne dein!

Arndt himself is a fascinating example of how a sense of national identity is frequently being formed in relation to experiences of a national 'other'. He grew up on the island of Rügen in the Baltic Sea – then part of the Swedish state. Until the turn of the century he thought of himself primarily as a Swede. It was only in the context of his enmity towards Napoleon that he fully discovered his own 'Germanness'.

Nationalist propaganda directed against Napoleonic France was not only funded by Prussia. Austria also became very active after 1809. Romantic nationalists such as Friedrich Schlegel were hired to highlight Austria's unity with other German-speaking states in central Europe and convince the latter that their interests were coterminous with those of Austria. Once again the common language was the most important marker of German unity. The anti-Prussianism of Austrian propaganda led to theories which distinguished between north Germans and south Germans, who allegedly had two different national characters. Whereas the former kept themselves to themselves and were sinister, gloomy, strict and hard, the latter were supposed to be more peaceful, educated, jolly, free-spirited and willing to mix with other peoples. *Gemütlichkeit* (inadequately translated as 'cosiness') was at home in southern Germany, not in the north. Unsurprisingly, the appeal of Romantic nationalism was limited in the Protestant north, since authors such as Schlegel (or Novalis for that matter) glorified the medieval *Reich* and its alleged unity of emperor and pope. That era was constructed as a golden age of Germandom, in which the Catholic popes had been the guarantors of peace and stability. The knights were German heroes who had extended the borders of

48 Hans-Dietrich Schultz, 'Land–Volk–Staat: Der geografische Anteil an der Erfindung der Nation', *Geschichte in Wissenschaft und Unterricht*, 51 (2000), pp. 4–16. See generally David Hooson, ed., *Geography and National Identity* (Oxford, 1994).

49 Ernst Moritz Arndt, 'Des deutschen Vaterland' [1813], in Karl Otto Conrady, ed., *Das große deutsche Gedichtbuch* (Königstein im Taunus, 1985), p. 392.

the Empire. Adherence to the universalism of the Catholic church went hand in hand with notions of a greater Germany (*Germania magna*).

Romantic nationalism was by no means restricted to Austria. In Berlin Achim von Arnim founded the 'Christian–German Table Society' (*Christlich–deutsche Tischgesellschaft*) in 1811, which brought together everyone who was aspiring to be someone in Berlin's intellectual life. The strong Christian slant of Romantic nationalism was at times combined with a vicious antisemitism. Non-Christians, in particular Jews, became enemies of the German nation *qua* religion. They could not be assimilated into a people defined primarily by a religious culture. German and Jewish national characters were juxtaposed as incompatible and the Jewish presence in the midst of Germany was constructed as threatening the nation with 'impurity'. The Jew was perceived as a parasite on the healthy German national body. Arnim, together with other well-known Romantics, such as Clemens Brentano and Adam Müller, all harboured antisemitic sentiments and refused to mix with Jews socially.[50] Such antisemitism persisted at a time when many discriminations against the Jewish members of individual German states were relinquished in acts of emancipation (e.g. in Baden in 1808; in Prussia in 1812). Jews could now become citizens of their respective states, but many restrictions (not least of movement) and discriminations remained in place. In most German states Jewish immigrants were not welcome.

In the early nineteenth century citizenship became increasingly important in defining who belonged to a particular state and who was entitled to benefits provided by that state.[51] In the Holy Roman Empire membership in a particular municipality had been all-important. Municipalities had their own codifications of who belonged and who did not. The very term 'citizen' (*Staatsbürger*) only came into wider usage in the late eighteenth century. In the absence of a unified German nation state, citizenship laws were developed by the German territorial states. Austria was first to define Austrian citizenship in the *Allgemeine Bürgerliche Gesetzbuch* (ABGB) of 1811. The idea behind such a codification was to give unity to what were very disparate territories. One citizenship law was supposed to bind very different people together. Once again the French Revolution had led the way: the idea of citizenship had been a powerful emotional tool capable of mobilizing the masses behind the revolutionary ambitions. In France, the place of birth was the decisive criterion for citizenship (*ius soli*): those born in France were French. In Austria and in the German states which subsequently adopted citizenship laws, the decisive criterion was ethnicity. Having been born

50 Susanna Moßmann, 'Das Fremde ausscheiden: Antisemitismus und Nationalbewußtsein bei Ludwig Achim von Arnim und in der "Christlich-deutschen Tischgesellschaft"', in Hans-Peter Herrmann, Hans-Martin Blitz and Susanna Moßmann, eds, *Machtphantasie Deutschland: Nationalismus, Männlichkeit und Fremdenhaß im Vaterlandsdiskurs deutscher Schriftsteller des 18. Jahrhunderts* (Frankfurt/Main 1996), pp. 123–60.

51 The importance of citizenship laws for national identity is discussed extensively in Dieter Gosewinkel, *Einbürgern und Ausschließen: Die Nationalisierung der Staatsangehörikeit vom Deutschen Bund bis zur Bundesrepublik Deutschland* (Göttingen, 2001); Andreas Fahrmeier, *Citizens and Aliens: Foreigners and the Law in Britain and the German States, 1789–1870* (Oxford, 2000); Rogers Brubaker, *Citizenship and Nationhood in France and Germany* (Cambridge, Mass., 1992).

the child of an Austrian, Badenese, Prussian etc. father (regardless of the location) determined citizenship (*ius sanguinis*).

There was, however, no straightforward dichotomy between French and German citizenship laws. The Austrian law already knew a *ius domicilis*: after ten years of living in Austria, one could apply for citizenship. As migration, communication and economic relations between the German states intensified in the first half of the nineteenth century, a series of mutual agreements came to regulate the flow of 'foreign' nationals from one German state to the other. All of these treaties were based on the *ius domicilis*, i.e. the decisive criterion for citizenship was place of permanent residence. Overall, passports became a powerful mass symbol of belonging to the nation state. Possessing a passport meant the difference between receiving benefits and being deported, imprisoned or even killed.

High hopes and disillusionment: the national idea from the wars of liberty to the Karlsbad decrees

In many textbooks on German history the wars against Napoleon between 1812 and 1815 have been described as 'wars of liberation' (*Befreiungskriege*). The term 'wars of liberty' was, however, the contemporary one. It linked nationalism firmly to demands for liberty and an end to all oppression. Such nationalism could be directed against Napoleon as well as against the German princes. Subsequently, throughout the nineteenth century, the legacy of these wars of liberty was deradicalized and sanitized. A new term, 'wars of liberation', now foregrounded the aspect of liberation from 'foreign' French rule and downplayed the aspect of liberty. By the time of the 1913 centenary celebrations in Germany, almost everyone was talking about the 'wars of liberation'. A conservative, monarchist and antiliberal interpretation of events, in which the people were merely the loyal servants of the crowned heads of the German states, had triumphed. The people's wider aspirations for freedom, democracy and constitutionalism had been written out of the history books.

Nationalism was, in any case, at best a minority opinion in the wars of liberty. The memorialization of that war after 1815 was a far more important vehicle for nationalism than the war itself. Events and battles were commemorated in festivals, theatrical performances, tournaments, processions and through the ringing of church bells.[52] Nationalist myth-making connected to the period of the wars of liberty abounded. One of most powerful myths concerned the spontaneous uprising of volunteers who rallied to the anti-Napoleonic cause and joined either the regular militia, the *Landwehr*, or special volunteer riflemen's organizations, the so-called *Freikorps*. Of Prussia's 300,000-strong army, militia units made up 120,000 men. They played an important military role, for example, in the Battle of Leipzig. The model of the *Freikorps* became the Lützow Rangers (*Lützowsche Schar*), a battalion

52 Christopher Clark, 'The Wars of Liberation in Prussian Memory: Reflections on the Memorialization of War in Early Nineteenth-Century Germany', *Journal of Modern History*, 68 (1996), pp. 550–76.

which included famous poets, such as Theodor Körner, who celebrated the war as the moment of national awakening. The Lützow Rangers were certainly unusual in that they swore allegiance not to the Prussian king but to the German nation. Intellectuals such as Bettina von Arnim demonstrated their commitment to the national cause by plans to name her son (who was born in 1812) Landstürmche. Luckily for him, she eventually settled for Freimund. But, more to the point, despite the best efforts of nationalist intellectuals, the *Landwehr* had nothing to do with the German people arming themselves. It was organized by Prussia from above and many 'volunteers' were forced into the *Landwehr* at gunpoint. And the *Freikorps* presented only a very small percentage of mainly young people – not more than 30,000 in total, few of whom were fighting for an illusory German nation. A much stronger Prussian patriotism at the time was bound up with loyalty towards the dynasty rather than towards a non-existent German nation. As Jörg Echternkamp has succinctly put it: 'The national rising did not happen.'[53]

Körner, who died in the wars of liberty, became a national hero – a poet and a national warrior who had sacrificed his life 'on the altar of the fatherland'. He fitted into the new cult of the citizen-soldier fighting a holy war for the nation that was propagated by Arndt and others at the time. Later in the nineteenth century his civic virtues, commitment to a cosmopolitan humanism and intellectual qualifications were increasingly demoted and the emphasis was more on discipline, heroism and virility.[54] The 'patriotic and soldierly citzens' hero' gave way to the 'Reich national warrior hero'. The First World War was to see the rise of the new 'technological heroes', such as the flying ace Manfred von Richthofen or the U-boat captain Otto Weddigsen. War heroes were given clear male gender attributes, and 'heroic manliness' became a byword for soldierly values.[55]

Yet the wars of liberty were not only fought by men. Some women, subsequently dubbed 'sword virgins' (*Schwertjungfrauen*), enlisted under the name of men [Figure 1.2]. Twenty-three are known to us, and none became more famous than Eleonor Prochaska who was celebrated by nationalists as a 'German Jean d'Arc'. Such direct involvement of women in the war effort was becoming the exception in the nineteenth century and their actions could only be justified with reference to the extraordinariness of the situation and the depth of national despair. National military service in peacetime was explicitly to exclude women, and their inability to serve would be an important justification for denying them full citizenship rights.

A separate spheres ideology had been codified in law during the eighteenth century which made the public realm the affair of men and aimed to restrict women to the private sphere.[56] But that was an idea which was constantly being

[53] Echternkamp, *Aufstieg*, p. 216 (see note 36).

[54] René Schilling, 'Die soziale Konstruktion heroischer Männlichkeit im 19. Jahrhundert: Das Beispiel Theodor Körner', in Karen Hagemann and Ralf Pröve, eds, *Landsknechte, Soldatenfrauen und Nationalkrieger: Militär, Krieg und Geschlechterordnung im historischen Wandel* (Frankfurt/Main, 1998), pp. 121–44.

[55] René Schilling, *'Kriegshelden': Deutungsmuster heroischer Männlichkeit in Deutschland 1813–1945* (Paderborn, 2002).

[56] Marion W. Grey, 'Men as Citizens and Women as Wives: The Enlightenment Codification of Law and the Establishment of Separate Spheres', in Duchhardt and Kunz, eds, *Reich*, pp. 279–97 (see note 43).

Eleonore Prochaskas tödliche Verwundung im Gefecht an der Göhrde. Nach einem alten Holzschnit von W. Lindenschmitt.

Figure 1.2 Eleanor Prochaska, one of the 'sword virgins' fighting in the wars of liberty for a more liberal and a more unified German nation.

challenged and undermined by women seeking to perform 'national duties' in the public realm. National wars were to give them many opportunities. In this respect the wars of liberty established patterns of women's behaviour and gender roles which remained valid for much of the nineteenth and twentieth centuries.[57] Nationalist discourse claimed the unity and equality of all members of the nation, but at the same time it institutionalized gender differences. Especially the equation between nation and family in the 'people's family' (*Volksfamilie*) allowed the construction of a gender order which was perceived as the foundation of a stable state and nation. The nation was imagined as a family with men and women occupying different but complementary roles: active, creative and passionate men were juxtaposed to loving, gentle, caring and beautiful women.[58] In times of war heroism was male and sacrifice female. If women could not be soldiers, they could be 'heroic mothers' (*Heldenmütter*), 'wives of soldiers' (*Soldatenfrauen*), 'warriors' brides' (*Kriegerbräute*) and 'nurses' (*Krankenpflegerinnen*).

During the wars of liberty, 573 women's associations were founded.[59] Their membership ranged from ten to one hundred women; with the exception of the eighteenth-century reading societies, it was the biggest associational movement ever. It dwarfed the male associations founded to support the war effort. Women

[57] Karen Hagemann, *'Männlicher Muth und teutsche Ehre': Nation, Krieg und Geschlecht in der Zeit der antinapoleonischen Kriege Preußens* (Paderborn, 2002).

[58] Karen Hagemann, 'Of "Manly Valor" and "German Honour": Nation, War and Masculinity in the Age of the Prussian Uprising against Napoleon', *Central European History*, 30 (1997), pp. 187–220.

[59] Dirk Alexander Reder, *Frauenbewegung und Nation: Patriotische Frauenvereine in Deutschland im frühen 19. Jahrhundert, 1813–1830* (Cologne, 1998).

in these organizations became involved in charity work: collecting money, providing clothing for the soldiers, caring for the wounded and the ill as well as the permanently disabled. They accepted the predominant discourse of male warriors and female helpers, but the women had to fulfil an important national duty. Some women directly related the women's role in the home to the state of world affairs. Thus Betty Gleim wrote in her pamphlet, *What Has the Reborn Germany to Demand of its Women?* (1814):

> Women, much has been entrusted to you; you, miraculously, hold in your hands the *government of the world*, although you might not be conscious of it! Whether, generally speaking, things go well or not depends on you and is your doing. If *you* govern the house wisely, then a wise government will delight *country* and *people*. But if your seemingly small regiment is poor, then do not be surprised that things outside will be pitiful, and it is a shame to live in such a state which has been brought to its knees by women who have forgotten their duty.[60]

The realm of politics was redefined so that the private sphere became political. Public happiness depended on women's role in the private sphere. But the demands of women for participation stayed mostly within the boundaries of the dominant patriarchal gender discourse. Hence it is not surprising that most of these women's associations were dissolved at the end of the war in 1815. Only a minority survived by reorienting themselves to caring for the poor and turning to social welfare.

The strong connection between gender order and nationalism is also very visible in the mythologies surrounding Queen Luise of Prussia (1776–1810).[61] Johann Gottfried Schadow made a famous bust of Luise as early as 1795 which idealized her female beauty. Subsequently Luise became the *mater patriae* who assembled in her person all the virtues of German women. In 1800 a *Pocket Book for Noble German Women* portrayed Luise as role model for all German women. She was a model wife and mother who loved her husband and educated her children herself. She had human warmth, discipline and a practical mind which combined modesty with homeliness. She was the least scandalous of royals imaginable. A succession of famous German writers – Jean Paul, Wieland, Goethe and Kleist come to mind – wrote about her. In the nineteenth century Luisen memorials and altars could be found all over Prussia. Primary-school reading books in Prussia invariably carried stories about Luise. In 1870/71 Prussian troops carried her portrait into battle. Schools and orphanages were named after her. In the twentieth century films were made about her and when, in the midst of the Weimar Republic, a monarchist women's association was founded in 1923, it took the name Luisen Association (*Luisenbund*).

Women shared in the nationalist agitation which was a prominent feature of the wars of liberty. But when it came to reordering the map of Europe in 1815 nationalists, men and women, were going to be disappointed. The Congress of

60 Cited in Karen Hagemann, ' "Deutsche Heldinnen": Patriotisch-nationales Frauenhandeln in der Zeit der antinapoleonischen Kriege', in Ute Planert, *Nation, Politik und Geschlecht,* p. 101 (see note 28).

61 Günter de Bruyn, *Preussens Luise: Vom Entstehen und Vergehen einer Legende* (Berlin, 2001).

Vienna, masterminded by Count Metternich, established a German Confederation (*Deutscher Bund*), which, like its predecessor, the Holy Roman Empire, was a federation of quasi-autonomous territorial states [Map 2]. Yet the centralization of territories in the 1800s could not be reversed. Hence it was a federation of far fewer and often larger states: 38 territories and four free city states in total. They did not want strong central government but preferred sovereignty. As all major European powers were wary of a strong and unified German nation state in central Europe, the German Confederation had few and relatively weak central institutions. It boasted a confederal army which was supposed to protect the alliance of sovereign states from outside threats. It also had a confederal diet in Frankfurt am Main, where each state was represented. The nominal head of the Confederation was the Austrian emperor, but de facto the two biggest powers within the Confederation, Prussia and Austria, dominated the north and south respectively. Both were multi-national states which incorporated large numbers of subjects who could not be classed as German by any stretch of the imagination. After 1815, however, Prussia was the more German of the two empires. It lost many of its Polish lands to Russia and instead gained territories in central and western Germany. Nevertheless, around 1815, those propagating Prussia's mission to unify Germany were a tiny minority. Especially in Austria and in the 'third Germany' (territories outside Prussia and the Habsburg Empire), many were mistrustful of Prussia's national rhetoric and saw it as a barely veiled attempt to expand Prussian territory and influence.

Within the Confederation processes of state-building were carried out within the territorial states rather than at the national level.[62] Many of the states had changed their shape considerably between 1803 and 1815 and they wanted to consolidate their authority over their territories. Constitutions and citizenship laws were meant to create a new sense of territorial identity. The interests of the territorial state were being pursued against all special interests, in particular those of the nobility, who lost many of their special privileges. The idea of divine-right monarchies and absolutism had been fatally undermined by the French Revolution. Almost everywhere in the German lands, and especially in the 'third Germany', monarchs became constitutional monarchs. They were careful to present themselves as popular monarchs, in harmony with their subjects. The strength of indigenous liberal movements forced monarchies to change: monarch and people now became a unity, where previously they had been two separate entities.

Attempts to create strong and integrated unitary states at the territorial level tended to acknowledge the existence of a German nation. Only in Bavaria can we see sustained efforts to bolster the notion of a separate Bavarian national identity. In all other states attempts were made to reconcile sentiments of Germanness with territorial state-building. The assumption was that a centralized nation state would not be in line with German national traditions. Once again federalism was constructed as the key characteristic of Germany. Many

[62] The importance of these state-building processes has been emphasized by Abigail Green, *Fatherlands: State-Building and Nationhood in Nineteenth-Century Germany* (Cambridge, 2001).

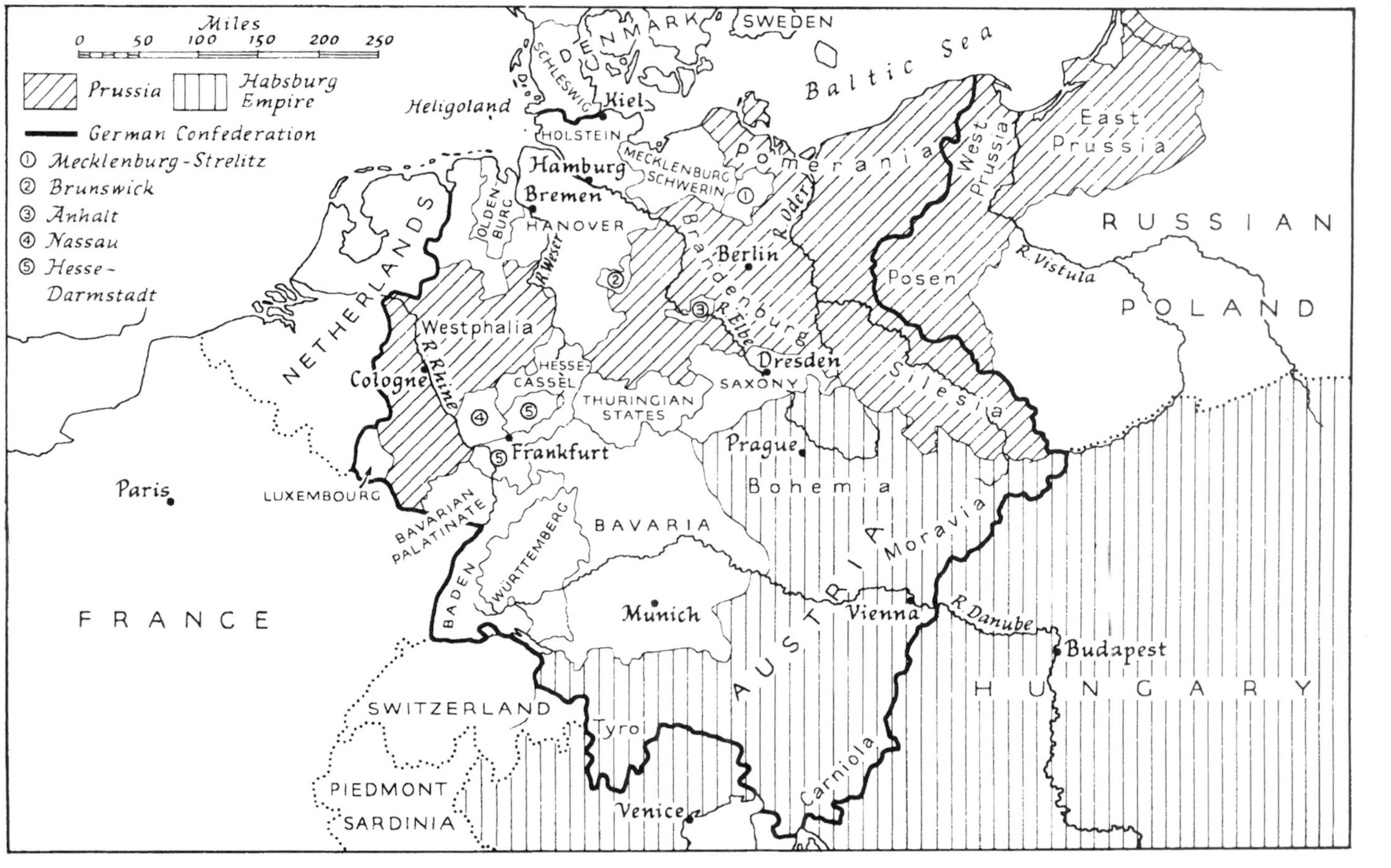

Map 2 The German Confederation, 1815.

individual German states inside the Confederation were successful in engendering state loyalties which survived the end of the Confederation in 1866. National monuments often had a regional touch, as had all state-sponsored cultural activities and, incidentally, postage stamps. National histories were mediated through the regions. Regional newspapers (which also carried national news) remained the norm in Germany (until today). When the *Deutsche Zeitung* appeared in 1847 it was the first time that a newspaper actually carried the word 'German' in its title. Communication networks such as the railway systems were based on the territorial states and often re-enforced regional rather than national identities.

After 1871 'small-German' nationalists condemned the Confederation as unworkable, just as they depicted the Holy Roman Empire as a monstrosity. The nationalist historian Heinrich von Treitschke, for example, described the Confederation's constitution as the worst ever given to a great people. But many others accepted the framework provided by the Confederation and worked hard to develop it into a more unified nation state. After all, the Confederation functioned reasonably well and it was widely accepted by its member states.[63] It kept the German states out of war and guaranteed internal peace and stability. If the Confederation could become not a federation of sovereign princes but of the German people, along the lines of the federal constitutional system of the United States of America, this would allow a United States of Germany to emerge which would avoid the disadvantages of a centralized unitary state. Making the central institutions of the Confederation responsible to a national parliament would be a first step in the right direction. For many moderate adherents to the national idea it was by no means a foregone conclusion that the Confederation would never be able to develop into something resembling a nation state.

Nationalists organized in a multitude of voluntary associations, such as informal friendship circles, social clubs, scholarly societies and private libraries during the first half of the nineteenth century. Associations became the most successful form of social mobilization in this period. Their members practised a new kind of sociability which involved an element of social levelling, as all members emphatically related to each other as equals.[64] Self-regulating bodies, they laid down their own forms of often democratic decision-making. They created their own statutes, held membership assemblies and elected society officers. They provided a public sphere which played a crucial role in the formation of public opinion and paved the way for a more participatory society. The most important nationalist associations were those of the gymnasts (*Turnvereine*), the students (*Burschenschaften*), the choral societies (*Gesangsvereine*), and the gun clubs (*Schützenvereine*).

63 Helmut Rumpler, ed., *Deutscher Bund und deutsche Frage 1815–1866* (Munich, 1990).

64 Otto Dann, ed., *Vereinswesen und bürgerliche Gesellschaft in Deutschland* (HZ Beiheft NF 9, Munich, 1984), pp. 55–115; Dieter Düding, 'Die deutsche Nationalbewegung als Vereinsbewegung: Anmerkung zu ihrer Struktur und Phänomenologie zwischen Befreiungskriegszeitalter und Reichsgründung', *Geschichte in Wissenschaft und Unterricht*, 42 (1991), pp. 601–24.

In the 1810s, 150 gymastics associations organized approximately 12,000 gymnasts, mainly in Prussia and North Germany.[65] They perceived the regular exercise of a healthy body as laying the foundations for a healthy nation. Gymnasts were often also singers and members of gun clubs (*Schützen*), and, in the case of students, members of the *Burschenschaften*. The young were over-represented. Membership of most associations was socially diverse and often incorporated artisans, although the majority came from the educated middle classes. The values all of these organizations espoused were bourgeois ones: discipline, decency, morality, order, manliness and a healthy lifestyle.

Two years before the first gymnastics associations were founded, Friedrich Zelter organized the Berlin Song Board (*Berliner Liedertafel*) in 1809. It became a model for other choral societies in Prussia. Its membership was restricted to those with musical talent coming from the upper echelons of society. Their nationalism was primarily Prussian rather than German. The choral associations in southern Germany, which emerged from the 1820s onwards, were a different matter. They were socially more inclusive and aimed at propagating a broader German national consciousness through song. They continued an eighteenth-century tradition, which regarded music as the most German of arts and of central importance in the task of nation-building.[66] People's songs were perceived as part and parcel of national education. Choral societies, like the gymnasts, excluded women. Male voices were supposed to be better suited to singing than female ones. For the gymnasts fitness and paramilitary training was also regarded as an all-male affair. The specific sociability within these associations was a male form of comradeship. But women played an important part in the festival culture of the gymnasts, choirs and gun clubs: they stitched the flags, handed out the prizes and were simply present as spectators, joining in the increasingly popular 'people's festivities' (*Volksfeste*). In line with the separate spheres ideology women fitted in, above all, as mothers, sisters and wives.

The gymnasts and the singers became major pillars of the national movement. On the eve of the 1848 revolution the gymnasts had 80–90,000 members and the choral societies could muster about 100,000 members. The gun clubs looked back on a much older history. Their golden age was in the fifteenth and sixteenth centuries, after which they declined. Increasingly they resembled sport and social associations. They still practised their shooting, which gave their activities a paramilitary character similar to those of the gymnasts. The social side of their festivities, especially drinking and singing, were, however, at least equally important. The new students' associations (*Burschenschaften*), founded in 1815, abhorred the drinking and gambling of their fellow students and denounced the widespread use of prostitutes by students. Some of the founding members had fought

[65] Michael Kruger, 'Body Culture and Nation Building: The History of Gymnastics in Germany in the Period of its Foundation as a Nation-State', *International Journal of the History of Sport*, 13 (1996), pp. 409–17.

[66] Mary Sue Morrow, 'Building a National Identity with Music: A Story from the Eighteenth Century', in Nicholas Vazsonyi, ed., *Searching for Common Ground: Diskurse zur deutschen Identität 1750–1871* (Cologne, 2000), pp. 255–69; Conrad L. Donakowski, 'Music, Politics, and Popular Culture: Nineteenth-Century Choral Singing, Especially in Regensburg, Bavaria', *Consortium on Revolutionary Europe, 1750–1850: Proceedings*, 23 (1994), pp. 224–32.

with the *Freikorps* in the wars of liberty. Their flag was the same as that of the Lützow Rangers: three stripes of black, red and gold. Their national and democratic orientation marked them out from their main rivals, the regionalist *Landsmannschaften*. Their first major public festival took place at the Wartburg on 18 October 1817 to commemorate the 300th anniversary of the Reformation and the fourth anniversary of the Battle of Leipzig. The students merged Protestant nationalism with the memorialization of the wars of liberty as a time when a greater national consciousness was taking shape. The Wartburg was also a key symbol of German culture. In the Middle Ages, Hermann of Thuringia (1190–1217) made it a centre of literary and artistic encounters. Two of the most well-known German medieval poets, Walther von der Vogelweide and Wolfram von Eschenbach, were protégés of Hermann. The Wartburg was also the refuge of Martin Luther and the place where he translated the New Testament into German. Hence it seemed appropriate for some 500 students from about eleven German universities to assemble here, south-west of Eisenach in Thuringia, to celebrate both the Reformation, which allegedly freed the German nation from papal despotism, and the victory at Leipzig, which freed the German nation from Napoleon's despotism. Books believed to be antinational and antidemocratic were burnt, as were symbols of absolutist rule. Liberty, freedom, democracy and national unity were among the key demands of the students.

The Wartburg festivities demonstrated the desire of the nationalist movement to rally around national symbols. Joseph Görres had already proposed the idea of a national monument in 1814. As a Catholic Rhinelander he suggested the Cologne dome – a massive gothic Cathedral which had remained an unfinished torso since the Middle Ages. The Gothic style was perceived as a typically German form of architecture. That it had been under construction for centuries seemed to symbolize the inner disunity of the German lands. Building the dome as a monument to Germany would be a symbolic gesture. It would demonstrate the desire of Germans to build a unified nation state, a new *Reich*. Over the next decades, the project was remarkably successful. Donations came in from all parts of Germany. The Prussian monarchy took an active interest. And the special festivities to celebrate the beginning and the end of the final construction period in 1842 and 1880, as well as the 600th anniversary of the dome in 1848, became genuinely popular events with a strong nationalist appeal.[67]

If nationalism was becoming more popular in the first half of the nineteenth century, it was also an opposition movement. The powers which had determined the settlement at the Congress of Vienna viewed it with suspicion. In 1817, the unruly events at the Wartburg alarmed conservatives in all German states. When two years later, in 1819, a member of the *Burschenschaften*, Karl Ludwig Sand, murdered an antiliberal and antinational writer, August von Kotzebue, the Confederation, led by the formidable Metternich, passed the Karlsbad decrees (*Karlsbader Beschlüsse*) of 1819. In essence they were common policing measures aimed at the repression of the liberal-democratic and national movement in the German lands. In particular their associational activities were the target of

[67] Thomas Nipperdey, 'Der Kölner Dom als Nationaldenkmal', *Historische Zeitschrift*, 233 (1981), pp. 595–613.

oppression. Jahn himself was imprisoned between 1819 and 1825. Even after his release he had to report to the police regularly and his freedom of movement was restricted. Jahn, the crank, with whom we opened this chapter, was rehabilitated by Frederick Wilhelm IV in 1840. Two years later, gymnastics became a school subject in Prussia, and in the 1840s a Jahn revival took place which celebrated the 'father of gymnastics' (*Turnvater*) as the father of the German nation to be. He had travelled a long way from marvelled-at eccentric to doyen of a growing national movement in the German lands.

Yet, by 1819, the making of Germans was still only the preoccupation of a minority. Most people living in the German lands did not yet think of themselves as primarily German. Local, regional, religious, occupational and cosmopolitan, transnational identities were all still far more important. Those who did have a strong national consciousness could draw on a wide and diverse range of ideas. National discourses were cultural, political and historical: they could idealize a Kantian rational republic or celebrate the Holy Roman Empire. By and large, they represented a *bricolage* of disparate ideas which, as we will see over the next chapters, could be put together in a number of different ways and to very diverse effects.

2

Nationalism in search of a mass audience, 1819–1871

In 1859 about 500 towns and cities across Germany celebrated the centenary of the birth of the man who had become the intellectual founding figure of the German nation: the dramatist Friedrich Schiller.[1] Tens of thousands of people from very different social, confessional and regional backgrounds came together in what was the biggest mass festival in nineteenth-century Germany. Schiller, who had died of tuberculosis in 1805, only 45 years old, became *the* national poet in Germany, because his writings seemed to symbolize the values of the bourgeois nation. His dramas such as *Die Räuber* (1782) and *Don Carlos* (1787) championed the freedom of the individual and of the people against absolutist tyrannies. He time and again defended the universality of human rights and criticized a society in which people were ordered into separate estates according to birth (*Kabale und Liebe*, 1784). *Wilhelm Tell* (1802–4) – the biggest sales hit in nineteenth-century German literature – and his *Geschichte des Abfalls der Vereinigten Niederlande von der Spanischen Regierung* (1788) made the right of the people to form their own nations a direct topic. 'We want to be a single nation of brothers,' was a line from *Wilhelm Tell* which was to ring a chord with the national movement. Yet Schiller never was an ardent nationalist, such as Arndt or Jahn. He was always proud that the French had made him an honorary citizen of the Republic in 1792 and remained sceptical of political attempts to create a unified German nation state.

This, however, could not prevent his thorough nationalization in the nineteenth century. When his intellectual soulmate, Johann Wolfgang von Goethe, wrote a memorial poem for his friend shortly after his death, he repeatedly used the verse 'Because he was ours!' (*Denn er war unser!*). Although this was not meant in a national sense, it was quickly interpreted as such. Volunteers in the wars of liberty were reported to have sung with enthusiasm the *Reiterlied* from Schiller's *Wallenstein's Lager*. And the liberal national movement began to organize the national admiration for Schiller in the first half of the nineteenth century.

[1] Otto Dann, 'Schiller', in Etienne François and Hagen S. Schulze, eds, *Deutsche Erinnerungsorte*, 3 vols (Munich, 2001), Vol. 2, pp. 171–86.

Georg Gottfried Gervinus, in his five-volume *History of the Poetical National Literature of the Germans* (1835–40), canonized the classical period of German literature, symbolized by the intellectual partnership of Goethe and Schiller in Weimar, as the high point of German literary culture.

The Schillerfest in Stuttgart in 1839, where a memorial to the national poet was unveiled, already demonstrated the dead poet's ability to rally thousands to the national cause. Twenty years later all the registers of an elaborate national festival culture were drawn to confirm Schiller's status as arch-symbol of the German national movement [Figure 2.1]. National festivities followed specific patterns: solemn processions to central festival squares were accompanied by the ringing of church bells and the firing of cannons. People wore what they believed to be national costume and the festival square (sometimes the entire town) was decorated with national insignia. Flags were prominent, as were oak leaves. The oak had been the holy tree of the Germanic tribes. It became a symbol for steadfastness and strength – allegedly core ingredients of the German 'national character'.[2] The black, red and gold increasingly became the flag of the national movement: black standing for the dark present, gold for the bright future and red for the bloody struggle which lay in between. The nationalists would read out patriotic poems and speeches – all of this accompanied by renditions of national songs. They would light fires and swear allegiance to the fatherland on holy national flames. These festivals addressed themselves to all Germans, regardless of age, social status, gender or profession, and they were successful in mobilizing support which went beyond the core of middle-class intellectuals who had been the standard-bearers of the national idea until the nineteenth century.

Schiller was not the only iconic figure to be fêted in this way. Other prominent 'Germans' who were similarly remembered included the inventor of the printing press, Johann Gutenberg, the painter Albrecht Dürer and, of course, the reformer, Martin Luther. The prime attraction of Schiller, however, lay in his ambivalence: as with nationalism itself, different people could read different things into Schiller. Reference to his writings could legitimate diverse versions of the nation. Thus, the socialist labour movement championed Schiller as the revolutionary who had detested tyranny and stood up for the freedom of the people. This did not prevent the political right in Germany from emphasizing Schiller's concern for the unity of the nation in the face of 'foreign' oppression. Hence Schiller always remained a different 'ours' to different groups constructing different versions of Germany.

In the first part of this chapter the road to the liberal national revolution of 1848 will be discussed. Analysing the extent and the limits of repression under the Karlsbad decrees, the focus will be initially on the developing institutions, networks and discourses of the liberal national camp. The second part of this chapter will then deal with the national side of the 1848 revolution. Nationalism as an ideology was used by diverse groups, such as women, workers and Jews, to claim greater inclusivity in the nation state. The continuing impact of strong particularist identities will be looked at in the context of the emerging 'small-German' and 'greater-German' schools. Due consideration will be given to the

2 See below, p. 65.

Figure 2.1 The centenary of Schiller's birth was celebrated by all sections of the national movement. Commemorative drawing from the *Gartenlaube*, 10 November 1859: representatives of different regions and different social classes come to pay tribute to the poet. The heading reads: 'the only thing and the only one'; the subtitle is: 'wherein Germany is united'. In the background you see people celebrating in America and other continents.

struggle over the memorialization of 1848. While conservatives, as we shall see, increasingly learned the language of the nation, around 1848 it was the urban middle classes who still dominated the national discourse. In the final part of this chapter the impact of 1848 on the development of national thinking will be examined. The reorientation of liberal nationalists towards power politics, the popularity of economic definitions of Germanness, the continued dualism between pro-Austria and pro-Prussian nationalism and the eventual Bismarckian 'revolution from above' will all be considered.

From repression to revolution, 1819–48

The associationalism which was the backbone of the national festival culture – above all choirs, gymnasts, shooting societies and students' associations – had suffered severe repression under the infamous Karlsbad decrees of 1819. In particular the intellectual leaders of the national movement were denounced as demagogues. They were sacked from their positions at the universities and the civil service. Police informants infiltrated their circles. They were repeatedly interrogated by the authorities and many were imprisoned. Thousands of liberal nationalists were prosecuted. Tough new censorship laws were introduced and applied to all publications except long and expensive books. The *Burschenschaften* (students' associations) were dissolved and their members portrayed as dangerous criminals. Repression was particularly effective in Austria, where the government successfully curbed the intellectual exchanges between the Habsburg Empire and other German lands. In 1825 all non-Austrian students had to leave Austrian universities and after 1829 Austrians were not allowed to study abroad. Gymnast and singing associations could not be formed in the Habsburg Empire. All communication between Austria and the rest of the German lands was tightly controlled.

But repression had its limits. The decrees were handled differently in different parts of the German Confederation. Not all governments were as severe as the Austrian one. And complete control of public opinion remained elusive. Censorship rules were undermined in a variety of ways. Networks of liberal nationalist circles were maintained throughout the period of repression between 1819 and 1842. When they marshalled their forces in 1832 at Hambach, 30,000 people came together at the first mass nationalist rally in the German lands to call for a free and united Germany. In particular the universities remained centres of nationalism throughout the nineteenth century. Professors saw themselves as intellectual mandarins educating the nation. Historians, theologians and economists became champions of the national idea.[3] Employed by the territorial states, they often sought to merge loyalty to their paymasters with a national commitment, mediating between the allegiances demanded by the territorial state and the ambitions of the national movement. Following the enforced dissolution of the *Burschenschaften*, national-minded professors encouraged their students to reassemble in friendship circles or reading societies and to maintain contact with national-minded student circles at other universities. Wearing 'German attire'

[3] Hedda Gramley, *Propheten des deutschen Nationalismus: Theologen, Historiker und Nationalökonomen (1848–1880)* (Frankfurt/Main, 2001).

now became a symbol of resistance to the Karlsbad decrees. From the 1820s onwards the national movement became socially more inclusive. Middle-class students attempted to interest artisans in the national topic. Often they appealed to the egalitarian features of nationalism and held out promises of breaking down social barriers. The national movement was thus depicted as a great alliance of different social strata united by a common national desire and identity.

Liberal national values and activities were carried from the universities into the schools. Teachers who had been caught up in the national movement of the 1810s introduced their pupils to the national literature from the wars of liberty. History teachers used textbooks such as Friedrich Kohlrausch's *Teutsche Geschichte* to construct a national past, which celebrated ancient Germanic tribes and their freedoms, glorified medieval German peasants and knights and criticized German feudalism for squandering both liberty and national unity. As literacy rates throughout the German lands were high by European standards and school attendance was enforced more and more, their efforts to spread the national message had some effect. Teachers portrayed themselves as educators of the nation out of conviction, but nationalism also legitimated their demands for more pay and higher social status. Since a German state did not exist, teachers were by no means tools of state-induced nationalism. In fact they were employed by the territorial states, where subjects such as history, religion and geography were used to strengthen the ties of the pupils with their respective territory. Thus many teachers had a dual loyalty: to the territorial state that paid them and to the imagined nation state of the future. Bringing the two into harmony was not always an easy task.

History teachers were often actively involved in the mushrooming historical associations, which worked hard to bring the many stories about the diverse regions and territories of the German lands together into a common national story. History, however, could be the servant of many masters. Regionalists used it to legitimate the existence of territorial states while nationalists used it to justify their demands for a unified nation state. Liberals and democrats used it to underpin their demands for constitutionalism just as much as conservatives used it to construct antimodernist and antiliberal traditions.

Yet in the course of the nineteenth century the national perspective undoubtedly gained ground as territorial, dynastic and confessional histories all declined in importance. Anthropological, ethnological and cultural perspectives had been prominent in fostering a historical sense of nation within the multitude of historical associations in the German lands.[4] The foundation of the *Monumenta Germaniae Historica* by the Freiherr vom Stein in 1819 was motivated by Stein's desire to construct a historical narrative of German national identity. What could be better suited to this purpose than a historical institution collecting and editing the German sources of the Middle Ages. The foundation of the Germanic National Museum at the first meeting of the German *Geschichts- und Altertumsforscher* in Dresden in 1852 was also motivated by national didactics. The Nuremberg-based museum (which still exists today) was to complement the collections and museums

[4] Georg Kunz, *Verortete Geschichte: Regionales Geschichtsbewußtsein in den deutschen Historischen Vereinen des 19. Jahrhunderts* (Göttingen, 2000).

in the individual German states and to strengthen national consciousness and love for the entire fatherland.[5]

Not only history but architecture and art too were developing a close affinity to nationalism.[6] Major national monuments, such as the Valhalla near Regensburg (1842) were built in classical style. The Valhalla's tympanums depicted German heroes from the times of the Germanic tribes to the contemporary period, but it did so in the form of a classcial Greek temple in Doric style. National monuments were not built in a new national style. Classicism and the view of humanity created in classical literature became the guiding light of many in the national movement. But adherents to other architectural styles also sought to bolster their preferences by relating them to alleged 'national style'. Thus the Gothic style came to be regarded as typically German – despite the fact that its origins lay demonstrably in medieval France rather than Germany. If history was useful to legitimate national ambitions, historical paintings were widely regarded as the pinnacle of artistic endeavour, and many of the masterpieces ably underpinned national myths and identities.

Architecture, art and the sciences (*Wissenschaften*) more generally put themselves at the service of the nation at the same time as they themselves underwent a profound process of nationalization. Biologists, for examples, determined national characteristics through evolutionary theories; geographers mapped out nations, and economists developed recipes for the economic welfare of their respective nations. The early nineteenth century witnessed the foundation of a range of subject-based academic societies meeting in public, usually on an annual basis. Scientific congresses were not only a means to exchange scientific opinions and arguments; they also were a way to escape censorship and surveillance under the strict regime of the Karlsbad decrees. And they contributed to the establishment of scientific communities which were increasingly national in their orientation, i.e. transcending the borders of the territorial states which maintained the upkeep of universities. The biologist Rudolf Virchow even argued that it was a specific national intellectual style of the Germans which made them better natural scientists than others (in particular the French). Research projects became of national significance, as scientific advances were celebrated as signs of national superiority. It was precisely the fact that professors could speak in the name of science which made them such effective propagators of the national idea.[7] It endowed the national movement with scientific legitimacy, i.e. it made the establishment of a nation state not the desire of particular interests in society, but the logical conclusion of an objective developmental process.

5 Peter Burian, 'Das Germanische Nationalmuseum und die deutsche Nation', in Bernward Deneke and Rainer Kahsnitz, eds, *Das Germanische Nationalmuseum Nürnberg 1852–1977* (Munich, 1978).

6 See generally Heinrich Schlie, *Die Nation erinert sich: Die Denkmäler der Deutschen* (Munich, 2002). On monuments and, incidentally, festivals, see also George L. Mosse, *The Nationalization of the Masses* (New York, 1975).

7 On the emerging 'scientificity' of the historical profession see Heiko Feldner, 'The New Scientificity in Historical Writing around 1800', in Stefan Berger, Heiko Feldner and Kevin Passmore, eds, *Writing History: Theory and Practice* (London 2003), pp. 3–22.

As these developments indicate, all attempts to repress a strong associational culture were futile and could not prevent the emergence of a strong urban civil society in the German lands which championed the national idea. That there was no simple retreat of the liberal national movement after 1819 is particularly evident in the enthusiastic support of German nationalists for both the Greek and the Polish struggle for national independence.[8] Small groups of volunteers went to Greece to fight against the Ottoman Empire between 1821 and 1829. Closer to home, newly founded associations looked after Greek refugees and collected money to support a national struggle which enthused liberal nationalists all across Europe. In the German lands parallels between the Greek struggle and the wars of liberty were quickly drawn. Middle-class elements dominated the Greek associations, but they also included artisans and skilled workers; women often were very active and members of different religious denominations worked alongside each other.

When Polish nationalists rose up against tsarist rule in November 1830 a similar wave of national solidarity swept through Europe. In the German lands Polish associations sprang up to look after the Polish émigrés. Liberal nationalists often combined pro-Polish sentiments with anti-Prussian ones. After all, as they reminded the public, Prussia and Russia had colluded in the separation of Poland. The remarkable solidarity shown by liberal nationalists to 'foreign' national movements is a timely reminder that early nineteenth-century nationalism had a strong cosmopolitan streak. Cosmopolitan nationalism was about the co-operation of European peoples inhabiting their respective nation states leading to the perfection of mankind. Repression of national movements elsewhere was compared with the repression of the national movement under the Karlsbad decrees, and activities on behalf of Greeks and Poles became a protest against the situation in the German lands.

A similar motivation underlay the penchant of liberal nationalists to cite the idea of 'English freedoms' as exemplary. They had allegedly been brought to England by the Anglo-Saxons. But in England these Germanic freedoms had been retained and developed into a system of constitutional government, whereas in the German lands this had not taken place. Anglo-Saxonism could thus form the basis of powerful notions of a spiritual alliance between Britain and Germany. A constant exchange of ideas between British and Prussian liberals took place around the mid-nineteenth century, but, as John Breuilly has shown, the very different societal contexts of these ideas meant that actual influences remained rather limited.[9] Still, on the eve of German unification Max Müller, a German-born academic at the University of Oxford, could claim:

> There is no country where so much interest is taken in the literature of Germany as in England, and there is no country where the literature of England is so much appreciated

[8] R. Quack-Eustathiades, *Der deutsche Philhellenismus während des griechischen Freiheitskampfes 1821–1827* (Munich, 1984); G.W. Strobel, 'Die deutsche Polenfreundschaft 1830–1834: Vorläuferin des organisierten politischen Liberalismus und Wetterzeichen des Vormärz', in Karl-Ernst Jeismann, ed., *Die deutsch-polnischen Beziehungen 1831–1848: Vormärz und Völkerfrühling* (Brunswick, 1979).

[9] John Breuilly, 'Variations in Liberalism: Britain and Europe in the Mid-Nineteenth Century', *Diplomacy and Statecraft*, 8 (1997), pp. 91–123.

> as in Germany [...] And the strong feeling of sympathy between the best classes in both countries holds out a hope that, for many years to come, the supremacy of the Teutonic race, not only in Europe, but all over the world, will be maintained in common by the two champions of political freedom and of the liberty of thought – Protestant England and Protestant Germany.[10]

It is noteworthy that Anglo-German solidarity here is not only ethnically and culturally underpinned, it is also religiously motivated. Both nations are referred to as Protestant nations. Protestant nationalism in Germany went back to the time of the Reformation.[11] In the nineteenth century the Reformation was constructed as a key event in the long history of German nation formation.[12] Heinrich Heine thought the link so strong that he compared Luther's chorale 'Ein' feste Burg is unser Gott' with the Marseillaise as key symbols of national identity in Germany and France respectively. Throughout the nineteenth century German cities and towns became littered with Luther statues and paintings. The Reformation was given a Germanic interpretation. After all, it was no less a person than Hegel who had pointed out that the Reformation had only been successful in Germanic countries: Scandinavia, Britain and the German lands. A nationalist cult emerged around the Swedish king Gustavus Adolphus, who had led the Protestant forces in the Thirty Years' War.[13] Via the Reformation the German nation constituted itself against Catholic universalism.

Many Protestant nationalists looked north and west, to Scandinavia and Britain for models of constitutional monarchies. But many liberal nationalists also showed a keen interest in French constitutional development. They idealized the French constitution of 1830 and followed the intellectual debates in Paris closely. Their negative counter-model was the autocracy of tsarist Russia. Ideas of freedom, progress and national unity continued to be connected closely by most liberal nationalists. They liked to talk about 'the people' as it was through the people that they justified their demands for national unity and constitutional government. But liberals drew a clear line between the uneducated and unpropertied masses (*Pöbel*), who could not be entrusted with the affairs of the nation state and at best had to be educated towards full inclusion in it, and themselves: a propertied and educated elite moving with the times and secure in the knowledge that history itself was on their side. In the 1830s radical democratic movements, such as 'Young Germany' (*Junges Deutschland*) criticized such elitism and avant-gardism. Their ambition was to create a more encompassing democratic public sphere. The split between liberals and democrats became especially sharp in the 1840s, but the championing of republicanism, majority

10 Cited in Maike Oergel, 'The Redeeming Teuton: Nineteenth-Century Notions of the "Germanic" in England and Germany', in Geoffrey Cubitt, ed., *Imagining Nations* (Manchester, 1998), p. 88.

11 See above, p. 19.

12 Hans R. Guggisberg and Gottfried Krodel, eds, *Die Reformation in Deutschland und Europa: Interpretation und Debatten* (Gütersloh, 1993).

13 Kevin Cramer, 'The Cult of Gustavus Adolphus: Protestant Identity and German Nationalism', in Helmut Walser Smith, ed., *Protestants, Catholics and Jews in Germany 1800–1914* (Oxford, 2001), pp. 97–120.

rule and the full equality of all citizens regardless of property and education became the rallying cry of only a small minority.[14]

That the national movement was increasingly disunited over definitions of freedom became obvious in the so-called Rhine crisis of 1840. When the French government, for domestic political reasons, revived its claims to the left bank of the Rhine, threatened war and concentrated its army in the Alsace, anti-French nationalism flared up across the German lands. Memories of the wars of liberty were mobilized and defending the 'German Rhine' was portrayed as an all-German affair. Nikolaus Becker's 'Rheinlied' became the rallying cry of German nationalists. It ended with the line: 'They shall not have it, the free, German Rhine.' Anti-French outbursts were genuine, but there were also those who argued that any fight for German freedom would not begin with fighting the French but with a struggle against the German princes who did not grant more participatory political systems.[15] Radicals, such as Arnold Ruge, insisted that nationalism had become the enemy of liberty, as it was deflecting from the real issue of bringing about a more liberal democratic order inside Germany and replacing this political issue with xenophobic sentiments directed against other nations.[16]

The revolution of 1848 and the national question

Splits within the liberal nationalist camp came to the fore again in the 1848 revolution, which sought to bring about a more liberal and a more national state. Most liberals shied away from questioning dynastic legitimacy and monarchic rule. But the issue of democratic republicanism was powerful enough to split the whole of the 1848 movement. Take, for example, the gymnasts: they formed a united national organization for the first time in the context of the revolution only to split into two almost immediately. The Democratic Gymnasts' Association (*Demokratischer Turnerbund*) was committed to achieving a free and united Germany, while the German Gymnasts' Association (*Deutscher Turnerbund*) decided to drop the word 'free'.

1848 was not just about a liberal national order; many demands focussed on social reforms within the existing territorial states. Fear of social revolution was in fact an important reason why many middle-class liberals were anxious to co-operate with rather than antagonize the monarchical governments in the German states. While 1848 cannot be narrowed down to liberal nationalism,[17] it did see

14 On the history of the terminologies 'liberal' and 'radical' see Jörn Leonhard, *Liberalismus: Zur historischen Semantik eines Deutungsmusters* (Munich, 2001).

15 Jörg Echternkamp, *Der Aufstieg des deutschen Nationalismus (1770–1840)* (Frankfurt/Main, 1998), p. 478.

16 Arnold Ruge, *Der Patriotismus* (reprint, Frankfurt/Main, 1968).

17 A broad discussion of all the diverse aspects of 1848 in its European dimensions is provided by Dieter Dowe, Heinz-Gerhard Haupt and Dieter Langewiesche, eds, *Europa 1848: Revolution und Reform* (Bonn, 1998). See also H.J. Hahn, *The 1848 Revolutions in German-Speaking Europe* (Basingstoke, 2001)

the first sustained attempt to create a unified German nation state. Festivals of national unity were celebrated up and down the country in 1848. Their common symbolic elements amounted to a 'festive discourse of the nation',[18] which owed much to the one developed by the French Revolution. However, very different conceptions of the nation lurked behind diverse festivities: some celebrated the dynastic nation represented by the royal houses, while others hailed the people's nation, and all of them revealed sharp political, social and confessional differences. Ironically, these festivals of national unity displayed the fundamental disunity in the German lands.

Yet nationalism moved from the realm of the spiritual to the realm of political action in 1848. The very word 'nation state' began to appear more frequently in the political language. Before, notions of national unity, national literature, national theatre, national feeling, national love, national church and national characteristics abounded, but few people talked about a nation state. 1848 was to change all that. Liberals from diverse German states assembled at the so-called Pre-Parliament in Frankfurt/Main and announced plans for the dissolution of the German Confederation and its diet. They prepared national elections for a new national assembly at the Frankfurt Paulskirche. A generous male franchise gave broad sections of the population the vote and, depending on the region, between 40 and 75 per cent of those eligible turned out to make their choice. Those elected were, by and large, the very middle-class elite who had been the main carriers of the national movement. Among the 799 parliamentarians only four artisans and no worker could be found. The members of parliament started to work on a new Bill of Rights and a liberal constitution for the whole of Germany.

But what *was* the whole of Germany? The issue of how to define Germany territorially came to haunt the Frankfurt parliamentarians. After centuries of alleged national humiliation and weakness, many were obsessed with creating a strong and powerful Germany. Yet voices of reason and moderation were not absent from the debates. Many parliamentarians showed themselves aware of and open to the ethnic heterogeneity of the German lands. They celebrated diversity, encouraged the use of other languages than German and refused to make language a requirement of citizenship. Varnhagen von Ense, for example, argued in the midst of debates about the borders of the German nation state: 'nationality is not the sole, not even the most important basis on which to form states. Shared laws and freedoms are undoubtedly much more important than ethnic ties, especially when these ties have been broken and obscured.'[19] With many parliamentarians, however, such civic elements of thought were closely intertwined with ethnic ideas. Civic and ethnic notions of the nation were not neatly separated and the Frankfurt parliamentarians cannot be divided into followers of either ethnic or civic nationalism. Both elements came to be formative for the national imagination.[20]

18 Jonathan Sperber, 'Festivals of National Unity in the German Revolution of 1848', *Past and Present*, 36 (1992), pp. 114–38.

19 Varnhagen von Ense, *Kommentare zum Zeitgeschehen: Publikzistik, Briefe, Dokumente 1813–1858* (Leipzig, 1984), p. 172.

20 Brian Vick, *Defining Germany: The 1848 Frankfurt Parliamentarians and the National Question* (Harvard, 2002).

Many nationalists in 1848 used notions of a hegemonic medieval *Reich* to legitimate territorial demands in the present: the Netherlands, the Flemish part of Belgium, Alsace and Lorraine, the Balkans, Bohemia, Moravia, the Polish-speaking Prussian province of Posen, Trieste and southern Tyrol – all were now declared part and parcel of the German nation, even if only a minority of their population was German-speaking. Germany was to stretch as far as possible from the North and Baltic seas in the north to the Adriatic and Black seas in the south. Parliamentarians were keen to wage war on Denmark in order to secure the disputed provinces of Schleswig and Holstein for Germany. Plans were made for a massive German navy. The predominant culturalism of the German national movement, which defined nationhood through language, traditions and history, now came into its own, justifying demands for expanding the borders of the new German nation far beyond the borders of the German Confederation. To ease the problems of Austria, with diverse Slav nationalisms, the parliament had adopted a territorial definition of the nation, but this was a tactical ploy to allow Austria into Germany. In debates on other regions, especially Poland, cultural definitions of the nation came to the fore, justifying demands for territories outside the borders of the German Confederation. Territorial and cultural definitions of the nation co-existed and were both used in order to ensure the greatest possible expansion of the new Germany.[21]

Such imperial ambitions of the Frankfurt parliament caused tensions with other national movements in Europe. The idea of a harmonious co-operation of peoples and nations, which had been at the heart of the Greek and Polish associations in the 1820s and 1830s, gave way to rivalry and mutual contempt. The Prussian Germanization policies in the province of Posen in the 1830s had already strengthened the Polish national movement. In the emerging 'Polish question' German voices emphasized the superiority of German over Polish culture and formulated a civilizing mission of the Germanic people in Slav Eastern Europe. This in turn produced a strong reaction from Polish and other Slav nationalists. The Czech national movement in Bohemia and Moravia boycotted the elections to the Frankfurt parliament and František Palacký assembled a separate Slav parliament at Prague to underline the national ambitions of diverse Slavic peoples. Slav and Italian nationalists protested at demands for Trieste and southern Tyrol.

In 1848 constructions of Germany were becoming more expansionist and more inclusive. Thus, for example, Louise Otto, one of the founding figures of the German women's movement, combined xenophobia with calls to incorporate women into the German nation.[22] She wanted to reduce foreign influences on the education of German women as far as possible. But at the same time Otto argued that women should have more of a say in the nation state because they were central to the nation and felt passionately for the nation. In the first German women's newspaper, the *Frauen-Zeitung*, edited by Otto, she demanded a more thorough

21 Dieter Gosewinkel, *Einbürgern und Ausschließen: Die Nationalisierung der Staatsangehörikeit vom Deutschen Bund bis zur Bundesrepublik Deutschland* (Göttingen, 2001), p. 117f.

22 Ute Planert, 'Die Nation als "Reich der Freiheit" für Staatsbürgerinnen: Louise Otto zwischen Vormärz und Reichsgründung', in Ute Planert, ed., *Nation, Politik und Geschlecht: Frauenbewegungen und Nationalismus in der Moderne* (Frankfurt/Main, 2000) pp. 113–30.

education for women and portrayed the 'daughters of Germania'[23] as the proud descendants of the wives and mothers of the Germanic warrior tribes who, according to Tacitus, went to war alongside their husbands and were regarded as equal comrades. She reminded her audience of the long list of distinguished women who had brought pride and honour to the German nation – none more so than the Prussian Queen Luise. Otto and nationally-minded women like her suffered under the exclusion of women from more active participation in the national movement. In 1848 democratic women's associations protested at the exclusion of women from the Paulskirche parliament. Their protests led to 200 seats in the spectators' gallery being reserved for women when the national parliament was opened in Frankfurt. Women such as Mathilde Franziska Anneke, Emma Herwegh and Amalia Struve were to be found on the barricades in 1848. The latter in fact served 205 days of solitary confinement in Freiburg following the defeat of the revolution.

When Otto and her compatriots founded the General German Women's Association (*Allgemeine Deutsche Frauenverein*, ADF) in 1865 they consciously chose to do this in Leipzig on 18 October, the anniversary of the battle of Leipzig against Napoleon. The ADF argued in favour of greater incorporation of women into the nation and more equal rights on the basis of a theory of gender difference. Men and women were constructed as biologically different. Women were destined to become mothers and motherhood formed a powerful argument in favour of empowerment.[24] Asserting the mother–child bond as of primary importance, women criticized patriarchy and the patriarchal nation. The nation, they argued, could only prosper on the basis of motherly virtues and values, such as patience, love, harmony, hope, co-operation and faith. Women were the main educators of the future generations on whom the welfare of the nation depended. If the nation was a family and should be loved like a family, then surely women, who were a central part of the family, also had a place in the nation. The women's organization of the home gave them a place in the public sphere, where a variety of social and charitable work awaited them.

If women used 1848 to present more inclusive visions of the nation, so did workers and artisans. They were hardly represented in parliament, but the revolution witnessed the formation of the first German labour movement. The Brotherhood of Workers (*Arbeiterverbrüderung*), led by Stephan Born, managed to build up a skeletal national organization with an estimated membership of about 15,000 in 1848. From 23 August to 2 September 1848 it organized the first German workers' congress, which discussed ideas for political reform, social justice and national unity. The Brotherhood strove for a centralist national organization of workers which deliberately ignored the borders of the territorial states.

23 On the Germania figure in German national mythology see Lothar Gall, *Germania: Eine deutsche Marianne?* (Bonn, 1993). The figure of Germania was chosen for the first national monument erected after unification of the country in 1871, the Niederwald Monument on the river Rhine between Koblenz and Mainz. See Patricia Mazon, 'Germania Triumphant: the Niederwald National Monument and the Liberal Moment in Imperial Germany', *German History*, 18 (2000), pp. 162–92.

24 Ann Taylor Allen, *Feminism and Motherhood in Germany 1800–1914* (New Brunswick, 1991).

Brotherhood members used 'German greetings' and addressed each other as 'German brother' in their correspondence. The black, red and gold flag was used prominently and described as the 'workers' flag' alongside the traditional red flags of the workers' movement. Born and his followers tended to support the democratic wing of the liberal movement. National unity and the democratic nation state were portrayed as preconditions for social reform. The nation state of the workers was one which had to be inextricably linked to social justice.[25]

Social revolution was the aim of the small Association of Communists (*Bund der Kommunisten*) founded by Karl Marx and Frederick Engels in 1847. They welcomed the formation of a German nation state as a necessary step on the further development of the capitalist economic order. The struggle of workers against capitalism would have to be fought along national lines, but nationalism as such was declared meaningless: 'the workers have no fatherland. One cannot take from them what they have not got ... national differences and antagonisms between peoples are vanishing more and more ... The rule of the proletariat will make them vanish even more.'[26] Alas, this proved to be wishful thinking, but it is important to note here that not all representatives of the workers allocated nationalism such a low priority. Many, including the influential Ferdinand Lasalle, combined nationalism with calls for democratization and social reform.[27] Lasalle, a disciple of Fichte and Hegel, firmly believed in the superiority of cultural nations and the special spiritual mission of the German nation. Thus he justified Prussia's annexation of Poland's western provinces as a victory of German culture over Slav barbarity. Such anti-Polish and anti-Slav sentiments had been rare in the national discourse of the Brotherhood, but it crept into the language of the labour movement as the nineteenth century progressed.

The debates about borders, foreign 'others', women and workers in 1848 demonstrate the potential of national constructions for both inclusion and exclusion. The same is true for the debates about Germans of Jewish faith. Attempts to construct German national identities sat next to Jewish efforts to establish a Jewish *Volksgeist*. In 1819 philologists, historians, philosophers and other, overwhelmingly middle-class Jews had founded the Association for the Culture and Science of the Jews (*Verein für Cultur und Wissenschaft der Juden*) in Berlin. Self-styled 'keepers of the Jewish identity' they portrayed the history of Jews as the history of suffering and persecution of an ethnic tribe.[28] The classical example was

[25] Walter Schmidt, 'Arbeiterverbrüderung, soziale Emanzipation und nationale Identität 1848/49', *Beiträge zur Geschichte der Arbeiterbewegung*, 36 (1994), pp. 20–36; Thomas Welskopp, *Das Banner der Brüderlichkeit: Die deutsche Sozialdemokratie vom Vormärz bis zum Sozialistengesetz* (Bonn, 2000), pp. 523–65. See also Jonathan Sperber, *Rhineland Radicals: The Democratic Movement and the Revolution of 1848/49* (Princeton, 1991).

[26] Karl Marx and Friedrich Engels, *Manifest der Kommunistischen Partei* (1844; 44th edn, Berlin, 1980), p. 66.

[27] For Lasalle see D. Footman, *Lasalle* (New York, 1969). The cult which developed within German Social Democracy around Lasalle is described by Andrew G. Bonnell, 'The Lasalle Cult in German Social Democracy', *Australian Journal of Politics and History*, 35 (1989), pp. 50–60.

[28] Ernst Schulin, *'The Most Historical of all Peoples': Nationalism and the New Construction of Jewish History in Nineteenth Century Germany* (London, 1996), p. 15.

Heinrich Graetz's twelve-volume *History of the Jews*, published between 1853 and 1876. Yet the search for Jewish identity was not yet bound up with the search for a Jewish state. In fact, the vast majority of Jews sought ways of further improving their integration into the German nation. They were alarmed by antisemitic pogroms such as the Hep-Hep riots which spread across Germany in 1819.[29] Pogroms accompanied the revolutionary crises of 1830 and 1848.[30] Some German nationalists continued to construct the Jew as an inner enemy of the German nation who could not be assimilated – a foreign and alien part on the national *Volkskörper*.[31]

The vast majority of Jews living in the German lands were not prepared to accept such exclusion from the nation. They searched for ways to enter respectable national society: one possibility was conversion to Christianity – a road taken by many. Another was military service: when the Prussian king announced plans to exempt Jews from military service in 1842 – despite the fact that Prussian officers tended to be full of praise for the exemplary soldierly behaviour of their Jewish recruits – Jewish organizations protested vigorously. They regarded this as an attempt to exclude them from the nation, a backward step on the road to full equality as citizens.[32] Despite the presence of antisemites in the Frankfurt parliament of 1848, the constitution of 1848 made Jews full members of the German nation. In the period from 1848 to 1871 the integration of German citizens of Jewish faith made significant progress. Hardly any acts of collective violence against Jewish communities were recorded during this period. Emancipation laws in Baden in 1862 and Württemberg in 1864 and the constitutions of 1869 and 1871 completed the legal emancipation of German Jews. Antisemitism was largely absent from public political debates, and despite individual antisemites among the professoriate, universities in the German lands showed few signs of discriminating openly against Jews.[33] Jews were prominent in the national movement before 1871.[34] Moses Mendelssohn became the key symbol of an integrated German Jew who had allegedly managed to balance both sides of his identity – Jewishness and Germanness.[35] Mendelssohn's portrait began to appear on vases, cups and plates. Busts of Mendelssohn or copies of his books, in particular his translation of the Bible, were popular presents at the bar mitzvah, as was, later on, Sebastian Hensel's book about the family Mendelssohn.

The Mendelssohns represented the dream of equality of Jews in the German nation. One of Moses's grandsons was the celebrated composer Felix

[29] Jacob Katz, *Die Hep-Hep-Verfolgungen des Jahres 1819* (Berlin, 1994).

[30] Stefan Rohrbacher, *Gewalt im Biedermeier: Antijüdische Ausschreitungen in Vormärz und Revolution (1815–1848/49)* (Frankfurt/Main, 1993).

[31] See above, p. 36; see also Klaus Holz, *Nationaler Antisemitismus: Wissenssoziologie einer Weltanschauung* (Hamburg, 2001).

[32] Ute Frevert, *Die kasernierte Nation: Militärdienst und Zivilgesellschaft in Deutschland* (Munich, 2001; English trans. forthcoming, see p. 33, note 46), pp. 95ff.

[33] Gramley, *Propheten*, p. 409 (see note 3).

[34] Andreas Biefang, '"Volksgenossen": Nationale Verfassungsbewegung und "Judenfrage" in Deutschland 1850–1878', in Peter Alter, Claus-Ekkehard Bärsch and Peter Berghoff, eds, *Die Konstruktion der Nation gegen die Juden* (Munich, 1999), pp. 49–64.

[35] See above.

Mendelssohn. He had been christened, and he composed, among other things, much church music. He felt himself intensely German and could have been a model of the smooth integration of Jews into the German nation, had it not been for Richard Wagner. In 1850 Wagner published his pamphlet *Das Judentum in der Musik* (Jews in Music) where he denounced Mendelssohn's 'Jewish music' as sentimental, vacuous and without real content. The nationalist Wagner denied Jews like Mendelssohn any genuine national feelings. Although Wagner was arguably more committed to his vision of total art as an aesthetic experience than to nationalism, his musical dramas became a powerful symbol for German nationalism.[36] He might have been a revolutionary, fighting on the barricades in 1848, but his *Meistersinger*, first performed on the eve of the Franco-Prussian war, was celebrated as a national opera. After all, the final refrain of the German hero of the opera, Hans Sachs, explicitly denounced 'welscher Dunst' and 'welscher Tand'. Total art was, according to Wagner, a German vocation. He had already contrasted the profoundness of German culture with the shallowness of Western intellectualism in his *Die deutsche Oper* (German Opera) of 1834. His *Ring der Nibelungen* took up national medieval mythology, and, although not intended as a celebration of nationalism, was read as such by generations of German nationalists. After Wagner's death in 1883, his widow Cosima played a major role in highlighting Wagner's nationalist, anti-French and antisemitic sides. But already in the mid-nineteenth century Wagner's antisemitic pamphlet was a powerful reminder of the limits of the Jewish dream of inclusion into the German nation.

Nationalist antisemitism was not only to be found in music. The popular novels by Gustav Freytag, such as *Soll und Haben* (1855) and *Die verlorene Handschrift* (1864) were full of antisemitic images. In his stories, decent middle-class German heroes, representatives of a German national culture characterized by efficiency, competence and energy, typically struggle against scheming, devious and rootless Jews. In his *Bilder aus der deutschen Vergangenheit* Freytag argued that every people is historically constituted and characterized by unique features. If the German ones were unambiguously positive, Jews and Poles provided negative counter-models.[37] With reference to German cultural icons such as Wagner and Freytag, the continued exclusion of Jews from the German nation was justified by many educated Germans.

If both the internal and external borders of the new German nation state remained highly contentious, most members of the Frankfurt parliament agreed that any such state would have to include the German-speaking parts of Austria. Yet when the antirevolutionary forces regained control in Vienna in the autumn of 1848, the Austrian government demanded the integration of the whole of the Habsburg Empire into the new Germany, something it knew would not be acceptable to the majority of parliamentarians in the Paulskirche. With a small

36 Julian Führer, ' "Deutschester Mensch" und europäisches Genie: "Der Fall Wagner" ', in Constanze Carcenac-Lecomte *et al.*, eds, *Steinbruch Deutsche Erinnerungsorte: Annäherung an eine deutsche Gedächtnisgeschichte* (Frankfurt/Main, 2000), pp. 85–98.

37 Peter Schumann, 'Vom "bösen" Juden und "guten" Deutschen', in Gerd Krumeich and Hartmut Lehmann, eds, *'Gott mit uns': Nation, Religion und Gewalt im 19. und frühen 20. Jahrhundert* (Göttingen, 2000), pp. 73–90.

majority, the Frankfurt parliament decided to attempt the formation of a small-German nation state without Austria and offered the German crown to the Prussian king, Frederick Wilhelm IV. But Frederick Wilhelm declined in April 1849 after restoring his authority in Berlin. Not only did he think the constitution far too radical, he was even more concerned that his acceptance might provoke war with Austria. Many members of parliament subsequently left Frankfurt in May, disillusioned about their ultimate failure to combine greater political participation with the monarchical principle in a unified nation state. The others moved to Stuttgart, where troops put an end to the life of the first national parliament on 18 June.

The debates in Frankfurt had highlighted the existence of two distinct roads to German unity: a small-German one, focussed on Prussia, and a greater-German one, focussed on the inclusion of Austria. Liberal nationalists, pinning their hopes on Prussia, stressed its modernity. They emphasized the modernizing influence of Frederick II, the 'philosopher king', who had abolished torture in 1740. The Prussian law code (*Allgemeines Preußisches Landrecht*) was hailed as the most modern law code of its time. Frederick's Prussia had practised confessional tolerance: he had given asylum to both the Catholic Jesuits and the Protestant Huguenots. Prussia had also been the first state to form a friendship and trade treaty with the newly independent USA – a country widely celebrated as a model of a liberal and federal political order. The early nineteenth century had seen the rise of Berlin from a mere garrison town to a European capital. It had Europe's most prestigious university, and the Prussian education system had become the envy of the world. The Prussian civil service was a byword for efficiency and modernity. Finally, Prussia was one of the most rapidly industrializing states in Europe after 1850. It was obvious why liberals looked to a strong Prussian state as the motor of German unity, but they hoped for a liberal and constitutional Prussia to emerge as the champion of a unified Germany. Their hopes were raised with the accession to the throne of Frederick Wilhelm IV in 1840. He had taken a strong interest in the construction of the Cologne dome and was familiar with the nationalist idiom of the times. He had reappointed Arndt to his Bonn professorship and he had stopped the police surveillance of Jahn. But ultimately his national sentiments were not in tune with liberal thought, as 1848 was to demonstrate.

Small-German liberals were largely Prussian. Non-Prussians still distrusted Prussian hegemony in a united German nation state. It was no coincidence that the 1848 constitution defined citizenship in a federal manner. A German citizen was defined as a citizen of one of the German states making up Germany. In the Frankfurt parliament south German liberals in particular stressed the federal traditions and the regional territorial solidarities. Lawyers, who were prominently represented in the Paulskirche, argued that the history of German law did not justify a unitary state but would find adequate expression only in a federal state. German federalism relied heavily on the idea of Germanic tribes or peoples (*Stämme*) who occupied their own territories. Ignoring the fact that, in the light of the Napoleonic reordering of the map of Europe, one could hardly speak of an organic development of territorial states, these states had put a considerable amount of effort and money into stabilizing their respective identities after 1815.

Frightened by the nationalist propaganda of the 1848 revolution, most German states doubled their efforts to construct collective identities at the state rather than the national level. For each national festival there were at least ten regionalist festivities in nineteenth-century Germany, and many national festivals, monuments and symbols had distinct regionalist flavours.[38] Prussianness, Bavarianness and Saxonness were not supposed to dissolve into Germanness but to flourish alongside it. The different states were frequently imagined as the different parts of the national body coming together to form a whole. The body was nothing without their proper co-operation, but at the same time the parts retained their separate functions and identities. Ludwig Bamberger's statement of 1850 that 'there is no German history in as much as Germany as a political unit is unknown in history'[39] rang a bell with many liberal federalists in the German lands.

The national imagination came in liberal, democratic and socialist guises; it could be Protestant, Catholic and Jewish; it was always gendered; and it was framed as small-German, greater-German and federal. It was even making converts among conservatives, some of whom moved from a position of strict antinationalism to the appropriation of the national idea. Throughout much of the first half of the nineteenth century conservatives had been the great enemy of the egalitarian, participatory idea of the nation. For them the social order was determined by birth, which gave access to privilege.[40] Christian teachings defined the mutual obligations of different estates in society, which formed a strict social hierarchy with the monarch at the top. If liberal nationalism was based on strong associationalism, the same could be said of conservatism. In fact, membership figures for conservative antinational associations were far higher than membership figures for liberal pronationalist groups throughout the first half of the nineteenth century.[41] The Gerlach brothers, who were prominent in Prussian court circles in the 1850s, were representative of such a traditional conservative antinationalism. But their position had been seriously dented by the 1848 revolution which demonstrated the strength of nationalism in mobilizing political loyalties.

Many conservatives now argued that it was not enough to be antinational. A more constructive engagement with the idea of the nation involved the search for a nationalism which stressed loyalty to dynasty, nobility and religion but rejected the participatory claims of liberal-democratic variants of nationalism. Protestant Pietism[42] and nationalism began to merge in the mid-nineteenth century. Christian revival movements were often linked to demands for social

[38] For details see Abigail Green, *Fatherlands: State-Building and Nationhood in Nineteenth-Century Germany* (Cambridge, 2001), pp. 137ff.

[39] Cited in Dieter Langewiesche, *Nation, Nationalismus, Nationalstaat in Deutschland und Europa* (Munich, 2000), p. 61.

[40] Robert M. Berdal, *The Politics of the Prussian Nobility: The Development of a Conservative Ideology, 1770–1848* (Princeton, NJ, 1988).

[41] Eckhard Trox, *Militärischer Konservatismus: Kriegervereine und 'Militärpartei' in Preußen zwischen 1815 und 1848/49* (Stuttgart, 1990).

[42] Pietism was a religious movement within German Protestantism originating in the late seventeenth century. It emphasized an individualist and subjective religiosity and championed forms of practical Christian life, often in collectives or communities.

reform and national unity. Pietist circles often viewed the wars of unification after 1864 in terms of divine intervention and justice.[43]

After 1848 a growing number of conservatives put forward plans for monarchical reform of the German Confederation in an attempt to put the monarchs at the helm of the national movement and identify the interests of the monarchy with those of the nation. Stabilizing the constitutional monarchies, which had been established almost everywhere in the German lands after 1848, involved placating the nationalist movement. One way of doing this was to make monarchism a national ideology.[44] Some aristocrats and supporters of the monarchical order wanted to 'dis-invent' the nation altogether, but far more successful were those who argued that conservatives needed to adapt the national concept for their own purposes.[45] Friedrich Julius Stahl, one of the best known conservative thinkers before 1871, argued that a nation was not constituted through the will of its people to participate in political affairs, but through ethnicity, language and history. Government thus remained in monarchical hands.

Political romanticism often backed up such monarchical and conservative visions of the nation.[46] Its representatives such as Clemens Brentano and Joseph von Eichendorff went in search of a glorious past which could underpin constructions of German identity in the present. Their 'discovery' of the cultural roots of the German nation not only produced collections of fairy tales and folk songs; it also led them to the idealization of the social order of the medieval Holy Roman Empire. Against the rationalism of the Enlightenment and the French Revolution they idealized the Christian Middle Ages when a society based on estates allegedly produced the kind of organic harmony that the romantics wanted to recreate. They put feeling and emotion against rationalism and modernity. The irrational, dionysian and ecstatic were celebrated as characteristics of German culture and Germanness more generally. The inner development of the self (*Innerlichkeit*) was more important than the struggle for political rights and interests. Their politics in fact did not recognize any plurality of competing interests. As the inner self strove towards wholeness, so the entire nation was to act as one. Romanticism also entered academic discourses; take, for example, Wilhelm Heinrich Riehl's 'science of the people' (*Wissenschaft vom Volke*) which aimed to demonstrate that the people were 'naturally' ordered into estates. Patriarchy, authority (especially

43 William R. Hutchison and Hartmut Lehmann, eds, *Many are Chosen: Divine Election and Western Nationalism* (Minneapolis, 1994).

44 Peter Burg, 'Monarchism as a National Ideology', in Hartmut Lehmann and Hermann Wellenreuther, eds, *German and American Nationalism: A Comparative Perspective* (Oxford, 1999), pp. 71–96.

45 Matthew Levinger, *Enlightened Nationalism: The Transformation of Prussian Political Culture, 1806–1848* (Oxford, 2000), Chapter 7. See also William J. Orr Jr, 'The Prussian Ultra Right and the Advent of Constitutionalism in Prussia', *Canadian Journal of History*, 11 (1976), pp. 295–310.

46 An attempt to recreate the lifeworld of key representatives of the Romantic movement can be found in Richard van Dülmen, *Poesie des Lebens: Eine Kulturgeschichte der deutschen Romantik 1795–1820* (Cologne, 2002). See also Frederic C. Beiser, *Enlightenment, Revolution, and Romanticism: The Genesis of Modern German Political Thought* (Cambridge, Mass., 1992), and Robert W. Lougee, 'German Romanticism and Political Thought', *Review of Politics*, 21 (1959), pp. 631–45.

the authority of the monarch and the noble estates) and piety were the ingredients which held up the 'natural' social order. The nation was not constituted politically but emerged 'naturally' out of the social life of its people which, for Riehl, was made up of language, customs, tribes and settlements.

Images taken from nature, particularly prominent in German Romanticism, were frequently used to underline the organic unity and 'naturalness' of the nation. Riehl had already distinguished between 'forest people' like the Germans and 'field people' like the British and French. When Ludwig Tieck, another key representative of the Romantic movement, coined the neologism 'forest loneliness' (*Waldeinsamkeit*) in 1797, it was the beginning of a whole forest ideology in German national thought. The Romantic desire for nature made droves of poets, painters and composers search for the German soul in the German forests. The oak became the tree symbolizing the national character of the Germans: sturdy, reliable and strong. Like an oak the German nation had roots and it grew; it germinated, matured and came to fruition. The deep roots of the German oak represented the Germans' closeness to nature. The idea that Germans were somehow in tune with nature also served as basis for a growing resentment of urban and industrial spaces and gave rise to the glorification of an allegedly more natural peasant and country life. French gardens were denounced as artificial and cities were described as resembling prisons. The 'naturalness' of national orders was underlined by comparing the nation to a human being. The nation as humanoid was imagined as either sleeping or awakening, ill or healthy. The image of the nation as human body, by assuming oneness, also alleged that the nation had one will and one interest only. Diversity and differences of interests just as conflicts over interests were not part of such an understanding of the nation.

The systematic research into German antiquities and peasant cultures of Jacob and Wilhelm Grimm helped to shift the identification of the people from the urban middle classes to the peasants, who were allegedly living more in tune with nature. The Grimm brothers are best known for their collection of fairy tales, which were meant as an archive of German folk poetry. Although the stories were strongly edited by the brothers and although many of their informants were not uneducated peasants but well-educated middle-class people, the Grimms claimed that their fairy tales preserved German cultural memory. Fairy tales were one means of strengthening national identity. The peasant ideology of German Romanticism emphasized the economic autarky, long traditions and rootedness of German peasant culture. The Grimm brothers, though, were not traditional conservatives. Jacob Grimm had been among the famous Göttingen Seven who protested against the abolition of the Hanoverian constitution for which they were dismissed from the university in 1837. Nor were they narrow-minded nationalists. Throughout their lives they retained a strong cosmopolitan interest in the fairy tales and folk cultures of other nations. Their glorification of peasant cultures was by no means an exclusive conservative ploy, but one which was shared by many liberals. Peasants, folk culture and nature were used in different argumentative contexts – sometimes for entirely different constructions of national identity. Conservative versions tended to imagine the nation as an ethnic and cultural rather than a political community. They constructed their own national narratives in an attempt to blunt what they perceived as a dangerous instrument in the hands of liberals and democrats. As Joseph von Radowitz put it just two years before the revolution of 1848: nationalism 'will remain a dangerous weapon in the hands of the party of revolution for as long as it has not been taken out of its hands'.[47]

The struggle of different political factions over the construction of German national identities was also always a struggle over the memorialization of 'national' events such as the 1848 revolution. Those who championed liberal-democratic ideals wanted to keep the memory of the March rising of 1848 alive by visiting the graves of the victims of the barricade fights, who were buried at the cemetery in Berlin-Friedrichshain. The authorities in turn attempted to prevent access to the graves.[48] They organized official celebrations to celebrate the sacrifice of the soldiers who had died in March 1848. A 48-metre-high column was erected to their memory in Berlin between 1850 and 1854. But there were limits to the extent to which national memory could be guided by the state. Despite its best efforts, the state could not prevent the memorialization of the March rising of 1848 becoming a central ingredient in the national memory of the democratic left and the early labour movement. In remembering the revolutionaries of 1848 they celebrated a different nation from the one established in 1871. On the 25th anniversary of the revolution in 1873 more than 20,000 people attended the March celebrations at Berlin-Friedrichshain. Berlin Social Democracy repeated them every year, and red as well as black, red and golden ribbons decorated the wreath laid at the grave of the revolutionaries.

From the 'revolution from below' to the 'revolution from above', 1848–71

The defeat of the liberal national movement in 1848 had, above all, one lesson for liberal nationalists. The striking powerlessness of the Frankfurt parliament had underlined the all-importance of power for the establishment of a nation state. The revolutionaries had not been short of either imagination or competence, but they were short of power. Who was going to provide that power in future? There were only two contenders: Prussia and Austria. The latter was limited by its need to maintain a multinational empire in which diverse nationalisms were gaining ground. Austria had repeatedly shown itself as the determined enemy of a unified German nation state. Greater-German positions were characterized more by their rejection of small-German nationalism than by their advancement of realistic plans of their own for German unification. Small-Germans, by contrast, argued with some conviction that if what was needed to make Germany was a strong state, then Prussia was the ideal candidate. The Prussian historian Heinrich von Treitschke developed the idea of a strong German state under Prussian leadership guaranteeing not so much democracy and the equal participation of citizens in the state as the 'inner freedom' of individuals. Treitschke

[47] Joseph Maria von Radowitz, 'Gespräche aus der Gegenwart über Staat und Kirche' [1846], in Wilhelm Corvinus, ed., *Ausgewählte Schriften*, Vol. 1 (Regensburg, 1911), p. 213.

[48] Rüdiger Hachtmann, *Berlin 1848: Eine Politik- und Gesellschaftsgeschichte der Revolution* (Bonn, 1997), pp. 850–6.

powerfully merged statism with nationalism and gave it an antiliberal turn. Characteristically, in his writings the West, notably France and Britain, did not any longer figure as models, but their idea of freedom was now contrasted with a specific 'Germanic' idea of freedom.[49]

It was not only a strong state which made Prussia the ideal candidate for unifying Germany. Prussia, on the eve of German unification, had the strongest economy in the German lands. Economic constructions of national identity received an important boost by small-Germans.[50] The customs union (*Zollverein*), established between Prussia and some other German states in 1834, became a powerful focus for such an economic identity. But there was no straight line between 1834 and 1871. The notion that political unity followed logically from economic integration was part of a nationalist mythology which was created *after* 1871. Hardly anyone thought much about politics when the Customs Union came about. Initially its main purpose was not even economic, it was fiscal. One of its main propagandists, the liberal economist Friedrich List, did however argue from early on that economic integration should lead to political unity. List, who had lived for years in the United States, where he had gone to escape political persecution, championed the USA as a model of economic and political development. With his *The National System of Political Economy*, published in 1841, he became one of the founding figures of the national school of economics in Germany. List allocated a central role to government in the development of the economy. By providing a strong education system, the state fostered a productive merger between the worlds of business and academic science. List was also a pioneer of railway construction in Germany. Railways were linking industrial centres and facilitating the exchange of goods and the effective build-up of markets. The democratization of travel, first through steamboats and, from the 1830s, through railways, was connecting the different parts of the nation allowing for greater communication and interchange. The geographical mobility of people increased. National festivals could attract larger audiences than ever before. Railway stations became national symbols, as in the city of Cologne, where the main station was built right next to the cathedral.

At the time List committed suicide in 1846, his idea of linking economic development to the project of achieving national unity was not prominent, but it was to gain in popularity over the next decades, as Prussia's industrialization proceeded apace. By the 1860s Prussia's economy was the fastest growing and most dynamic in the German lands. *Zollverein* administration and tariff policy was organized along Prussian lines. Prussia's liberal economic policies were hailed by liberals across the German lands. The middle-class entrepreneurs were the most enthusiastic supporters of the customs union and at the same time they were likely to be active members in national organizations. In academic circles a national school of economics emerged which attempted to draw lessons from economic history so as to allow for the better development of the economy in the present. Economic prosperity was seen as the key to national great power status.

[49] Andreas Dorpalen, *Heinrich von Treitschke* (New Haven, 1957).

[50] Harold James, *A German Identity 1770–1990*, rev. edn (London, 1990), Chapter 3.

The future, national economists argued, belonged to big united states with considerable economic potential.

Historians took up the idea of the economy being the key determining factor in historical development. Johann Gustav Droysen, for example, demonstrated in his biography of the Swedish king Gustavus Adolphus (published in 1869) how Sweden became a great European power through the development of its trade and commerce in the seventeenth century. And Karl Marx, of course, built his entire theory on the assumption that economic development was the basis for everything else. Economic nationalism could be politically conservative or radical. Nation-building could be portrayed as a series of institutional arrangements to benefit the overall prosperity, i.e. it could become a nationalism with the politics left out. Equally, as again Marxist political thought demonstrates, it could also be the stepping stone for a programme of radical political change. What is important is that, from very different political vantage points, Germany was increasingly imagined economically. Even where states were wary of Prussian expansionism, *Zollverein* revenue was too important for them to make leaving the customs union a viable option.

However, unification was not ultimately the result of economic integration but of war. It was the rivalry between Prussia and Austria which produced deadlock for any attempts to reform the German Confederation. Austria attempted to enter the *Zollverein* twice and was rebuffed by Prussia on both occasions. But Prussia's increasing economic prowess was not matched by political clout. In November 1850 Austria had forced Prussia in the Olmütz agreement to abandon plans for greater political union in north Germany. Instead, the Dresden conference of 1851, attended by all German states, restored the German Confederation in more or less the same way as it had existed before 1848. The confederal diet established an appropriately named Reactionary Committee which aimed at unmaking most of the revolutionary reforms. Freedom of assembly was restricted. The press became more tightly regulated. Revolutionary constitutions were abolished. A police association became the first genuinely national institution transgressing state borders. Once again the liberal national movement found itself harassed and repressed.

What went on between 1849 and 1858 was, however, not so much the restoration of an old order, but rather the significant modification of the new order of 1848. Almost nowhere in the German lands were constitutions entirely withdrawn; they were amended. In Prussia, for example, the amendment of the constitution of 1850 introduced the infamous three-class franchise to the lower house (*Landtag*) and made the upper house (*Herrenhaus*), dominated by the old nobility, the more important institution, but it still retained considerable potential for the constitutionalization of Prussian politics in the 1850s.[51] The veterans of '48 did not just disappear. Throughout the 1850s and 1860s they kept awake ideas of liberty and national unity.[52] Many became professional journalists and politicians – sometimes

51 Rainer Paetau, 'Die regierenden Altliberalen und der "Ausbau" der Verfassung Preußens in der Neuen Ära (1858–1862)', in Bärbel Holtz and Hartwin Spenkuch, eds, *Preußens Weg in die politische Moderne: Verfassung—Verwaltung—politische Kultur zwischen Reform und Reformblockade* (Berlin, 2001), pp. 169–91.

52 Christian Jansen, *Einheit, Macht und Freiheit: Die Paulskirchenlinke und die deutsche Politik in der nachrevolutionären Epoche 1849–1867* (Düsseldorf, 2000).

after returning from years of exile in France, Britain or the United States. Their ideals and values changed over the decades, and we have already alluded to the stronger economic and power political leanings of liberals in the post-1848 period. But 1848 had changed the entire framework of politics: even conservatives no longer denied the power of liberal nationalism to mobilize the people. It had forced monarchies in the German lands to change. Parliaments, however limited, provided the focus for the development of political parties and state-wide political organizations after 1848. The extension of the public sphere seemed unstoppable.

In 1858 liberal nationalists in Prussia were hopeful that the period of repression would come to an end. Prince William succeeded Frederick Wilhelm IV on the Prussian throne. Before both houses of the Prussian parliament he swore to govern constitutionally, hinting at his desire to put himself at the helm of the national movement in Germany. Hopes for a more liberal and a more national policy were further enhanced by Italian unification in 1859. Small-Germans wanted Prussia to play the part that Sardinia–Piedmont had played in Italy. Under the impression of events in Italy they now formed a National Association (*Nationalverein*), which, at its zenith in 1862/63, had 20–25,000 members. It can best be described as a proto-political party focussed on encouraging the unification of Germany along small-German lines.[53]

The National Association was ably supported by a Prussian school of historiography which wrote the Prussian vocation in Germany backwards into history.[54] One of its founding figures was Johann Gustav Droysen, who spent thirty years of his life, from the 1850s to his death in 1884, writing a multi-volume history of Prussia which depicted the foundation of the German nation state in 1871 as the logical conclusion of hundreds of years of Prussian history. The wars of liberty, he argued, were the birth hour of modern German nationalism. The more popular historical novels of the nineteenth century were also often set against heroic national backgrounds, in particular the wars of liberty.[55] Prussianism was well supported by a dense network of liberal newspapers, but it was by no means speaking with one voice. Some imagined Germany to be created by a popular movement from below, along the lines of 1848. The 1849 democratic constitution of the Paulskirche had many supporters in the National Association. Others abhorred the mobilization of a mass movement and argued for closer co-operation with the Prussian government in a common endeavour to unite Germany. Many liberals had come to fear the masses. Their elitist stance was reflected in the setting of very high membership dues for the National Association, which exluded poorer artisans and workers. The Prussian government did nothing to repress this revival of the liberal-national movement which also found an expression in the foundation of the German Gymnasts' Association

[53] Andreas Biefang, *Politisches Bürgertum in Deutschland 1857–1868: Nationale Organisationen und Eliten* (Düsseldorf, 1994).

[54] Stefan Berger, *The Search for Normality: National Identity and Historical Consciousness in Germany since 1800* (Oxford, 1997; pb edn with new foreword, 2003), Chapter 1.

[55] Brent O. Peterson, 'German Nationalism after Napoleon: Caste and Regional Identities in Historical Fiction: 1815–1830', *German Quarterly*, 68:3 (1995), pp. 286–303; Michael Limlei, *Geschichte als Ort der Bewährung: Menschenbild und Gesellschaftsverständnis in den deutschen historischen Romanen (1820–1890)* (Frankfurt/Main, 1988).

(*Deutsche Turnerschaft*) in 1868. Nationalism played a major role in the remarkable growth of gymnasts' associations throughout the 1860s.[56]

If Prussia tolerated and even encouraged a small-German national movement after 1858, Austria did not remain idle. The National Association had a greater German counterpart in the Reform Association (*Reformverein*).[57] It was generously supported in central and southern Germany, where mistrust of Prussian hegemony ran high. If there was a wide spectrum of views in the pro-Prussian National Association this was even more the case for the pro-Austrian Reform Association. It ranged from those who supported very diverse plans for a reform of the German Confederation to those who favoured the creation of a unified *Grossdeutschland* led by Austria. In August 1863 Austria organized a congress which discussed reform of the German Confederation. Almost all German princes were in attendance with the exception of the Prussian king and those who were too dependent on Prussia to risk antagonizing it. The congress signalled, above all, Austria's will not to leave Germany to Prussia. It put itself forward as champion of a reformed federal union. Given the strength of federal national sentiment in the German lands, this was by no means an unrealistic perspective.

But Austria's attempts to champion the national cause lacked a popular base. Austria had been more successful than any other German state in suppressing the national movement before 1848. The revolution itself was restricted to a few urban centres and it was never supported by a strong extra-parliamentary movement. After 1848 the Habsburgs returned to a policy of repressing all popular national movements. It did not allow the gymnasts and singing societies to organize; national festivals could not be held on Austrian territory; and the strong connections between Protestant Pietist circles in Prussia found no parallel in Austria. Support for Austria in other German states, particularly in the southwest, was not so much pro-Austrian as anti-Prussian. Austrian historians tended to be no match for their Prussian counterparts. This was partly due to the fact that the Austrian universities were not as well endowed as their Prussian rivals. But more importantly, Austria was a multinational empire, which made it difficult to construct a narrative around an Austrian national history. Dynastic history could not be combined with national history in the way that this was possible for Prussia. The most effective greater German historians were first and foremost anti-Prussian. They were more likely to counter the Prussian narrative than present their own counter-narrative. Onno Klopp, for example, published a biography of Frederick II in 1861, which depicted one of the prime heroes of the Prussian school of history as aggressive, repressive and absolutist. Greater-Germans tended to agree with Edmund Jörg's dictum that Prussia had 'only a stomach for Germany, never a heart'.[58]

56 Michael Krüger, *Körperkultur und Nationsbildung: Geschichte des Turnens in der Reichsgründungsära* (Schorndorf, 1996); Berit Elisabeth Dencker, 'Popular Gymnastics and the Military Spirit in Germany 1848–1871', *Central European History*, 34 (2001), pp. 503–30.

57 Nicholas Hope, *The Alternative to German Unification: The Anti-Prussian Party, Frankfurt, Nassau and the two Hessen 1859–1867* (Wiesbaden, 1973), Chapter 1.

58 Cited in James J. Sheehan, *German History 1770–1866* (Oxford, 1989), p. 848.

The newfound enthusiasm of the small-Germans for the Prussian monarchy came to an abrupt end with the appointment of Otto von Bismarck as minister president in the midst of the constitutional crisis of 1862. Bismarck was widely regarded as an unbending conservative. In 1848 he had been one of the most rabid antirevolutionaries, advocating measures of extreme violence against the revolution. The 1862 crisis had broken out over the question of army reform in Prussia. Liberals did not dispute the need for a stronger army, but they favoured a people's army over professional soldiers. They feared a standing army as a potential instrument of a military state which could be directed against its own citizens. The loyalty of the Prussian army to the counter-revolution in 1848 was still vivid in the memory of many liberals. Hence they argued that a constitutional state needed a citizens' army, but this was an idea unacceptable to the Prussian king. Armed citizens, organized in *Volks-* and *Bürgerwehren*, had often been fighting on the side of the revolutionaries in 1848 and had been duly disbanded after 1849. The conflict between the liberal majority in the lower house of parliament and the king reached stalemate, and Bismarck only solved the problem by pushing through the army reforms without the consent of parliament and ruling unconstitutionally between 1862 and 1866. Had it been reasonable to assume for Prussian liberals that a liberalizing Prussia would take the lead in unifying Germany in 1858, it now appeared as though a very illiberal Prussia was pursuing different priorities. Bismarck's friendship with the antinational Gerlach brothers – influential players at the Prussian court – was well-known. What good could come from him?

Liberal anxieties about Bismarck were understandable, but liberals were wrong to depict him as an arch-conservative aristocratic country bumpkin (*Krautjunker*). He was, in Lothar Gall's famous phrase, the 'white revolutionary',[59] whose deal with liberal nationalism would pave the way for the formation of the first German nation state in 1871. He had built his career on fighting liberal nationalism, hence he was well aware of its aims and ambitions. One of his most consistent aims was to destroy the Austrian-Prussian dualism in the German Confederation and achieve Prussian domination over the German lands. Yet the idea of a long-term Bismarckian master plan resulting in three carefully planned 'wars of unification', at the end of which German unity would emerge, is nothing but another nationalist myth created after 1871. He did not fight the war against Denmark in 1864 as a national crusade. The conflict had been provoked by Denmark's decision to incorporate the province of Schleswig into the Danish kingdom and thereby violate the longstanding indivisibility of the two duchies of Schleswig and Holstein, which were under Danish rule. It provoked outrage among the German national movement. *Nationalverein* and *Reformverein* were united in their stance against Denmark. A national network of Schleswig-Holstein associations preached an aggressive nationalism and provided ideological ammunition for a people's war against Denmark. The gymnasts were certainly ready to volunteer. Many sought to emulate Garibaldi's corps in Italy. But in the end the regular Prussian and Austrian armies waged that war. Still, the

[59] Lothar Gall, *Bismarck* (London, 1986).

national movement was delirious, but only for a short moment. The Danes were quickly defeated but that smooth military victory did not lead to the incorporation of the two provinces into the German Confederation. Instead Prussia occupied Schleswig and Austria Holstein. Far from emerging as national champion, Bismarck's negative perception in liberal circles was confirmed by this outcome of the war against Denmark.

The 1866 'German civil war'[60] between Prussia and Austria can also hardly be described as anything else than a traditional cabinet war for supremacy in the German Confederation. This was a war that Bismarck had definitely wanted, but it was about great power interests, not about national unity. Official Prussian and Austrian pronouncements made use of national arguments in their war propaganda, but the national movement itself was terrified by this war. Most of the south-west German states of the Confederation fought alongside Austria against Prussia. There was no public pressure to go to war; rather the opposite: the National Association was badly divided between those who supported Prussia and those who shrank away from the idea of a civil war. The war itself produced Prussian, not German nationalism. On the day of the all-decisive Königgrätz battle, elections to the lower house of the Prussian parliament brought a heavy defeat for the liberal national parties.[61] Following the defeat of Austria, small-German voices in Berlin celebrated the outcome as the precondition for German unity, but greater-German voices lamented the outcome of the civil war as destruction of the German nation. In the famous words of Franz Grillparzer: 'You think you have founded an Empire, but you have only destroyed a people.'[62]

The military defeat itself, though, does not explain the rapid retreat of Austria from Germany. Most great powers in Europe would have looked favourably on a continued presence of Austria in Germany and most of the south-west German states still were more favourably inclined towards Austria than towards Prussia. The Habsburg dynasty had been wearing the German imperial crown for centuries, and many had looked to Austria to build a more coherent German nation state. But Austria faded out of Germany, because it could not combine a national commitment to Germany with a multinational empire focussed on the Habsburg dynasty. There was no effective way of imagining an Austrian-led German nation state which went further in integrating the German states than the Confederation. The existing political structures had been broken down in 1866. In Austria and the south-west German states feelings of defeat were overwhelming. Many south-western states suffered under Prussian occupation. They were not in a hurry to join a Prussian-led Germany. But the high ground of imagining Germany was increasingly being occupied by the small-Germans. On the eve of German unification popular nationalist organizations had tens of thousands of dedicated members, most of them middle class, most of them highly educated, most of them Protestant. They held key positions in the economy and

60 Sheehan, *German History*, pp. 899–911 (see note 58).

61 John Breuilly, *The Formation of the First German Nation State 1800–1871* (Basingstoke, 1996), p. 83.

62 Cited in Heinrich Lutz, *Zwischen Habsburg und Preussen: Deutschland, 1815–1866* (Berlin, 1985), p. 485.

in public opinion formation. They were influential within a rapidly expanding public sphere and they put forward an ideal of a militarized, authoritarian and homogeneous national community understood as a new political religion.[63]

So successful were their constructions of a Prussian mission in Germany that even Bismarck firmly believed that no successful politics could be made without the support of the liberal and national middle classes. He recognized them as powerful social forces and he attempted to rope them in – against the advice of his former conservative allies. Bismarck was a skilful manipulator of public opinion who used bribery and harassment to get his own way. He knew of the power of public opinion in modern politics and he knew that it was the liberal national camp which dominated public opinion. Bismarck had no emotional attachment to imagining Germany, but he believed that those forces who did could not be excluded from politics forever. This is why he put forward the so-called Indemnity Bill in 1866, which signalled his intention to return to constitutional government in Prussia.

The liberals divided into a smaller group, which was opposed to any deal with Bismarck which would annul four years of unconstitutional rule, and a larger group, which accepted what was on offer in the hope that it would give liberals a greater say in the shaping of any future German nation state. It was especially among the younger generation of liberal nationalists that the compromise with Bismarck was quickly and more wholeheartedly adopted. The older generation of liberals, who still had direct memories of 1848, were dubious.[64] Prussian business elites were also, on the whole, very willing to work with Bismarck, as they could look back on a range of positive experiences with his government after 1862. It might have been antiliberal, but it showed its willingness to satisfy the needs of industrial capitalism.[65] Thus the year 1866 marked the beginning of a close co-operation of the National Liberal Party with Bismarck which lasted over a decade. In the newly created North German Federation, liberal nationalists, led by the Prussian minister of commerce, Rudolf von Delbrück, were responsible for a great deal of unifying legislation in the realms of banking, trade, currency, civil rights and citizenship.

However, any national programme put forward by Bismarck and his new National Liberal allies did not appeal in south and south-western Germany. Suggestions made in 1867 for a customs parliament (*Zollparlament*) uniting the northern and southern states of Germany were meant as a first step on the road to national unity. It was an attempt to use the economic strength of Prussia to achieve political unity. But it badly backfired. Liberal nationalists suffered defeats across south-west Germany in the elections of 1868, which turned out to be a plebiscite against Prussian-led national unity in the south.

---

[63] Dietmar Klenke, 'Nationalkriegerisches Gemeinschaftsideal als politische Religion: zum Vereinsnationalismus der Sänger, Schützen und Turner am Vorabend der Einigungskriege', *Historische Zeitschrift*, 260 (1995), pp. 395–448.

[64] Peter Brandt, 'Youth Movements as National Protest Cultures in Germany', in Lehmann and Wellenreuther, eds, *Nationalism*, p. 396 (see note 44).

[65] James M. Brophy, 'The Juste Milieu: Businessmen and the Prussian State during the New Era and the Constitutional Conflict', in Holtz and Spenkuch, eds, *Preußens Weg*, pp. 193–223 (see note 51).

Two years later Bismarck provoked war with France, skilfully manipulating the international crisis which had broken out over the question of whether a member of the Hohenzollern dynasty should succeed to the vacant Spanish throne. Convinced that it was wise to deal with the French threat to Prussia sooner rather than later, he also perceived the potential of a 'national war' against France. If France could be portrayed as attacking Prussia, Bismarck reckoned that an outbreak of mass national sentiment would bring even the southern states into the war. A successful outcome of the campaign would further strengthen national sentiments and ensure the success of a Prussian programme of national unity. Much more than the 1866 conflict with Austria, the Franco-Prussian war was cast in national terms by Prussian war propaganda. Although there was no general enthusiasm for the war, nationalist sentiments were indeed raised. The south German singing associations, which had been steadfastly greater German until 1870, now began to support the formation of a small-German state.[66] Nationalist sentiment also demanded a harsh treatment of the defeated France. Alsace and Lorraine were annexed by the new Germany on the basis that, by language and ethnicity, its inhabitants were German rather than French. And France had to pay massive reparations. The peace treaty was to haunt Franco-German relations for the first half of the next century.

Nationalist sentiment did indeed produce the climate in which the monarchs of the south-western German states could be largely bribed by Prussia to join a Prussian-dominated German empire. This empire was proclaimed in the Hall of Mirrors at Versailles on 18 January 1871. The date underlined the Prussian nature of the new German *Reich*: 18 January was the date of the crowning of the first Prussian king in 1701. The location, Versailles, was chosen not primarily to humiliate France but because it was almost the only place where it was acceptable to crown a German emperor. The German princes would most certainly have objected to Berlin. The most famous depiction of the Versailles ceremony is an officially commissioned painting by Anton von Werner, entitled *The Proclamation of the Emperor at Versailles*. It shows the German princes toasting the German emperor and it highlights the central role of Bismarck by painting him in a white uniform, which he did not actually wear on the day, but which makes him stand out against his surroundings. It does not show any representatives of the people, and there were indeed none present when Bismarck read out his statement: 'To the German Nation'. German unity was constructed from above: it was a unity of princes and monarchs, and it was a fragile unity. The toast itself had become the subject of heated controversy. Should it be 'Long live Wilhelm, Emperor of Germany', as suggested by the Prussian king himself? Or should it be 'Emperor of the Germans', as favoured by the crown prince, who was more in tune with popular liberal nationalism? Bismarck was looking for a phrase which would please the Prussian king but not offend the south-western monarchs and therefore opted for 'German emperor'. In the end the Grand Duke of Baden, who actually gave the toast, came up with a solution which satisfied no one. 'Long live Emperor Wilhelm' left it entirely open what he was emperor of.

[66] Dieter Langewiesche, *Nation, Nationalismus, Nationalstaat in Deutschland und Europa* (Munich, 2000), p. 161f.

The incident is of wider significance, as it indicated the persistence of strong territorial and regional sentiments in the new Germany. Nationalism in 1871 was a forceful movement in the German lands. Its imagination had contributed significantly to the making of a German nation state. But among the population at large nationalism was still relatively weak. Large sections of the population remained little affected by it and identified more with their locality or their region than with the nation. Furthermore, nationalism continued to be badly divided along the lines of confession and class. Catholics and socialists were not necessarily antinational, but they were, for the most part, sceptical about the shape and content of the new German nation state. How would the new nation state cope with strong particularist, class and religious identities? 1871 was not so much the conclusion to the making of Germans than the beginning. Both the Holy Roman Empire and the German Confederation were frequently described by their enemies as crumbling edifices and their eventual collapse was applauded by many nationalists, but the nationalists' own house was one still very much under construction. This, however, did not prevent Prussian liberal nationalists from celebrating in 1871. Their sentiments were summarized in a famous letter written by the Prussian historian Heinrich von Sybel to Hermann Baumgarten on 27 January 1871:

> Time and again my eyes wander over to the special edition [of the newspaper announcing the proclamation of the German Empire] and tears run down my cheeks. How did one earn God's grace to experience such big and mighty things? And how shall we live afterwards? What has been, for twenty years, the content of all desires and strivings has now been fulfilled in such an endlessly glorious way![67]

But was 1871 really what liberal nationalists had been fighting for between 1819 and 1871? And how indeed would the nation be imagined now that a unified state had been created?

[67] Cited in Heinrich August Winkler, *Der lange Weg nach Westen*, Vol. 1 (Munich, 2000), p. 212.

3

Making Germans, 1871–1914

Two months before the outbreak of the First World War, Heinrich Mann put the finishing touches to his novel *The Loyal Subject*. Because of censorship rules during wartime, it could only be published in 1918. The book, which Mann had started to work on as early as 1906, is a satire about the bourgeoisie in Imperial Germany, whose representatives are portrayed, among other things, as dynastic, antidemocratic, militaristic and antiliberal nationalists. The reader follows the development of the book's main character, Diederich Hessling, from childhood to local notable in the small town of Netzig. Hessling is an industrialist, combining fervent nationalism with a belief in the modernity of industrial Germany. He is a careerist looking for his own economic advantage and social advancement wherever possible. He is portrayed as being submissive towards his perceived superiors and a tyrant over his family and his workers. Aggressive and timid in equal measure, his talk about culture and morality is revealed throughout the novel as vacuous. A philistine at heart, Hessling is obsessed with the loud, arrogant and almost theatrical staging of the nation. In his festive speech on the occasion of the official opening of the memorial to Wilhelm I in Netzig Hessling dwells at length on the topic of the fatherland:

> 'Your Excellencies, my Lords and Gentlemen, it is a hundred years since the great Emperor, whose monument is being unveiled by His Majesty's representative, was given to us and the Fatherland. At the same time – to lend more significance to this hour – it is almost a decade since his illustrious grandson ascended the throne! Why should we not first of all cast back a proud and grateful glance over the great times which we ourselves have been privileged to experience?' Diederich glanced back. He alternately celebrated the unparalleled upsurge of commerce and of nationalism. He discussed the ocean for a considerable time. 'The ocean is indispensable to the greatness of Germany. In the ocean we have a proof that there can be no decision, on the seas and beyond them, without Germany and the German Emperor, for today world commerce is our chief concern.' [...] Diederich drew an unflattering picture of the previous generation which, led astray to licentious beliefs by a one-sided humanitarian education, had no sense of dignity in national affairs. If that had now been fundamentally changed, if we now formed one single national party, in the just consciousness that we were the most competent people in Europe and the whole world, despite mean-spirited and captious critics – whom had we to thank for it? 'Only His Majesty,' Diederich answered.

> [...] 'Rendered efficient to an astonishing degree, full of the highest moral strength for positive action, and in our shining armour, the terror of all enemies who enviously threaten us, we are the elite among the nations and represent an unprecedented height of Germanic master-culture which will never be surpassed by any people be they who they may!' [...] 'A master-nation, however, does not achieve such an incomparable flowering in the slackness of peaceful ease. No. Our ancient Ally has deemed it necessary to test the German gold with fire. We had to pass through the fiery furnaces of Jena and Tilsit, and in the end we have been able to plant our victorious colours everywhere, and to forge the imperial crown of Germany upon the field of battle.' [...] 'Our ancient Ally bears witness! We are not like the others. We are serious, loyal and true! To be a German is to do a thing for its own sake. Who among us has ever made money out of his loyalty? Where could corrupt officials be found? Here masculine honesty is united with feminine purity, for woman leads us ever onward and is not the tool of ignoble pleasure. This radiant picture of true German character, however, rests upon the solid earth of Christianity, and that is the only true foundation; for every heathen civilization, however beautiful and fine, will collapse at the first breath of disaster. And the soul of the German being is the veneration of power, power transmitted and hallowed by God, against which it is impossible to revolt. Therefore we must, now as always, regard the defence of our country as the highest duty, the Emperor's uniform as the supreme distinction, and the craft of war as the most dignified labour.'[1]

Historians disagree about the value of Mann's novel as a historical source. Thomas Nipperdey called the picture painted of a society of loyal subjects as at best a 'partial truth', whereas Reinhard Alter has argued that the novel provides valuable perspectives on the social history of the bourgeoisie in Imperial Germany.[2] Even allowing for the satirical treatment of the subject-matter, it is remarkable how many prominent features of the national imagination are present in Hessling's speech: xenophobia, antisocialism, antipluralism, monarchism, Social Darwinism, the merging of Protestantism and nationalism, pride in the modernity of a strong industrial nation which combined with a fin-de-siècle mood of cultural despair, an excess of *Weltpolitik*, navalism and militarism as well as a concern with monumental representations of the past – all of this features strongly in Mann's novel, and in the discussion below.

In the first part of this chapter the weakness of nationalism in the 1870s will be examined in the context of the new constitutional settlement and the ongoing search for powerful national symbols. Subsequently we will discuss the construction of internal and external enemies of the nation and the role of women in the national imagination. We will also assess the strength of antipluralism and militarism in Imperial German society and analyse the impact of German desires for great power status on definitions of the nation. Finally, this chapter will explore the significance of *Heimat* discourses and of *völkisch* ideas for diverse constructions of the nation.

1 Heinrich Mann, *The Loyal Subject*, ed. Helmut Peitsch (New York, 1998), pp. 339–42.

2 Thomas Nipperdey, 'War die Wilhelminische Gesellschaft eine Untertanengesellschaft?', in *idem*, *Nachdenken über die deutsche Geschichte: Essays* (Munich, 1986), p. 175; Reinhard Alter, 'Heinrich Manns *Untertan* – Prüfstein für die "Kaiserreich-Debatte"?' *Geschichte und Gesellschaft*, 17 (1991), pp. 370–89.

The continuing weakness of nationalism and the search for national symbols

The first national elections in the German Empire of 1871 showed the electorate's considerable resistance to the national idea [Map 3]. Only 51 per cent of those eligible to vote bothered to do so. Half of those opted for parties which were either lukewarm or forthrightly sceptical about the new nation state and the specific form it had taken: the Catholic Centre Party, the Socialists, Left Liberals, Prussian Conservatives and the representatives of national minorities within the borders of the new Germany. The parties in full support of the new nation state did best in urban areas, whereas the population in many rural locations remained little affected by nationalism.

Confusion continued to reign among nationalists about the shape of the new nation state. Significant territories of the new empire had not been part of the German Confederation: Alsace, Lorraine, Schleswig and Holstein. About 7 per cent of Germans in the Empire did not speak German as their mother tongue in the 1870s. At the same time millions of German-speakers remained outside the Empire. The German parts of the Habsburg Empire were still regarded by many nationalists as an integral part of Germany. Confusion sometimes brought disillusionment. Popular nationalism was a declining phenomenon in the 1870s. Gymnastic and singing associations concentrated more on general educational and less on political aims.[3] Gymnasts still argued that a fit and healthy body of the individual (as idealized in the male body of ancient Greek sculpture) was the fundamental precondition for a healthy body of the nation and the people (*Volkskörper*), but fewer members joined the gymnasts and the movement stalled. When liberal nationalists in Berlin opened a monument to the 'father of the gymnasts', Jahn, in 1872, no representative of the Hohenzollern monarchy attended. The kind of nationalism from below, represented by Jahn, was suspect. Instead, in 1873 the monarchy erected the Victory Column in Berlin as a monarchical monument to the nation unified by the Prussian military and the Prussian monarchy. It bore the inscription 'The Grateful Fatherland to the Victorious Army' and the reliefs at the bottom of the column depicted scenes from all three wars of unification.

The constitution of Imperial Germany added to the general confusion. Its hybrid character seemed to satisfy hardly anyone in the new Germany. It was an uneasy compromise between a democratic and an authoritarian state, between the dynastic and the national principle and between a federal and a unitary state. Was the new Germany an enlarged Prussia, or was it, as Wilhelm I had argued with obvious regret, the end of the old Prussia? Did the bourgeoisie become feudalized in the new Germany or did the aristocracy become more bourgeois? Was Imperial Germany primarily a military state or a cultural state or was it not, first and foremost, one of the most dynamic industrial states in Europe and a pioneer of the welfare state? Governments in Imperial Germany were responsible to the monarch and not to parliament. But a democratic male franchise mobilized

3 Svenja Goltermann, *Körper der Nation: Habitusformierung und die Politik des Turnens, 1860–1890* (Göttingen, 1998).

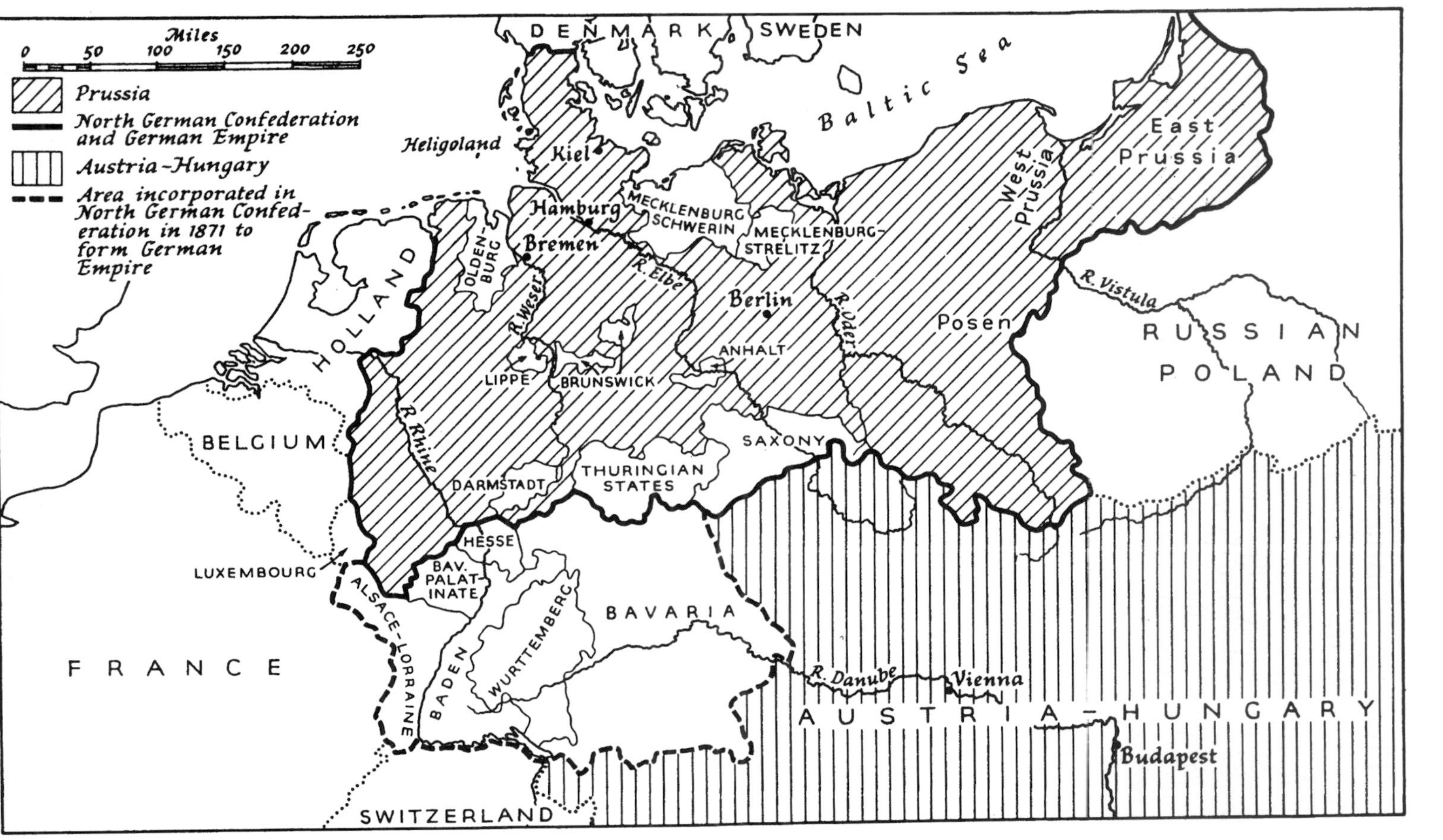

Map 3. The German Empire, 1871.

voters in national politics and contributed to a dynamic political culture and a vibrant interest politics. It was increasingly difficult for national governments to ignore public opinion and parliament altogether.

Bismarck's championing of federalism was meant as a check on democracy, but as the central state became stronger over time and a modern intervention state formed at the national level, so democratic tendencies revived. Prussian administrators dominated the federal constitutional set-up and legislative processes. Prussia was not only the biggest territory in the *Reich*, it also had the largest population and was easily the most powerful state in economic and military terms. In 1871 the Prussian state had acquired a nation which was grounded in an uneasy compromise between the old and the new. Statism was to become important in forging a German identity from above over the next decades. In German political thought the state preceded both politics and the nation. The state represented the interests of the entire nation whereas party politics by its very nature had to remain always sectional and partisan. Most German constitutional lawyers regarded the people only as the object of power, and many German historians, most notably Georg von Below, spilt an enormous quantity of ink attempting to prove the existence of a German state in the Middle Ages.

Yet the Imperial German constitution was an agreement between dynastic states. Vital powers over taxation, education, welfare and cultural policies were retained by the individual states making up the German Empire. Those states used their powers over educational and cultural domains to foster particularist support for their territorial states. The vast majority of monuments in Imperial Germany still carried regional rather than national overtones. As we shall see below, *Landespatriotismus* could go hand in hand with nationalist sentiments but it certainly did not decline after 1871. Political parties continued to have their organizational centres in the territorial states rather than at the national level long after 1871. Last but not least, the military remained organized along federal lines. The everyday life of most Germans continued to be much more determined by the policies of the territorial states than by the nation state.

But, as we have seen in the previous chapters, the perception of cultural, political and economic unity had been growing since 1800. The National Liberals pushed through a significant amount of unifying legislation between 1866 and their fall from power in 1879. Weights and measures, the currency and the banking system were all standardized. A national market was created and a unified civil law code was introduced in 1900. The successful delivery of the economic goals of unification through a booming Prussian economy was absolutely vital for the medium-term success of the unification project. Creating and boosting a 'national memory' became one of the major tasks of schools in the *Kaiserreich*.[4] The state sought to foster the national appreciation of cultural achievements: thus, for example, it initiated a range of prestigious projects documenting the

4 Stefan Zahlmann, ' "Der Bestand und die stetige Fortentwicklung der Nation ...": Die Schulerziehung der Jahrhundertwende und die Idee des Nationalen Gedächtnisses', in Clemens Wischermann, ed., *Die Legitimität der Erinnerung und die Geschichtswissenschaft* (Stuttgart, 1996), pp. 149–74; Katherine D. Kennedy, 'Visual Representation and National Identity in the Elementary Schoolbooks of Imperial Germany', *Paedagogica Historica*, 36 (2000), pp. 225–45.

central place of music in German national identity and it encouraged the establishment of strong musicology departments at German universities.[5] How successful would the new nation state be in propagating a national identity which would be acceptable for the citizens of that new state and bind them together beyond the many social, economic and political differences?

Imperial Germany's difficulties with national symbols highlighted the difficulties of the new state in coming up with a national language. The nation never had an official anthem. *Deutschland, Deutschland über alles* had democratic 1848 connotations and was therefore suspect. Hence, at most official occasions the Prussian monarchical war hymn *Heil Dir im Siegerkranz* was set to the melody of *Deutschland, Deutschland über alles*. Equally a long protracted debate about the national flag eventually ended in yet another uneasy compromise: the black, red and gold of the national movement had again been tainted by 1848 in the eyes of the Imperial German political elites. Hence, a red stripe was added to the black and white of the Prussian flag.

If national symbols were problematic, the Prussian-led state sought to develop a medieval *Reich* and emperor mythology as a means of integrating Germans around the dynastic state. The importance of monarchism in the national imagination was clearest in the 400 or so monuments dedicated to Wilhelm I in Imperial Germany – most of which depicted him on horseback. They were mostly erected during the reign of his admiring grandson, Wilhelm II, but they were financed largely by voluntary associations, and inscriptions typically read: 'From his thankful people'. Wilhelm was mythologized as Barbablanca (White Beard) in direct parallel to the medieval Emperor Frederick Barbarossa (Red Beard). The most famous was the Kyffhäuser memorial built between 1892 and 1896. It is located on the site of the ruined castle Kyffhäuser which had been rebuilt by Barbarossa in the middle of the twelve century. The myth was that Barbarossa's spirit was still haunting the castle and that he, himself, was sitting inside the mountain at a stone table with his red beard growing through the stone table top waiting for the completion of the *Reich*. The year 1871 had seen that very completion by the hands of Barbablanca, and the symbolism of the monument carefully merged ancient, medieval and contemporary German history to demonstrate the inner continuity of the German nation.[6] Dynastic nationalism was also highly visible in the bombastic avenue of marble statues of Hohenzollern monarchs in the Avenue of Victory (*Siegesallee*) dedicated by Wilhelm II in 1901.

The 400 memorials to Wilhelm I were still dwarfed by the more than 700 memorials to Bismarck, largely erected by about 300 Bismarck associations after the death of the 'iron chancellor' in 1898.[7] Most of them memorialized him as

[5] Celia Applegate and Pamela Potter, 'Germans as the 'People of Music': Genealogy of an Identity', in *idem*, eds, *Music and German National Identity* (Chicago, 2002), pp. 15, 18f.

[6] Monika Arndt, 'Das Kyffhäuser Denkmal – ein Beitrag zur politischen Ikonographie des Zweiten Kaiserreiches', *Wallraff-Richartz Jahrbuch*, 40 (1978).

[7] Lothar Machtan, ed., *Bismarck und der deutsche Nationalmythos* (Bremen, 1994); Mark A. Russell, 'The Building of Hamburg's Bismarck Memorial, 1898–1906', *Historical Journal*, 43 (2000), pp. 133–56.

founder of the *Reich* and a political leader who had successfully overcome the many internal divisions in German society. His admirers were not restricted to Protestant Germany, and the Bismarck associations recruited from broad social strata testify to the genuine popularity of Bismarck in Imperial Germany. One of the most impressive statues can be found in Hamburg: it is 15 metres high, a giant Bismarck in stone complete with armour and sword. The heraldic figures at the bottom of the monument represent the agreement of the diverse German tribes to Bismarck's unification of Germany. The monument was part and parcel of Hamburg's imperial iconography which carefully mediated between national and regional identity.

Monuments were crucial to imagining the nation in Imperial Germany. The vast majority of them emphasized that the nation was being built on the twin pillars of monarchy and the military.[8] Nowhere were the mythical foundations of Imperial Germany emphasized more than in the Hermann memorial in the Teutoburg forest near Detmold[9] [Figure 3.1]. Hermann, previously better known by his Roman name Arminius, had been an integral part of thinking about Germany since the humanists of the sixteenth century.[10] The memorial depicted a 26-metre-high Germanic warrior figure on top of a dome. The raised sword in his right hand carried the inscription: 'Germany's unity is my strength, my strength is Germany's power.' The shield in his left carried the inscription: 'steadfast in loyalty' (*treufest*). The Germanic warrior who had defeated the Romans in AD 9 prefigured the struggles against France in 1813/14 and again in 1870/71. The battle in the Teutoburg forest created the illusion of a foundational act of the German nation, allowing the nationalists to create a teleology of German national development which culminated in 1871.

Hermann's sword was directed against Rome, and at the height of the struggle against the autonomy of the Catholic church (*Kulturkampf*) this was widely interpreted as the nation struggling for unity in the face of the alleged transnationalism of the Catholic church. Hermann was primarily a symbol for the unity of the Protestant nation, although Catholics at least attempted to relate their own national sentiments to this 'Germanic warrior-hero'. Left Liberals and Social Democrats, by contrast, retained their distance from a monument which was difficult to relate to their respective conceptions of the nation. Like the 1848 festivals celebrating nationality, the Hermann cult, meant to bring about unity, ultimately only revealed the deep divisions in the German national imagination. The anti-French and anti-Catholic symbolism of the Hermann monument, however, indicates the importance of 'national enemies' for the construction of the nation in Imperial Germany.

8 Reinhard Alings, *Monument und Nation: Das Bild vom Nationalstaat im Medium Denkmal – zum Verhältnis von Nation und Staat im deutschen Kaiserreich* (Berlin, 1996).

9 Charlotte Tacke, *Denkmal im sozialen Raum: Nationale Symbole in Deutschland und Frankreich im 19. Jahrhundert* (Göttingen, 1995); Andreas Dörner, 'Der Mythos der nationalen Einheit: Symbolpolitik und Deutungskämpfe bei der Einweihung des Hermannsdenkmals im Jahre 1875', *Archiv der Kulturgeschichte*, 79 (1997), pp. 389–416.

10 See above, p. 18.

Figure 3.1 Hermann monument near Detmold, 1875, © Bildarchiv Preussischer Kulturbesitz, Berlin.

The construction of internal enemies of the nation

Anti-Catholicism united liberal and Protestant nationalists who perceived Catholicism as backward, reactionary and antinational. When the pope, locked in battle with Italian nationalists, first published the *Syllabus of Errors* in 1864, it included nationalism. Subsequently, in 1870, when he declared the doctrine of papal infallibility, Protestants and liberal nationalists found their worst fears confirmed. But by then, they, in alliance with the devout Protestant Bismarck, had already begun what they perceived as an epic struggle against Catholicism which became known as the *Kulturkampf*. This literally means cultural struggle, and it was very much perceived as a fight of the forces of culture against the forces of superstition and ignorance. It saw the banning of the Jesuit order from Germany and various attempts by the state to control the church and abolish as much autonomy over its internal affairs as possible. The freedom of movement of Catholic priests was severely restricted; many were forcibly expatriated and imprisoned, including, at one point, five of the eleven Prussian bishops. The Catholic press and associations were placed under permanent police supervision. Civil marriages became obligatory, but the attempt to freeze the Catholic church completely out of school education was eventually unsuccessful.

The persecution of Catholics was committed in the name of a Protestant Germany. Protestant theologians celebrated the military defeat of France in 1871 as victory for German Christian spiritualism and idealism against the rationalist principles of the French Revolution. They propagated the idea of a 'Protestant emperor' guarding the Protestant nation against its Catholic enemies. A well-financed and well-equipped Protestant historiography legitimated notions of a Protestant nation. Protestants regarded Protestantism as the national religion of the Germans and denied Catholics national sentiments.[11] That had not always been the case. In the first half of the nineteenth century attempts had been made to incorporate both major denominations into the national movement. From mid-century onwards, however, and particularly after 1871 the confessional cleavage became more marked in German nationalism. The 400th birthday of Martin Luther in 1883 was the highpoint of a public symbiosis of Protestantism and nationalism. Confessional affiliation became the biggest single divide in German national identity.[12]

Protestants and Catholics came up with mutually exclusive and radically different images of the nation. Protestant national discourse regarded Catholics as the 'inner France' and feminized Catholicism in order to exclude it from the proper male and Protestant nation.[13] Catholicism was perceived as a disease eating away at the soul of the nation and a brake on the forward march of national civilization. Where Protestants and Catholics came too close physically, as was the case in the new industrial centres, such as the Ruhr, violence and psychological warfare between the two confessional camps ensued. Conflict between Protestants and Catholics became the 'outstanding religious feature of the Second Reich'.[14] Catholic integration into what was a predominantly Protestant state structure became one of the key problems of nation-building in Imperial Germany. Persecution and exclusionary practices only strengthened an increasingly tight-knit Catholic milieu. In comparison with the 1871 elections, the Catholic Centre Party doubled its votes in 1874, and confessional affiliation remained the single most important determinant of voting behaviour in the *Kaiserreich*.[15]

[11] Arlie J. Hoover, *The Gospel of Nationalism: German Patriotic Preaching from Napoleon to Versailles* (Stuttgart, 1986); Horst Zillessen, ed., *Volk, Nation, Vaterland: Der deutsche Protestantismus und der Nationalismus* (Gütersloh, 1970).

[12] Helmut Walser Smith, *German Nationalism and Religious Conflict: Culture, Ideology, Politics, 1870–1914* (Princeton, 1995).

[13] Boruta Manuel, 'Das Andere der Moderne: Geschlecht, Sexualität und Krankheit in den antikatholischen Diskursen Deutschlands und Italiens (1850–1900)', in Werner Rammert *et al.*, eds, *Kollektive Identitäten und kulturelle Innovationen* (Leipzig, 2001), pp. 59–75.

[14] Oded Heilbronner, 'From Ghetto to Ghetto: The Place of German Catholic Society in Recent Historiography', *Journal of Modern History*, 72 (2000), pp. 453–95.

[15] Jonathan Sperber, *The Kaiser's Voters: Electors and Elections in Imperial Germany* (Cambridge, 1997).

By the end of the 1870s, Catholics were undoubtedly more wary of the state than they had been before, but the stamp of antinationalism, imposed on them by their liberal and Protestant nationalist adversaries, did not fit either before or after the *Kulturkampf*. German Catholic women in the 1840s often felt passionately about the nation.[16] Catholics, as we have seen, had been prominent members of the national movement in the first half of the nineteenth century, when nationalists tended to downplay the religious cleavage. Where Protestants did identify their religion with the nation, Catholics pointed out that Catholicism should be regarded as the essence of German nationality, as it could lay claim to a centuries-old tradition. Catholics had presented the German nation for a long time before the Reformation. And we have noted how the Cologne dome, a Catholic cathedral, had become one of the prime symbols of the national movement in the nineteenth century.[17] What Catholics opposed was the equation of religion with nationalism that was such a characteristic feature of Protestantism. Catholics had championed the national cause in 1848 because they had hoped to achieve more independence of the church from the state. The constitution of the Paulskirche had obliged them by giving churches the widest possible autonomy. Catholic nationalism had naturally tended to be greater German and pro-Austrian. But after 1866 realist political forces in the Catholic church, such as the Bishop of Mainz, Wilhelm Emmanuel von Ketteler, conceded that the only option for German unity was the Prussian one. He was content with a plea for a close alliance between this new Germany and fellow Germans in the Habsburg Empire. Catholics tended to be strong federalists in the new Germany, as they perceived a federal state structure as the best defence against an over-mighty Protestant Prussia.

1871 undoubtedly caused anxieties: Catholics had formed the majority of Germans in the Holy Roman Empire (60:40 divide). In the German Confederation the confessions had been finely balanced, but in Imperial Germany Protestants outnumbered Catholics at a ratio of 70:30. But it was only the persecution of Catholics which led to the ghettoization of a Catholic popular culture maintained by strong social and religious associations, such as the Kolping associations for journeymen or the St Barbara brotherhoods for miners. That Catholic milieu, especially in south-west Germany, was not anti-German, but its members were intent on retaining a dual identity as Catholics and Germans. The revival of popular Catholicism in the second half of the nineteenth century stood in marked contrast to a Protestantism badly affected by secularization.[18] But even if many middle-class Protestant liberal nationalists might have displayed fewer signs of devoutness, they clung to the idea of a 'cultural Protestantism' which equated the Protestant nation with progress and the Catholic nation with reaction. Throughout the history of Imperial Germany Catholics made repeated attempts to fight Protestant accusations of antinationalism and demonstrate

16 Sylvia Paletschek, *Frauen und Dissens: Frauen im Deutschkatholizismus und in den freien Gemeinden, 1841–1852* (Göttingen, 1989).

17 See above, p. 45.

18 David Blackbourn, *The Marpingen Visions: Rationalism, Religion and the Rise of Modern Germany* (London, 1995).

their own commitment to the national idea. The foundation of the Görres Society in 1876 and the publication of the *Historisches Jahrbuch* after 1880 were attempts to counter the dominance of Protestant national narratives. After the Centre Party had become a party of government in 1897 it supported the naval programmes and increases in military budgets as well as the broad outlines of German colonial policy. Catholic politicians surged forward to declare their loyalty to *Kaiser* and *Reich*. One way of demonstrating national reliability was adherence to antisocialism – which brings us to the second important group labelled 'internal enemy' in the *Kaiserreich*.

In 1878 the Anti-Socialist Law was passed in parliament which allowed the Socialist party to put forward candidates in elections but otherwise forbade them to organize and campaign.[19] It was renewed several times during the 1880s and remained on the statute books until 1890. During twelve years of persecution approximately 330 organizations were dissolved, 1300 publications were banned, 900 Socialists were expatriated, and the law courts sentenced about 1500 Socialists to a total of 1000 years of imprisonment. In a letter to his wife dated February 1887, an imprisoned August Bebel, leader of the Socialist party, wrote: 'O Germany, you national prison!'[20] The passing of the law followed two assassination attempts on the life of the emperor. The Socialist party had distanced itself from such acts of terrorism, but it was an obvious target. Bismarck dubbed Socialists 'enemies of the Reich' (*Reichsfeinde*) and 'vagrants without a fatherland' (*vaterlandslose Gesellen*). Had Socialists not criticized Prussia for its actions in the Franco-Prussian war and had they not refused to grant the war budgets? Had Bebel not championed the Paris Commune and warned, in a famous speech in parliament, that the Commune had only been the beginning of the struggle which would see the end of the existing social and economic order? Were the Socialists not a revolutionary party which wanted to do away with the whole edifice of the state that had been created in 1871? Was it not committed to working-class internationalism and did it not put class before nation, thereby threatening the national unity of the *Reich*? It was easy to find reasons why the Socialists should be banned. Bismarck's real motivation, however, had little to do with the threat of socialism, which was hardly very real in 1878 – with the Socialist party staying regularly below 10 per cent of the vote for Reichstag elections. The chancellor wanted to weaken the National Liberal party, which originally refused to support a law in such flagrant breach of liberal principle. It was only under the impact of a heavy electoral defeat in 1878 that the National Liberals came round to supporting the law.

Whatever the origins of the law, its impact was wide-reaching. For a start, it marked the breakthrough of Marxist ideology in the Socialist party. Until the 1880s Marx had been one among other theoretical influences, but the Anti-Socialist Law seemed to confirm to many Socialists Marx's teachings about class war and class rule. The state was obviously a tool in the hands of ruling classes intent on repressing the workers. Ferdinand Lasalle's idea of a democratized

19 Stefan Berger, *Social Democracy and the Working Class in Nineteenth- and Twentieth-Century Germany* (London, 2000), pp. 72ff.

20 Ursula Hermann, ed., *August und Julie Bebel: Briefe einer Ehe* (Bonn, 1997).

state as ally of the workers in their struggle for emancipation seemed far-fetched in the context of the 1880s. Few Socialists, either before or after the Anti-Socialist Law, familiarized themselves with the finer points of political theory, but from the 1880s onwards many were convinced of the repressive potential of the state. They did not have to read *Das Capital* in order to experience that. As a result, the Socialists remained alienated from the existing nation state long after the Anti-Socialist Law was lifted in 1890. As with the Catholics, they built up their own milieu and kept themselves to themselves. A Socialist was a Socialist 'from cradle to grave'. They visited Socialist kindergartens and went to Socialist youth groups before joining a Socialist trade union and eventually the Socialist party. They spent their leisure time cycling in Socialist cycling clubs or singing in Socialist choirs and they were members of Socialist lending libraries. Even after they died, they would be buried by the Socialist burial association. Socialist trade union halls or people's houses (*Volkshäuser*) represented the power of the Socialist milieu to the outside world. They were often imposing buildings situated in strategic locations in many German cities and towns.

Socialists continued to be among the strongest critics of the official nationalism in Imperial Germany. Rather than celebrating Sedan Day on 2 September, Socialists remembered the dead of the Paris Commune and of the barricade fighting in Berlin in 1848 every 18 March. They did not vote in parliament for millions of Reichsmarks to be spent on a Kaiser Wilhelm memorial in Berlin, and instead of a Bismarck cult they developed a cult surrounding their former leader Ferdinand Lasalle. August Bebel, not Wilhelm II, was their 'emperor'. Socialism in Imperial Germany was infused with radical democratic antimilitarism.[21] Imperial Germany, according to the Socialists, resembled a 'garrison state' run by a clique of Prussian Junkers for their own interests. The egotistical, militarist, antidemocratic, narrow-minded and backward-oriented Junker symbolized everything that was wrong about the nation. In their antimilitarism and their anti-Junker stance Socialists were heavily influenced by liberal national traditions of the *Vormärz* period.

If Socialists were critical of the existing nation they were by no means antinational. The myth of the revolution and class allegiance did not replace the myth of the nation in Socialist thought. In the 1870s and 1880s Socialists expected the revolution to be fairly imminent but, as the stability of the newfound nation state became increasingly obvious, they had to accommodate themselves to its existence. Simply by virtue of operating within a national political framework Socialists were drawn into the fabric of the Imperial German nation state. In parliament they fought hard to bring about social reforms which would benefit workers. They by and large supported social welfare policies, such as the introduction of accident (1881), sickness (1884) and old age (1888) insurance. They welcomed more rigid factory inspection regimes and greater protection for women and children. Parliament itself was widely perceived as the holy grail of

[21] Nick Stargardt, *The German Idea of Militarism: Radical and Socialist Critics 1866–1914* (Cambridge, 1994), who also points out that democratic antimilitarism gave way to pacifist sentiments motivated not so much by a domestic critique of the state in Imperial Germany as by concerns about German *Weltpolitik*.

people's sovereignty by Socialist leaders. In the south-western states of Germany, Socialists were increasingly co-operating with other political parties to bring about practical reforms. Despite the continuing antisocialism of both major denominations, of the judiciary, the churches, the army and most other political parties in Imperial Germany, Socialists were adamant that they were patriots too. Veterans' organizations refused Social Democrats membership and the Imperial League Against Social Democracy (*Reichsverband zur Bekämpfung der Sozialdemokratie*) started an officially supported and well-endowed propaganda campaign against the 'internal enemy of the nation'. But Socialists themselves begged to differ. The SPD's famous organizational patriotism, which made it the strongest and electorally most successful Socialist party in the world before 1914, gave rise to the notion that the German proletariat had a special historical mission in the inevitable evolution towards socialism. German Socialists thus nurtured their own nationalist feelings of superiority vis-à-vis other weaker labour movements elsewhere in Europe.

In their attempt to develop their own brand of left-wing patriotism, Socialists insisted that love for one's fatherland could go hand in hand with international class solidarity. Bebel famously declared his readiness to shoulder his rifle should Germany be threatened by reactionary Russian Tsarism. Many Socialists believed in the right of a 'higher culture', i.e. the German one, to defend itself against attack from a 'lower culture', i.e. the Slav one. The left-wing Socialist Konrad Haenisch confessed that for him it was a moment of cathartic release when, in August 1914, he could sing the refrain of *Deutschland, Deutschland über alles* for the first time. And Philipp Scheidemann recalled in his memoirs how his whole political experience had taught him one thing: 'I learnt what it means to be truly patriotic; it means being a Social Democrat! Patriotism means love for one's country. No one can love his Fatherland more than we Social Democrats.'[22] Socialist nationalism in Imperial Germany was miles apart from the official nationalism. Socialists were the self-styled heirs to the universalist, cosmopolitan and liberal nationalism of the first half of the nineteenth century. They attacked the liberals for selling out their erstwhile democratic concept of the nation to Prussian authoritarianism. All the same though, Socialist nationalism had significant overlaps with the xenophobic, aggressive, militarist and predominantly ethno-cultural nationalism that characterized the official nationalism in Imperial Germany.[23]

Antisocialism was frequently connected to antisemitism. Antisocialists did not tire of pointing out that many leading Socialists were also Jews and that socialism itself was a Jewish conspiracy to undermine and destroy the German nation. On the far right of the political spectrum a range of antisemitic parties and *völkisch* groups routinely depicted Jews as fat spiders sitting in their webs of deceit and conspiracy, engulfing and endangering the German nation. Jews were not only supposed to be behind socialism, they were also representatives of capitalism,

22 Philipp Scheidemann, *Memoirs of a Social Democrat*, Vol. 1 (London, 1929), p. 12f.

23 Stefan Berger, 'British and German Socialists Between Class and National Solidarity', in Stefan Berger and Angel Smith, eds, *Nationalism, Labour and Ethnicity, 1870–1939* (Manchester, 1999), pp. 31–63.

pacifism and feminism – all equally abhorred by different groups of antisemites. The economic crisis of 1873 known as the *Gründerkrach* produced an economically motivated antisemitism. For organizations such as the Imperial German Mittelstand League, Jews became scapegoats for the economic problems of many of their members. Antisemitism was also mobilized in the campaign against any further immigration of Jews from Russian-occupied Poland in the late 1870s. This issue formed the backdrop of the Berlin Antisemitism Dispute,[24] in which von Treitschke wrote the fateful sentence 'The Jews are our misfortune', which became the motto of Julius Streicher's infamous Nazi journal *Der Stürmer*, founded in 1923. It was left overwhelmingly to Jews to contradict Treitschke and defend themselves against his accusations. The exception among non-Jews was Treitschke's former liberal ally and fellow history professor, Theodor Mommsen, who spoke out against antisemitism. Cultural antisemitism also surfaced in the debates surrounding a Heinrich Heine memorial in his home town of Düsseldorf between 1887 and 1893. Heine had an ambiguous relationship to Germany, which always swayed between love and hatred. He was one of the sharpest critics of German politics, and spent much of his life in his beloved Paris. But he was also the writer of the most famous Romantic poems about Germany and German landscapes, including the one on the Lorelei drawing the fishermen of the Rhine to their death, which starts:

Ich weiss nicht, was soll es bedeuten,
Das ich so traurig bin;
Ein Märchen aus alten Zeiten,
Das kommt mir nicht aus dem Sinn.[25]

Antisemites hated Heine as a Jew and alleged national traitor, and in Düsseldorf they were successful in scuppering plans for the memorial. It was to take almost another century before the city of Düsseldorf decided to name its new university Heinrich-Heine-Universität.

Christian-motivated antisemitism was also highly notable in the *Kaiserreich*. Religion remained a major focus for people's identities,[26] and religiously motivated antisemitism had a long history. Catholics often equated liberalism with prominent Jewish leaders of the liberal parties and argued that their desire to destroy Catholicism in the *Kulturkampf* was yet another Jewish plot.[27] The Protestant conservative *Kreuzzeitung* and the Protestant court chaplain Adolf Stoecker were vociferous in their antisemitism. Otto Böckel, the 'king of the peasants', established a popular antisemitic movement in the 1880s which combined calls for agrarian reform and greater participation of the rural population

[24] Christhard Hoffmann, 'Geschichte und Ideologie: Der Berliner Antisemitismusstreit 1879/81', in Wolfgang Benz and Werner Bergmann, eds, *Vorurteil und Völkermord: Entwicklungslinien des Antisemitismus* (Freiburg, 1997), pp. 219–51.

[25] 'I don't know what it means / that I feel so sad; / An old fairy tale / Keeps coming back into my mind.'

[26] Hugh McLeod, ed., *European Religion in the Age of Great Cities 1830–1930* (London, 1995).

[27] Olaf Blaschke and Aram Mattioli, eds, *Katholischer Antisemitismus im 19. Jahrhundert: Ursachen und Traditionen im internationalen Vergleich* (Zurich, 2000).

in the affairs of the state with attacks on Jews. Violent antisemitic disturbances rocked the towns of Skurz in 1884, Xanten in 1891 and Konitz in 1900. In each case accusations of ritual muder of Germans by Jews initiated ugly pogroms.[28] German polite society seriously discussed the question whether Jews could be invited to dinner parties. Antisemitism was socially acceptable.[29]

Jewish integration into German society had its limits, but the vast majority of the approximately half a million Jews living within the borders of the German *Reich* in 1871 (about 1 per cent of the total population) firmly believed in the possibility of a dual identity as Germans and Jews. The middle-class intellectual leaders of the Jewish community in particular identified almost completely with German culture and emphasized their belonging to the German nation through the German language.[30] By adopting the German language, they argued, they had become German and felt themselves as part and parcel of the German national spirit. The Jewish people could portray themselves as yet another tribe making up the whole of the nation. Assimilation had given rise to Reform Judaism which sought to overcome what were regarded as the more backward elements in the Jewish religion. Reform Jews found it particularly easy to adhere to notions of a 'German-Jewish symbiosis'. They self-confidently belittled signs of antisemitism. The Central Union of German Citizens of Jewish Faith (*Centralverein deutscher Staatsbürger jüdischen Glaubens*), which had 34,000 members in 1912, campaigned for civic equality and challenged political and economic forms of discrimination in the law courts.[31]

Many German Jews perceived the supporters of antisemitic parties, whose fortunes declined in the 1890s, as complete outsiders and cranks. They were not taken seriously as a threat to the Jewish community. Were Jews not far more integrated into German society than Catholics? Many Jews received official state honours; Jewish students attended German universities and German academia was, if anything, more open to Jews than universities in Britain.[32] Many state officials might still harbour antisemitic sentiments, but the authorities dealt swiftly with any outbreak of violence against Jews. Before 1914, far more vicious antisemitic states existed in Europe – notably Tsarist Russia and the Habsburg Empire. Zionism, Jewish nationalism propagating a homeland of the Jews in Palestine, was particularly strong in Russia and Austria-Hungary. A Zionist Association for Germany was founded in 1897, but most German Zionists prided

[28] Christhard Hoffmann, Werner Bergmann and Helmut Walser Smith, eds, *Exclusionary Violence: Antisemitic Riots in Modern German History* (Chicago, 2002).

[29] Oded Heilbronner, 'From Antisemitic Peripheries to Antisemitic Centres: The Place of Antisemitism in Modern German History', *Journal of Contemporary History*, 35 (2000), pp. 559–76.

[30] Dietz Bering, 'Jews and the German Language: The Concept of *Kulturnation* and Anti-Semitic Propaganda', in Norbert Fintzsch and Dietmar Schirmer, eds, *Identity and Intolerance: Nationalism, Racism, and Xenophobia in Germany and the United States* (Cambridge, 1998), pp. 251–91.

[31] Avraham Barkai, *'Wehr Dich': Der Centralverein deutscher Staatsbürger jüdischen Glaubens 1893–1938* (Munich, 2002).

[32] Thomas Weber, 'Anti-Semitism and Philo-Semitism among the British and German Elites: Oxford and Heidelberg before the First World War', *English Historical Review*, 118 (2003), pp. 86–119.

themselves on being German. A Jewish state in Palestine was supported as the best means for liberating the oppressed and persecuted Jews in Eastern Europe. German Jews, it was felt, had no need for it. But, as we have noted, the ideological world of antisemitism and its strong connections to nationalism were already in place in Imperial Germany. In the 1920s and 1930s they were retrievable.

The construction of external enemies and the role of women in the national imagination

Catholics, Socialists and Jews were the most prominent 'internal enemies' of the nation, but nationalism in Imperial Germany also relied extensively on the construction of external foes. France, in particular, was regarded as the 'hereditary enemy' who would forever remain 'the other' in German nationalist discourse – regardless of the fact that social etiquette in Germany continued to follow France. But with the rising Anglo-German antagonism before 1914,[33] 'perfidious Albion' was also widely attacked for attempting to suppress their up-and-coming German rival. And, of course, Slav Russia and Eastern Europe were perceived as culturally backward, politically reactionary and racially inferior. German xenophobia was reflected in the treatment of non-German ethnic minorities who were subjected to ruthless Germanization policies. In the annexed Alsace, Alsatians spoke a German dialect but many identified more with France than with Germany. More than a third of the population left after 1871 and moved to France. 2.8 million French-speakers remained within the borders of the *Reich* and had to accommodate themselves to the fact that they were part of a German *Reichsland* ruled directly from Berlin. Alsace and Lorraine became known as the 'garrison of the *Reich*' with one soldier to every fourteen civilians. The brutal treatment of civilians by German officers in the small town of Zabern in 1913 created an uproar among the indigenous population and demonstrated how volatile the integration of the annexed territories into Germany remained. On the other hand, by 1914 their political and economic structures had become closely interwoven with those of Germany and a specifically Alsatian identity, which regarded itself as neither fully French nor fully German, was in the making.[34] In 1914 Alsatian MPs were just as enthusiastic as other members of parliament about war. 380,000 Alsatians and Lorrainers fought in the German army during the First World War and many were severely hurt by the continual mistrust they encountered from the German authorities.

The 140,000 Danish-speakers living in North Schleswig or Southern Jutland (as the Danes called the territory) also suffered under attempts to Germanize the area. In 1888 German became the sole language of instruction in schools. Only four hours of religious instruction could be held in Danish for children of Danish-speaking parents. Danish nationalist agitators were forcibly expatriated and moved to Denmark. The bitter conflict was channelled into somewhat

[33] Paul Kennedy, *The Rise of the Anglo-German Antagonism* (London, 1980).

[34] Jena M. Gaines, 'The Politics of National Identity in Alsace', *Canadian Review of Studies in Nationalism*, 21 (1994), pp. 99–109.

quieter waters after 1907 when Denmark officially accepted the northern borders of the *Reich* and Germany toned down its anti-Danish policies in North Schleswig.

No such compromise was made with Polish nationalism in the east. Poland as a state was non-existent on the map of Europe after it had been divided by Prussia, Russia and Austria-Hungary in 1793. But 2.5 million Polish-speakers and 150,000 Lithuanian-speakers lived largely in the eastern territories of Prussia. Tens of thousands of them migrated to the new industrial centres of Germany, in particular to the Ruhr, where many worked in the coal mines. They included Polish-speaking but Protestant Masurians who, by and large, identified more with Germany than Poland. Yet, for those Germans who used ethnic and linguistic criteria for 'objectively' defining nationhood, Masurians, regardless of their 'subjective' choice, could not be German.[35] In Polish-speaking areas German was made the obligatory language of instruction in schools in 1872/3. It became the only valid official language in 1886. After 1899 Polish-speaking miners in the Ruhr had to demonstrate their ability to speak German before they could be employed in the mines. In 1885 mass expulsions of Poles who had lived on German territory for generations but did not possess Prussian citizenship caused international protests. In 1908 an expropriation law sought to reduce the area of land held by Polish-speakers in Eastern Prussia. Fear of the Polonization of Prussia's eastern territories led the government to restrict immigration of Polish-speakers from Russian-occupied Poland despite the fact that German agricultural interests lobbied hard for such immigrants, who were the cheapest labour force for seasonal harvesting. Where the government did give in to economic interests, it did everything possible to prevent the naturalization of foreign labourers.

The reform of the citizenship law in 1913 underlined such restrictive immigration practices and the xenophobic tendencies of the German imagination more generally. Between 1842 and 1913 the law moved further and further away from a territorial definition of citizenship (*ius domiciles*) and towards a definition that prioritized ethnic homogeneity (*ius sanguines*). Dual citizenship became ever more difficult to obtain and the naturalization of foreigners became rare. Known Socialists, Poles and Jews were almost never naturalized; the 'enemies of the nation' were kept before the gates. The 1913 law scrapped the stipulation that Germans living abroad lost their citizenship after ten years. This was in line with official efforts to lure ethnic Germans back to the fatherland, maintain their allegiance to Germany and keep track of ethnic Germans living abroad. After 1900 the national census sought to register systematically all Germans living abroad.

While voluntary entry into the German nation became more and more difficult, those living inside the German borders were subjected to Germanization policies which relied heavily on the suppression of non-German languages. This was regarded as all the more important, because Germany was not at all linguistically unified. Provincial languages persisted after 1871. Dialects such as Alemanian, Bavarian, Hamburgian and Masurian were almost impossible to

[35] Richard Blanke, *Polish-Speaking Germans? Language and National Identity among the Masurians since 1871* (Cologne, 2001).

understand by other German-speakers. As a result, attempts to codify a standard high German were stepped up – now with the explicit support of the state. In the preface to the first of his famous dictionaries, published in 1872, Konrad Duden made the explicit link between a single German orthography and national unity.[36] Linguistic nationalism led to the foundation of a German Language Association (*Deutscher Sprachverein*) in 1885, which sought to purge the German language of foreign words (*Fremdwörter*) and heighten German national awareness more generally. Its slogan 'No foreign word when a good German expression is available'[37] reflected its concern for linguistic purity. 'Contamination' by other national languages, notably Latin, French and English, the association argued, had to be avoided if the German language was to play a world role in future. However, an older concern with using German, in order to allow more ordinary people to understand what was being said,[38] remained present in the socialist labour movement. Thus Wilhelm Liebknecht in his defence of the Erfurt programme was adamant that foreign words in the programme were only used where no appropriate German word existed.[39]

But in the struggle against linguistic and ethnic 'others', language became a means of exclusion rather than inclusion. The German Ostmark Association (*Deutsche Ostmarkenverein*) lobbied the government and initiated public campaigns on behalf of stricter Germanization policies meant to prevent the Polonization of the 'German east'. They proposed settlement schemes for Germans in the east and economic policies which would disadvantage Polish-speakers. Germans, the propagandists of the association argued, had to fulfil a civilizing mission in the barbaric Slav east. The rebuilding of the Marienburg after 1882 was a conscious attempt to remind the public of the medieval colonization of Eastern Europe through the Order of the German Templars (*Deutschritterorden*).[40] It underlined German claims of a civilizing influence in Eastern Europe. The Hohenzollern dynasty was described as the 'protector of the Ostmark'. Given the rigidity and aggressiveness of anti-Polish policies in Imperial Germany it can hardly be surprising that Polish nationalism grew substantially from the last third of the nineteenth century onwards. The Poles may have been Prussian citizens but they formed their own tight-knit communities. A specifically Polish milieu was held together by Polish-speaking Catholic priests, a Polish press, Polish trade unions, political parties and cultural associations.

The Ostmark Association had a prominent women's wing, the German Women's Association for the Ostmarks (*Deutscher Frauenverein für die Ostmarken*). It was founded in 1896 to counter the activities of Polish women in

36 Martin Durrell, 'Political Unity and Linguistic Diversity in North-Central Germany', in Maiken Umbach, ed., *German Federalism: Past, Present, Future* (Basingstoke, 2002), p. 96.

37 Cited in Michael Townson, *Mother-tongue and Fatherland: Language and Politics in Germany* (Manchester, 1992) p. 98f.

38 See above, p. 26f.

39 Protokoll, 1891, pp. 330–4.

40 Hartmut Boockmann, 'Das ehemalige Deutschordens-Schloß Marienburg 1772–1945: Die Geschichte eines politischen Denkmals', in Boockmann, Arnold Esch, Hermann Heimpel, Thomas Nipperdey and Heinrich Schmidt, eds, *Geschichtswissenschaft und Vereinswesen im 19. Jahrhundert* (Göttingen, 1972), pp. 99–161.

the Polish national movement. Women were to encourage and bolster German cultural life in the east and spread the use of the German language, traditions and customs. This was just one of several women's organizations in Imperial Germany concerned with strengthening German nationalism. One of the most successful, with 600,000 members in early 1914, was the Patriotic Women's Association (*Vaterländischer Frauenverein*).[41] It performed a multitude of tasks, especially in areas of social welfare and social work. Recruiting overwhelmingly among the Protestant middle and upper classes it was self-consciously anti-socialist and emphasized its loyalty to the nation and to the emperor in particular. Its construction of womanhood was one of service to the nation as good samaritans. Women were imagined as the healing element of the nation which contrasted the male world of destructive warriordom. Like other right-wing national women's associations, it marginalized and excluded Jewish women, who were forced to set up their own organizations.[42]

National women's associations were part of the bourgeois women's movement in Germany which founded the Federation of German Women's Associations (BdF) as an umbrella organization in 1894. Within the BdF the idea of motherhood was a crucial link between demands for greater emancipation and nationalist commitment. Women were not only bringing children into the world. They were also responsible for their future well-being and education. As children were the future of the nation, women had a key responsibility for the well-being of the nation. The civil law code in Imperial Germany maintained strict punishments for women seeking to limit their number of children through birth control or abortion. The state clearly did not see motherhood as a choice, but as a national duty. Bourgeois women activists were willing to accept this, but in return they demanded more rights. Thus Hedwig Dohm, for example, argued in *The Scientific Emancipation of Woman* (1874) that women died in childbirth in the course of their national duty of producing the next generation of soldiers. The fact that they did not do military service was irrelevant, especially as many men didn't serve either. The Socialist August Bebel, in his hugely popular *Woman and Socialism* (1879), agreed: the toll of lives of women who died in childbirth was equal to the army service of men. Furthermore the participation of women in the wars of unity between 1864 and 1871 as nurses in hospitals and in other areas of social welfare was held up as the best proof that women could be entrusted with having their say in the nation state. If motherhood was a service to the nation, then, some women argued, it also entitled them to citizenship. Maternalist discourses were an important gateway through which women could legitimately enter the realm of the nation.[43]

Next to maternalism, the construction of the idea of the German *Hausfrau* (housewife) served as an important anchor for women in their claims for national belonging. Advice literature for married women, housewives' organizations and magazines as well as domestic science courses in schools and adult education

41 Helen J. Quataert, 'German Patriotic Women's Work in War and Peace Time, 1864–1890', in Stig Förster and Jörg Nagler, eds, *On the Road to Total War: The American Civil War and the German Wars of Unification 1861–1871* (Washington, DC, 1997), pp. 449–77.

42 Irmgard Maya Fassmann, *Jüdinnen in der deutschen Frauenbewegung 1865–1919* (Hildesheim, 1996).

43 Ann Taylor Allen, *Feminism and Motherhood in Germany, 1800–1914* (New York, 1991).

relentlessly hammered home the point that German housework was part and parcel of German quality workmanship. Non-German housewives were regarded as poorer housekeepers than German ones, whose ideals of cleanliness, order and thrift excelled those of any other nation.[44] Family and domesticity thus played a major role in the construction of Germanness. This is confirmed by a study of Christmas as a specifically German national holiday.[45] Christmas combined sentimental notions of social cohesion with peculiar consumption patterns of a material culture to arrive at a set of rituals which celebrated Christmas as the prime example of German inwardness (*Innerlichkeit*) and homeliness. Christmas came to stand for a harmonious family life in a harmonious national community free of strife and interest clashes. Women, with their special responsibilities for homeliness and harmony, naturally occupied a central role in the success of any German Christmas. If many bourgeois and proletarian women's associations sought to allocate women a more central place in the nation, far right-wing groups denounced women's emancipation as part and parcel of a racial process of degeneration. A German League to Combat Female Emancipation, founded in 1912, campaigned with much public support against a woman's movement which was allegedly undermining the natural gender order and thereby the health and strength of the nation.[46]

More progressive, left-of-centre women's groups were wary of women subscribing to a male-centred perception of gender relations and propping up a gender order of separate spheres, in which the national discourse could be feminized but the public sphere of the state remained the exclusive preserve of men. Especially the Social Democratic women's associations and the more middle-class Association of Progressive Women's Associations (*Verband fortschrittlicher Frauenvereine*), founded in 1899, were unhappy with the imagination of the nation state as a patriarchal family in which the fathers and husbands would speak for the whole family. When the citizenship law of 1913 did not change the rule that women's citizenship followed their husbands', veteran women campaigner Helene Lange commented bitterly: 'Women have no fatherland.'[47]

Antipluralism, monarchical government and the quest for a world political role

The construction of external and internal enemies was meant to contribute to the process of nation-building, but it only divided the nation further and resulted

[44] Nancy Reagin, 'The Foreign Housewife and the German Linen Cabinet: Household Management and National Identity in Imperial Germany', in Ute Planert, ed., *Nation, Politik und Geschlecht: Frauenbewegungen und Nationalismus in der Moderne* (Frankfurt/Main, 2000), pp. 198–214.

[45] Joseph Parry, 'The Private Life of the Nation: Christmas and the Invention of Modern Germany' (Ph.D. thesis, University of Illinois at Urbana-Champaign, 2001).

[46] Ute Planert, *Antifeminismus im Kaiserreich: Diskurs, soziale Formation und politische Mentalität* (Göttingen, 1998).

[47] Bärbel Clemens, *'Menschenrechte haben kein Geschlecht!' Zum Politikverständnis der bürgerlichen Frauenbewegung* (Pfaffenweiler, 1988), has argued that many right-wing women's organizations constructed theories of biological difference which undermined a more emancipatory human rights discourse.

in a proliferation of competing, overlapping but also often mutually exclusive national imaginations. Such a plurality of national constructions was deeply suspect in a nation state where antipluralism was widespread. Yes indeed, civil society was strong in Imperial Germany: economic and social interests were highly organized, political parties mobilized millions of voters, and voluntary associations were plentiful. Not for nothing did Germans have the reputation of being associational human beings (*Vereinsmensch*). But there is no necessary connection between a strong civil society and a tolerant pluralism. Civil society can encourage inequalities, social distancing and discriminatory practices just as much as it can foster plurality, social inclusion and tolerance. If civil society is in many respects the enemy of totalitarianism, it also has its darker side – hence Frank Trentmann has rightly drawn our attention to the 'paradoxes of civil society'.[48] Furthermore, the strong civil society of Imperial Germany was deeply divided, and these divisions in turn produced longings for greater unity. This was particularly the case since civil society in Germany was often not seen to be in opposition to the state (as was the case in Britain) but in harmony with it. The German term *Staatsbürger* carried very different notions to that of the British *citizen* or the French *citoyen*: it included a more passive, subject-like element, where the egotistical activities of the indvidual had to be controlled and guided by the state and its laws.[49] Most German liberals, champions of civil society, famously abhorred conflict between state and civil society. They idealized harmony and were critical of partisan conflict.

Hence it is hardly surprising that party politics were often accused of fatally dividing the nation and preventing the formation of a more organic national community. Even as particularist parties lost influence and the political system was nationalized, the reputation of party politics remained dubious. Parties were being charged with dividing and fragmenting the nation. In Bismarckian Germany even debating national identity politics was frowned upon, as it allegedly weakened the young nation state. Only after 1890, when Imperial Germany became a more stable nation state, did a public discussion about the diversity of national images and ideas get under way.[50]

When the new *Reichstag* was being built in monumental and imperial style between 1884 and 1894 its iconography hardly referred to parliamentary traditions in Germany at all. Wilhelm II intervened to prevent the words 'To the German People' being placed on the building's gable and routinely referred to the *Reichstag* as his 'imperial monkey house'. Ferdinand Tönnies's famous distinction between 'community' and 'society' became an ideological tool with which to reject modern pluralist industrial society. A mechanistic society ruled by the atomization of individuals, rationalism and contractual obligations could

48 Frank Trentmann, ed., *Paradoxes of Civil Society: New Perspectives on Modern German and British History* (Oxford, 2000).

49 John Keane, 'Despotism and Democracy: The Origins and Development of the Distinction Between Civil Society and the State', in *idem*, ed., *Civil Society and the State: New European Perspectives* (New York, 1988), p. 63.

50 Mark Hewittson, '*Nation* and *Nationalismus*: Representation and National Identity in Imperial Germany', in Mary Fulbrook and Martin Swales, eds, *Representing the German Nation: History and Identity in Twentieth Century Germany* (Manchester, 2000), pp. 19–62.

be juxtaposed with the deep spiritual roots of an organic national community. When the director of the Hamburg art museum, Alfred Lichtwark, talked about the topic of 'The German of the Future' in 1901, he developed a programme for a national education which sought to overcome materialism and intellectualism. Instead it would bring a people, divided into classes, confessions and castes, together in an organic whole and renew national life through culture.[51] The *Sammlungspolitik* of the Imperial German governments of the 1890s was based on the idea of a grand alliance of industry and agriculture and of liberalism and conservatism. The middling classes of society in particular were meant to come together under the banner of the national common interest. The strength of authoritarian corporatist thought in Imperial Germany was based on the ideal of a possible harmonization of interests with the politics left out.[52]

This illusive search for the unity of the nation found one of its most powerful expressions in the idea of monarchical government. The monarch represented the interests of the whole nation. Wilhelm I remained at heart a Prussian and it was only under his grandson Wilhelm II that the monarchy became thoroughly nationalized and enthused with images of modernity and imperialism. Wilhelm II was frequently portrayed as a youthful emperor leading a young and ambitious nation. Youth itself became a cult ideology, with strong Protestant, Catholic and proletarian youth movements establishing themselves before 1914. The largely middle-class *Wandervogel* in particular sought to merge youth and national sentiment in an attempt to reinvigorate the national principle. Its members abhorred what they regarded as the stifling, materialist, self-satisfied, vacuous and hypocritical nationalism of the older generation. Instead they longed to return to what they hoped would be a more idealistic, natural and unconventional espousal of national sentiments. Walking (*wandern*) was propagated as part and parcel of a comprehensive renewal of the Germanic lifestyle. An unprecedented *Wanderlust* of young Germans was catered for by a dense network of cheap student hostels. One of the *Wandervogel's* mentors was the popular right-wing philosopher Arthur Moeller van den Bruck who wrote in his book about the Germans in 1904: 'The nation needs a change of blood, an uprising of the sons against the fathers, the replacement of old age by youth.'[53]

If the cult of youth generated considerable generational conflict, it was also useful to portray a youthful Germany and a youthful emperor replacing older, allegedly declining powers in the existing world system. German assertiveness in European and world politics found expression in concepts of German hegemony over central Europe (*Mitteleuropa*) and in the search for a German colonial empire. Germany's geographical position in the middle of Europe was perceived as a natural starting point for economic and political hegemony on the European continent. Nationalist academics, such as the sociologist Max Weber, argued

[51] Klaus von See, *Freiheit und Gemeinschaft* (Heidelburg, 2001), pp. 160–5. On the diverse facets of German high culture see Matthew Jefferies, *Imperial Culture in Germany 1871–1918* (Basingstoke, 2003).

[52] Stefan Berger, 'Germany in Historical Perspective: The Gap Between Theory and Practice', in Stefan Berger and Hugh Compston, eds, *Policy Concertation and Social Partnership in Western Europe: Lessons for the 21st Century* (Oxford, 2002), pp. 125–38.

[53] Arthur Moeller van den Bruck, *Die Deutschen*, Vol. 1 (Minden, 1904), p. 142.

that the future belonged to grand world states. Germany could either push forward and try and be among them or it would be left behind: 'We have to understand that the unification of Germany would have been a youthful prank, which the nation committed in its old age and which, because of its economic costliness, would have done better to refrain from, if it was meant as the end point and not the beginning of a German bid for world power.'[54] Protestant middle-class Germans overwhelming supported such claims of the nation as global power-political player. Further to the right, mass nationalist organizations such as the Pan-German League (*Alldeutscher Verband*), the Navy League, the Ostmark Association and the German Colonial Association (*Deutscher Kolonialverein*) had hundreds of thousands of members and propagated an aggressive, expansionist and xenophobic nationalism.

Colonialism became a national task and lack of support for colonialism was regarded as unpatriotic. When the Centre Party's refusal to grant more monies in parliament for a genocidal war against the Herero tribe in German south-west Africa brought down the government in December 1906, chancellor Bülow called new elections and effectively mobilized nationalism in the so-called Hottentotten elections of 1907 to boost the electoral fortunes of the Conservatives and National Liberals. The alleged colonial calling of Germany included the categorization of different peoples according to race and culture. The biological concept of the nation, based on race, can be traced back to the 1770s, when it was first developed by the Göttingen professor of philosophy, Christoph Meiners.[55] In his writings colonized people make an appearance as naturally and permanently inferior people, and colonial rule is justified by reference to the racial superiority of colonizing people. If his ideas had been regarded as eccentric in the late eighteenth century they moved into the mainstream by the late nineteenth century. The emperor's advice to the German troops sent out to fight the Boxer rebellion in China in 1900 was: 'Behave like the Huns'. The natives had to be taught a stern lesson to accept the superiority of the white German race and culture.

Early explorers became national heroes in the pantheon of German colonialists. Alexander von Humboldt, who had travelled much and written extensively about central and southern America in the early nineteenth century, was now stylized as the 'German Columbus'. Imperial adventurers such as Carl Peters achieved notoriety, and the popular panoramas often depicted scenes from the colonies.[56] Colonial natives were put on tour to be displayed like circus animals. Ethnology museums (*Völkerkundemuseen*) were founded in several German cities to display a range of artefacts brought back from the colonies by explorers, adventurers and academics. German expressionism was fascinated by African art and culture. The colonial discourse was a highly gendered one with a variety of colonialist women's associations attempting to forge close links between womanhood, nationalism and colonialism.[57] Overall, the influences of colonialism

[54] Max Weber, 'Der Nationalstaat und die Volkswirtschaftspolitik', in *idem*, *Gesammelte politische Schriften* (Munich, 1921), p. 23.

[55] Susanne Zantop, *Colonial Fantasies: Conquest, Family and Nation in Precolonial Germany 1770–1870* (Durham, NC, 1997).

[56] Arne Perras, *Carl Peters and German Imperialism 1856–1918* (Oxford, 2004).

[57] Lora Wildenthal, *German Women for Empire, 1884–1945* (Durham, NC, 2001).

on German national culture and the national imagination were considerable in Imperial Germany,[58] even if in the longer term and in comparison with countries such as Britain or France, empire had a relatively negligible influence on the shaping of German identities.

From the 1890s onwards a youthful *Weltpolitik* was pursued in the spirit of a young, self-confident and progressive nation. The technical and economic abilities of the new nation seemed limitless. Industrialization and urbanization proceeded at breakneck speed. Attitudes towards material progress were jubilant. The dynamism of pre-war German society was the envy of many other European nations. In 1896 an Englishman, E. E. Williams, published a book entitled *Made in Germany*.[59] To its British audience it was a lament about the decline of Britain and a dire warning that Germany was about to outdo and overtake Britain. The book was quickly translated into German and to its German readers it was confirmation of their own upbeat and optimistic predictions for their nation. In the early nineteenth century the German lands had been a byword for an industrial backwater of Europe. Now German industrial products had a reputation for being reliable, durable, secure, powerful and innovative. German progress in science and technology had fed into Germany's economic strength. Science and industry enjoyed a close and mutually beneficial relationship. The foundation of the Kaiser-Wilhelm Society in 1911 was a deliberate attempt to maintain and expand German scientific superiority. World exhibitions served as showcases for the economic, scientific and cultural achievements of Germany.[60] The German Museum in Munich, opened in 1906, celebrated the applied sciences and their contribution to the success of German industry. German products carried patriotic names such as the 'Wotan' lightbulb produced by Siemens. When the British White Star Line publicized plans for massive and luxurious passenger ships, the *Titanic* among them, the German shipbuilding company, Hapag, the biggest shipbuilders in the world, announced that it would build even bigger and more luxurious ones. The *Imperator*, *Fatherland* and *Bismarck* all went to sea between 1912 and 1914. Wilhelm II took a keen interest in this Anglo-German contest and directly influenced the patriotic names given to the ships. They were a fitting symbol for the global naval ambitions of Imperial Germany. Britain was no longer going to be the only nation ruling the seas.

Youthful optimism and modern dynamism were finely balanced by self-doubt and insecurity. A fin-de-siècle mood combined with a penchant for draping the nation in historical costume. A series of prominent anti movements accompanied the rapid transformation of German society: anti-materialism, anti-urbanism, anti-modernism, anti-industrialism. The medievalism of the Hohenzollern cult and the idealization of a medieval social order, for example in Ludwig II's Bavarian castles, stood in marked contrast to the images of a powerful industrial, urban

[58] Birthe Kundrus, *Moderne Imperialisten: Das Kaiserreich im Spiegel seiner Kolonien* (Weimar, 2003); *idem*, ed., *Phantasiereiche: Zur Kulturgeschichte des deutschen Kolonialismus* (Frankfurt/Main, 2003).

[59] David Head, *Made in Germany: The Corporate Identity of a Nation* (London, 1992), for a thorough discussion of the book and the long history of its title.

[60] Eckhardt Fuchs, 'Das Deutsche Reich auf den Weltausstellungen vor dem ersten Weltkrieg', *Comparativ*, 5/6 (1999), pp. 61–88.

and modern nation discussed above. The economic depression lasting from 1873 to 1896 had a major impact on the intellectual climate. It produced a cultural pessimism, which tended to reject much of contemporary society and its alleged decadence. Julius Langbehn's *Rembrandt as Educator*, published anonymously in 1890, depicted the Germans as in need of a spiritual awakening.[61] They had forgotten their idealist dispositions and their national identity had to be regenerated through art.

The philosophers Friedrich Nietzsche and Arthur Schopenhauer came to symbolize the strong dissatisfaction with materialism and the search for a more inward and authentic nation. They had nothing but scorn for a country which seemed to sway between the crassest materialism and a trivialized Romanticism finding expression in, for example, the popular allotment movement (*Schrebergärten*), the praise for German *Gemütlichkeit* and the country's reputation for heavy consumption of beer (which became *the* national drink of the Germans in the last third of the nineteenth century). The pathetic care that was lavished on the neatness and decorativeness of the allotment became a symbol of the conventional uprightness, and the philistine bourgeois conformism of the age. The national imagination in Imperial Germany incorporated both the critique of the shallowness of contemporary civilization and the enthusiasim about limitless technological progress. The critics of modernization rarely wanted to do away with modernity altogether. Rather, they aimed for a 'different modernity',[62] one in which technology would return to service traditional cultural values and in which the perceived artificiality of modern life would give way to more 'natural' lifestyles. Technology had to be perfected and nature had to be reconciled with technology. Both the thorough commitment to modernity and the advocacy of cultural pessimism often lived within one and the same German soul. Take for example Walther Rathenau, one of the most successful industrialists in Imperial Germany: he built successful high-tech companies on his understanding of and enthusiasm for technology, yet he also wrote knowledgeably about the dangers of a technology which ran riot and cut itself loose from human concerns.

Militarism, *Heimat* and the rise of *völkisch* nationalism

The bourgeois public celebrated the wars of unification as major achievements of the Prussian army and the Prussian state with only a minor role being allocated to the people.[63] The wars of unification had raised the status of the army considerably and contributed to the militarization of society in Imperial Germany.[64]

61 On Langbehn and other philosophers of 'cultural despair' see Fritz Stern, *The Politics of Cultural Despair: A Study in the Rise of the Germanic Ideology* (Berkeley, 1961).

62 Thomas Rohkrämer, *Eine andere Moderne? Zivilisationskritik, Natur und Technik in Deutschland 1880–1933* (Paderborn, 1999); see also *idem*, 'Cultural Criticism in Germany 1880–1933: A Typology', *History of European Ideas*, 25 (1999), pp. 321–39.

63 Frank Becker, *Bilder von Krieg und Nation. Die Einigungskriege in der bürgerlichen Öffentlichkeit 1864–1913* (Munich, 2001).

64 Bernd Ulrich, Jakob Vogel and Benjamin Ziemann, eds, *Untertan in Uniform: Militär und Militarismus im Kaiserreich 1871–1914. Quellen und Dokumente* (Frankfurt/Main, 2001).

War gave a boost to nationalism in many other European nation states,[65] but nowhere was war so instrumental in bringing about the nation state. The Sedan celebrations, commemorating the defeat of the French army at the battle of Sedan on 2 September 1870, were an annual national festival with a strongly Protestant flavour. The German Protestant Association (*Deutscher Protestantenverein*) had originally suggested it to foster the religious-cultural renewal of the nation. The state never officially endorsed it, Socialists remained hostile from the start and Catholics referred to it as 'Satan's Day'. Many Catholic clerics expressly forbade the ringing of church bells on the occasion.[66] The confessional nature of this national festival limited its appeal from the start, despite attempts to keep Sedan Day out of the day-to-day political conflicts which tended to accompany military festivals in France.[67] Although the popularity of Sedan Day celebrations waned after 1900, Sedan panoramas, the biggest of which stood in Berlin and measured 20 by 40 metres, acquired genuine popularity. As a contemporary newspaper put it: 'The nation was delighted to be able to view at long last its victories in a form befitting of their greatness ... the poorest peasants travelled for days only to see the place ... where their sons had fought.'[68]

The army as creator of the nation became the school of the nation. Male autobiographies underlined that those who served came out of the army identifying with a manly image of the nation: 'Having finished one's military service, one feels as citizen and as a true man.'[69] The regiment became part of the family. Regimental histories complete with heroic stories usually involving the regimental flag were being written as a means to construct collective identity.[70] Geographically and socially the army brought the nation closer together. As recruits often served far away from their hometowns and villages, the nation became a more experienced and less abstract category. Recruits from rural areas got a taste of life in a garrison town and urban recruits intermingled with people from rural backgrounds. The physical skills of a labourer could count for more in the army than the social standing of an industrialist's son. But the army also undertook more deliberate attempts to implant the idea of nationhood. Hours of harsh physical exercise were followed by a daily hour of instruction. Instruction manuals, handbooks and journals aimed at producing loyal subjects, fervent nationalists and enthusiastic soldiers.

[65] Michael Howard, 'War and the Nation State', in *idem*, *The Causes of Wars and Other Essays*, 2nd edn (Cambridge, Mass., 1983), p. 26f.

[66] Ute Schneider, 'Einheit ohne Einigkeit: Der Sedantag im Kaiserreich', in Sabine Behrenbeck and Alexander Nützenadel, eds, *Inszenierungen des Nationalstaats: Politische Feiern in Italien und Deutschland seit 1860/1871* (Cologne, 2001); Claudia Lepp, 'Protestanten feiern ihre Nation – die kulturprotestantischen Ursprünge des Sedantages', *Historisches Jahrbuch,* 118 (1998), pp. 201–22.

[67] Jakob Vogel, *Nationen im Gleichschritt. Der Kult der 'Nation in Waffen' in Deutschland und Frankreich 1871–1914* (Göttingen, 1997).

[68] Cited in Stephan Ostermann, *Das Panorama: Die Geschichte eines Massenmediums* (Cologne, 1980), p. 79.

[69] Michael Schwab, a journeyman and later industrialist, cited in von See, *Freiheit*, p. 125 (see note 51).

[70] Ute Frevert, *Die kasernierte Nation: Militärdienst und Zivilgesellschaft in Deutschland* (Munich, 2001; English trans. forthcoming, see p. 33, note 46), pp. 245ff.

In the 1860s the National Liberals had risked a constitutional crisis over their desire to see the creation of a citizens' army.[71] Under the impact of the wars of unification they made their peace with the standing army. National Liberals now celebrated generals such as Roon and Moltke as national heroes. Former liberals such as the historian Treitschke denounced parliament as symbol of German division and celebrated the army as symbol of German unity: 'The German army has become without any doubt the most real and effective band of national unity and not, as one had hoped previously, the Reichstag. The latter has contributed to the deplorable state of affairs in which Germans hate and slander each other.'[72] Where many members of the liberal middle classes had originally disliked military service, it now became a mark of distinction and went alongside the idealization of all things military. Being able to join the rank of reserve officer was a sign of high social status and promised rapid advancement and a steep social career. By 1914, there were 91,000 reserve officers compared with 29,000 active officers in the Imperial German armies. Reserve officers were even known to propose to their beloveds in full military uniform.

Instead of the transformation of soldiers into citizens, Imperial Germany witnessed the militarization of civilian life. During national festivals weapons, military uniforms, insignia and flags were everywhere. The War Associations (*Kriegervereine*) were the focus of national festivities in each and every small town; together with other nationalist mass organizations such as the Kyffhäuser Association and the Navy League they dominated the official memory of the wars and the nation brought about through war. With 3 million members (in 1913) the War Associations were by far the biggest mass organizations in German society. They were socially inclusive and celebrated the soldier as unpolitical manly warrior who was loyal to emperor and nation.[73]

In a popular pamphlet entitled *Das Volk in Waffen* (The People Armed), published in 1883, a Freiherr von der Goltz called on his fellow Germans to be constantly alert and ready for war. Being a warrior was described as a national virtue of the Germans. The centenary of the wars of liberty in 1913 brought innumerable speeches emphasizing that Germany, if necessary, was ready to follow the example of 1813. Middle-class boys were often dressed in military uniforms [Figure 3.2]. After 1890 naval dress proved especially popular. Military training became increasingly in vogue in various youth groups across Germany. Organizations such as the *Zentralausschuss zur Förderung der Volks- und Jugendspiele* (1891) and the *Jungdeutschlandbund* (1911) taught young Germans to develop a warlike mentality.[74] The most popular symbol used to refer to Germany in the mid-nineteenth century, the German Michel, was a nightcap-wearing figure, a bit simple-minded perhaps, but honest, gentle, and, above all, slightly dreamy. Following the wars of unification the Prussian aristocrat

[71] See above, p. 71.

[72] Heinrich von Treitschke, *Politik: Vorlesungen gehalten an der Universität zu Berlin*, Vol. 2 (Leipzig, 1922), p. 357.

[73] Thomas Rohkrämer, *Der Militarismus der 'kleinen Leute'. Die Kriegervereine im deutschen Kaiserreich 1871–1914* (Munich, 1990).

[74] Hans Doderer, 'Die vormilitärische Erziehung der deutschen Jugend in der Kaiserzeit', *Geschichte in Wissenschaft und Unterricht*, 49 (1998), pp. 746–53.

Figure 3.2 Little boy as soldier, around 1890.

(Junker) complete with monocle and spiked helmet (*Pickelhaube*) replaced the Michel in satirical magazines across Europe. The so-called *Zwölfender*, non-commissioned officers with twelve years of service who had a claim to a job in the lower echelons of the civil service, could be found almost anywhere in the sprawling local, regional and state administrations.

Despite this cult of the military, most people thought of the nation not foremost as an idealized garrison, but rather as a piece of *Heimat*. The *Heimat* idea mediated between the everyday experience of the local and the more abstract notion of national belonging. Imagining the local or regional *Heimat* became the first step towards imagining the nation. National culture consisted, it was argued by *Heimat* ideologues, of a rich diversity of local and regional cultures.[75] 400 *Heimat* museums were founded between 1871 and 1918. Innumerable *Heimat* books were being published, divided into history, folkore and customs. *Heimat* associations were legion and *Heimat* studies became part of the primary school (*Volksschule*) curriculum. The *Heimat* movement argued that the different landscapes incorporated the collective memory and culture of the nation and its people. The German Association for the Protection of Heimat (*Deutscher Bund Heimatschutz*), founded in 1903, explicitly linked the preservation of monuments and landscapes to the strengthening of national identity.[76] The early environmental movement stressed the need to protect the *Heimat*.[77] As industrialization and urbanization destroyed rural landscapes nature conservation became a national duty.

> In old books and travel descriptions, it is often written that Germany is an endlessly beautiful land in whose cities, villages and forests it is a pleasure to wander. Such words will one day be only a dream from forgotten times for our children. We are confronted with the fact that Germany is losing its character as our beloved homeland, becoming an abode for the dullest kind of sobriety. [...] There will be no more delightful gardens, no churches, no bridges to round out the landscape into a harmonious picture. The former beauty of our land will be ruined forever.[78]

Nature was portrayed as a great healing power for the divisions of society. National monuments were developed in close alliance with perceptions and representations of nature.[79] Harmony between nature and society was the first step on the road to a happy and unified nation.

While the national imagination worked through *Heimat* motif, not all constructions of a local *Heimat* necessarily involved the nation. Especially in the south-west of Germany *Heimat* celebrations of folklore customs and regional traditions adopted a strong anti-Prussian tone and became sceptical of the new Prussianized nation state. The *Heimat* movement was, after all, a deeply provincial movement which juxtaposed a healthy local and often rural culture with a

75 Alan Confino, *The Nation as Local Metaphor: Württemberg, Imperial Germany and National Memory 1871–1918* (Chapel Hill, 1997); Celia Applegate, *A Nation of Provincials: the German Idea of Heimat* (Berkeley, 1990).

76 Matthew Jefferies, 'Back to the Future? The Heimatschutz Movement in Wilhelmine Germany', *History*, 77 (1992), pp. 411–20.

77 William H. Rollins, *A Greener Vision of Home: Cultural Politics and Environmental Reform in the German Heimatschutz Movement 1904–1918* (Ann Arbor, 1997).

78 Paul Schultze-Naumburg, the president of the German League for Heimat Protection, at its founding congress in 1904; cited in John Alexander Williams, ' "The Chords of the German Soul are Tuned to Nature": The Movement to Preserve the Natural Heimat from the Kaiserreich to the Third Reich', *Central European History*, 29 (1996), pp. 339–84, quote on p. 347.

79 Wilfried Lipp, *Natur, Geschichte, Denkmal: Zur Entstehung des Denkmalbewußtseins der bürgerlichen Gesellschaft* (Frankfurt/Main, 1987).

decadent and cosmopolitan national and often urban centre. It rejected cities, industrialization, liberalism and socialism.[80] The heart of the nation was in rural Germany. The Germanic forests became a positive antisymbol to modern industrial class society. Richard Duesberg's *The Forest as Educator* (1910), for example, drew a parallel between the organic life of the forest and the ideal of the 'people's community' (*Volksgemeinschaft*). The order of the forest, he argued, had to be introduced into social relations. The popular novels of Ludwig Ganghofer, Franz Lienhard and other *Heimat* writers identified the nation with specific German landscapes which were invariably wild, romantic and rural. The strong anti-urbanism in late nineteenth-century Germany was the direct result of rapid urbanization.[81] Berlin grew from 800,000 to over 2 million before the First World War. Villages in the Ruhr valley became huge industrial centres. By 1914 two-thirds of all Germans lived in cities. The rapidity of the change brought unease, which in turn made cities into symbols for amorality, sexual depravity, restlessness, materialism, secularism and ill health. Antimodernism could be characteristic of *Heimat* movements, but more recent research has insisted that this was not necessarily so. The aim of preserving the traditions of the past could be pursued equally in line with accepting the inevitable advances of modernity.

As the proliferation of museums, tourist guides, postcards and monuments indicated, *Heimat* and with it the nation consisting of diverse *Heimats* was transformed into a commodity. The national past became a spectacle to be consumed by increasing numbers of tourists. Mass tourism began in the decades before the First World War. Tourist guides became important places for the reflection and self-reflection of national identity.[82] No lesser figure than Wilhelm II became a powerful symbol of the merger between tourism and nationalism. Nicknamed *Reisekaiser* (travel emperor), he was especially fond of visiting historic sites, holding historic ceremonies and celebrating in historical surroundings. Wilhelm united in his person the diverse facets of German nationalism in the empire. He was the youthful emperor representing an industrial and modern nation; he was the militarist glorifying the medieval past and desperate to appear in historical uniforms. He was the embodiment of the commodification of the nation and he also adapted and espoused the new racial nationalism expressed in particular by *völkisch* groups.[83]

Völkisch ideas and groups emerged in the last decade of the nineteenth century. The Deutschbund, formed in 1894, and the journal *Heimdall*, founded in 1896, were two of the most influential *völkisch* institutions before the First World War.[84] Language, race and religion were the three key concepts in the

80 Klaus Bergmann, *Agrarromantik und Großstadtfeindschaft* (Meisenheim am Glan, 1970), pp. 39–49, who focusses on Wilhelm Heinrich Riehl as a prophet of the *Heimat* movement.

81 Anthony McElligott, *The German Urban Experience: Modernity and Crisis, 1900–1945* (Oxford, 2001).

82 Rudy Koshar, *German Travel Cultures* (Oxford, 2000), p. 63.

83 On Wilhelm see Chris Clark, *Kaiser Wilhelm II* (Basingstoke, 2000), and, at much greater length, John Röhl, *Young Wilhelm: The Kaiser's Early Life, 1859–1888* (Cambridge, 1998).

84 Uwe Puschner, *Die völkische Bewegung im wilhelminischen Kaiserreich: Sprache, Rasse, Religion* (Darmstadt, 2001). See generally on the history of the extreme right in Germany Lee McGowan, *The Radical Right in Germany: 1870 to the Present* (Basingstoke, 2003).

völkisch Weltanschauung. Völkisch ideologues rehashed ideas of Herder and Fichte about the superiority of the German language, rid them of their tolerant cosmopolitanism and merged them with ideas of race. Race, they argued, determined the fate of the individual. A crude Social Darwinism led to analogies being drawn between nature and nation. Following the publication of Charles Darwin's *Origins of Species* in 1859 (translated into German in 1860) many writers sought to transfer his findings about the evolution of the natural world to the development of societies and nations. The disciplines of biology and anthropology thrived from the 1860s onwards. Scientists began measuring skulls and testing millions of people for hair and eye colour. The racial characteristics of the *Volk* allegedly decided between success or failure in the inevitable 'survival of the fittest' competition. A strict hierarchy of races put the Germans top and the Jews and Slavs bottom. Concern about the purity of German blood also led to rigorous attempts to prevent marriages between Germans and members of the indigenous population in the German colonies. Many governors expressly forbade such marriages after 1905. It was almost impossible for children of mixed marriages to acquire German citizenship, even if in principle German citizenship still followed paternity rather than race.[85] Those concerned about the purity of racial stock also worried about the 'degenerates' among their own population: they interpreted alcoholism, homosexuality and criminality as part and parcel of a racial decline which threatened healthy Germandom. To *völkisch* groups race became a dogma of religious quality. The German race was of divine descent and it followed a divine mission: to redeem the world. Paul de Lagarde and Houston Stewart Chamberlain became the most important ideologues of race in Imperial Germany.

Völkisch monuments began to become more prominent. The most famous was the Monument to the Battle of Nations (*Völkerschlachtdenkmal*) in Leipzig (1913). The *völkisch* propagandist Langbehn spoke of the 'fine barbarism' of a Germanic artistic style revealed in the monument. It was a 91-metre-high pyramidical structure – the biggest memorial in Europe at the time. Its symbolic language emphasized the sacrifices, courage, manliness and strength of a German warrior people. The nation had become one, the monument alleged, through sacrifice in war. The people (*Volk*) had been consecrated through war.

War was also a major theme of one of the most popular expressions of the new *völkisch* paradigm – Felix Dahn's three-volume novel *Struggle for Rome* (1876). It went through thirty editions between 1876 and 1900 and sold approximately 600,000 copies. No lending library in Germany was complete without one, and it was a book in heavy demand. It told the story of the struggle of the Goths against the Roman Empire. At a time when about 20 per cent of all historical novels dealt with the Germanic tribes,[86] this was a popular theme. In the context of the *Kulturkampf* it could be read as confirmation of the importance

[85] Dieter Gosewinkel, *Einbürgern und Ausschließen: Die Nationalisierung der Staatsangehörikeit vom Deutschen Bund bis zur Bundesrepublik Deutschland* (Göttingen, 2001), pp. 303–9.

[86] H. Eggert, *Studien zur Wirkungsgeschichte des deutschen historischen Romans 1850–1875* (Frankfurt/Main, 1971), p. 90; on the importance of Germanic myths to the national imagination in Imperial Germany see also Rainer Kipper, *Der Germanenmythos im Deutschen Kaiserreich: Formen und Funktionen historischer Selbstthematisierung* (Göttingen, 2002).

of the struggle against the Catholic church. But the Goths in Dahn's novel were not religious. They had substituted a belief in the *Volk* for a belief in God. The historical Goths had converted to Christianity, but in the novel they were described as heathens critical of the Christian religion. They were depicted as a people of courageous, loyal and honest peasants led by the nobility. The family was celebrated as the basis of their society – with a clear separation of spheres: women were mothers and carers, men were warriors. The urban middle classes, for so long the standard-bearers of the national idea in the nineteenth century, were completely absent from the novel. Dahn's idealization of peasant life was also a hallmark of the propagandist efforts of agricultural pressure groups such as the Association of Farmers (*Bund der Landwirte*), founded in 1893. Hans Grimm and Adolf Bartels belonged to the most popular blood and soil ideologues praising peasant life and contrasting it positively with the degenerate city life of urban tradesmen. Public support for the Boers in the Boer War was frequently connected to ideas of an organic peasant people of Germanic origin being suppressed by the cunning of a hypocritical tradespeople, the English.

The final volume of Dahn's novel dealt with the demise of the Goths, who were depicted as being surrounded by envious and devious enemies planning their downfall. It was read widely as an analogy to the young and dynamic Germany which was allegedly surrounded by envious enemies scheming to prevent the German nation from occupying its leading place in the world. The success of Dahn's novel demonstrated the potential popularity of *völkisch* ideas. At the same time it needs to be emphasized that racial nationalism remained a minority position in Imperial Germany. All suggestions to bring together the various *völkisch* groups, which were divided by many internal differences, came to nothing before 1914. A *völkisch* party could not be founded, and mainstream political thought often ridiculed the crankiness of *völkisch* ideas [Figure 3.3]. Highbrow cultural nationalism and the banal nationalism of the everyday remained far more important than the integral nationalism of the political right. Yet the pre-war *völkisch* movement already contained all the ideological ingredients of National Socialism's racial nationalism, which moved into the mainstream in the inter-war period – as a direct consequence of the First World War.

We started off this chapter by asking how successful the new nation state would be in engendering feelings of national identity. Undoubtedly massive steps had been taken on the road to an effective nationalization of the masses between 1871 and 1914. On the eve of the First World War the vast majority of people living in Germany, including many Catholics, Socialists and Jews, who had been dubbed 'internal enemies' of the nation, felt German. The kinds of Germany that were imagined, however, were manifold: dynastic, authoritarian and militarized constructions stood next to democratic, liberal and participatory ones. The division of Imperial Germany into milieux (Protestant national, Socialist and Catholic) produced competing national imaginations which could be overlapping at times. Images of a dynamic economic and imperial nation blended with images of a cultural nation in crisis. Local and regional loyalties produced significant synergies with national sentiments. A racialized discourse of a *völkisch* nation challenged older forms of liberal and dynastic nationalism but remained marginal before 1914. Representations of the nation as progressive and

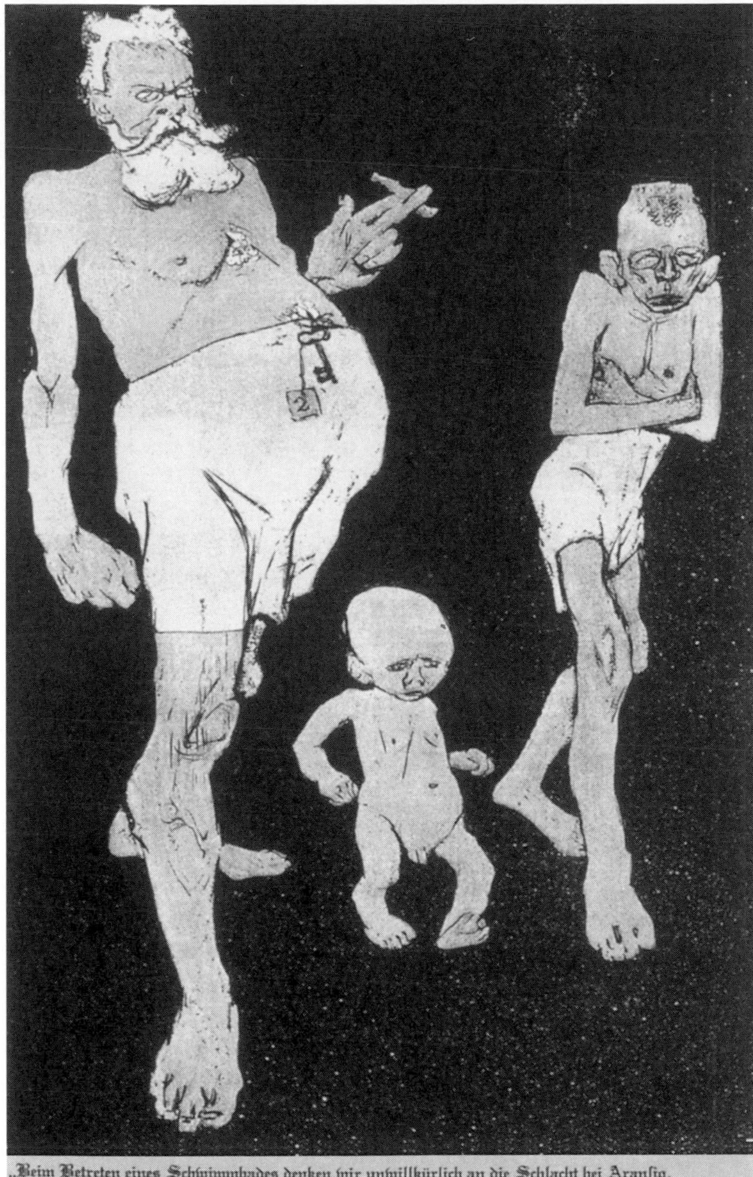

Figure 3.3 Poking fun at the racists: caricature from *Simplicissimus* 7, 1902, no. 24. The subtext reads: 'Walking into a swimming pool we naturally think of the Battle of Aransio, where our courageous ancestors terrified the Romans through the mere sight of their bodies.'

forward-looking stood next to celebrations of Germanic virtues and a historist inclination to package the nation in historical costume. Women were not full members of the nation state, but they could imagine themselves and were imagined by men as a vital part of national life. A vibrant civil society produced and organized a plurality of interests but rejected pluralism in favour of concepts of national unity which sought to dissolve all differences and integrate diverse interests.

Overall we have encountered a perplexing variety of different ways of imagining the nation in Imperial Germany. National identity was far from fixed; it was extraordinarily fluid and under construction. As we shall see in the next chapter, the First World War was going to have a major impact on which of these constructions would have greater power in the first half of the twentieth century.

4

The mythologies of war and the republican nation, 1914–1933

When war broke out in August 1914, the vast majority of intellectuals greeted it with open arms. In line with the fin-de-siècle mood of cultural despair that was such a prominent part of the national imagination after 1900, writers thought of war as a unique opportunity for purifying the nation. It was perceived like a clearing thunderstorm which would end all materialistic falseness and the philistinism of the Wilhelmine period. Take for example the expressionist poet Richard Dehmel's *Lied an alle* (Song to all):

Be blessed, earnest hour, Which finally unites us in steely determination; Peace was in everyone's mouth, Suspicion paralysed friend and foe – Now war is coming, The honest war!	Sei gesegnet, ernste Stunde, die uns endlich stählern eint; Frieden war in aller Munde, Argwohn lähmte Freund und Feind – Jetzt kommt der Krieg, Der ehrliche Krieg!
Dull greed with blunt claw Haggled for pleasures and splendour; Now suddenly everyone feels What alone will bring us happiness – Now peril is coming, The holy peril!	Dumpfe Gier mit stumpfer Kralle feilschte um Genuß und Pracht; jetzt auf einmal ahnen alle, was uns einzig selig macht – Jetzt kommt die Not, Die heilige Not!
Fiery clarity will now hover Over dust and smoke of guns; Not for life, not for life Man is leading the struggle for life – Death will always come, The divine death!	Feurig wird nun Klarheit schweben Über Staub und Pulverdampf; Nicht ums Leben, nicht ums Leben Führt der Mensch den Lebenskampf – Stets kommt der Tod, Der göttliche Tod!
Believers, we defend ourselves, For the spirit in our blood; People, defend your honour,	Gläubig greifen wir zur Wehre, Für den Geist in unserm Blut; Volk, tritt ein für deine Ehre,

Man, your happiness is sacrifice –
Then victory will come,
Wonderful victory!

Mensch, dein Glück heißt Opfermut –
Dann kommt der Sieg,
Der herrliche Sieg![1]

The nation, ran Dehmel's message, would find itself and a new idealism through war. One and a half million German war poems expressed sentiments like these. The 'August experience' of 1914 became a powerful figure of speech in nationalist discourse, suggesting as it did that the deep class, confessional and other divisions in German society could be overcome. The *Kaiser* himself had declared on 1 August: 'I do not recognize parties any more, I only know Germans.' Even the allegedly unpatriotic Social Democrats had voted for war credits in parliament. At long last the nation would overcome all sectional interests and internal divisions and come together in one people's community (*Volksgemeinschaft*) to demonstrate the superiority of Germanness over Slav barbarity and the shallowness of Western civilization.[2]

In this chapter we shall examine the deep impact of the First World War on constructions of the nation in the Weimar Republic. First, the 'ideas of 1914' and their contribution to the radicalization of the national imagination will be analysed. Secondly, the end of the war was almost as important for conceptions of national identity as its beginning. Hence we need to explore reactions to defeat and the Versailles peace treaty. Thirdly, the segmentation of the national imagination, already prominent in Imperial Germany, became even more marked after 1918. Therefore we shall discuss three different casts of national imagination: the Communist, the republican and the right-wing antirepublican. By way of conclusion we shall reflect on why the political right was ultimately so much more successful than anyone else in capturing the concept of the nation in the Weimar Republic.

The 'ideas of 1914' and the radicalization of the national imagination

Intellectuals wrote about the war not so much as a power-political struggle, but as a clash of national cultures and ideals. The German 'ideas of 1914' were juxtaposed to the French ideas of 1789. German order, discipline, idealism, selfless sacrifice and community contrasted with Western materialism, sensuousness and search for profits. Expressionist artists such as Franz Marc celebrated their own Germanic art as more expressive and metaphysical than anything produced by 'Western' artists. Expressionism was declared the truest artistic form of Germanness.[3]

Thomas Mann, in his infamous 'Declarations of an unpolitical man', pitted the depth of German culture, music, literature and philosophy against the failure of Western democracies to produce truly great works of art. According to Mann,

1 Richard Dehmel, *Hundert ausgewählte Gedichte* (Berlin, 1922), p. 95; also: www.richard-dehmel.de/rdehmel/ richard%20dehmel/texte.html; see generally Thomas Anz and Joseph Vogel, eds, *Die Dichter und der Krieg: Deutsche Lyrik 1914–1918* (Munich, 1982).

2 Jeffrey Verhey, *The Spirit of 1914: Militarism, Myth and Mobilization in Germany* (Cambridge, 2000).

3 Joes Segal, 'The Work of Art as a Mirror of National Identity: Public Debates on Art and Culture in Germany during World War I', *European Review of History*, 4 (1997), pp. 9–17.

it was the authoritarian state which allowed the flourishing of art and culture by preventing artists from getting involved in politics:

> Politics itself is alien and poisonous to the German soul; [...] I am deeply convinced that the German people will never be able to love political democracy, for the simple reason that it cannot love politics itself. The much maligned authoritarian state is and remains the type of state most appropriate and beneficial for the German people and it is basically the one that it wants. [...] My deepest inner self, my national instinct rebelled against the cry for 'politics' in the spiritual sphere: it is the 'politicization of the spirit', the false renaming of the spirit-concept into the one espoused by the do-good Enlightenment and by revolutionary philanthropy which affects me like poison [...]; and I know that my disgust and protest are not something meaningless and personal or bound to a specific time and place, but that it is the national essence itself which speaks through me. [...] The difference between spirit and politics contains the one between culture and civilization, between soul and society, between freedom and voting rights, between art and mere literature; and Germandom is culture, soul, freedom, art and *not* civilization, society, voting rights and literature.[4]

German *Innerlichkeit* did not have to take the highbrow artistic expression given to it by Thomas Mann. A more popular example was the German family Christmas under the Christmas tree. In the nineteenth century it had been a German export article. Prince Albert famously brought it to Britain. But it was during wartime, first in 1870/1 and especially after 1914 that Christmas became a powerful symbol of Germanness: 'And even if aligned against us in battle, / The dark hatred of the entire world: / You will not rob the German soul / The dear and golden Christmas light.'[5] Protecting the innermost sanctum of Germanness went hand in hand with racist and militarist declarations in favour of the German war effort, such as the so-called 'manifesto of the 93': it was signed by more than 4000 Germans – a kind of *Who's Who* of German cultural life. A counter-manifesto, drafted, among others, by Albert Einstein, which reminded the combatants of their common European heritage, only carried four signatures.

Not all Germans, however, welcomed war. The enthusiasm of the intellectuals was not representative of all segments of society. Undoubtedly there was war euphoria in the big demonstrations and marches on the streets and squares of major German cities. Young urban middle-class Germans were most affected by forms of collective hysteria. But equally there was much fear about the lives of sons and anxiety about the harvest in rural areas. The population in border regions was less enthusiastic than the people in the urban centres. Even in urban areas, working-class districts greeted the news of war with far fewer signs of nationalism than middle-class districts. The national unity of August 1914 was always an imagined one, but it was one which was supported by the vast majority of intellectuals, which explains its staying power as a nationalist myth long after the end of the First World War. Opposition to the war surfaced in 1915 and developed into a mass movement by 1917. Mass strikes were an expression of frustration

4 Thomas Mann, 'Bekenntnisse eines Unpolitischen' [1918], in *idem*, *Aufsätze, Reden, Essays*, Vol. 2: *1914–1918* (Berlin [O], 1983), p. 185f.

5 Cited in Doris Foitzik, 'Weihnachten', in Etienne François and Hagen S. Schulze, eds, *Deutsche Erinnerungsorte*, 3 vols (Munich, 2001), Vol. 3, p. 159; see also above, p. 96.

with working conditions and the inadequate supply of food and clothes, but they were also a vote for democratization and peace. Ultimately the war deepened internal divisions and the loss of the war coincided with revolution and civil war.

If the experience of the First World War did not produce unity, much of the writing about the war confirmed and radicalized existing national concepts. The war was welcomed by many intellectuals because it facilitated, in the words of Max Scheler, the 'recognition ... of the reality of the nation as having a collective spiritual personality'.[6] Many authors depicted the war as a fight for the existence of the German nation. They re-enforced notions of the superiority and homogeneity of Germanness, and strengthened xenophobic reactions towards Germany's external enemies. *Gott strafe England* (God punish England) became a popular everyday greeting during the war and Anglophobia reached unprecedented heights[7] [Figure 4.1]. The deepening of wartime hostilities carried over into the inter-war period. French desires to make territorial gains on the left bank of the river Rhine, for example, led to renewed public debates about the Rhine as a German river. Culminating at the time of the Ruhr occupation in 1923, much ink was spilt over the defence of the 'German Rhine', and the memory of 1840[8] was invoked to present to German contemporaries an image of heroic national resistance to French expansionism.

Militant nationalism affected both the Protestant and Catholic churches. Forgotten was the *Kulturkampf* of the 1860s, as Protestant pastors and Catholic priests vied with each other over declarations describing the German war effort as God's commandment. In Protestant theology links were forged between the idea of Christianity and the defence of a racially defined *Volk*. Christianity, Protestant theologians argued, found its highest expression in the German people; by defending the German nation, the Germans were de facto defending the essence of Christianity.

The unity of the German people had been at the heart of the 'August experience'. The same theme was developed further by the idea of the 'community of the trenches'. The social history of the First World War leaves us with no doubt that social divisions were often replicated at the front. The everyday experience of the war was different depending on social status, which explains the many complaints among ordinary soldiers about the arrogance of their officers. But the idea that the common experience of trench warfare overcame all social and other divisions and forged the German soldiers together in one indivisible community became an influential myth. It was represented powerfully in the writings of war veteran Ernst Jünger. Wounded several times, he emerged from the war a highly decorated officer who gave expression to his belief that the meaning of true life was only revealed in moments of war when the individual was staring death in the face. He described battle as an ecstatic moment:

> The enthusiasm spurs on manliness to such a degree that the blood is pulsating in the veins and runs fierily through the heart. This is a frenzy above all wild frenzies, an unleashing which bursts all boundaries. It is a rage which knows no limits or considerations,

6 Max Scheler, 'Der Genius des Krieges und der deutsche Krieg', in *Gesammelte Werke*, Vol. 4: *Politisch-pädagogische Schriften* (Bern, 1982), p. 81.

7 Matthew Stibbe, *German Anglophobia and the Great War, 1914–1918* (Cambridge, 2001).

8 See above, p. 55. On the Ruhr crisis see Conan Fischer, *The Ruhr Crisis 1923–1924* (Oxford, 2003).

Figure 4.1 'Christmas in England. Whereas previously no Englishman would have socialized with coloured people, the dark-skinned military allies have now become the dominant element in London society. Some of them may even give the traditional Christmas kiss under the mistletoe to a fair-haired lady.' Caricature from *Simplicissimus*, 22 December 1914.

comparable only to the forces of nature. That is the moment when the human being is like the roaring storm, the raging sea and the bellowing thunder. Then he is one with the cosmic forces, he rushes onto the dark gates of death like a bullet towards the aim. […] When we [the soldier and his adversary] meet in the midst of fire and smoke, then

> we become one, we are two parts of one power, fused together to one body. To one body – this is a parable of special significance.[9]

War as an existential experience was merged with the idea of war as an opportunity to sacrifice one's individual body on the collective altar of the nation. At the battle of Langemarck (better known in English as the battle of Ypres) wave upon wave of young, mainly middle-class, German volunteers ran into the machine-gun fire of the British army singing: '*Deutschland, Deutschland über alles*'. 80,000 soldiers were killed on both sides, a few trenches and hills were taken and lost. Overall, the front hardly moved at all. But the tale of Langemarck spoke of individual and collective heroism which attempted in vain to overcome the mechanized killing of trench warfare. It told of the nation at arms producing the 'people's community', for which German soldiers had been willing to die regardless of social class, status or confession. In the inter-war period countless literary and historical depictions of the battle of Langemarck made it the central focus for the idealization of a manly soldierly nationalism. After 1928 German students celebrated 'Langemarck Day' on every 19 November.[10]

The war produced some important antiwar novels, in particular Erich Maria Remarque's *All Quiet on the Western Front* (1929). But for every one antiwar novel dozens celebrated the war and the wartime experience of the soldiers. Some of the most popular authors included Werner Beumelburg, Hans Carossa, Walter Flex, Hans Grimm, Herman Löns and Felix Luckner. None of their works merits rereading today but their books were popular, especially among the younger people in the Weimar Republic who had not experienced the 'community of the trenches' themselves. They were also the ones who flocked to the many war movies shown in the cinemas which vividly conveyed the myths of the community of the trenches, the heroism of dying for the fatherland and the comradeship of sacrifice. Historical films, such as the ones on Frederick II, were immensely popular among cinema-goers, and their battle scenes deliberately reminded the audience of the heroism of German soldiers in the First World War. By contrast, when *All Quiet on the Western Front* became a Hollywood movie in 1930 the Nazis organized major protests, arguing that the film belittled the German war effort and the heroism of the German soldier.

Film itself rose to prominence as a tool of nationalist propaganda in the context of the First World War.[11] Nine hundred German soldiers' cinemas were established on the western and eastern fronts and a Photo and Film Office was founded to produce documentaries about the war effort. The Universum-Film-Aktiengesellschaft (UFA) was established in December 1917 as a private company, but in fact the government held about one-third of shares and was behind the whole project. Where nationalists had often attacked the cinema for morally

[9] Ernst Jünger, quoted in Christian Krockow, *Von deutschen Mythen* (1995), p. 61f.

[10] Karl Unruh, *Langemarck: Legende und Wirklichkeit* (Koblenz, 1986); also George L. Mosse, *Fallen Soldiers: Reshaping the Memory of the World Wars* (Oxford, 1990).

[11] Susanne Brandt, ' "Zerborstene Türme, tote Trümmer fragen die Welt: wer sind die Barbaren": Filme im ersten Weltkrieg und kollektives Erinnern', in Vittoria Borsò, Gerd Krumeich and Bernd Witte, eds, *Medialität und Gedächtnis: Interdisziplinäre Beiträge zur kulturellen Verarbeitung europäischer Krisen* (Stuttgart, 2001), pp. 259–87.

corrupting the nation, they now praised it as a means of strengthening nationalist sentiments. The UFA news programme, *Wochenschau*, was nothing if not consistent in its nationalist messages, which is perhaps not too surprising given that UFA was controlled by Alfred Hugenberg, media magnate and leader of the German conservative party (DNVP) after 1928. Not all of the German film production in the inter-war period was nationalist. It was too big for that. In fact, in the 1920s it was the only serious rival of Hollywood and with expressionist film it created its own distinctive artistic image. War films were overwhelmingly nationalist, however, and their messages reflected the power of the nationalist myths surrounding the First World War.[12]

Apart from the cinema, it was radio which transmitted a variety of national imaginations to millions of Germans in the inter-war period. Around 1930 approximately 4 million radio sets could be found in German households. Depending on where they were located in Germany they received very different messages about the state of the nation, as radio was controlled through regional politics. In regions with republican centre-left majorities listeners would hear much about the achievements of the 1918 revolution and about political and social reform in the Weimar Republic. By contrast, in regions controlled by the antirepublican right, the radio talked about the humiliation of Versailles. It reminded audiences of the splendour of Imperial Germany and pondered about the lost empire or about ways and means to regain Germany's former strong position in continental Europe.[13] If radio differed in the kinds of national images it transmitted, it was intensely nationalist everywhere. In 1926 the *Deutsche Welle* was specifically founded to strengthen national sentiment among those Germans living outside the borders of the Weimar Republic. Overall, novels, the cinema, the radio and last but not least, museums[14] were all important means of extending the memories of the war experience well into peacetime.

Thirteen million German men had served in the army. Two million lost their lives. Four million returned permanently disabled. Their experience was by no means homogeneous.[15] But the war was of crucial significance to the memory of each and every one of the survivors. A vibrant battlefield tourism, which started soon after the end of the war, underlined the power of the war memories. The memory landscape of the war marked the continuation of the war in peacetime.[16] It was among the most highly contested areas of memory politics in the inter-war

---

[12] Siegfried Kracauer, *From Caligari to Hitler: A Psychological History of the German Film* (Princeton, 1947); Bernadette Kester, *Film Front Weimar: Representations of the First World War in German Films from the Weimar Period (1919–1933)* (Amsterdam, 2002), for a more recent and differentiated look at inter-war German film.

[13] Joachim-Felix Leonhard, ed., *Programmgeschichte des Hörfunks in der Weimarer Republik*, 2 vols (Munich, 1997).

[14] Susanne Brandt, 'The Memory Makers: Museums and Exhibitions of the First World War', *History and Memory*, 6 (1994), pp. 95–122.

[15] Gerhard Hirschfeld, Gerd Krumeich, Dieter Langewiesche and Hans-Peter Ullmann, eds, *Kriegserfahrungen: Studien zur Sozial- und Mentalitätsgeschichte des Ersten Weltkrieges* (Essen, 1997). On the huge impact of the First World War on post-war Germany see generally Richard Bessel, *Germany after the First World War* (Oxford, 1993).

[16] Bernd Ulrich and Benjamin Ziemann, eds, *Krieg im Frieden: Die umkämpfte Erinnerung an den ersten Weltkrieg* (Frankfurt/Main, 1997); Jörg Duppler and Gerhard P. Gross, eds, *Kriegsende 1918: Ereignis, Wirkung, Nachwirkung* (Munich, 1999).

period. One of the crucial questions was how the war should be remembered. How was one to give meaning to the mechanized mass death, the tearing apart of bodies and the suffocation through nerve gas? The memorialization of war and of the national war dead fell largely to the veterans' and regimental associations. Their war memorials became national altars on which the citizen was celebrated as soldier. This marks an interesting contrast with France, where the citizen in uniform was the focus of war memorialization. France also saw the depiction of many more non-heroic memorials depicting widows, orphans or older men mourning their dead sons. In Germany the depiction of heroic warriors dominated.[17] There were exceptions to the rule, such as Käthe Kollwitz's granite figures of mourning parents at the Roggevelde war cemetery in Flanders. But most monuments selectively remembered heroic aspects of the war and constructed meanings which underpinned the myths of the 'people's community' and of the 'community of the trenches'. Manly honour, Christian sacrifice and youthful nationalism had to be cast in stone. War memorials in German war cemeteries were often located in so-called 'heroes' groves' (*Heldenhaine*), where oak trees symbolized German reliability and solidity [Figure 4.2].

The official war memory of republican Germany after 1918 found it difficult to come to terms with the war dead. The war had not been its war, and the memory of the war was hegemonized by the antirepublican right. They used the war and its multiple myths of community as a potent weapon against the republic. Yet leading republican politicians found it difficult to distance themselves emotionally from the 'national war effort'. It was only in 1929 that the Social Democratic minister president of Prussia, Otto Braun, determined that the Berlin Neue Wache should become the central war memorial. The largely empty interior contained only a monolith of black granite on top of which lay an oak reef. The sobriety of its interior decoration was in marked contrast to the heroism of many other war memorials, but it never functioned as a central war memorial in the same way that, for example, the London Cenotaph became *the* central war memorial in Britain after 1918. The German memory of the war was far more divided than the British one.[18]

The myth of the betrayal of the nation and the outcry over the Versailles treaty

When the war was lost, Imperial Germany democratized with breakneck speed in the hope that a more constitutional and democratic Germany would be able to

[17] Michael Jeisman and Rolf Westheider, 'Wofür stirbt der Bürger? Nationaler Totenkult und Staatsbürgertum in Deutschland und Frankreich seit der französischen Revolution', in Reinhart Koselleck and Michael Jeismann, eds, *Der politische Totenkult: Kriegerdenkmäler in der Moderne* (Munich, 1994); Reinhart Koselleck, 'Zur politischen Ikonologie des gewaltsamen Todes: ein deutsch-französischer Vergleich', in Alexandre Escudier, ed., *Gedenken im Zwiespalt: Konfliktlinien europäischen Erinnerns* (Göttingen, 2001), p. 59; also: Jay Winter, *Sites of Memory, Sites of Mourning: The Great War in European Cultural History* (Cambridge, 1995).

[18] Sven Oliver Müller, *Die Nation als Waffe und Vorstellung: Nationalismus in Deutschland und Großbritannien im ersten Weltkrieg* (Göttingen, 2002).

Figure 4.2 German oaks. Postcard of Luther and Bismarck standing beneath an oak tree. 'A strong castle is our God', the first line of Luther's famous chorale, and Bismarck's famous quotation, 'Us Germans, we fear God and nothing else on this world', are written on the bottom of this postcard which was sent by many German soldiers from the front, © Altmärkisches Museum Stendahl.

achieve a more favourable negotiated peace settlement with the allies. But the revolution overtook the political reform process and forced a change of pace which was to end the constitutional monarchies all over Germany and see a republican Germany emerge from the rubble of war. The military leadership of Imperial Germany used the revolution to put into circulation the 'stab-in-the-back myth' (*Dolchstoßlegende*), according to which the German army had not been defeated in battle by the enemy. Instead it had been stabbed in the back by the socialist revolutionaries who had undermined morale at the home front and in the army. The constitutional assembly established a parliamentary enquiry into the defeat of Germany in the First World War. Germany's wartime leader, Paul von Hindenburg, spoke as a witness about the secret and deliberate subversion of the army and navy. Military operations had failed, he argued, as a direct consequence of the work of the revolutionaries. Hindenburg's text had been written by his former deputy, Erich Ludendorff, in conjunction with one of the leading politicians of the DNVP, Karl Hefferich. The whole antirepublican right in the republic repeated its basic argument: the defeat of Germany in the war was primarily the result of treason by the democratic and left-of-centre political parties.

The Old High German national epic of the Nibelungen was invoked to underline the main accusation of treason. The *Nibelungenlied*, first described as the 'German Iliad' in the context of the wars of liberty against Napoleon's armies, described the struggle of the noble Burgund-Nibelungen against the barbaric Huns. Before the war the relationship between Imperial Germany and the Habsburg Empire was frequently described as one of Nibelungen loyalty: one would stand by the other like brothers. Now, after the war, the nationalist imagination dwelt on treachery and the gallant German army became Siegfried, hideously murdered from behind by the socialist Hagen.[19]

Republicans found it difficult to counter the 'stab-in-the-back' myth. The fact of the matter was that Ludendorff, at the end of the war, had pleaded with the government to sign an immediate armistice, as it was only a matter of days (at best) before the Allied troops would break through the German lines. But republican politicians did not want to appear unpatriotic. Friedrich Ebert, the socialist leader of the revolution and first president of the republic, who had lost two sons in the war, famously greeted the homecoming troops in Berlin on 11 December 1918 with the words: 'I salute you, who return unvanquished from the field of battle.' When the war ended the German army still stood deep on French territory. Germany itself had never been occupied by Allied troops. Hence the myth could take root and become one of the most potent weapons of the antirepublican right. The republic could be described as the child of the revolution and those who had been its midwife, i.e. the republicans, were denounced by the right as 'the dregs of the nation', who lacked manly and national substance.[20]

If the antirepublican right was successful in blaming the republic for the lost war, this was particularly potent in the context of a harsh peace treaty which was perceived by everyone in Germany as a national humiliation. Defeat itself came as a nasty shock to most Germans. Wartime propaganda had not prepared them for it. The war aims programme of Chancellor Bethmann von Hollweg envisaged a German-dominated Europe with vast annexations, vassal states and a central European economic union under German leadership. The demands of the Pan Germans were on a grander scale still. When a majority of the *Reichstag* published

19 Fritz Lang's film version of the Nibelungen of 1924 came up with another popular parallel: the struggle of the Nibelungen against the Huns resembled the struggle of German civilization against Slav barbarity in the East.

20 On antirepublican thought in the Weimar Republic see Kurt Sontheimer, *Antidemokratisches Denken in der Weimarer Republik* (Munich, 1978).

the Peace Resolution in 1917, demanding a negotiated peace based on a compromise with the Allies, the nationalist right responded by forming the Fatherland Party (*Vaterlandspartei*). Chaired by Admiral Tirpitz, it propagated the aim of total victory and nourished dreams of a German-dominated continental Europe. The Fatherland Party was a huge success. In July 1918 it was the biggest political party in Germany with one and a quarter million members. By contrast, the left liberal People's Association for Freedom and Fatherland (*Volksbund für Freiheit und Vaterland*), founded as a direct response to the Fatherland Party, advocated moderate war aims as well as social and political reforms in the *Kaiserreich*, but it could only muster 2800 members by October 1918.

For four years the soldiers at the front had suffered terribly, and civilians at home had also endured much, especially in the terrible hunger winters of 1916/17 and 1917/18, in which the Allied blockade led to a severe shortage of food. Everyone had held out in the hope of victory and of a better, brighter future at the end of the war. When the war was lost and the victors announced their peace proposals, disillusionment in Germany was complete. The nation was to lose one-seventh of its territory and one-tenth of its population. One-third of its coal and three-quarters of its iron ore resources were gone. It was not going to be a colonial power any more. It was not allowed a strong army and it had to pay massive reparations. On top of all that, the Versailles treaty in Article 231 declared Germany the only guilty party in the outbreak of the war. The Social Democratic chancellor, Philip Scheidemann, resigned over the question of whether or not to accept the treaty and summed up the feeling of almost everyone: 'Which hand would not wither if it laid these chains on itself and on us?'

If republican politicians ultimately signed the peace treaty, they did so under protest and with the intention of safeguarding Germany from a worse fate, such as the threatened occupation by Allied troops. The nationalist right, however, was to use this acceptance of Versailles and subsequent attempts to comply with the demands of the treaty as another powerful weapon in its incessant struggle against the republic. Not only had republicans stabbed the German army in the back and caused the loss of the war, they had also signed the 'treaty of shame' and enslaved the German nation for generations to come. The Western nations, in particular France, were regarded as the chief oppressors of the German people, but their allies in Germany were the representatives of the republic who espoused Western political ideas and implemented a Western-style parliamentary democracy. The national struggle had to be fought not only against the victorious Western allies but also against the import of their value systems and political ideas into Germany and against those espousing such values inside Germany.

In order to counter the perceived Westernization of the German nation, the right appropriated the language of the *Volk* to serve its purposes. The term *Volk* took centre stage in the German political vocabulary after 1914. It was used by democrats to highlight the fact that the people had become the political sovereign of the German nation in the 1918 revolution. Yet it was the antidemocratic right which dominated the discourse of *Volk*. They linked the wartime search for true national community with the belief in the need to bring *Volk* and state together as one. Cultural, linguistic and racial definitions of the *Volk* spread like wildfire in and after the First World War.

A *völkisch* nationalism combined with the rise of a new *Reich* ideology. The idea of the *Reich* became the most powerful alternative to the republic, and in its territorial ambitions the new *Reich* transcended the Imperial German *Reich* of 1871. With the collapse of the Habsburg Empire in 1918, the new *Reich* was 'greater-German' in that it aimed for the inclusion of Austria. It also wanted to include all of those who were ethnically German but lived outside the borders of the republic. *Reich* and *Volk* inspired the national imagination in the Weimar Republic like no other concepts could. *Völkisch* ideas entered mainstream historical-cultural discourses in the inter-war period and rivalled older state-oriented ideas of nationalism that had been dominant in Imperial Germany. Within the various *Heimat* organizations, which boomed in the inter-war period, genetic determinism and racist ideas became stronger. They shared with the political right a common language of *völkisch* nationalism and propagated the past as one vast expression of German cultural and ethnic superiority.

In the most German of all arts, music, German musicologists were busy producing and upholding an international canon of classical music that was essentially German-dominated.[21] Some genres, such as the *Lied*, were, of course, almost by definition German. De-anglicizing George Frideric Handel and emphasizing the Germanic roots of Gregorian choral music had long been preoccupations of nationalist musicologists. In the Weimar Republic the political right closely associated music with Germanness. Composers such as Hans Pfitzner saw themselves struggling valiantly against Jewish-Bolshevist internationalist influences in music and identified totally with what they believed to be true German music. *Völkisch*-nationalist amateur and semi-professional groups such as the Spielschar Ekkehard espoused their own variant of *völkisch* nationalism in music. In 1924 musicologists embarked on a project which attempted to provide a comprehensive overview of the musical folk heritage in Germany celebrating a nationalist *Heimat* discourse in music.[22]

Völkisch discourses underpinned the struggle of the political right against the republic and against Versailles. Republicans, however, were also opposed to Versailles and a succession of republican governments sought ways and means of achieving the revision of the Versailles treaty. The non-acceptance of the post-war territorial order was particularly evident in the map war which became a prominent part of Germany's attempts to prove to the world how much of an injustice the Versailles treaty represented. Various mapping projects were brought under way with official government support to legitimate claims that particular territories were German and to refute Allied claims that they were not.[23] German geographers accused the Allies of having used falsified maps in the

21 Pamela M. Potter, *Most German of the Arts: Musicology and Society from the Weimar Republic to the End of Hitler's Reich* (New Haven, 1998).

22 Michael H. Kater, 'Culture, Society and Politics in the Cosmos of "Hans Pfitzner the German" '; Bruce Campbell, '*Kein schöner Land*: the Spielschar Ekkehard and the Struggle to Define German National Identity in the Weimar Republic'; Philip Bohlman, 'Landscape—Region—Nation—Reich: German Folk Song in the Nexus of National Identity', all in Celia Applegate and Pamela Potter, eds, *Music and German National Identity* (Chicago, 2002), pp. 105–39, 178–89.

23 Guntram Henrik Herb, *Under the Map of Germany: Nationalism and Propaganda, 1918–1945* (London, 1997), Chapter 3.

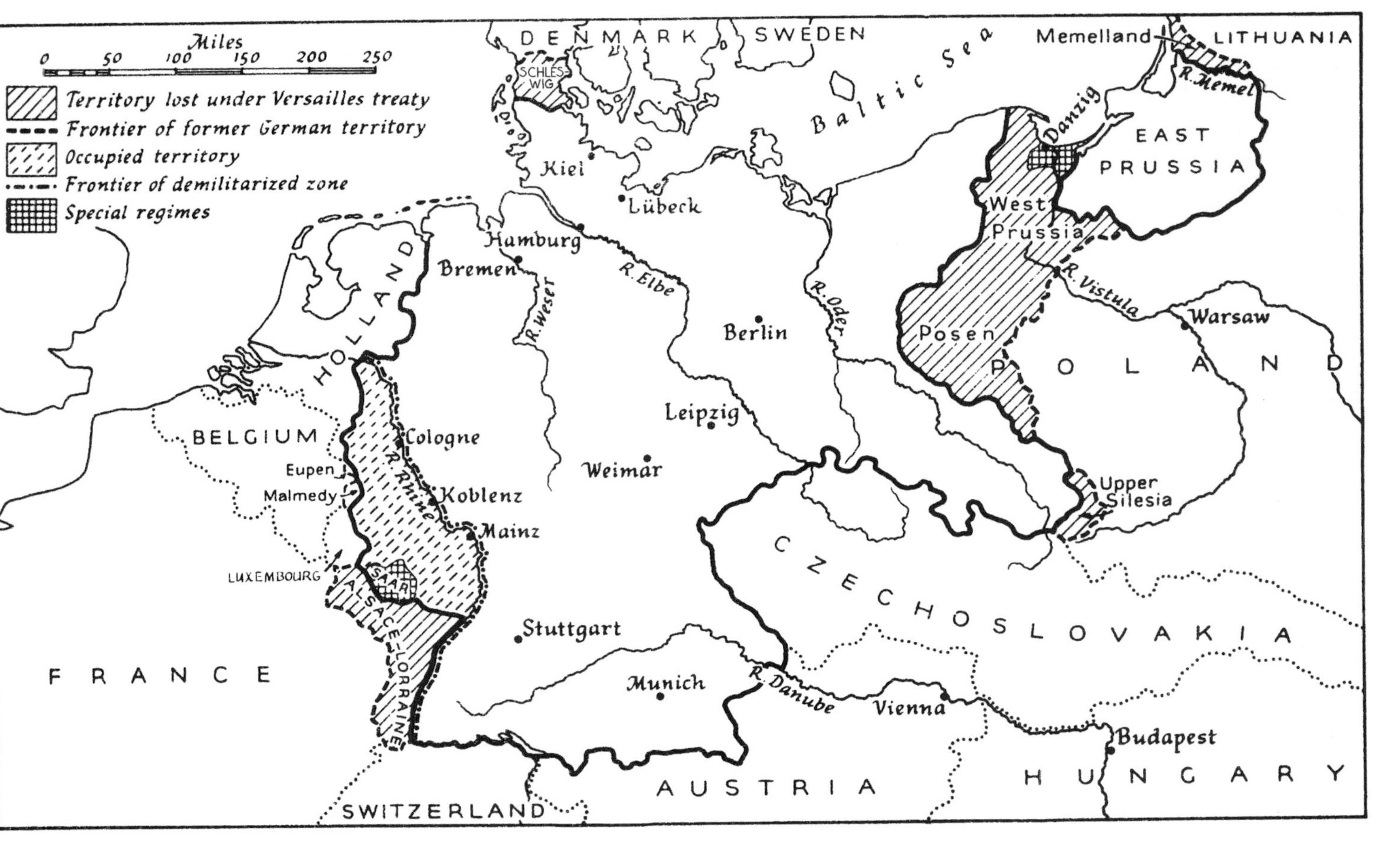

Map 4 Germany after the First World War, 1919.

peace settlement of Versailles. Maps in German schoolbooks clearly showed lost territories as German ones, where the same maps before 1914 had often indicated that these same territories had not been sufficiently German.[24]

Historians were similarly useful to German attempts to revise Versailles. The Department for Questions Relating to German War Guilt in the Foreign Office (*Kriegsschuldreferat*) employed and co-operated with well-known German historians in an attempt to influence public consciousness at home and abroad.[25] The major edition of sources, entitled *Great Politics of the European Cabinets 1871–1914*, published in forty volumes between 1922 and 1927, was deeply clouded by apologetic tendencies. Research on the German East (*Ostforschung*) legitimized the 'German urge eastwards'. Scientific research underpinned German expansionist claims and cultural-historical racism increasingly underpinned academic studies.[26] Preservationists participated prominently in these culture wars by designating the heritage of particular places as specifically German.[27] The protection of German monuments and the preservation of a German past outside the borders of the German state became a major concern in the inter-war period. The republican state, often in line with *völkisch* organizations, promoted *Heimat* organizations especially in the German borderlands. *Heimat* travel became popular and *Heimat* studies (*Heimatkunde*) were introduced as a new subject area in primary and secondary schools.

The pillarization of the national imagination I: the Communist nation

The lost war, the revolution and the Versailles treaty marked a deep caesura in the German national imagination. In 1918/19 it seemed to many in Germany that one kind of nation had come to an end while a completely different one was about to begin. Segments of German society welcomed these developments, while others deplored it. During the Weimar Republic the national imagination remained, as in the *Kaiserreich*, highly contested. The deep divisions in the political culture of Weimar were replicated in different political-social milieux which in turn produced highly diverse constructions of Germanness.

On the far left the Communist Party of Germany (KPD) put forward a foreign national model, the Soviet Union, as fatherland of the proletariat. Their prime allegiance as Communists was not to the nation but to the Soviet Union and the working class. Social identity was more important than national identity. Hence Communists tended to regard nationalism as an ideology of mass mobilization

[24] Rainer Bendick, 'Wo liegen Deutschlands Grenzen? Die Darstellungen des Deutschen Reiches in den deutschen und französischen Schulkarten vor und nach dem Ersten Weltkrieg', *Geschichte in Wissenschaft und Unterricht*, 51 (2000), pp. 17–36.

[25] Ulrich Heinemann, *Die verdrängte Niederlage: Politische Öffentlichkeit und Kriegsschuldfrage in der Weimarer Republik* (Göttingen, 1983).

[26] Wolfgang Wippermann, *Der 'Deutsche Drang nach Osten': Ideologie und Wirklichkeit eines politischen Schlagwortes* (Darmstadt, 1989); Michael Burleigh, *Germany Turns Eastwards: A Study of 'Ostforschung' in the Third Reich* (Cambridge, 1989).

[27] Rudy Koshar, *Preservation and National Memory in the Twentieth Century: Germany's Transient Past* (Chapel Hill, 1998), pp. 87–106.

in the service of the capitalist system. Where it affected workers, nationalism became a classic case of 'false consciousness'. In the Weimar Republic the KPD was among the strongest critics of the nationalist right. But the party also attempted to tap into nationalist working-class sentiments to rally support, most famously during the 1923 Ruhr crisis, when Karl Radek pronounced the member of the National Socialist Workers' Party (NSDAP), Leo Schlageter, a national martyr, after he had been tried and shot by the French army for acts of sabotage. It was relatively easy for the KPD to criticize the French occupation of the Ruhr and the Versailles treaty, as Communists saw all international politics through the lens of capitalist-imperialist struggles. Capitalist-imperialist rivalry was responsible for the outbreak of the First World War, as it was for the harsh peace treaty and for the French occupation of the Ruhr. Any specific German war guilt could easily be refuted with reference to such international capitalist rivalries. There was no justification, according to the KPD, for making German workers suffer under the conditions of the Versailles treaty.

Communists had their own national martyrs in the shape of their murdered leaders Karl Liebknecht and Rosa Luxemburg. The annual Liebknecht–Luxemburg celebrations at the Berlin Friedrichsfelde cemetery commemorated their violent deaths at the hands of the paramilitary Freikorps during the Communist rising of January 1919. Many Freikorps members held extreme right-wing beliefs; brutalized by their wartime experiences, these former soldiers developed an extremely violent imagery of the nation in which a feminized and racialized 'national enemy' was legitimately raped, tortured and murdered.[28] It had, however, been a Social Democrat, Gustav Noske, who was in command of the military operations against the Communists during that rising.

In many German cities and regions former socialists, who were now members of separate parties, found themselves on different sides of what amounted to a form of civil war in Germany between 1919 and 1923. The *putsch* in January 1919 was not the only attempt to force the coming of a Soviet Germany. The Munich and Bremen council republics, the mass strikes of spring 1919, the formation of a Red Ruhr Army in the wake of the right-wing Kapp *putsch* in 1920, the setting up of proletarian paramilitary formations in Saxony and Thuringia in 1923 – they all were signs that Communists envisaged a different kind of Germany and had the support of significant sections of the German working class. The KPD was, after all, the biggest Communist party outside of the Soviet Union, and many Communists firmly believed that for world Communism to succeed, it had to conquer Germany first.

But that was not to be. For sure, a strong Communist movement was the source of much anxiety, especially among middle-class Germans, which explains the violent anti-Communist propaganda of the nationalist right in the Weimar Republic. For Protestants and Catholics alike, Bolshevism was the anti-Christ. Even republicans used the spectre of Bolshevism to portray the republic as a bulwark against the Sovietization of Germany. A strong KPD was a powerful rival for the SPD, which shared the same Protestant working-class milieu. In fact Social

[28] Klaus Theweleit, *Male Fantasies*, Vol. 1: *Women, Floods, Bodies, History* (Minneapolis, 1987); *idem*, *Male Fantasies*, Vol. 2: *Psychoanalysing the White Terror* (Oxford, 1989).

The republican nation failed to deliver its promises in the economic and political sphere. In the realm of foreign policy, while the republic was not without its successes, its overriding rationale of revising the Versailles treaty was the same as that of its enemies on the right. The road to that goal was different, but the right successfully lambasted the republic for not making rapid enough progress and selling out German interests in the attempt to fulfil the conditions of Versailles. Republican politicians were denounced as 'fulfilment politicians' (*Erfüllungspolitiker*).

Republicans, in turn, promoted international reconciliation and rejected the right's desire for revenge. Germany's admission to the League of Nations in 1926 was a powerful symbol for a republican Germany developing peacefully alongside other nations in Europe. Gustav Stresemann's foreign policy was no less revisionist and intent on restoring Germany to great power status than that of less republican governments after him, but he wanted to achieve this through international diplomacy using the existing international system.[33] Progress on the road to Franco-German reconciliation, as advocated by the left-liberal intellectuals assembled in the Association New Fatherland (*Bund Neues Vaterland*) and symbolized by the Locarno pact of December 1925, seemed to throw open the path to greater European integration. Communists frequently attacked Europe as a capitalist plot and the nationalist right saw it as a sinister conspiracy to sell out the national interest. But the republican vision of the German nation was eminently compatible with Europeanism. However, even among republicans, pro-Europeanism was often bound up with national interest politics. Stresemann's pro-Europeanism, for example, was connected to the overriding aim of the revision of the Versailles treaty. 'Greater German' pro-Europeanism was linked to the goal of enabling Austria to become part of Germany.[34]

In the cultural sphere the republican nation was not without its supporters. Architecturally, the Bauhaus became closely associated with the new democratic style of the republic. It was all about clarity, honesty and usefulness of lines and materials. There was to be no pretence. What was useful was also beautiful. Aesthetics merged with a new social vision. Modernist architecture formed a powerful alliance with social reform projects designing some of the best known housing estates in the Weimar Republic. The political right started a prominent hate campaign against the Bauhaus and attacked its style as 'unGerman'. But the leading representative of the Bauhaus school, Walter Gropius, was himself deeply motivated by a perceived mission to contribute to the making of a new Germany after the war, from which he emerged a highly decorated officer. His fellow modernist architect, Bruno Taut, expressly sought to use architecture in order to counter the revisionist nationalist discourses which sought revenge for the lost war and a return to Imperial German definitions of the nation.[35]

[33] On all aspects of Stresemann see Jonathan Wright, *Gustav Stresemann: Weimar's Greatest Statesman* (Oxford, 2002).

[34] Wolfgang Burgdorf, '*Chimäre Europa*': *Antieuropäische Diskurse in Deutschland 1648–1999* (Bochum, 1999), pp. 172–88.

[35] Koshar, *Preservation*, p. 130 (see note 27).

The republican nation received support not only from modernist architects. The 'new sobriety'[36] went far beyond architecture and could be found in the New Realism (*Neue Sachlichkeit*) of literature. Artists such as Otto Dix and George Grosz attacked the German elites hankering after the Imperial past and criticized their continuing influence in the Weimar Republic. Thomas Mann, so sceptical of any Western imports into Germany in 1917, came round to defend a republican vision of the nation in the 1920s. His novel *Magic Mountain* marked the moment of conversion of one of the best known German writers, who was awarded the Nobel Prize for Literature in 1929. In 1930, in his famous 'German speech' in Berlin, he explicitly called on the German middle classes to rally to the support of Social Democracy and defend the republic against its right-wing enemies. Many in the audience were not impressed and Mann was heckled and interrupted frequently. In Weimar culture the outsiders of Imperial Germany had become the insiders,[37] but such a move led to some powerful counter-reactions. Many intellectuals were sceptical of the republic and could be found either on the extreme left or the extreme right. Ultimately the republican nation failed to convince economically, politically and culturally.

The pillarization of the national imagination III: the political right

Weimar has often been described as a republic without republicans. Certainly committed 'republicans of the heart' (*Herzensrepublikaner*) were in the minority. More numerous were those who supported the republic because they saw it as the only reasonable alternative (*Vernunftrepublikaner*). Their attitude was exemplified by the national liberal historian Friedrich Meinecke: 'I remain oriented towards the past, at heart a monarchist, but, facing the future, I will become a republican out of reason.'[38] Those like Meinecke accepted the political realities of the Weimar Republic and were willing to play by the rules of the game. But they longed to mediate between what they regarded as an alien Western political system, forced upon Germany at the end of the war, and German traditions such as statism and Romantic nationalism. At heart they remained sceptical of the natural law traditions of the West and adhered to a more traditional German understanding of the state standing above society and party politics. They praised the merits of strong government and efficient bureaucracy and they were proud of the excellence of the German educational system and the country's industrial achievements.

Antipluralism remained strong, even among those who had shaped the Weimar constitution. They sought to counterbalance 'parliamentary absolutism' with institutions, such as the presidency and the civil service, which were designed to be disinterested and above sectional party politics. Many Germans continued to

36 John Willett, *The New Sobriety, 1917–1933: Art and Politics in the Weimar Period* (London, 1978).

37 Peter Gay, *Weimar Culture: The Outsider as Insider* (London, 1969).

38 Cited after Werner Weidenfeld, *Der deutsche Weg*, 2nd edn (Berlin, 1991), p. 75.

imagine the nation as a homogeneous society in which interest fragmentation was unknown. They harked back to the wartime *Volksgemeinschaft* ideal which in turn gave a boost to radical nationalist forces in the Weimar Republic.[39] Antipluralism penetrated deep into the republican forces. Within the Catholic Centre Party support for a corporate state and a society ordered according to different social estates alienated sections of the Catholic milieu from the democratic and republican nation. Social Democratic pluralists, such as Gustav Radbruch and Hermann Heller, abandoned the idea that a truly socialist society would not know any interest fragmentation. Precisely because the existence of diverse interests was characteristic of every society, the maintenance of individual rights through the rule of law (*Rechtsstaat*) became of prime importance. The democratic state became the ideal state form for Social Democracy as it alone was capable of solving the existing class conflicts by extending the idea of the rule of law to other areas of society, notably to the economy. But such a view was not consensual inside the SPD. Many socialists clung to antipluralist Marxist ideas of a classless society in which the interests of the government would fall into one with those of the governed.[40]

If republicans found it difficult to endorse pluralism wholeheartedly, antirepublicans portrayed it as 'unGerman'. Few Germans seemed willing to defend the monarchy against the revolution in 1918/19. But soon afterwards conservative nationalists idealized the old political and social order. Especially the Protestant Prussian middle classes and the East Elbian Junkers hankered after the old unity of throne and altar. Monarchists continued to celebrate 18 January as the day of the foundation of Imperial Germany. When Hindenburg was elected president in 1925 as candidate of the right, he was widely perceived as 'substitute emperor', underlining the mistrust in parliamentary democracy and the strength of pro-monarchist sentiments in German society.

Yet sections of the political right saw monarchism as a spent political force. Monarchical nationalism seemed outdated. Its symbols were the ones attributed to a long-gone age. Instead, many on the right were looking towards the future, and they thought they had seen that future in the trenches of the First World War. It was the 'community of the people' (*Volksgemeinschaft*) and a racialized definition of the *Volk* which was held up as radical nationalist alternatives to both monarchical and republican nationalism. Right-wing veterans' organizations supported such a radical redefinition of the nationalist terrain in the Weimar Republic. The German Warriors' Assocation (*Deutscher Kriegerbund*) and the Kyffhäuser Assocation, both going back to Imperial Germany, united in 1921 to form the German Reich Warrior Association Kyffhäuser. Its 42,000 branches mustered more than 4 million members. In addition the Stahlhelm was an association of veterans closely allied to the DVP and DNVP. Its annual gatherings (*Reichsfrontsoldatentage*) became the organizational focus for Protestant

[39] On the attractiveness of the *Volksgemeinschaft* ideal in Weimar Germany see Peter Fritzsche, *Germans into Nazis* (Cambridge, 1998).

[40] Stefan Berger, 'Democracy and Social Democracy', *European History Quarterly*, 32 (2002), pp. 13–38.

middle-class associationalism in the Weimar Republic.[41] In 1929/30 it had 400,000 members. Millions of disabled veterans were looked after much better by a far more generous state in Germany than was the case in Britain, but the war-disabled, in line with the right-wing veterans' organizations, were among the strongest critics of the republican nation and tended to give their support to far right-wing political forces.[42] The soldier having seen active service at the front (*Frontkämpfer*) became the true opposite to the republican politician in the imagination of the political right.

Right-wing intellectuals pointed out that the *Frontkämpfer* had brought about the *Volksgemeinschaft* in the First World War. Looking back on his wartime experience, Ernst von Salomon, wrote: 'We felt ourselves to be Germany.'[43] Their struggle to overcome the republican nation was a struggle to recreate that mythical wartime collectivity. Representatives of the so-called 'conservative revolution' rejected the bourgeois liberalism and parliamentary democracy of the post-war era. Instead they propagated a 'revolution from the right'[44] which would lead to the renaissance of a new *Reich*, in which a strong leader would unite all social groups, generations and confessions in a *Volksgemeinschaft* reminiscent of the First World War. They were not monarchists, but they built on the critique of civilization, the cultural pessimism and the *völkisch* traditions which had been present in Imperial Germany.[45] Not the monarch, but the warrior was the key figure integrating the nation of the future. A *völkisch* definition of the people put the *Volksgenosse* at the heart of national constructions. The *Volksgenosse* of the future had been shaped by the war experience. He was defined by courage, manliness, heroism and endurance – the kind of 'superman' described by the philosopher Friedrich Nietzsche. Nietzsche had become *the* nationalist philosopher in the context of the First World War, as his writings celebrated war as redemption, the end of decadence and the rebirth of the nation. Throughout the interwar period, the political right celebrated a Nietzsche cult which put the mad professor from Basle, who had famously renounced his Prussian citizenship, at the heart of the national imagination.[46] The 'conservative revolution' was ably supported by right-wing publishers such as J.F. Lehmann who shared its anti-republican and *völkisch* sentiments.[47]

The politics of cultural despair could build on considerable anti-urban sentiments directed at big cities, in particular Berlin. Berlin was the European equivalent to Chicago in the 1920s – a metropolis of distraction, with its museums, theatres, cabarets, restaurants, cinemas, nightclubs and bordellos. During the golden

41 Peter Fritzsche, *Rehearsals for Fascism: Populism and Political Mobilization in Weimar Germany* (Oxford, 1990).

42 Deborah Cohen, *The War Come Home: Disabled Veterans in Britain and Germany, 1914–1918* (Berkeley, 2001).

43 Cited in Ulrich Bielefeld, 'Die Nation als Geheimnis: Ernst von Salomon und das angedrehte "Wir" des Volks', *Mittelweg*, 6:1 (1997), p. 7.

44 Hans Freyer, *Revolution von rechts* (Leipzig, 1931).

45 See above, pp. 100ff.

46 Steven Aschheim, *The Nietzsche Legacy in Germany 1890–1990* (Berkeley, 1992).

47 Sigrid Stöckel, ed., *Die 'rechte Nation' und ihr Verleger: Politik und Popularisierung im J.F. Lehmanns Verlag 1890–1979* (Berlin, 2000).

by them. Where the Allies violated their own principle of national self-determination, as in Upper Silesia in 1921, German outrage was immediate and genuine. The Allies were prepared to give four-fifths of Upper Silesia to Poland, including many cities and territories which had voted overwhelmingly to remain with Germany in the plebiscite of March 1921. However, such instances could not hide the fact that much of the territories lost in the 'German east' were in fact populated by majorities which were not German-speaking.

If the linguistic and cultural character of the population was insufficient to justify territorial claims, geographers, historians and other social scientists engaged on 'border studies' made use of the distinction between 'people's' and 'cultural' soil (*Volksboden* and *Kulturboden*). German cultivation in the east, they argued, had left signs in the physical landscape. German culture, therefore, far extended the territory in which a German-speaking majority lived.[52] In other words, the *Kulturboden* was much wider than the *Volksboden*. The experience of German occupation of Eastern Europe in the First World War had given a major boost to such notions of 'cultural soil'. Experts brought in by the German military authorities to survey the land and the people and to provide an efficient administration were busy orientalizing the east and describing it in terms of the primitive 'other' in need of cultivation. The 'mindscape of the East' consisted of vast spaces and manipulable races which had to be ordered and civilized by German culture.[53] Part and parcel of such 'othering' was the feminization of the Slav east. People and landscape were depicted as bride of the German soldier and colonizer. The Germanization of Polish place names was a straight analogy to the wife taking the name of the husband after marriage.

The imagery began to change following the 'loss of the German east' in 1919: male Poles now appeared as rapists of a German 'mother *Heimat*'.[54] Such images were meant to appeal to German manliness to bring about the revision of the Versailles treaty. But it was not only men who strongly identified with the 'honour of the nation'. Women had been an integral part of the homefront during the First World War. Traditional household duties were being revalued and the war offered greater employment opportunities for nationally minded women. Any construction of a solidaristic people's community was incomplete without them. It was not by chance that women received the vote at the end of the war. It was their reward for national service, as Ebert explicitly stated in October 1918: 'What would the German homefront be without the tireless work of the women in the workshops, the bureaus, the hospital wards and in all areas of war-related social care! Who does not admire the quiet heroism of women and would wish to reward them through giving them the same political rights as those already enjoyed by men.'[55]

The republican nation gave 19 million women the right to vote and boosted claims for women's emancipation. Thus, for example, Weimar witnessed ferocious

---

52 Herb, *Under the Map*, Chapters 4 and 5 (see note 23).

53 Vejas Gabriel Liulevicius, *War Land on the Eastern Front: Culture, National Identity and German Occupation in World War I* (Cambridge, 2000).

54 Angela Koch, *DruckBilder: Stereotype und Geschlechtercodes in den antipolnischen Diskursen der 'Gartenlaube' (1870–1930)* (Cologne, 2002).

55 *Die Gleichheit*, 3 (1918), p. 18.

debates surrounding 'the politics of the body', including the question whether motherhood should be redefined as a more voluntary concept.[56] Despite offering greater opportunities for women, republicans found it difficult to convince many women that the republican nation looked after their interests. While the almost exclusively male self-image of the KPD foregrounded its concern with male factory workers and prevented many proletarian women from identifying with Communism,[57] the far right was much more successful in mobilizing women against the republic. Especially Protestant conservative women's associations became associated with the antirepublican milieu.[58] They did not join the BdF which they regarded as too democratic and internationalist. The BdF indeed continued to advocate women's rights in areas such as employment, education and politics. At times it worked closely with republican governments to revise the Versailles treaty, attempting to use its international links wherever possible. Gertrud Bäumer, one of the strong women of the BdF, saw in the bourgeois women's movement 'perhaps the purest power for the unification of our nation which is not hampered by political or other party loyalties'.[59]

But conservative women's associations outside of the BdF had an altogether different service to the nation in mind. They mobilized the female conservative vote, and portrayed themselves as 'conscience of the nation', whose task it was to enlighten and educate future generations about their *völkisch* duty. Theirs was not a struggle for women's rights but for the rights of the nation which they increasingly defined in *völkisch* terms. Tapping into the radicalized nationalism of the right, they saw women's vocation in serving their *Volk* and their nation.[60] This is also the theme of Ina Seidel's popular novel *Wunschkind* (Wanted Child) of 1930. Its central heroine is a middle-class owner of a country estate who willingly sacrifices her beloved son in the war, because his death for the nation is described as the return of the child into the mother's womb. The message was clear: the German nation could only hope for redemption through its mothers.

Women's associations were actively involved in bolstering Germandom in territories outside the borders of the *Reich*. Culture wars took place in Alsace on the Franco-German border,[61] but above all on the German-Polish border in east-central Europe. German research on the German east and Polish research on the

[56] Cornelie Usborne, *The Politics of the Body in Weimar Germany: Women's Reproductive Rights and Duties* (Ann Arbor, 1992).

[57] Eric D. Weitz, *Creating German Communism, 1890–1990: From Popular Protests to Socialist State* (Princeton, 1997), Chapter 6.

[58] Andrea Süchting-Hänger, *Das 'Gewissen der Nation': Nationales Engagement und politisches Handeln konservativer Frauenorganisationen 1900–1937* (Düsseldorf, 2002).

[59] Gertrud Bäumer, 'Die Einheit der Nation und die Einheit der Frauen', in Elisabeth Altmann-Gottheiner, ed., *Jahrbuch des Bundes deutscher Frauenvereine 1920* (Leipzig, 1920), p. 51.

[60] Elizabeth Harvey, 'Serving the Volk, Saving the Nation: Women in the Youth Movement and the Public Sphere in Weimar Germany', in Larry E. Jones and James Retallack, eds, *Elections, Mass Politics, and Social Change in Modern Germany: New Perspectives* (Cambridge, 1992), pp. 201–21.

[61] J.E. Craig, *Scholarship and Nation Building: the Universities of Strasbourg and Alsatian Society 1870–1939* (Chicago, 1984); Samuel Goodfellow, 'From Germany to France? Interwar Alsatian National Identity', *French History*, 7 (1993), pp. 450–71.

Polish west attempted to underpin their respective nation's territorial claims.[62] Naturalization of Slav Eastern European immigrants remained extremely rare in Weimar Germany, because they were still perceived as people inhabiting a lower cultural level. In particular the 'Eastern Jew' (*Ostjude*) represented everything that was wrong with migrants from Eastern Europe.[63] The Tannenberg myth served to underline the belief in German cultural superiority over the Slav east. In 1410 a Polish-Lithuanian army defeated an army of the German Templars at Tannenberg. All too often a 'great moment' of one nation's national history spelt humiliation for another nation. Hence, when German troops defeated a Russian army near Tannenberg at the end of 1914 it was quickly dubbed the battle of Tannenberg, mark II. Celebrated as revenge for 1410, its memorialization after 1924 served as a permanent reminder in stone of the cultural superiority of the Germanic over the Slav races. The Tannenberg memorial, stylistically a mixture between a Germanic cultic site, castle and war grave, was opened in 1927 and immediately associated with the cult surrounding the hero of Tannenberg, the then President Hindenburg. Tannenberg became Weimar's closest equivalent to the Sedan celebrations in Imperial Germany – another military victory which served as reminder of the lost territories in the east which had to be regained.

Like so many myths about the First World War, Tannenberg was closely tied to the idea of the people's community. This notion of *Volksgemeinschaft* was the glue binding together all antirepublican forces on the right and the most important single bridge between the conservative milieu and the National Socialists. Conservatives and Nazis found common ground in their rejection of the parliamentary system of Weimar and in their extreme nationalism. By the early 1930s both subscribed to the idea of a German people's nation (*Volksnation*) which was racially defined. The NSDAP had already stated in its 1920 programme that only *Volksgenossen* of Aryan descent should become German citizens. The German student movement (*Deutsche Burschenschaft*), once the flagship of an oppositional liberal nationalism,[64] decided in 1920 only to accept German students of Aryan descent. The student body in Weimar moved decisively to the right and was relatively solid in its opposition to the republican nation.[65] Students turned to National Socialism earlier than any other social group. The ideal of the *Volksgemeinschaft* allowed the Nazis to appeal to Germans of different social classes, generations and genders.[66]

---

62 Jan M. Piskorsi with Jörg Hackmann and Rudolf Jaworski, eds, *Deutsche Ostforschung und polnische Westforschung im Spannungsfeld von Wissenschaft und Politik. Disziplinen im Vergleich* (Osnabrück, 2002).

63 Dieter Gosewinkel, *Einbürgern und Ausschließen. Die Nationalisierung der Staatsangehörigkeit vom Deutschen Bund bis Zur Bundesrepublik Deutschland* (Göttingen, 2001), pp. 328–68.

64 See above, pp. 44f. and 50f.

65 Peter Brandt, 'Youth Movements as National Protest Cultures in Germany', in Hartmut *German and American Nationalism: A Comparative Perspective* (Oxford, 1999) Lehmann and Hermann Wellenreuther, eds, pp. 371–428.

66 Jürgen Falter, *Hitlers Wähler* (Munich, 1991); also *idem*, 'How Likely Were Workers to Vote for the NSDAP?' in Conan Fischer, ed., *The Rise of National Socialism and the Working Classes in Weimar Germany* (Oxford, 1996); and *idem* and Detlef Mühlberger, 'The Anatomy of a Volkspartei: The Sociography of the Membership of the NSDAP in Stadt- and Landkreis Wetzlar, 1925–1935', *Historical Social Research*, 24 (1999), pp. 58–98.

The extent to which their racial nationalism was constructed against Jews boded ill for the Germans of Jewish faith. Antisemitism had already been officially endorsed by the infamous Jew count in the army in 1916.[67] It had been a reaction to popular complaints that Jews were shirking army service. The results of the count, which were not published until well after the war, showed that Jews fought and died in the German army in numbers which were entirely in line with their proportion in the German population. The Weimar Republic integrated Jews into the mainstream of German society. Institutional discrimination was rare and the majority of Jews remained convinced that the 'German-Jewish symbiosis' was their only worthwhile orientation.[68] On the far right the Association of National German Jews, founded in 1921 by Max Naumann, propagated an authoritarian, *völkisch* and antirepublican German nationalism.[69] On the far left, the Jewish anarchist revolutionary Ernst Toller argued that neither his Jewishness nor his socialism alienated him from his Germanness. Was Germany not, he asked, 'the country in which I grew up, the air that I breathe, the language that I love, the spirit which formed myself?' He concluded: 'and when someone asks me where do I belong I would reply: "I have been born to a Jewish mother, Germany has nourished me, Europe has educated me, my *Heimat* is the earth and the world my fatherland.'[70]

Jewish intellectuals also became prominent spokespersons for the republican centre-left, which was one of the reasons why the political right blamed Jews for all the problems of the defeated Germany and the young republic. Jews were behind Bolshevism and behind defeat; they were the cause of inflation and revolution; they were pulling the strings behind unemployment and the policy of fulfilling the terms of the Versailles Treaty. The republic itself was denounced as 'Jewish republic' (*Judenrepublik*). White-collar workers, peasants and students were among the social groups worst affected by antisemitism, but it was an accepted part of political rhetoric from the Catholic Centre Party to the *völkisch* groups on the far right. The *völkisch* paramilitary organizations gave antisemitism a militancy that had been largely absent before 1918. Calls to kill Jews like one would kill vermin were now being heard regularly. Artur Dinter's bestselling novel *Die Sünde wider das Blut* (The Sin against the Blood), published in 1917, described the terrible consequences of any mixing of Jewish and German blood. There was a direct line between the propagation of such racial theories and the passing of the Nazis' Nuremberg race laws in 1935.

The slow and gradual demise of the Weimar Republic after 1930, when presidential cabinets undermined the spirit of parliamentary democracy, was carried out in the name of the nation. When Franz von Papen replaced Brüning as chancellor in 1932, the president asked him to build a 'government of national

67 Werner T. Angress, 'Das deutsche Militär und die Juden im Ersten Weltkrieg', *Militärgeschichtliche Mitteilungen*, 19 (1976), pp. 77–146.

68 See above, p. 91f.

69 Matthias Hambrock, *Die Etablierung der Außenseiter: Der Verband nationaldeutscher Juden 1921–1935* (Cologne, 2003).

70 Ernst Toller, *Eine Jugend in Deutschland* (1933; Reinbek, 1963), p. 162; see also the English translation *I was a German: An Autobiography* (London, 1934).

concentration'. When Hitler was appointed chancellor a year later, his government was officially called a government of 'national alliance'. The Nazis themselves referred to their coming to power as 'national revolution'. On balance, the national theme was captured most effectively by the political right after the First World War and it served the purpose of undermining parliamentary democracy – the much hated 'system'. Republican forces attempted to construct their own national images and symbols in an effort to strengthen the republican nation, but their labours remained pale and weak by comparison with the powerful myths created by the political right. Most of them were rooted in and around the experience of the First World War. The war fundamentally restructured the national imagination. Above all, the 'August experience' and the 'community of the trenches' gave rise to the idea of the *Volksgemeinschaft* – a people united by race. If one was to believe the Nazis in 1933, this idea was about to become reality in Germany.

5
The racial nation, 1933–1945

Do you hear the daffodils
Rejoice?
Thus we never before
Understood the meaning of the festival
As today ... Because Germany itself is
Resurrected in all its glory.

Do you hear the daffodils
Rejoice?
Germany too suffered its Golgotha
And was nailed to the cross –
Now the bitterness of what occurred
Has born wonderful fruit.

Do you hear the daffodils
Rejoice?
Germany too had many a mother
With the sword through their bleeding
  hearts
Now the high spirits of Easter lets them
Forget all sorrows.

Do you hear the daffodils
Rejoice?
Germany's grave is also empty today:
The people have found home –
And however heavy the stone was,
It has been moved.

Do you hear the daffodils
Rejoice?
Thus we never before
Understood the message so deeply –
Because Germany, like the Holy Christ,
Is arisen in all its glory!

Hörst Du die Osterglocken
Frohlocken?
So haben wir noch zu keiner Frist
des Festes Sinn verstanden
wie heute ... Denn Deutschland selber ist
Leuchtend auferstanden.

Hörst Du die Osterglocken
Frohlocken?
Auch Deutschland erlitt sein Golgatha,
und ward ans Kreuz geschlagen –
nun hat das Bittere, das ihm geschah,
Herrliche Frucht getragen.

Hörst Du die Osterglocken
Frohlocken?
Auch Deutschland hatte der Mütter viel
mit dem Schwert im blutenden Herzen –
nun läßt sie das österlich-hohe Ziel
Vergessen alle Schmerzen.

Hörst Du die Osterglocken
Frohlocken?
Auch Deutschlands Grab ist heute leer:
Das Volk hat heimgefunden –
und war der Stein auch noch so schwer,
Es hat ihn überwunden.

Hörst Du die Osterglocken
Frohlocken?
So haben wir noch zu keiner Frist
die Botschaft tief verstanden –
denn Deutschland ist, wie der Heilige
  Christ,
Leuchtend auferstanden![1]

1 Heinrich Anacker, 'Deutsche Ostern 1933', in Wolfgang Gast, ed., *Politische Lyrik: Deutsche Zeitgedichte des 19. und 20. Jahrhunderts* (Stuttgart, 1973), p. 30.

the idea of the *Volksgemeinschaft* and sought to demonstrate its 'reality' in a variety of ways.[7] After all, the 'people's radio' (*Volksempfänger*), nicknamed 'Goebbels snout', allowed the Nazis to claim that the Führer's voice could be heard in all German living rooms. Hitler time and again emphasized the central importance of the *Volksgemeinschaft* idea: 'Today we witness the foundation of a new state for which it is characteristic to see in the *Volksgemeinschaft* the primary aim. ... Never before in German history was there such unity of spirit, will and leadership. Many generations before us have hoped for this and we are the happy witnesses of the fulfilment of their dreams.'[8] The Nazi *Volksgemeinschaft* was forged in the trenches of the First World War, and its appeal built on the strength of antipluralism, the desire for wholeness and the rejection of conflictual interest politics. The idea of the *Volksgemeinschaft* was paramount in producing an extraordinary social consensus behind the regime which included the widespread persecution of alleged enemies of that 'people's community'.[9] On the other hand the *Volksgemeinschaft* remained a projection, an idea which could barely hide the manifold and often bitter divisions between Germans which produced dissent in the Third Reich.[10] But the Nazis' propagation of the ideal of the *Volksgemeinschaft* led to extremely polarized, dichotomous and Manichean constructions of the nation. One could only be for or against them, one was friend or foe, and Germany awaited either victory or defeat, survival or annihilation.

Accordingly, the Nazi *Volksgemeinschaft* rigidly excluded all those who were constructed as its internal or external enemies. Communists, Social Democrats, representatives of the hated 'Weimar system', pacifists, feminists, homosexuals, Jehovah's Witnesses, and, above all, gypsies and Jews: they were the political, cultural and racial 'other', representing everything that threatened the German nation. Terror against these groups started immediately after the Nazis had come to power. They were rounded up by the SA, maltreated, humiliated, tortured and murdered. The infamous concentration camps were soon full with those deemed enemies of the nation. Those who were forced into exile were denaturalized: they lost not only their German citizenship, but also their property and social rights. German universities colluded with the Nazis to revoke academic titles from those deemed unworthy of Germandom.

External enemies were equally important in sustaining the homogeneity of the nation. In Hitler's thinking, France remained the 'hereditary enemy'. The Franco-German antagonism would have to end with the subjugation of one nation by the other. Similarly older stereotypes about the materialistic, self-seeking and hypocritical (essentially Jewish!) character of the ruling elites of the British nation informed Nazi images of Britain. The United States were even more racially depraved. Yet traditional anti-Western images tended to be accompanied by a

7 Inge Marßolek, '"Aus dem Volke für das Volk". Die Inszenierung der "Volksgemeinschaft" im und durch das Radio', in *idem* and Adelheid von Saldern, eds, *Radiozeiten: Herrschaft, Alltag, Gesellschaft (1924–1960)* (Potsdam, 1999), pp. 121–35.

8 Cited in Frank-Lothar Kroll, *Utopie als Ideologie: Geschichte und politisches Handeln im Dritten Reich* (Paderborn, 1998), p. 41.

9 Robert Gellately, *Backing Hitler: Consent and Coercion in Nazi Germany* (Oxford, 2002).

10 Ian Kershaw, *Popular Opinion and Political Dissent in the Third Reich* (new edn, Oxford, 2002).

grudging respect for the achievements of these nations. Plans for Hitler's new capital of Germany, Germania, designed by his favourite architect Albert Speer, were meant to make Berlin a bigger and better version of the French capital. Hitler admired the British Empire and saw it as a model of how to govern a Germanized Eastern Europe after the successful conclusion of the war. And America provided not only the inspiration behind much of Nazi advertising and propaganda; it also was exemplary in its mass consumerism and technological modernity.

If we move to the Eastern European neighbours of Nazi Germany it was an altogether different matter. Slavs were 'subhumans' (*Untermenschen*) who lacked any higher culture or civilization. The infamous *Generalsiedlungsplan Ost* during the Second World War foresaw the ethnic cleansing of 50 million Slavs and the resettlement of German working-class and peasant families whose task it would be to civilize these regions. Millions of members of the Slav nations' middle classes, in particular the intelligentsia, were marked out for physical annihilation. The rest would operate as slaves to the 'German master race'. Jewish Bolshevism was the ultimate ideological enemy of the Nazis, and hence the war against the Soviet Union was not only fought for living space (*Lebensraum*), it was a racial war. On 30 March 1941 chief of staff General Franz Halder noted in his war diary: 'Struggle of two world views against each other. Annihilating judgment about Bolshevism, equals asocial criminality. Communism immeasurable danger for the future. We must move away from the viewpoint of soldierly solidarity. The Communist can never be a fellow soldier. We are dealing with a war of annihilation.'[11] Political commissars in the Soviet army were not taken prisoner, they were shot straightaway. Hundreds of thousands of civilians were starved to death. Of the 5.7 million Soviet prisoners of war 3.3 million died.[12] Most were starved to death or died in epidemics in the overcrowded prisoner of war camps, left without any medical attention.

But the worst enemy of the Nazi racial nation was 'the Jew'. Jews were systematically robbed of all citizenship rights and transformed into subhumans who could only be annihilated. The 1935 Nuremberg laws created the new crime of 'race defilement' for any sexual contact between Germans and Jews. Most Jewish synagogues were burnt down in the 1938 'Night of Broken Glass' (*Kristallnacht*). Exhibitions such as 'The Eternal Jew' or 'Debased Art' and 'Debased Music', which featured, above all, Jewish artists and musicians, constructed the Jew as the mirror opposite of the German. Jews were portrayed as the incarnation of everything that was evil, the soulless enemy of common humanity. Redemption could only come through the Aryan people eliminating the Jews. The central ingredient of the Nazi construction of the nation was the Shoah, the systematic murder of approximately 7 million European Jews. The importance of antisemitism to the Nazi construction of the nation is beyond any doubt,[13] but the Holocaust was

[11] Franz Halder, *Kriegstagebuch* (Stuttgart, 1963), Vol. 2, p. 335.

[12] Christian Streit, *Keine Kameraden. Die Wehrmacht und die sowjetischen Kriegsgefangenen* (Stuttgart, 1978), p. 136.

[13] Claus-E. Bärsch, 'Die Konstruktion der kollektiven Identität der Deutschen gegen die Juden in der politischen Religion des Nationalsozialismus', in P. Alter, C.-E. Bärsch and P. Berghoff, eds, *Die Konstruktion der Nation gegen die Juden* (Munich, 1999), pp. 191–223.

not a long-term national project of the German nation hooked on some kind of 'eliminatory antisemitism'.[14] Antisemitism in nineteenth-century Germany was weaker than elsewhere in Europe, and studies on the perpetrators of the Holocaust have shown conclusively that many were motivated by a broad variety of considerations, of which antisemitic hatred was not necessarily the most important one. Career prospects, male peer pressure, belief in authority and duty were among a complex web of reasons why 'ordinary men' became ruthless killers in the context of the radicalization of warfare on the eastern front during the Second World War.[15]

The descendants of Moses Mendelssohn had to watch helplessly, as the Leipzig memorial to Felix Mendelssohn-Bartholdy was removed in November 1936, as their property was Aryanized and as they were hounded out of Germany. Their dream of a 'German-Jewish' symbiosis had reached a cul-de-sac, even if the proponents of this dream refused to accept it. One of the leading members of the Jewish Women's Association, disbanded in 1933, Hannah Kaminski, defiantly challenged her exclusion from the German nation: 'It hardly deserves mentioning that our belief in the German spirit, our rootedness in German culture cannot be shaken by anything. Never have we felt this more strongly than in these weeks, when one attempts to exclude us from contributing to German culture.' Visiting her close friend and associate, Cora Berliner, in 1942 to say good-bye before Berliner was transported to her death in the east, she found her friend sitting in the garden reading Goethe.[16] For many the idea of symbiosis ended in Auschwitz. Others, who had gone into exile, still attempted to link their Jewishness to German culture. Elias Canetti, for example, wrote in 1944:

> The language of my spirit will remain German, and that is because I am a Jew. What remains of this terribly maimed country, I will preserve for myself as a Jew. Their fate also is mine; but I additionally carry a common human heritage. I want to give their language back what I owe to it. I would like to contribute so that there is something for which one can be thankful to them.[17]

Biology as destiny

The construction of the German nation against the Jews was the clearest sign that the Nazis defined the *Volksgemeinschaft* in racial terms.[18] The *Volk* was defined as community of blood. Blood and race, not culture and territory, defined belonging to the nation. The 1935 Law for the Protection of German Blood and Honour introduced a new category of *Reichsbürger* for those of 'German or German-related

[14] Daniel Jonah Goldhagen, *Hitler's Willing Executioners: Ordinary Germans and the Holocaust* (New York, 1996).

[15] Christopher Browning, *Ordinary Men: Reserve Police Battalion 101 and the Final Solution in Poland* (New York, 1992).

[16] Cited in Birgit Seemann, 'Stieftöchter der "deutschen Nation": der Jüdische Frauenbund 1904–1938 und in der Bundesrepublik', in Ute Planert, ed., *Nation, Politik und Geschlecht* (Frankfurt/Main, 2000), p. 314f.

[17] Elias Canetti, *Die Provinz des Menschen. Aufzeichnungen 1942–1972* (Munich, 1973), p. 54.

[18] Michael Burleigh and Wolfgang Wippermann, *The Racial State: Germany 1933–1945* (Cambridge, Mass., 1991).

blood' only. The nation in all its diverse aspects, history, culture and geography, was comprehensively biologized. Under Weimar, the *Volk* had been 'ill'; it had been penetrated by parasites (*Volksschädlinge*), especially the omnipresent Jews. The nation had to be cured by 'cleansing' it of all elements who had contributed to its 'illness'. The SS was particularly vociferous in its belief in the principles of 'breeding' and 'elimination'. The national history was the history of the racial struggle of the Germanic people to keep their Aryan race pure. The SS developed its own Germanic cult complete with runes on tombstones for dead SS members, SS ancestral shrines (*Ahnstätten*) and their own castles (*Ordensburgen*), such as the Wewelsburg near Paderborn. Heinrich Himmler believed himself to be the reincarnation of the medieval Welf duke, Heinrich the Lion, and made Heinrich's burial place, Brunswick cathedral, the centre of an elaborate SS cult. Himmler's 'black order' celebrated the Saxon duke, Widukind, as oldest known ancestor of the Germanic race. National Socialist dramatists, who sought to make a name for themselves in the Third Reich, wrote dozens of Widukind dramas for stage which depicted the 'honest' Saxons and their national 'other', the 'devious' Franks led by the 'slaughterer of the Saxons', Charlemagne. Mainstream Nazi propaganda, however, also portrayed Charlemagne as an emperor who had attempted to unite Europe. Parallels between Hitler and Charlemagne were not uncommon.

The racial nation bred SS occultism, but it had a much greater impact on the lives of people through its rigid separation of 'desirable' from 'undesirable life'. Race hygiene and National Socialist population science was busy categorizing people into different races and selecting some for special breeding and others for extermination. The Social Darwinist construction of the nation put great emphasis on the performance principle: efficiency, strength and endurance had to be guaranteed by 'good breeding', just as any weakness had to be thoroughly uprooted. The Law for the Prevention of Genetically Deficient Offspring from July 1933 led to the enforced sterilization of thousands of Germans deemed asocial or otherwise genetically deficient. Criminality was widely seen as genetically determined and the popular 'research on the body of the people' (*Volkskörperforschung*) sought to solve a whole range of social problems through rigid birth control and race policies. Much of this aimed at the maintenance of a pure genetic pool which was not polluted by forms of inter-cultural or inter-ethnic contact. To qualify as German citizen everyone in the Nazi nation had to provide proof that three generations of Aryan blood was running in their veins. For members of the SS, which referred to itself as an 'aristocracy of the blood' (*Blutadel*), Aryan descent had to be traced back to 1648.

The ideal of the Aryan warrior, willing to struggle, fight and die for the nation was put in stone by Arno Breker's Nazi sculptures depicting powerful, belligerent and self-confident male nudes.[19] War and struggle were of central importance to the Nazi definition of Germandom. Violence characterized fascist lifestyles and was aestheticized in fascist rituals, symbols and actions.[20] The whole language of

[19] J.A. Mangan, 'Icon of Monumental Brutality: Art and the Aryan Man', *International Journal of the History of Sport*, 16 (1999), pp. 128–52.

[20] For a comparison of the SA with the Italian Squadristi see Sven Reichardt, *Faschistische Kampfbünde: Gewalt und Gemeinschaft im italienischen Squadrismus und in der deutschen SA* (Cologne, 2002). On the importance of symbols and rituals see also Simon Taylor, 'Symbol and Ritual under National Socialism', *British Journal of Sociology*, 32 (1981), pp. 504–20.

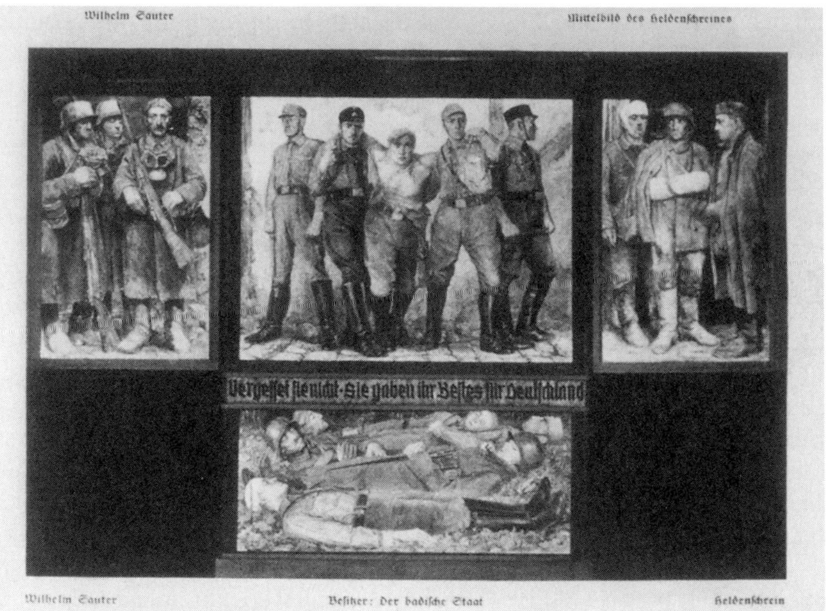

Figure 5.1 Wilhelm Sauter, 'Heldenschrein' (1936), 'Forget them not: they gave their best for Germany'; soldiers from the First World War and SA men as Nazi national heroes.

the Third Reich, the Lingua Tertii Imperii,[21] was characterized by a warlike rhetoric of struggle. The Nazis presented a nation on the march, *Volksgenossen* in uniform. Much of Nazi architecture, for example Albert Speer's designs for the grounds of the Nuremberg party rallies, was designed for such uniformed spectacles of the fighting spirit of the nation. The emphasis on struggle and war incorporated the belief in sacrificing oneself for the community of the nation. In the Social Darwinist world-view of the Nazis the struggle for the survival of the fittest nation was inevitable. Germany had to win that struggle or go under. The Führer demanded loyalty, obedience and sacrifice with reference to his own experiences in the First World War. Hitler stated on many occasions how the trenches of the First World War had been his true *Heimat*. Throughout the Second World War Hitler emphasized that he demanded nothing of his people that he had not endured himself.

Sacrifice for the nation in times of war was closely linked to an elaborate cult of the hero in Nazi Germany.[22] Every March the Nazis celebrated Heroes' Day (*Heldengedenktag*), remembering the self-sacrifice of the soldiers for the nation [Figure 5.1]. Every 9 November, the 'martyrs of the movement' were celebrated in Munich, 'the capital of the movement', through carefully staged torchlight processions from the Bürgerbräu Cellar to the place near the Feldherrnhalle

[21] Viktor Klemperer, *Language of the Third Reich: LTI, lingua tertii imperii; a Philologist's Notebook* (London, 2000).

[22] Sabine Behrenbeck, *Der Kult um die toten Helden: Nationalsozialistische Mythen, Riten und Symbole* (Vierow, 1996).

where the Nazis' attempt to stage a coup had ended in a hail of police bullets in 1923. Funereal music accompanied the carrying of the 'blood flag' to one of Nazism's most sacred places. Hitler himself described the blood of those who had died on 9 November 1923 as 'baptismal water of the Third Reich'.[23] Among the group of National Socialist 'blood witnesses' arguably the most famous was Horst Wessel, the author of what became the unofficial national anthem under the Third Reich.[24] His actual murder might have had more to do with his complicated love life than with his political convictions, but this did not prevent the Nazis from making him their arch-martyr. As 'singer of the movement', he could easily be connected to the myth of Langemarck and the young soldiers dying with the *Deutschlandlied* on their lips.[25]

Close to Wessel in the Nazi pantheon of martyrs came Albert Leo Schlageter, the Nazi who had been executed by the French occupants for acts of sabotage in the Ruhr in 1923.[26] The Nazis turned his Düsseldorf memorial into a 'national monument' (*Nationalehrenmal*) and Schlageter became 'the first soldier of the Third Reich'. A series of films produced after 1933, such as *SA Man Brand*, *Hans Westmar* and, of course, *Hitler Youth Quex* all made the theme of the National Socialist hero their subject. And in the Second World War the National Socialist cult of the soldierly hero sacrificing his life for the nation came to full fruition. The elaborate celebrations in honour of the war dead staged by the Nazis incorporated frequent references to the nation: 'The future of Germany and the German people has been saved with their blood.'[27] The absolute super-hero in the Third Reich was, of course, the Führer himself. In fact, Hitler and Germany were merged into one through the propagation of the 'Führer myth'[28] which included the total identification of the leader with the nation. Hitler was Germany.

Much of what has been said so far about the National Socialist construction of the nation underlines the degree to which it relied on a merger of many traditional elements of German nationalism with its own brand of racial theory. The eclectic nature of the images of the nation propagated by Nazism was visible in its heavy use of religious imagery, its tapping into many of the ideas of the 'conservative revolution', most importantly the notion of the *Volksgemeinschaft*, and, of course, its emphasis on a heroic nationalism based on the 'ultimate sacrifice'. Even before 1933 the millenarianism of the Nazis, which was closely connected to the theme of national renewal, was entirely in line with the multitude of pseudo-religious revival movements so popular in Weimar.[29] Their call for a 'Third Reich' was directly taken from the immensely popular book title of one of the key representatives of the 'conservative revolution', Arthur Moeller van den Bruck.[30] He had envisaged a future in which the breakdown of the nation in 1918 was followed by mass resistance and struggle of all truly nationally minded Germans

[23] Cited in Max Domarus, *Hitler: Reden und Proklamationen 1932–1945* (Munich, 1965), p. 458.
[24] Jay W. Baird, *To Die For Germany: Heroes in the Nazi Pantheon* (Bloomington, 1990).
[25] See above, p. 116.
[26] See above, p. 125.
[27] Cited in Behrenbeck, *Kult*, p. 523 (see note 22).
[28] Ian Kershaw, *The 'Hitler Myth': Image and Reality in the Third Reich* (Oxford, 1987).
[29] Ulrich Linse, *Barfüßige Propheten: Erlöser der zwanziger Jahre* (Berlin, 1983).
[30] Arthur Moeller van den Bruck, *Das dritte Reich* (Hamburg, 1923).

for a new *Reich* which would restore Germanness in all its glory. The National Socialists portrayed themselves precisely as the movement which could bring that about.[31]

Many of Nazism's internal 'antinational enemies' were the ones which had been traditionally excluded from the German nation. As far as external enemies were concerned, their construction could equally build on an existing pool of negative national stereotypes. Nazism tapped into the existing national imagination in a variety of other ways. Statism, for example, had been a central ingredient of nineteenth-century Prussian nationalism. With their Law for the Protection of the Unity of Party and State of 1 December 1933 the Nazis latched onto that tradition and declared the NSDAP the sole carrier of the German idea of the state. The party was to form an indissoluble union with the state. Nazi architecture was intent on demonstrating the omnipresence and power of the total state. Many of its monumental designs were meant to visualize the intended unity of nation.[32]

Like so many nationalists before them, the Nazis placed immense importance on the past and portrayed themselves as the logical successors to a thousand years of German history. Nazi archaeologists examined and analysed prehistoric Teutonic tribes as the forefathers of 'Aryan man'. Nazi propagandists celebrated German medieval traditions. This was particularly visible in the choice of Nuremberg as the site for Nazi party rallies after 1927. The 'treasure chamber' (*Schatzkästlein*) of the *Reich*, as it was frequently described, had been a powerful free city in the Holy Roman Empire and a place identified with key medieval artists such as Hans Sachs and Albrecht Dürer. It seemed to incorporate everything that was best about the German past and German traditions. What is more, architecturally the Middle Ages still seemed alive in a city surrounded by mighty walls and including an almost entirely medieval collection of houses. To top it all, the annual party conferences started with a performance of Richard Wagner's *Meistersinger*, the opera featuring the patriotic Hans Sachs in Nuremberg. Sachs is portrayed in the opera as safeguarding the best tradition of the German art of singing, but he is also the one who is aware of the need for permanent renewal and development of that heritage. This was precisely how the Nazis liked to see themselves. They represented and safeguarded the best of the German past but equally they were determined to renew that tradition and push it forward – towards the racial nation. Nuremberg was, after all, the place where the Nazi race laws originated in 1935.

Apart from prehistoric tribes and medieval German glory, the Nazis also stressed their links to the Second German *Reich*. They had merged the colours of the Imperial German flag with their own symbol, the swastika. It was most frequently depicted as a black swastika in a white circle against a red background. Prussian values, such as order, authority, obedience, loyalty, soldierly courage, and self-sacrifice were held in high regard by the Nazis. They frequently chose to stage party events at places closely associated with Prussianism, such as the palace of Frederick II in Potsdam. The handshake between Paul von Hindenburg, the leader

31 James M. Rhodes, *The Hitler Movement: A Modern Millenarian Revolution* (Stanford, 1980), talked about the 'apocalyptic themes' of the National Socialists in this context.

32 B. Miller Lane, *Architecture and Politics in Germany 1918–1945* (Cambridge, 1968).

of the Imperial army in the First World War and the 'hero of Tannenberg', and Adolf Hitler at the so-called 'Day of Potsdam' in March 1933 symbolized the alleged continuity between the Second and the Third Reich. The old general was handing over the baton to the young corporal. The famous postcard that the Nazis published on the occasion of Hitler's birthday in April 1933, depicting Frederick II, Bismarck and Hitler, hammered home the same message as did popular exhibitions such as 'Eternal Germany' or 'The German Face in the Mirror of Centuries': Nazi Germany was part and parcel of a continuity in German history that could be traced back over centuries, to Luther, Frederick Barbarossa and Arminius.

Yet Germany was not completely recast in Teutonic, medieval and Prussian garments. The Nazis carefully nourished the image of a modern industrial nation state, at the cutting edge of technology and promising a paradise for masses of consumers. Hitler preached not less but more intensive industrialization. Technical progress and new inventions were to pave the way for a more equal distribution of wealth along collectivist lines. A good example of the Nazis' championing of 'reactionary modernism'[33] was their fascination with the Autobahn. It was recognized as the most important means of revolutionizing transport in the twentieth century. The 1936 Berlin automobile show presented Germany as the hub of the new age of the automobile, and the idea behind the Nazi-owned 'people's car' (*Volkswagen*) was precisely the vision of an automobilized Germany. The Nazis were about more than a nostalgic longing for an imperial past. Their constructions of the nation incorporated a range of modern elements, where these could be tied to their vision of an undemocratic, dehumanized and racialized future in which the well-being of a biologized *Volk* was the prime focus for collective identity.

How much Nazi constructions of the nation were fluctuating uneasily between the old and the new became visible in the Nazis' espousal of militarism. The ideal of 'soldierly manliness' guided the education of boys from their earliest years in the Nazi state. The Nazis could build on a long tradition of paramilitary youth education in Imperial Germany. By 1936, 60 per cent of all children had joined the Hitler Youth and membership was made compulsory in 1939. The six months of Labour Service was further contributing to the militarization of young people in Nazi Germany, but the highpoint was the two years (after 1936) of military service. In the Nazi state, just as in Imperial Germany, men became full members of the nation only after serving in the army. Unlike in Imperial Germany, however, there were to be no more privileges for the university-educated. Everyone had to serve the same amount of time, and the Nazis insisted that soldiers from working-class backgrounds should have greater opportunities to rise through the ranks in the Nazi army. Race and skill should determine access to top positions, not class and education.

Many leading generals, after some initial scepticism, supported the Nazi state because they welcomed the strong definition of the nation in military terms. They

[33] Jeffrey Herf, *Reactionary Modernism: Technology, Culture and Politics in Weimar and the Third Reich* (Cambridge, 1984); also Thomas Rohkrämer, 'Antimodernism, Reactionary Modernism and National Socialism: Technocratic Tendencies in Germany 1890–1945', *Contemporary European History*, 8 (1999), pp. 29–50.

believed that the Nazis were putting into practice ideas about a *Wehrstaat* which had been so popular among leading representatives of the army in the Weimar Republic.[34] The swastika was worn on army uniforms and displayed on army flags. The Nazi salute was given and Wehrmacht units took part in Nazi party conferences. From August 1934 a personal oath of loyalty was sworn to Hitler by all new recruits. Military education inside the army was geared towards Nazi ideology. Soldiers, for example, were asked not to have any contact with Jews, who were systematically excluded from the army, as they were excluded from all areas of public life. The army chief of staff, General von Brauchitsch, put it this way in a decree to his officers from December 1938: 'With regard to the purity and honesty of the National Socialist world-view the officer corps shall not be surpassed by anyone else.'[35] One of the areas in which the military elites saw eye to eye with the Nazis was in the field of foreign policy. The Versailles Treaty had to be revised. The German army had to be rebuilt. Lost German territories had to be regained. Austria had to be brought into the Reich. And when war broke out, many generals were keen to achieve the hegemonic position in Europe that Germany, in their estimation, deserved.

The Nazi nation was a militarized nation with a proud military past. German history, more generally, took pride of place in the Nazis' comprehensive national education programme. History education in schools was used to indoctrinate pupils and prepare them for war.[36] Historians at the universities willing to serve the Nazis received generous funding and sometimes found themselves elevated to policy advisers. Representatives of the so-called *Volksgeschichte* built up huge research networks and became heavily implicated in legitimating and propagating genocide and the Nazi war effort.[37] *Volksgeschichte* was part and parcel of a wider *Volkstumsforschung* which intellectually prepared the new Nazi racial order in Europe. Scientists from many different areas, including archaeology, geography, biology, literature and philosophy, contributed. Geographers, for example, developed theories which defined space in relation to race and highlighted the importance of race in all areas of geographical enquiry. They produced maps which were extensively used for the purpose of Germanizing the landscape of Eastern Europe through ethnic cleansing and the Holocaust.[38]

As diverse academic disciplines were racialized, so was the long-established discourse on *Heimat*. Many conservationists and *Heimat* propagandists had already been close to the right-wing *völkisch* ideas prominent in the Weimar Republic and found it easy to support the Nazis after 1933. A 'healthy' *Heimat* and a 'clean' nature were now linked to the need to purify German landscapes from Jews and to practise 'racial hygiene' more generally. A racialized vision of

34 See above, p. 135.

35 Cited in Manfred Messerschmidt, 'Militarismus im Nationalsozialismus', in Wolfram Wette, ed., *Militarismus in Deutschland 1871–1945: Zeitgenössische Analysen und Kritik* (Münster, 1999), p. 88.

36 Horst Gies, *Geschichtsunterricht unter der Diktatur Hitlers* (Cologne, 1992).

37 For a review of the extensive new literature on historians and National Socialism see Stefan Berger, 'Nationalism and Historiography', *German History*, 18 (2000), pp. 239–59.

38 Guntram Henrik Herb, *Under the Map of Germany: Nationalism and Propaganda, 1918–1945* (London, 1997), pp. 119–77.

Heimat became the precondition for a 'healthy' *Volksgemeinschaft*.[39] The federal construction of the nation had been the backbone of *Heimat* sentiments.[40] Yet the Nazis mounted one of the most sustained attacks on German federalism.[41] On 30 January 1934 the powers of the *Länder* were transferred to the *Reich*. The federal system was replaced by a central one and the country was now subdivided into *Gaue* with a party *Gauleiter* at its head who was directly responsible to Hitler. Nazi propaganda had long stressed the theme of unity in the face of federal fragmentation. The *Volksgenosse* should be loyal to the nation, not the region. *Heimat* sentiments were, however, too deeply entrenched in popular constructions of the nation to be removed at the stroke of a pen. Many of the Nazi *Gauleiter* were hardened regional patriots who put the welfare of their region before anything else. They strengthened symbols of regional belonging and sought to merge them with Nazi ideology in the hope that it might strengthen their own legitimacy with the people.

National education in Nazi Germany was not only a matter for schools, universities and *Heimat* enthusiasts. The Nazis put great emphasis on the importance of the arts and of the entertainment industry in promoting national sentiment.[42] They generously financed the theatre, opera and film production which in turn won them much support among the people working in the culture and entertainment industries. The new Theatre Law of 15 May 1934 gave the theatres the express task to foster national education and put on stage a variety of German heroes with whom the people could identify. Musicologists, for example, were busy finding 'proof' of the superior German presence in the musical cultures of diverse European countries, thereby strengthening the already well-established assumption of the superiority of German over other national forms of music.[43] The Nazis sponsored highbrow German culture, but they paid at least equal attention to forms of popular entertainment.[44] Historical parades, for example, were popular with the Nazis, as they hoped to strengthen the emotional attachment to their national religion through such performances of the racial nation. The popularity of American jazz among young Germans led the Nazis to experiment with their own German version of jazz, dance music (*Tanzmusik*), which turned out, however, a major failure on the dance floor.[45] On a more mundane level,

[39] John A. Williams, ' "The Chords of the German Soul Are Tuned to Nature": The Movement to preserve the Natural *Heimat* from the Kaiserreich in the Third Reich', *Central European History*, 29 (1996), p. 381.

[40] See above, p. 105f.

[41] Jeremy Noakes, 'Federalism in the Nazi State', in Maiken Umbach, ed., *German Federalism: Past, Present, Future* (London, 2002), pp. 113–45.

[42] Alan Steinweis, *Art, Ideology and Economics in Nazi Germany: The Reich Chambers of Music, Theater, and the Visual Arts* (Chapel Hill, 1993); Karl Christian Führer, 'German Cultural Life and the Crisis of National Identity during the Depression, 1929–1933', *German Studies Review*, 24 (2001), pp. 461–86.

[43] Pamela Potter, 'Musicology under Hitler: New Sources in Context', *Journal of the American Musicological Society*, 49 (1996), pp. 70–113.

[44] The German language knows a rigorous distinction between *U(nterhaltungs)-Kultur* and *E(rnste)-Kultur*, 'entertainment culture' and 'serious culture'.

[45] On jazz in the Third Reich see Michael H. Kater, *Different Drummers: Jazz in the Culture of Nazi Germany* (Oxford, 2003).

the Nazis encouraged the collecting of cheap little cards (*Sammelbilder*), many of which depicted historical themes and landscapes which were supposed to strengthen a historical sense of national identity among the collectors.[46]

One of the biggest entertainment events stage-managed by the Nazis in the 1930s was the Olympic Games of 1936. Through exhibitions, endless shows, parades and receptions, the Nazis intended to impress on the world that a 'new' Germany was in the making. They even toned down their antisemitism (copies of *Der Stürmer* newspaper were not allowed to be sold on the streets) in an effort to highlight the positive achievements of national unity and the reality of the *Volksgemeinschaft*. The documentary film-maker Leni Riefenstahl made a film of the Olympics which was entirely in line with Nazi aesthetics, stressing the virility and power of the athletes' bodies as a symbol of the virility and health of the nation. Millions visited the exhibition accompanying the Olympic Games which was simply entitled 'Germany'. Exhibitions more generally played a key role in bringing the key concept of the racial nation and the *Volksgemeinschaft* to the people.[47]

The film industry delivered straightforward ideological propaganda, and political censorship was provided by the Department for Political Guidance in the Reich Film Chamber set up in July 1933. By and large, however, entertainment movies dominated the cinemas. They allowed a few hours of escapism for cinema-goers experiencing considerable levels of alienation in a highly industrial and modern world. Where Nazi films talked about national identity they often idealized pre-industrial organic communities and fostered a romantic longing for wholeness and naturalness. They glorified heroic death in the struggle for national values and ideas. The individual was portrayed as part and parcel of a greater national community. The 'othering' of internal and external enemies of the racial nation found its apogee in Veit Harlan's film *Jew Süß* of 1940.[48] Boasting a star-studded cast, high production costs and a script which uneasily moved between soap opera and crude ideological statements, it amounted to a systematic effort to help prepare the German public for the Holocaust. The full range of antisemitic stereotypes was used to hammer home one message: Jews were vermin, fit only for collective extinction. The Nazis were, however, always anxious not to bring details of their most gruesome project out into the open. They attempted (not with great success) to hide the systematic genocide from the German public – unsure whether the majority of Germans would support the 'final solution' to the 'Jewish question'.

The concept of the racial nation worked best where it combined 'the themes of traditional German nationalism with Nazi ideological motifs'.[49] Such a merger of traditional and new motifs of the nation deeply penetrated the national imagination. The racial nation intended to break down class barriers and proved a

46 Rudy Koshar, *Preservation and National Memory in the Twentieth Century: Germany's Transient Past* (Chapel Hill, 1998), p. 144.

47 Hans-Ulrich Thamer, 'Geschichte und Propaganda: Kulturhistorische Ausstellungen in der NS-Zeit', *Geschichte und Gesellschaft*, 24 (1998), pp. 349–81.

48 Linda Schulte-Sasse, 'Courtier, Vampire or Vermin? *Jew Süß's* Contradictory Effort to Rend the "Jew" Other', in Terri Ginsberg and Kirsten Moana Thompson, eds, *Perspectives on German Cinema* (New York, 1996), pp. 184–220.

49 David Welch, *The Third Reich: Politics and Propaganda* (London, 1993), p. 16.

powerful ideology of social integration which promised greater equality to millions of Germans. The egalitarianism of the 'community of the trenches' idea was transformed into the vision of *völkisch* community in which the 'ordinary man on the street' would experience unprecedented social mobility.[50]

The deep impact of the racial nation on German society

Millions of Germans willingly supported the racial construction of Germanness. This became particularly evident in the treatment of foreign labourers during the Second World War. By August 1944, 7.6 million foreign labourers served the German war economy, which would have collapsed much earlier without them. The Nazis introduced a finely graded racial hierarchy. Some Western Europeans were treated almost like indigenous German workers, but Russians, Poles and Jews were among those who were inadequately clothed, housed and fed. They worked long hours, were denied even the most basic medical care and often beaten and abused by their German superiors. They were to be 'exterminated through work' (*Vernichtung durch Arbeit*). For many Germans who encountered slave labourers, the 'practice of racism became a daily habit'.[51] Germans experienced upward social mobility as they were promoted to positions of foremen and supervisors, whilst the army of slave labourers would do all the unpleasant and dirty jobs. Under these circumstances the racial nation appealed to many ordinary Germans who, on balance, showed little interest in the fate of the slave labourers. Days before the end of the war thousands of so-called 'Eastern workers' (*Ostarbeiter*), including women and children, were murdered, not because they had done anything, but because they were perceived as a threat to the German population once the German army had capitulated. The Nazi propaganda of hordes of racially inferior barbarians plundering the German nation and polluting the purity of German blood had clearly struck a chord.

In the early 1940s many Germans dreamt of a new life as colonizer in the east after the successful conclusion of the war. Himmler talked about the 'socialism of the good blood' when referring to his plans to 'cleanse' Eastern Europe of Slavs and repopulate it with Germans. Hundreds of thousands of so-called 'foreign Germans' (*Auslandsdeutsche*) underwent individual examinations to determine precisely which race they belonged to. Race maps used pseudo-anthropological criteria to categorize people into different races. Those who had been affected too much by the mixing of races had to stay in their territories. Where there was doubt about the purity of their blood, they were sent home to the *Reich* for re-education. Only those who passed rigorous race tests were resettled with the promise of higher living standards, better homes and greater opportunities. German soldiers who took part in the campaign against the Soviet Union frequently referred to Nazi terminology when attempting to describe their experiences in the

[50] Götz Aly, *Rasse und Klasse: Nachforschungen zum deutschen Wesen* (Frankfurt/Main, 2003).
[51] Ulrich Herbert, *Hitler's Foreign Workers: Enforced Foreign Labour in Germany under the Third Reich* (Cambridge, 1997), p. 396.

east. In Walter Kempowski's impressive collage of thousands of autobiographical voices from the war in the east, one encounters references to 'subhuman Russians', 'cities infested with Jews' and 'primitive peoples' on almost every page.[52] The acceptance of racial nationalism among a considerable number of German soldiers also helps to explain the barbarity of the racial war on the eastern front.[53] The language of the racial nation penetrated deeply into the everyday life of Germans in the Third Reich.

It also affected the whole concept of welfare. Social welfare became racial welfare. The democratic welfare state in the Weimar Republic had patently failed to heal the wounds of the nation. The Nazis comprehensively biologized and medicalized social problems, building on an international eugenicist discourse already prominent in the 1920s.[54] The 'healthy' had to be 'separated' from the 'degenerate'. The body of the *Volk* gained priority over the body of the individual. In fact the mutilation or death of the individual body might be necessary to ensure the health of the *Volk* body. Elimination and welfare were two sides of the same coin in the racial nation.[55] But the Nazi welfare state also took great care to emphasize its continuities with the Bismarckian creation in the late nineteenth century. It was propagated as an important means of integrating workers into the nation and guaranteeing the advent of a true *Volksgemeinschaft*.[56]

The Nazis presented workers as key representatives of the 'new' nation. Not for nothing was the NSDAP called a 'workers' party'. Hitler believed that his party fused the greatest idea of the nineteenth century, nationalism, with the greatest idea of the twentieth century, socialism. Anticapitalism had been a part of National Socialist ideology from the beginning. Its 25-point programme of 1920 demanded the expropriation of big landowners, the breaking of the 'thraldom of interest' and the abolition and dissolution of trusts. The workers who had been following the Pied Piper of Marxism were regarded as the deluded victims of Communism and Social Democracy. It fell to them, the Nazis argued, to lure the workers away from internationalism and reconcile them with the nation. The Nazis loved to portray their leaders as young, charismatic and, above all, 'of the people'. Positive proletarian images of 'good Nazis' were contrasted with negative images of a cosmopolitan bourgeoisie depicted as effeminate, weak and corrupt. Although the anticapitalist wing of the NSDAP was largely emasculated by 1933/34, the continued promise of social integration struck a chord with many workers. The Nazis made 1 May, International Labour Day, a national holiday and praised the workers for their 'German quality work'. A variety of symbolical practices

52 Walter Kempowski, *Das Echolot – Barbarossa 41: Ein kollektives Tagebuch* (Munich, 2002).

53 Alf Lüdtke, 'The Appeal of Exterminating "Others": German Workers and the Limits of Resistance', *Journal of Modern History*, 64 (1992), pp. 46–67; Omer Bartov, *The Eastern Front 1941–45: German Troops and the Barbarization of Warfare*, 2nd edn (Basingstoke, 2001).

54 Paul Weindling, *Health, Race and German Politics: Between National Unification and Nazism 1870–1945* (Cambridge, 1989).

55 Detlev J.K. Peukert, 'The Genesis of the "Final Solution" from the Spirit of Science', in David F. Crew, ed., *Nazism and German Society 1933–1945* (London, 1994), pp. 274–99.

56 Sandrine Kott, 'Der Sozialstaat', in Etienne François and Hagen S. Schulze, eds, *Deutsche Erinnerungsorte*, 3 vols (Munich, 2001), Vol. 2, p. 494.

emphasized the 'honour of labour' in the Third Reich.[57] The National Socialists intended to meet German workers at exactly the place where a large part of their social identity was created, the workplace. The German Labour Front (DAF) sponsored organizations such as Beauty of Labour (*Schönheit der Arbeit*) and Strength through Joy (*Kraft durch Freude*, KdF) which promised better working conditions, greater social status and a better lifestyle to millions of workers.[58]

The DAF promised a welfare state which would provide services and leisuretime activities for workers and break down the social distinction between workers and other social classes. KdF holidays were meant to bring people from different walks of life together and increase their sense of national cohesion. A *Volksgemeinschaft* in leisure was to transcend social class and regional sentiments of belonging. KdF offered educational weekend tours and holidays, where holidaymakers could be educated about Germanic architecture and landscapes. Travel became an important means of affirming national identity in the Third Reich. A 1940 guidebook to the city of Posen, for example, emphasized the German character of the city. It denounced any Polish or Jewish influences on the cityscape and encouraged German settlement and cultural conquest. Similarly, guidebook literature presented Eastern Prussia as a 'land of castles' culturally civilized by the Teutonic Order with their fortress Marienburg as the jewel in the crown.[59] Many of the DAF's activities were propagandistic in nature and never went beyond the planning stage, but it presented workers with a construction of the nation which would at long last incorporate them as equal representatives. One of the DAF's most spectacular schemes involved the financing of the Volkswagen motor company in 1937. The Volkswagen became one of the most popular symbols of the *Volksgemeinschaft*. The motorization of the people was regarded as one more form of practical social policy.[60] Similarly Nazi housing policy was sold to the workers as 'sanitizing' decrepit city centres and improving living standards. The language of urban renewal was in line with the creation of a healthy *Volksgemeinschaft*, while the renewal itself destroyed working-class neighbourhoods which had sustained a proletarian culture in the 1920s.

If workers were one key addressee of Nazi constructions of the nation, peasants were another. In the racial nation 'blood' and 'soil' went together. A racially vibrant peasantry was the key to a racially healthy nation. Richard Walther Darré, the Reich Leader of the Peasants (*Reichsbauernführer*) looked to the Germanic tribes of the past for a lifestyle that was to become Germany's future. Civilization and modernity equalled cultural decay. Germany, Darré argued, had to be reinvented as an agrarian country. After 1933 Aryan peasants could not be expropriated any more, but equally they could not sell their land and were in fact tied to the soil. Markets and prices for agricultural products were tightly controlled by the state. In Goslar, the *Reich* City of the Peasants (*Reichsbauernstadt*), the annual

[57] Alf Lüdtke, 'The "Honor of Labor": Industrial Workers and the Power of Symbols under National Socialism', in Crew, ed., *Nazism and German Society*, pp. 67–109.

[58] Ronald Smelser, *Robert Ley: Hitler's Labour Front Leader* (Oxford, 1988).

[59] Rudy Koshar, *German Travel Cultures* (Oxford, 2000), p. 152f.

[60] Hans Mommsen and Manfred Grieger, *Das Volkswagenwerk und seine Arbeiter im Dritten Reich* (Düsseldorf, 1996).

harvest festival took place under the patronage of Hitler. A proliferation of 'peasant novels' idealized the rural way of life and equated it with true Germanness.[61] The German Society for Architecture laboriously catalogued and analysed German peasant architecture after 1933 and hundreds of rural *Heimat* museums exhibited what they believed to be Germanic peasant culture. A newly created Institute for German Music Research incorporated a large folk music department which was to trace the heritage of German rural musical customs. A rustic and rural Germanism found expression in the Nazi-propagated *Thingspiel*, vast open-air theatre performances with mass choirs and actors. The dominant theme of such open-air mass spectacles was the racial nation and popular titles included 'The Awakening of Germany', 'German Passion 1933' and 'The Play of Job the German'.[62]

Even during the war, the Nazis were careful not to overburden workers and peasants, the 'ordinary man' in the street who had been promised upward social mobility in the racial nation. The war itself and the German occupation of Europe was financed largely by exploiting the occupied territories and robbing European Jewry of its property. But the appeal of the Nazi racial nation was not restricted to the 'ordinary man'; it incorporated also 'ordinary women'. Collectively, women were not victims of the racialized *Volksgemeinschaft*. Certainly, Nazi ideology was anti-emancipatory, antifeminist and antinatalist. The few women who held any kind of position in the higher echelons of civil service, politics and the professions were dismissed after 1933. Those women excluded from the racial community, and they number in the hundreds of thousands, were forcibly sterilized and murdered.[63]

But equally the Nazis offered millions of Aryan German women a firm place in the racial nation. Women were to find their true vocation in caring for their families, their children and the future of the Aryan race. Motherhood was once again depicted primarily as a national vocation; women were the 'mothers of the Volk' (*Volksmütter*). The Nazis honoured motherhood, where the mother's blood was of the right kind. Mother's Day was made into a national holiday. A 'cross of honour' in bronze, silver and gold was introduced for Aryan mothers who had been particularly fertile.[64] Marriage loans made life easier for many newlywed German housewives. Exemplary population and family policies (of course, only for Aryans) benefited women. Pro-natalism was as integral a part of Nazi policies as was antinatalism. Many women gave crucial emotional support to Nazi men and upheld the Nazi vision of a racialized *Volksgemeinschaft*.[65]

[61] Peter Zimmermann, *Der Bauernroman: Antifeudalismus–Konservatismus–Faschismus* (Stuttgart, 1975).

[62] Rainer Stommer, *Die inszenierte Volksgemeinschaft: Die 'Thing-Bewegung' im Dritten Reich* (Marburg, 1985).

[63] Gisela Bock, 'Antinatalism, Maternity and Paternity in National Socialist Racism', in *idem* and Pat Thane, eds, *Maternity and Gender Policies: Women and the Rise of European Welfare States 1880s–1950s* (London, 1990), pp. 253–69.

[64] Irmgard Weyrather, *Muttertag und Mutterkreuz: Der Kult um die 'deutsche Mutter' im Nationalsozialismus* (Frankfurt/Main, 1993).

[65] Claudia Koonz, *Mothers in the Fatherland: Women, the Family and Nazi Politics* (New York, 1987).

Female diary writers during the Second World War identified strongly with Nazi ideology and widely perceived the future of the Nazi regime as identical with the future of Germany.[66] Racism and antisemitism were central to published women's writing during the Nazi years.[67] Even at the height of the Second World War the Nazis refused to introduce conscription for women, whose national service continued to be in the home and for the family.

But the Nazis did not restrict German women tightly to the sphere of family and housekeeping. The increasing feminization of the German workforce since the 1920s was not reversed by the Nazis. Nazi organizations, such as the Association of German Girls (BDM), the Reich Labour Service and the National Socialist Women's League offered millions of women a whole range of opportunities to broaden their social experience and gain spaces for recognition and status outside the sphere of the home.[68] A *völkisch* activist such as Else Frobenius shared the Nazis' anti-Slav and antisemitic ideas and wholeheartedly supported their construction of the racial nation.[69]

It was especially among the younger age groups which had been socialized in the National Socialist state that the national education of the Nazis bore terrible fruit in 1944/5. When it was clear to everyone that Nazi Germany had lost the war these youngsters remained among the most fanatical supporters of the Nazi regime. Thirteen- and fourteen-year-olds volunteered to fight the enemies of the nation and to sacrifice themselves as national heroes. Their devotion to the cause could, however, barely hide the fact that, by this time, the majority of Germans had turned their back on the Nazis' racial nationalism. Even when war broke out in September 1939 the majority of Germans reacted not with enthusiasm but with a kind of fatalist apathy. The devotion to the cause of a Nazified Europe grew with the rapid successes of the German armies between 1939 and 1942. As the Wehrmacht came to occupy vast areas of Europe the Nazis promoted fantasies of a racialized Europe in which Germans would be the dominant master race. Success breeds support and the Nazi nation promised to deliver the goods to those who were lucky enough to count themselves Aryans.

Yet an increasing disillusionment with the racial nation set in after the defeat of Stalingrad in 1943. When the tides of war turned, the destructive nature of Nazi nationalism became self-destructive. If Germany could not win, thus Hitler's dictum, it had to go under. This was entirely in line with the Nazis' Social Darwinist beliefs in a global race struggle which could end only in total success or total failure. Nazi propaganda now focussed on exhortations to hold out. Films such as *Kolberg*,

66 Susanne zur Nieden ' "Ach ich möchte ... eine tapfere deutsche Frau werden": Tagebücher als Quellen zur Erforschung des Nationalsozialismus', in Berliner Geschichtswerkstatt, ed., *Alltagskultur, Subjektivität und Geschichte: Zur Theorie und Praxis von Alltagsgeschichte* (Münster, 1994).

67 Ellen de Visser, *Frau und Krieg: Weibliche Kriegsästhetik, weiblicher Rassismus und Antisemitismus: eine psychoanalytisch-tiefenhermeneutische Literaturanalyse* (Münster, 1997).

68 Jill Stephenson, *The Nazi Organization of Women* (London, 1981).

69 Lora Wildenthal, 'Mass Marketing Colonialism and Nationalism: The Career of Else Frobenius in the "Weimarer Republik" and Nazi Germany', in Ute Planert, ed., *Nation, Politik und Geschlecht: Frauenbewegungen und Nationalismus in der Moderne* (Frankfurt/Main, 2000), pp. 328–45.

depicting the defence of the city of Kolberg against Napoleon in 1807 as a model for contemporary Germans, used the glorious Prussian past once more to rally Germans to the war effort. In the last months of the war many German cities did indeed become fortresses and the German people were told to fight for every house and every street. The famous 'Nero order' of Hitler (not carried out because of Speer's refusal to communicate it further down the line) called on the German army to destroy everything in its wake rather than leave it to the enemy. The scorched earth policy that the Wehrmacht had carried out in the Soviet Union was to be repeated on German soil. However, the majority of Germans had not minded total destruction too much, as long as it had affected others, but they were distinctly unwilling to agree to the Nazis' self-destructive impulses. A growing number of *Volksgenossen* opted out of the Nazis' construction of the racial nation. Nazi authority could only be maintained by means of terror. Most Germans awaited the end of the war and hoped that it might be quick.

The construction of the 'other' Germany

If disillusionment with Nazi constructions of Germany spread rapidly in 1944/45, what alternative constructions of Germanness were available? Those in the vanguard of opposition to Nazism, national-conservatives, Social Democrats, liberals, Christians and Communists, all developed their own national imaginations.[70] The national-conservative resistance included many high-ranking military officers, Prussian aristocrats, senior members of the civil service, and conservative politicians. For the most part they were traditional German nationalists. After 1933 many had been willing to accept the Nazi dictatorship. They tended to share some of the Nazis' key beliefs, such as anti-Communism, antisocialism and frequently antisemitism. They mostly preferred an authoritarian political order to a parliamentary democracy, which they saw as foreign to German traditions and alien to the German national character. Above all they applauded Hitler's plans to lead Germany to greatness again. Many supported the German war effort as long as Germany's armies were advancing in Europe. Some of the military men had their doubts about the racial warfare in the east. The national-conservative resistance included those with strong religious and ethical beliefs who did not share the barbaric underpinnings of Nazi racial nationalism. But many only turned firmly against the dictator when things began to go wrong for the German war effort. Like the majority of Germans, they were unwilling to follow the Nazis into national self-destruction. Instead they sought to come to an understanding with the Western allies which might yet safeguard what they perceived as Germany's national interests. Many even envisaged co-operating with the West to prevent the looming Bolshevization of Europe. And they were willing to kill Hitler to remove what they saw as the major obstacle on the road to a negotiated peace settlement with the Western allies.

[70] Hans Mommsen, 'German Society and the Resistance to Hitler', in *idem, From Weimar to Auschwitz. Essays in German History* (Oxford, 1991), pp. 208–23. See also Peter Hoffmann, *The History of the German Resistance 1933–1945* (Montreal, 1996), and David Clay Large, *Contending with Hitler: Varieties of German Resistance in the Third Reich* (London, 1991).

Defending the nation against the Nazis played a major role in the considerations of the national-conservative resistance. Colonel von Stauffenberg, the man who had left the bomb in a briefcase right next to Hitler in the Wolf's Lair in July 1944, before he was shot by the Nazis, cried out: 'Long live our sacred Germany.' The Germany Stauffenberg had in mind was not the racial nation of the Nazis, but neither was it the liberal democratic nation of the Weimar Republic. Some favoured an estates-based corporate state, others were monarchists and anti-modernists and yet others favoured some kind of authoritarian state with limited electoral rights and oligarchic government. Christian family values were important to many of them, and some, especially those resisters associated with the Kreisau Circle around Hellmuth James von Moltke, thought about a post-war European order in which the sovereignty of nation states would be limited by a European federation. Most, however, wanted to retain a powerful Greater Germany in its 1914 or even in its 1938 boundaries.

A very different nation was imagined by the democratic opposition to Hitler, foremost among which was the SPD. In his speech against the Enabling Law, the Social Democratic member of parliament Otto Wels rejected the Nazis' claim to represent the nation:

> The gentlemen of the National Socialist Party call the movement they have unleashed a national revolution [...] We Social Democrats have carried the burdens of responsibility during the most difficult of times [...] our achievements in the reconstruction of the state and economy, and in the liberation of the occupied territories, will stand before history. We have created equal rights for everyone and socially just industrial law. We have helped to make a Germany where the highest offices of the state are open not only to dukes and barons but to men from the working class. [...] we stand firmly by the principles of the rule of law, and the equal and social rights enshrined in it. In this historic hour we Social Democrats solemnly profess to our belief in the principles of humanity and justice, freedom and socialism.[71]

Many of the fundamental differences between the democratic and the national-conservative resistance are immediately apparent in this passage. The belief in parliamentary democracy made a compromise with dictatorship impossible. The Social Democrats in exile held up Western political models for a reconstructed Germany, above all the United States, Britain, France and Scandinavia. A post-Nazi Germany, they argued, had to be anchored firmly in Western political values. A democratic republic, a parliamentary system and a non-capitalist economy – those were the pillars on which a new Germany had to be rebuilt.[72] Whereas Hitler meant war, a democratic Germany would also be a peaceful Germany. Social Democrats rejected German power policy and the aim of making Germany the hegemonic power in Europe. Instead they supported a collective international

[71] *Stenographische Berichte über die Verhandlungen des Deutschen Reichstages*, Vol. 457, 1933, pp. 32–4.

[72] Rainer Behring, *Demokratische Außenpolitik für Deutschland: Die außenpolitischen Vorstellungen deutscher Sozialdemokraten im Exil 1933–1945* (Düsseldorf, 1999); Erich Matthias, *Sozialdemokratie und Nation: Ein Beitrag zur Ideengeschichte der sozialdemokratischen Emigration in der Prager Zeit des Parteivorstandes, 1933–1938* (Stuttgart, 1952); Anthony Glees, *Exile Politics during the Second World War: The German Social Democrats in Britain* (Oxford, 1982).

system guaranteeing peace and stability and a federal Europe in which the nations would lose some of their sovereign rights.

In the war Social Democrats sided with the Allies against their own Nazified nation. They had been shocked by the reports coming from those of their supporters who remained in hiding inside Germany about the high levels of support for the National Socialists in the 1930s. However, throughout the war, they upheld the distinction between Nazi Germany and the 'real Germany', which they themselves represented. Within the SPD in exile considerable differences of opinion existed as to the extent to which the Germans collectively had been affected by Nazism but the leadership ultimately insisted on the (unrealistic) assumption that underneath the façade of the Nazi nation was another layer of a non-Nazified nation. It showed above all how much Social Democrats identified with the German nation and how fervently they believed in defending what they perceived to be Germany's national interests. The latter had to be defended, if need be, also against the Western allies and their claims of a 'collective guilt' of Germans. The national commitment of the Social Democrats in exile and their vision of a democratic Germany made any rapprochement with the Communists highly problematic. Unlike in France and Spain, a united front between the two working-class parties never emerged in Germany, not even under the conditions of exile.[73]

The KPD had not been averse to using nationalist sentiment when it suited its purposes, such as in 1923,[74] but its construction of the nation took place within a wider Marxist framework of class war. Communism's official verdict on fascism saw in it nothing but 'the open terroristic dictatorship of the most reactionary, most chauvinist, and most imperialist elements of finance capital'.[75] As, according to Marxism-Leninism, the demise of capitalism was inevitable, Nazism was widely underestimated as a last-ditch attempt to bolster capitalist interests. Many Communists greeted Nazism almost triumphantly, claiming: 'after the Nazis it will be our turn'. The KPD put up the strongest resistance to Nazism inside Germany after 1933 and it had the highest number of victims. By 1935/36 almost all of its resistance groups inside Germany had been infiltrated by the Gestapo and its members were either dead or in concentration camps. Many Communists were in a state of shock when the Hitler–Stalin pact was announced in 1939 and Communist resistance to Nazism only slowly came under way again after Hitler's invasion of the Soviet Union in 1941. By now the KPD was far less triumphant than in 1933 and instead it emphasized the need for unity among all anti-Nazi forces.

Stalin's Order of the Day of February 1942 made a clear distinction between Nazis and Germans: 'The Hitlers will come and go, but the German people will go on.' Throughout the war, Soviet propaganda attempted to appeal to national sentiments among German officers and soldiers. The Soviet-backed National

[73] Gerd-Rainer Horn, *European Socialists Respond to Fascism: Ideology, Activism and Contingency in the 1930s* (Oxford, 1996).

[74] See above, p. 125.

[75] G. Dimitrov, General Secretary of the Communist International, 'Speech to the Seventh Congress of the Communist International, Moscow' [August 1935], in *idem*, *The Working Class against Fascism* (London: Lawrence, 1935).

Committee for a Free Germany not only included Communists, but also traditional nationalists such as Colonel von Einsiedel, a nephew of Otto von Bismarck. Stalin's aim was a Communist Germany (and, as far as possible a Communist Europe), but in order to achieve this aim, Communists were told to build alliance with other political forces. Antifascism was seen as the perfect glue to hold such alliances together. In particular the democratic and Communist constructions of the nation respectively were to have an important influence on the shaping of the Federal Republic of Germany (FRG) on the one hand and the German Democratic Republic (GDR) on the other, as we will see in the next two chapters.

6

Towards postnationalism? The Federal Republic of Germany, 1945–1990

A young Jew, Marcel Reich-Ranicki, fled Communist Poland in 1958 and decided to settle in the Federal Republic, despite the fact that he was the only surviving member of his entire family. He was, of course, to become one of the most famous literary critics of Germany. In his memoirs he talks about the significance of an event which happened on a rainy day in Warsaw in December 1970. The chancellor of West Germany, Willy Brandt, had gone to lay a wreath in front of the memorial to the Jewish rising in the Warsaw ghetto against their Nazi oppressors. Standing in front of the memorial, he fell to his knees in a powerful gesture of atonement [Figure 6.1]. The socialist Brandt, who had been exiled by the Nazis and actively fought against them, made a grand public gesture accepting German guilt before the eyes of the world. Reich-Ranicki writes of his strong feelings of gratitude towards Brandt: 'I still recall very well what went through my head, when, in 1970, I saw the photo of the kneeling German chancellor: at that moment I thought that my decision to return to Germany and to settle in the FRG in 1958 was, after all, not the wrong decision, that it was, after all, the right decision.'[1]

Victims of the National Socialist tyranny like Reich-Ranicki applauded Brandt, but not everyone agreed. Brandt polarized the West German public like no other chancellor in the history of the FRG. In the 1969 general election he was the object of an intense hate campaign initiated by his political opponents, who alleged that he had betrayed the nation in the Second World War. They tried to make heavy weather of his name change from Frahm to Brandt, which was connected to his illegal antifascist activities inside Germany during the Third Reich. Günter Grass, a staunch supporter of Brandt, picked up on the widespread resentment against the chancellor in his collection of vignettes on the twentieth century. He again focusses on Brandt's gesture in Warsaw, this time as seen through the

1 Marcel Reich-Ranicki, *Mein Leben* (Munich, 2000), p. 550f.

Figure 6.1 Willy Brandt kneeling in front of the Warsaw Ghetto memorial, 1970, © Bildarchiv Preussischer Kulturbesitz, Berlin. Photo: Hanns Hubmann.

eyes of a fictitious hostile journalist attending the event:

> My paper will never buy this. They'd like to have some waffle, such as 'Took all guilt upon himself ...' or 'Suddenly the chancellor fell on his knees ...' or even laying it on really thick: 'Kneeling for Germany!' They must be joking: suddenly! It was planned to the smallest detail. I am certain that this wily devil, you know, his interlocutor and negotiator,[2] has given him the idea of this special number. He knows how to sell the humiliating sell-out of arch-German land as a victory at home. And now his boss, this drunkard, behaves as though he is more Catholic than the Pope. As if he would believe in anything. All pure showbizz [...] This emigrant! How he gets on my nerves. Not because he is an illegitimate child ... That sort of thing can happen ... But otherwise ... His whole pompous behaviour ... And when he knelt there in the drizzle ... Sickening ... How I hate him. Well, he will be surprised when he gets home. They will tear him and his Ostverträge apart. Not only in my paper. But you have to give it to him, it was accomplished, this thing, simply onto his knees.[3]

Brandt's visit to Warsaw had been part of his government's policy of *Ostpolitik*. After decades in which the West German political elite refused to have any contact with Eastern European Communist regimes, the Brandt government, in line with a new international spirit of détente, opened a dialogue in the hope of achieving 'change through rapprochement'. For his efforts to overcome the stalemate and achieve reconciliation he was awarded the Nobel Peace Prize in 1971. The social-liberal government under Brandt marked a new beginning not only in relation to foreign policy, but also in terms of domestic policy. In his first speech as chancellor before parliament he stated:

> We want to dare to be more democratic. We will make government more transparent and be more forthcoming with information. [...] In the coming years one of the most powerful forces in various realms of our society will be codetermination and coresponsibility. [...] We want to create a society which offers more freedom and demands more coresponsibility. The government stands for dialogue; it looks for a critical partnership with all those who carry responsibility. [...] If we want to do what has to be done then we need to make use of all active forces in our society. [...] In our Federal Republic we are being faced with the necessity of comprehensive reforms. [...] In a democracy any government can only be successful if it is supported by the democratic engagement of the citizens. [...] We need people who are critical, who want to take decisions and carry responsibility. The self-confidence of this government will reveal itself as tolerance. It will value the kind of solidarity which expresses itself in criticism. We are not chosen, we are elected. This is why we are seeking a dialogue with all those who care for this democracy. [...] Over the last years some in this country have had fears that the second German democracy might follow the course of the first. I never believed this to be the case. Today I believe it less than ever. No: We are not standing at the end of our democracy, we are only just about to begin.[4]

What Brandt offered to do here was to integrate all those political forces who were discontented with Konrad Adenauer, with the long rule of Christian

2 Egon Bahr, close friend and advisor of Brandt and one of the key architects of the social democratic *Ostpolitik*. On Brandt's biography in English see Barbara Marshall, *Willy Brandt* (London, 1990). Also his autobiography: Willy Brandt, *My Life in Politics* (New York, 1992).

3 Günter Grass, *Mein Jahrhundert* (Göttingen, 1999), pp. 257, 260.

4 Willy Brandt, 'Aus der Regierungserklaerung des Bundeskanzlers, vor dem deutschen Bundestag, 28. Oktober 1969', in *idem*, *Mehr Demokratie wagen: Innen- und Gesellschaftspolitik 1966–1974* (Bonn, 2001), pp. 218–24.

Democracy over German politics, with the stifling authoritarianism of the 1950s and with the lack of serious debate about National Socialism. He offered to relegitimate the FRG for those who felt marginalized in Adenauer's state. At the end of the 1960s there was a strong feeling in large sections of German society that what was needed was a more tolerant, liberal, pluralist and democratic society. In other words, what was needed was a new beginning, and this was precisely what the young, popular and good-looking mayor of Berlin had to offer. The 1960s have been described as a 'hinge decade', in which the modernization of West German society, which had begun in the 1950s, accelerated and brought a break with many traditional aspects of German society.[5] Willy Brandt symbolized that break in both foreign and domestic politics. What he stood for was a new vision of the nation, a more democratic nation, for sure, but also a nation which would no longer orient itself towards the *Reich* nation, i.e. the one founded by Bismarck in 1871. When he talked about 'our country' he meant, first and foremost, the FRG, and he was willing to accept the (perhaps long-term) division of Germany as the outcome of German history in the first half of the twentieth century. This had been very different after the end of the Second World War.

This chapter will start off by analysing how Germany was reconstructed as victim rather than perpetrator post-1945 and how the invention of a 'good nationalism' emerged from the ashes of National Socialism. In the 1950s anti-Communism rather than antifascism was the key ideology legitimating the new state, but it was not the only one. We will explore the role of pro-Europeanism and of economic success in reforging Germanness after the end of the Second World War. As indicated above, the long 1960s (ranging from the late 1950s to the early 1970s) marked a major watershed in the history of the FRG. In the final sections of this chapter we will comment on the diverse ways in which West Germany redefined itself during this crucial decade. In particular we shall pay attention to constructions of Germany as a failed nation which gained wider currency in the 1980s.

Re-education and the construction of Germany as victim of Hitler

In 1945 Germany ceased to exist. The Allies insisted that any reinvention of Germany was to be done under Allied control. They feared the re-emergence of a German nationalism which was keen on revenge. Prussia, perceived by the Allies as the epicentre of everything that was wrong with Germany – militarism, expansionism, authoritarianism and unthinking obedience – was dissolved by Allied decree. At the Potsdam conference in 1945 they decided to drop plans to dismember Germany permanently. Instead they declared their intention to administer the occupied territories as one. They drew provisional new borders and legitimated the expulsion of millions of ethnic Germans from territories east of these new borders. Very soon, however, the Cold War would make any meaningful co-operation between the Soviet Union and the Western allies impossible. Their

[5] Axel Schildt, Detlef Siegfried and Karl Christian Lammers, eds, *Dynamische Zeiten: Die 60er Jahre in den beiden deutschen Gesellschaften* (Hamburg, 2000).

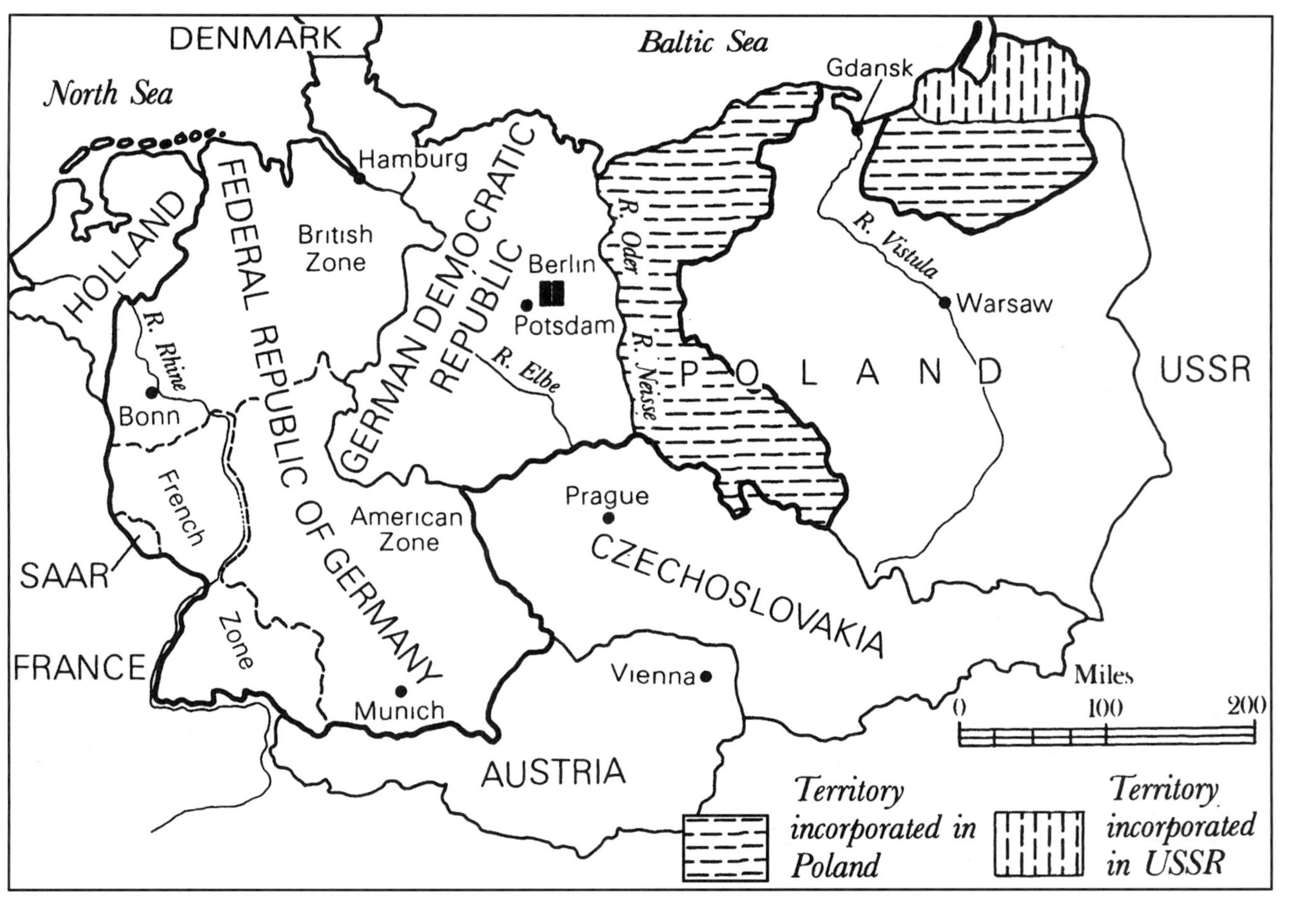

Map 5 Divided Germany, 1945.

ideas about how Germany was going to be reinvented proved mutually exclusive and the setting up of two German states in 1949 was the direct outcome of entirely different developments in the Western zones of occupation and the Soviet one.

The new political elites in the Eastern and Western zones of occupation were not in a position to resist the division of their country. They made a feeble attempt to discuss ways of preventing such a division at Munich in May 1947, but the East and West German delegations could not even agree on a common agenda. Hence West German politicians ultimately agreed in 1948 to Allied demands to set up a separate West German state. A constitutional assembly was to work on a constitution for that new state. The outcome, the FRG's Basic Law, was reinventing Germany as a liberal-democratic nation which had learnt its lessons from the demise of the Weimar Republic. A range of perceived structural weaknesses of the Weimar constitution were ironed out and the FRG constituted itself as '*wehrhafte Demokratie*' – a democracy which would actively fight the enemies of democracy. Bonn, in the famous phrase of Fritz René Allemann, was not going to be Weimar.[6] The Basic Law amounted to a bid of the reinvented West Germans to be accepted into the community of liberal-democratic nation states of the West which had positioned themselves against the Communist states of Eastern Europe. As this bid had been encouraged by the Western allies, there was going to be no problem with getting accepted. However, the relationship between the newly baptised democratic West Germans and the Western allies was not going to be entirely smooth and straightforward.

Many in the Allied camp believed firmly that the German 'national character' suffered from serious flaws and that the German people were in need of re-education after twelve years of Nazism. In 1945 they had used shock tactics to confront Germans with the results of the Holocaust: photos of piles of corpses in the liberated concentration camps were displayed in public. Germans were forced to march through the camps and witness the horrific results of the Nazi racial state. A film about the camps, *Die Todesmühlen*, was shown in all cinemas. The war crimes trials of leading Nazis in Nuremberg were given the widest possible exposure in newspapers and on the radio. The Allies wanted to encourage the development of feelings of guilt and remorse.[7] Their efforts were reflected in vigorous debates in the press. In August and October 1945, both the Protestant and the Catholic churches published official statements deploring their complicity in supporting the Nazi regime and in not having done enough to oppose its crimes. The philosopher Karl Jaspers, in a much-commented-on lecture series in Heidelberg in 1946, argued that Germans collectively were guilty as these crimes had been committed in the name of the German nation. But during the post-war years it became increasingly clear that the overwhelming majority of Germans was going to be unwilling to accept their casting in the role of perpetrator and villain. They perceived Allied denazification as victor's justice and resented Allied attempts to re-educate Germans towards democracy. Instead they reinvented Germany as victim of Hitler and the Nazis.

The newly founded FRG liquidated the legacy of Allied denazification. Broad amnesties were put in place in 1949 and 1954 and convicted war criminals were

6 Fritz René Allemann, *Bonn ist nicht Weimar* (Cologne, 1956).

7 Dagmar Barnouw, *Germany 1945: Views of War and Violence* (Bloomington, Indiana, 1996).

set free again. Nazi civil servants were re-employed generously and virtually all Nazis (except the top layer) could continue their careers in the FRG as long as they were willing to support the new political order and remain quiet about their past. The political boundaries to the far right were drawn rigorously. Neo-Nazism was not tolerated. But the ideal of the *Volksgemeinschaft* continued to have a deep impact on many Germans who were quick to demonstrate solidarity with persecuted former Nazi officials, but showed little concern for the victims of the National Socialist terror regime.[8]

It was, of course, impossible to be entirely silent about Nazism in the post-war period: 'far from being totally repressed and silenced, the Third Reich was everywhere: in everyday life, in gestures and modes of speech, in school text-books and films, in political rhetoric and novels, in tourist guidebooks and travelogues.'[9] But the appropriation of that most immediate past was highly selective. Take, for example, the foundation of the Institute of Contemporary History in Munich, initially named the Institute for Research on National Socialism, in 1950. It immediately set about researching Nazism, but certain aspects, such as the Holocaust and the socialist/communist exile and resistance did not become serious topics for research until the 1960s.

In films such as Roberto Rosselini's *Germania: Anno Zero* images of a morally bankrupt people in a totally destroyed country dominated. For decades Germany was to remain a 'post-war society', in which the diverse traumas of the war left deep imprints on national identities.[10] Immediately after 1945 there was much talk about the need for moral renewal. The historian Friedrich Meinecke called for the moral renewal of Germany through the foundation of Goethe societies which would promote religious values and classical German culture. Religion and culture went hand in hand to develop the themes of harmony, reconciliation and forgiveness without making the question of German guilt a major topic. The influence of the churches in the immediate post-war years was considerable. The Christian memory of the war was dominated by themes of sacrifice and redemption. The 200-year celebrations of Goethe's birth in 1949 reminded Germans of a national past untainted by Nazism. Intellectuals keen to overcome the legacy of Nazism called for a revival of humanistic German traditions. References to German cultural achievements at times served the purpose of opposing Allied attempts at re-education. The post-war West German nation preferred an image of the nation of poets and philosophers to an image of mass murderers. Hence national landmarks, including many churches, were being rebuilt across the FRG. References to wartime destruction did not incorporate references to Nazism or German guilt. The war appeared as a kind of natural disaster and biblical metaphors of floods and pestilence abounded. It was depicted as

8 Norbert Frei, *Adenauer's Germany and the Nazi Past: The Politics of Amnesty and Integration* (New York, 2002).

9 Alon Confino and Rudy Koshar, 'Regimes of Consumer Culture: New Narratives in Twentieth-Century German History', *German History*, 19 (2001), p. 150. See also Robert G. Moeller, 'What Has "Coming to Terms with the Past" Meant in Post-World War II Germany? From History to Memory to the "History of Memory"', *Central European History*, 35 (2002), pp. 223–56.

10 Klaus Naumann, ed., *Nachkrieg in Deutschland* (Hamburg, 2001).

something outside of human, let alone German control. The reconstruction of national monuments was a mechanism for distancing Germany from the responsibility for the Second World War.[11]

Feelings of guilt were drowned by feelings of self-pity. In a public letter Walter von Molo, author of historical novels, wrote to Thomas Mann after 1945 and asked him to return to Germany to demonstrate to the world that there were good Germans and to help heal the 'trampled hearts' of his fellow countrymen. His plea specifically included the conviction that the majority of Germans had stayed morally upright during the Nazi years. Thomas Mann's response was one of the most stinging rejections of this idea of German innocence:

> Are we to wipe these twelve years and their events from the board and can one pretend that they did not happen? The loss of the usual everyday life, of house and land, books, memorabilia and property, accompanied by miserable actions at home, rebuffs and rejections, was difficult enough, breathtaking enough, in 1933. ... What happened next, the wandering from country to country, the passport difficulties, the existence in hotels, while all the time the ears hurt when hearing the despicable stories which came daily from the country which one had lost, and which was turning increasingly wild and totally alien, all this was difficult enough. All of this, you, who swore loyalty to the 'charismatic Führer' (terrible, terrible, the drunken intellect!) and who did culture under Goebbels, have not experienced. I do not forget that later on you have gone through far worse which I escaped: but that you have not known: the emigrant's asthma of the heart, the experience of being uprooted, the nervous terrors of not having a *Heimat*. ... That everything came as it did is not my doing. How completely and utterly it is not! It is a result of the character and the fate of the German people – a people curious enough, tragically interesting enough that one endures many things from it. But then one should also accept the results and not let everything end in a banal 'Come back, everything is forgiven![12]

Mann was, in any case, one of the few who had been asked to come back. The West German government never asked those half a million people who had been hounded out of Germany by the Nazis to return. The 6 per cent who did find their way back often faced rejection: they had, after all, not been part of the national community. Their presence was an unpleasant reminder of how artificial the construction of Germany as victim of the Second World War was.[13] Compensation for victims of Nazism functioned according to the principle: too little too late. Especially communists and victims in Eastern Europe received nothing at all in the 1950s and 1960s. Payments to the state of Israel were made under pressure from the Western allies and were a calculated move to restore the credibility of the FRG. Any compensation payments to victims of National Socialism were deeply unpopular with the German population – another sign that there was little consciousness of guilt or remorse among ordinary Germans.

---

11 Rudy Koshar, *Preservation and National Memory in the Twentieth Century: Germany's Transient Past* (Chapel Hill, 1998), pp. 218ff. See also Peter Reichel, *Politik mit der Erinnerung: Gedächtnisorte im Streit um die nationalsozialistische Vergangenheit* (Munich, 1995).

12 Cited in Hermann Glaser, *Kulturgeschichte der Bundesrepublik Deutschland*, Vol. 1: *Zwischen Kapitulation und Währungsreform 1945–1948* (Munich, 1985), p. 96f.

13 Marita Kraus, *Heimkehr in ein fremdes Land: Geschichte der Remigration nach 1945* (Munich, 2001).

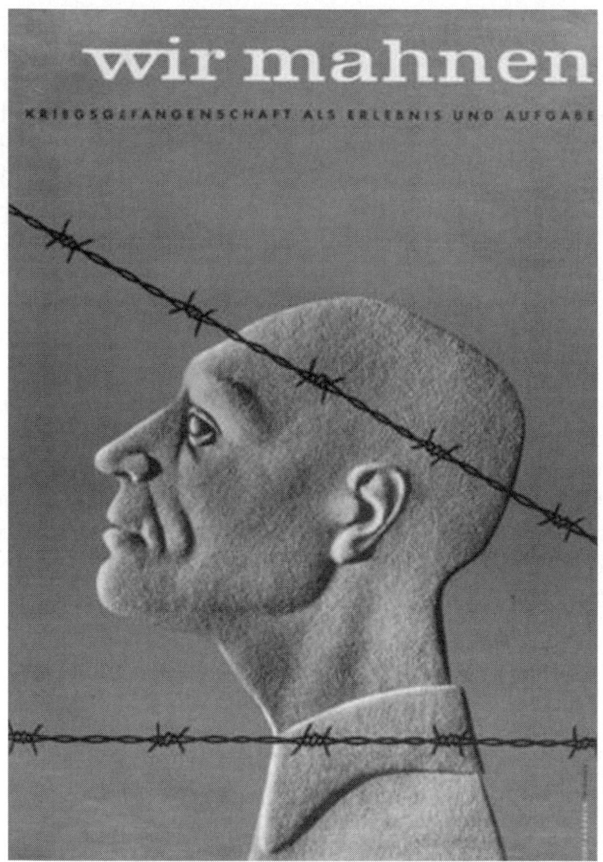

Figure 6.2 'Remember: prisoners of war, experience and task for the future'; exhibition poster of a travelling exhibition organized by the Society for War Returnees (1953), © Bundesarchiv Koblenz.

The criminal energies of the racial nationalism of the Nazis and its power of persuasion over many Germans were forgotten.

Not Jews, but German prisoners of war in the Soviet Union were remembered as the main victims of war in the 1950s. Several war films and exhibitions focussed on the honesty and suffering of the ordinary German soldier.[14] Germans were depicted as the real victims of war and National Socialism.[15] The image of prisoners with shaved heads behind barbed wire was not (yet) the archetypal image of the Nazi concentration camps but served to highlight the plight of the German prisoners of war in the Soviet Union[16] [Figure 6.2]. H.G. Konsalik's novel

[14] Robert G. Moeller, 'Geschichten aus der "Stacheldrahtuniversität": Kriegsgefangene im Opferdiskurs der Bundesrepublik', *WerkstattGeschichte,* 26 (2000), pp. 23–46.

[15] Michael L. Hughes, ' "Through No Fault of Our Own": West Germans Remember their War Losses', *German History*, 18 (2000), pp. 193–213.

[16] Robert Moeller, 'War Stories: The Search for a Usable Past in the Federal Republic of Germany', *American Historical Review*, 101 (1996), p. 1029.

The Doctor of Stalingrad celebrated the moral superiority of German prisoners of war over mean Soviet prison guards. Its sales figures were phenomenal compared to the relative obscurity of major memoirs by Holocaust survivors. Germans also felt themselves to be victims of the Allied aerial bombardment and of the post-war dismantling of German industries. But arguably the most powerful symbol of German suffering was the plight of the 12 million refugees and expellees who had to leave their homes in east-central Europe. They were often greeted by their West German compatriots with derision and treated badly, but the Equalization of Burdens Law (*Lastenausgleichsgesetz*) of 1952 provided for a major transfer of funds from those who had retained their homes in West Germany to those who had left everything in 'the German east'.[17]

The citizenship laws in the FRG remained essentially ethnic in character, allowing the rapid integration of all refugees and expellees of German origin. Article 116 of the Basic Law gave automatic citizenship rights to all those who had been citizens of the German *Reich* in 1937. Furthermore the Expellees' Law (*Bundesvertriebenengesetz*) of 1961 stated categorically that everyone was German who had felt himself to be German in his home country and who could demonstrate his belonging through ethnic descent, linguistic ability, education and culture. The memorialization of the experiences of the refugees and expellees was officially sanctioned and generously funded.[18] Politicians constantly spoke about their sacrifices, official monuments were dedicated to them, and historians embarked on a major historical research project between 1951 and 1961 to document their suffering comprehensively. The travelling exhibition 'German *Heimat* in the East', shown in all major German cities from 1950 onwards, emphasized that the 'lost territories in the East' were deeply imprinted by German culture and civilization. The violent removal of millions of Germans from these areas, it argued, created a void which could not be filled by the Slav population of these countries. The belief in the German civilizing mission in eastern Europe was still alive and well.

The reinvention of Germany as a victim of Hitler's war served as an effective barrier against Allied re-education efforts. However, Allied reinventions of Germany nevertheless left their mark on West Germany in a variety of ways. 'Fraternization' between Allied troops and German Fräuleins was widespread. In particular American technical equipment and consumer goods became objects of desire, especially for the young. West German radio emulated a model provided by the British BBC, and TV was geared towards American models. From the mid-1950s onwards younger male Germans sought their role models in America. James Dean and Marlon Brando became the heroes of a generation struggling against conformism and authoritarianism. Throughout the history of post-war

17 Michael L. Hughes, *Shouldering the Burdens of Defeat: West Germany and the Reconstruction of Social Justice* (Chapel Hill, 1999); Perrti Ahonen, *After the Expulsion: West Germany and Eastern Europe 1945–1990* (Oxford, 2004).

18 Wolfgang Benz, ed., *Die Vertreibung der Deutschen aus dem Osten: Ursache, Ereignisse, Folgen* (Frankfurt/Main, 1995); Dirk Hoffmann, Marita Krauss and Michael Schwartz, eds, *Vertriebene in Deutschland: Interdisziplinäre Ergebnisse und Forschungsperspektiven* (Munich, 2000).

West German film, images of the USA were crucially important: 'America functions as a site of projection, a place where unsure individuals see themselves in sharper focus. In the process America acts as a mirror image, a catalyst for self formation, a reflection against which one can better define oneself.'[19] Among intellectuals, the hunger for Western culture, long absent during the Third Reich, was considerable. Authors such as Ernest Hemingway and Joseph Conrad were now among the most popular in Germany. The libraries of the British Council and the America houses, as well as the Institut Française, served as important bridges for the cultural transfer of Western culture to the FRG. The avant-garde of West German composers turned its back on national traditions which, they felt, were irrevocably tainted by National Socialism. Instead they endorsed the atonalism of Arnold Schönberg and his school, and moved to serialism and esoteric electronic music.[20] A more popular rejection of Nazi cultural tastes was the highly successful import of jazz into post-war Germany. However, jazz was soon recommended as an antidote to rock and roll youth culture and it became a Cold War stick with which to beat the East German Communists, who repressed jazz music as expression of American imperialism.[21]

Western, in particular American, ideas also impacted on West German political culture.[22] The establishment of a bipolar party system with the CDU and the SPD representing different reinventions of Germany but accepting a common democratic framework was an important new beginning. In the 1950s the SPD underwent a long and complex transformation in which it sought to shed its traditional class-fixation and develop an appeal across the social classes. After 1945, the CDU had been founded as a self-conscious biconfessional Christian party. It wanted to overcome the ghettoization of the Catholic milieu and it successfully marginalized the old mouthpiece of political Catholicism, the Centre Party. The old milieu-fixation of the German party-political system disappeared. Parties reconstituted themselves as people's parties or catch-all parties which appealed to the broadest possible spectrum of voters. The rapid acceptance of the concept of people's parties, though, had arguably more to do with the lingering ideal of the *Volksgemeinschaft* than with Westernization: overcoming class and milieu boundaries and realizing what was best for the nation was something that had, after all, been preached by the Nazis.

Throughout the 1950s strong antiliberal and anti-Western forces were still at work, for example in German Protestantism, conservatism and among German journalists. But at the same time West German society was moving towards

[19] Eric Rentschler, 'How American is it: the US as Image and Imaginary in German Film', in Terri Ginsberg and Kirsten M. Thompson, eds, *Perspectives on German Cinema* (New York, 1996), p. 288.

[20] Gesa Kordes, 'Darmstadt, Postwar Experimentation and the West German Search for a New Musical Identity', in Celia Applegate and Pamela Potter, eds, *Music and German National Identity* (Chicago, 2002), pp. 205–17.

[21] Uta G. Poiger, *Jazz, Rock, and Rebels: Cold War Politics and American Culture in a Divided Germany* (Berkeley, 2000).

[22] Anselm Doering-Manteuffel, *Wie westlich sind die Deutschen? Amerikanisierung und Westernisierung im 20. Jahrhundert* (Göttingen, 1999).

'modern times'.[23] Institutions, values, habits, symbols and generally ways of doing things became recognizably more Western during the 1950s and helped to overcome the legacies of political Romanticism and anti-Enlightenment thinking that had played such a major role in nineteenth- and early twentieth-century Germany. American liberal ideals were introduced through the Congress for Cultural Freedom, and German trade unionism after 1945 was influenced through its contacts with its American and British counterparts. But Westernization did not happen overnight. The 1950s were a decade of transition in which a very traditional German society was still highly visible and a more Westernized Federal Republic was in the making.

Reconstructing a 'good nationalism' vis-à-vis a 'bad racism'

In post-war West Germany Nazism was almost exclusively identified with racism rather than racial nationalism. Racism was something to be eradicated, and the state made considerable efforts to deracialize Germanness, for example over the issue of the largely illegitimate mixed-race children, the product of liaisons between black occupation soldiers and German mothers.[24] Public debates about the impact of racial nationalism on German society and the popularity of Nazism as a genuinely national movement were, on the other hand, rare. Instead Hitler was demonized as an evil spirit in German history. The success of the Nazis was described as an almost inexplicable mystical breakthrough of the irrational, a kind of freak accident in Germany's national history.

In 1950 leading historians of Germany assembled in the Ranke Society to combat what they perceived as the one-sided and negative falsification of German national history.[25] They, like Hans Rothfels, head of the West German historians' association between 1958 and 1962, continued to idealize the 'splendour and authenticity' of the nationalism of the Langemarck volunteers.[26] Gerhard Ritter, another doyen of West German historiography, warned repeatedly not to abandon national pride but to recreate a strong and 'healthy' national identity. There were exceptions to the rule, such as Friedrich Meinecke, who at least began

[23] Axel Schildt and Arnold Sywottek, eds, *Modernisierung im Wiederaufbau: Die westdeutsche Gesellschaft der 50er Jahre* (Bonn, 1998). See also Arnold Sywottek, 'The Americanization of Everyday Life? Early Trends in Consumer and Leisure-Time Behaviour', in Michael Ermath, ed., *America and the Shaping of German Society 1945–1955* (Oxford, 1993); Axel Schildt, 'From Reconstruction to "Leisure Society": Freetime, Recreational Behaviour and the Discourse on Leisure Time in the West German Recovery Society of the 1950s', *Contemporary European History*, 5 (1996), pp. 191–222; Paul Betts, 'German Modernity as New Historical Object', *Journal of Urban History*, 25 (1999), pp. 874–82.

[24] Heide Fehrenbach, 'Of German Mothers and "Negermischlingskinder": Race, Sex and the Postwar Nation', in Hanna Schissler, ed., *The Miracle Years: A Cultural History of West Germany, 1949–1968* (Princeton, 2001), pp. 164–86.

[25] Manfred Asendorf, 'Was weiter wirkt. Die "Ranke-Gesellschaft" – Vereinigung für Geschichte im öffentlichen Leben', *1999*, 4 (1989), pp. 29–61.

[26] Hans Rothfels, 'Zur Krise des Nationalstaats', *Vierteljahreshefte zur Zeitgeschichte*, 1 (1953), p. 142.

to locate the 'German catastrophe' in specific German national traditions, such as Prussian militarism and the alleged weakness of the German bourgeoisie. But overall, the public debate about national identity during the first half of the 1950s was dominated by those who sought – behind a rhetorical smokescreen of lament about the loss of the nation state – to rescue and re-establish, in somewhat modified forms, many of the old nationalist apologias.

Imperial Germany was frequently glorified as the happiest hour of the German nation. The 'greater German question' was at long last put to rest after 1945, as Austria began the difficult path of reinventing its own separate national history from that of Germany.[27] The small-German identity focussed on the Bismarckian *Reich* became the anchor-point of all discussions about national identity in the early FRG. The search was on for positive national traditions which could lay to rest the arguments of those foreign and domestic critics that Germany's national history was one big failure culminating in the years between 1933 and 1945. Thus, for example, the centenary of the 1848 revolution provided ample opportunity to highlight indigenous liberal-democratic traditions. The Weimar Republic became another precedent on the road to liberal democracy. When, in 1952, the third stanza of the *Deutschlandlied* (which talked a lot about unity and freedom) became the national anthem of West Germany, one had to overlook the fact that the first stanza (which talked a lot about a greater Germany) had been sung by the Nazis, often alongside the Horst-Wessel-Song. Instead the song's roots in 1848 (its author Hoffmann von Fallersleben was a liberal democrat) were emphasized as was the fact that it had been made the national anthem of all Germans by the first Social Democratic president of the Weimar Republic, Friedrich Ebert, in 1922.[28]

Part of the good nationalism which could still be celebrated after 1945 was the German tradition of federalism. The FRG established a federal political system in which central and regional government were entangled in a complex web of devolved decision-making processes. Recourse to federalism was connected to a revival of the *Heimat* concept. Idyllic descriptions of *Heimat* figured strongly in post-war populur music (*Schlager*) and film.[29] *Heimat* films such as *Schwarzwaldmädel* (1950) and *Grün ist die Heide* (1951) consisted of idyllic scenes set in the beautiful German countryside to the tunes of traditional German folk songs. They highlighted themes of social harmony and love leading to matrimony and stable family life. This message appealed in an increasingly prosperous post-war cultural community intent on not talking too much about some of the most problematic aspects of the immediate Nazi past. The only time when the post-war national discourse happily took recourse to the Nazi years was when it came to celebrate the national-conservative resistance to the Nazi regime which served as a reminder that there had been a good nationalist Germany resisting the evil Nazis in the Third Reich. The opening of the Memorial

27 Ernst Bruckmüller, *Nation Österreich* (Vienna, 1994).

28 Margarete Myers Feinstein, 'Deutschland über alles? The National Anthem Debate in the Federal Republic of Germany', *Central European History*, 33 (2000), pp. 505–31.

29 André Port le Roi, *Schlager lügen nicht: Deutscher Schlager und Politik in ihrer Zeit* (Essen, 1998), p. 94.

to the German Resistance (*Gedenkstätte deutscher Widerstand*) was a deliberate attempt to provide role models for the new Germany and overcome popular prejudices which preferred to see members of the resistance as 'traitors to the nation' well into the 1950s.

Many Germans chose to take a break from politics after 1945 and to privatize their war experiences: compensation for the lost war was sought not in radical nationalist politics, as after the First World War, but in the spheres of family and work.[30] Reinventing the nation meant first and foremost reconstructing family life and the traditional gender order. Germany had 7.3 million more women than men in 1945. *Trümmerfrauen* (rubble women), rebuilding the destroyed German cities, are among the most enduring images of the immediate post-war years. Many households were headed by single, divorced or widowed women who acquired a strong sense of self-confidence and self-sufficiency. The men who returned from the war, by contrast, found it difficult to adapt to civilian life. Many, like Wolfgang Koeppen's fictitious Beckmann in the play *Draußen vor der Tür* (1946), were physically handicapped and psychologically damaged. Such an inversion of the traditional gender order was attacked by those intent on reconstructing a healthy new feeling of national consciousness. Women, fraternizing with the former enemy, were accused of betraying the nation:

> Germany is destroyed and dismembered. We have become completely destitute. Sorrow, desperation, despair oppress many. But in the midst of all this trouble and affliction, a sinister craze of pleasure-seeking runs through the Volk. Numerous German women and girls degrade themselves through licentious behaviour. [...] Such women and girls forget their honour and dignity; they forget the thousands of graves that surround them. They forget the frightful plague of starvation and dying in the East. They forget their husbands, brothers, sons, boyfriends, who are still imprisoned or missing. They forget the many thousands of war-wounded. They forget the entire plight and affliction of the Fatherland.[31]

Redomesticating women became one of the major aims of West Germany's family policy. Franz-Josef Wuermeling, family minister between 1953 and 1962, wanted to make the family the foundation stone of the emerging post-war social order. Both Nazism and Communism had, he argued, subjected the family to the needs of the state. In the FRG the family would come first and the state would be the servant of a strong and stable family life. School books portrayed women mainly as housewives, mothers and smaller sisters.[32] Article 3 of the Basic Law stated categorically that women and men were equal, and for the first time in German history women could determine their citizenship independently and regardless of whom they married. But even the so-called Equality Law of 1958 still made the right of women to gainful employment dependent on its compatibility with their 'duties in marriage and family'.

[30] Vera Neumann, *Nicht der Rede wert: Die Privatisierung der Kriegsfolgen in der frühen Bundesrepublik. Lebensgeschichtliche Erinnerungen* (Münster, 1999).

[31] A Protestant High Consistory (Oberkirchenrat) in Stuttgart, cited in Heide Fehrenbach, *Cinema in Democratizing Germany: Reconstrucing National Identity after Hitler* (Chapel Hill, 1995), p. 99.

[32] Christiane Schmerl, *Das Frauen- und Mädchenbild in den Medien* (Opladen, 1984), p. 74.

'Protecting motherhood' and its values of domesticity and clean living became one of the leading themes of post-war German reconstruction.[33] Any specifically female experiences of suffering in and immediately after the war as well as their experiences of empowerment were, by contrast, submerged in the general German national suffering.[34] Films such as *The Sinner* (*Die Sünderin*), released in January 1951 and featuring Hildegard Knef, became major public scandals not because of brief nudity scenes, but because they depicted strong and active women and juxtaposed them with weak and damaged men. Thereby they challenged the post-war project of re-domesticating women and re-empowering men.[35] Popular American Western movies such as *High Noon* supported ideas about manly courage in the service of the community and underlined traditional gender roles of a duty-bound masculinity and an obedient femininity.[36] Defeated, disillusioned and broken men regained their dominant position in various spheres of life during the 1950s: they became once again providers for families and architects of 'German quality workmanship' and the 'economic miracle'.[37]

One important means of gendering the nation in more traditional patriarchal ways was the representation of war veterans not as broken men but as conquerors of both Nazi and Communist inhumanity. This was precisely how the last German prisoners of war were presented as they returned from the Soviet Union in 1955.[38] They were portrayed as honest soldiers who had fought a senseless war on behalf of fanatical Nazis and who had suffered under the brutality of the Communists. Adenauer, 'the good father of Germany',[39] had returned them to their families. The refound unity of these families became a symbol of the ultimate goal of a unified Germany.

The image of the 'honest German soldier' not only helped to reconsolidate a patriarchal gender order, it also was a powerful argument legitimating the build-up of the West German army, the Bundeswehr. In April 1951 Adenauer went on record in parliament to defend the German soldier: 'Those war criminals which have violated the laws of humanity do not deserve our mercy ... But the percentage of those, who are really guilty, is so extraordinarily small that the honour of the former German Wehrmacht is not compromised.'[40] Germans could mourn their war dead as 'victims of war and dictatorship' – thus the inscription on the central memorial to the German war dead erected on the site of the North Cemetery in Bonn. The myth of a clean Wehrmacht allowed former Nazi generals to rebuild a West German army against the strong opposition of vast sections

33 Robert G. Moeller, *Protecting Motherhood: Women and the Family in the Politics of Postwar Germany* (Berkeley, 1993).

34 Elizabeth Heinemann, '"The Hour of the Woman": Memories of Germany's "Crisis Years" and West German National Identity', *American Historical Review*, 101 (1996), pp. 354–95.

35 Fehrenbach, *Cinema*, Chapter 4 (see note 31).

36 Uta G. Poiger, 'A New "Western" Hero? Reconstructing German Masculinity in the 1950s', in Schissler, ed., *Miracle*, pp. 412–27 (see note 24).

37 Robert G. Moeller, *War Stories: The Search for a Usable Past in the Federal Republic of Germany* (Berkeley, 2001).

38 Robert G. Moeller, 'Heimkehr ins Vaterland: Die Remaskulinisierung Westdeutschlands in den fünfziger Jahren', *Militärgeschichtliche Zeitschrift*, 60 (2001), pp. 403–36.

39 Cited in *ibid.*, p. 410. On Adenauer generally see Ronald Irving, *Adenauer* (Basingstoke, 2002).

40 *Stenographische Berichte des Bundestages, 1: Wahlperiode*, p. 4984.

of public opinion.[41] The 'Without Me Movement' (Ohne Mich Bewegung) of the 1950s and the protests against rearmament were, however, telling signs that, following the horrors of two world wars, the nation, in the eyes of many, had lost its right to demand from its citizens 'the ultimate sacrifice'. In 1946 the popular SPD politician Carlo Schmid had called on his fellow countrymen never again to send their sons into the garrisons.

Rearmament, therefore, did not mark the return to the kind of militarized nationalism that had characterized earlier periods of German history. The constitution enshrined the right to conscientious objection and although it was handled very restrictively until the late 1970s, an ever-increasing number of young people made use of their constitutional right. Army reformers, such as Wulf von Baudissin, developed the idea of soldiers as 'citizens in uniform'. They wanted to anchor the army firmly within the values of parliamentary democracy and combine civic and soldierly virtues. The impact of those ideals in practice has to remain doubtful.[42] Traditional ideals of obedience, duty and soldierly manliness dominated. Leading army generals were keen to honour the traditions of the German military which explicitly included the Nazified Wehrmacht.

If the Wehrmacht's deep implication in the Nazis' racial nationalism could be sidelined in the 1950s, Germany was not allowed to forget the Holocaust. Jews were recognized as victims of the Nazis from early on. Public antisemitism was taboo, as the case of Wolfgang Hedler demonstrates. In 1949 Hedler, a member of the German Party, a junior coalition partner of the CDU/CSU government, publicly voiced his concerns that too much was being made of Jewish suffering under the Nazis. The Nazis, he argued, had been justified in removing Jewish influence from German public life. These statements killed his political career, but it was ominous that a huge crowd of people, on hearing the news that he had been cleared of all charges, greeted him with a standing ovation when he left the law court. In 1952 37 per cent of all West Germans still thought it best not to have any Jews in Germany. When a nationwide campaign of antisemitic incidents in the late 1950s recorded 470 cases and culminated in swastikas being smeared on a Cologne synagogue, Adenauer reacted angrily. He called on his fellow citizens to give those responsible 'a good thrashing' if they should catch them. He was, of course, well aware that these incidents damaged Germany's image abroad, where public opinon immediately noticed any flaring up of racist violence. But Adenauer's recommendation is itself revealing: he recommended treating offenders as naughty little children would have been treated by many parents in the 1950s. Thus he was in effect belittling the continuing impact of antisemitism in Germany.

Ultimately, however, the sustained efforts of schools, the state and the wider public to fight antisemitism and overcome prejudices among the younger generations were successful. In 1983 only 9 per cent of West German citizens thought that it was better to live in a country without Jews. However, that figure rose again

[41] David Clay Large, *Germans to the Front: West German Rearmament and the Adenauer Era* (Chapel Hill, 1996).

[42] Ute Frevert, *Die kasernierte Nation: Militärdienst und Zivilgesellschaft in Deutschland* (Munich, 2001; English trans. forthcoming, see p. 33, note 46), p. 336.

to 13 per cent in 1987 and should be judged alongside data which document the continuously high ethnocentric and xenophobic orientations of many Germans after 1945.[43] Such a discontinuous decline of antisemitism in West Germany happened in a country where it was rare for young Germans to encounter Jews. Of the 15,000 Jews who had survived inside Nazi Germany and the 230,000 displaced Jewish persons in the Western zones of occupation fewer than 30,000 settled in the FRG. Very few Jewish exiles returned after 1945. For obvious reasons, few Jews wanted to settle in a post-Holocaust Germany. For those who did there was no easy way back to their erstwhile dreams of a 'German-Jewish symbiosis'. The Holocaust marked a deep and lasting divide between Germans and Jews, and even the official philosemitism of the FRG put Jews on a pedestal thereby still keeping them apart and distinguishing them from ordinary Germans.[44]

Totalitarianism, Europhilia and the 'economic miracle'

National Socialism was most frequently described not as something specifically German but as a totalitarian regime which shared most of its important characteristics with Communism. Totalitarianism and anti-Communism were the most important means of selectively appropriating the National Socialist past. Anti-Communism was an ideological bridge from the Nazi ideology to the liberal democratic ideals of the FRG. The mass rape of German women by Soviet soldiers at the end of the war and in the early days of occupation served as a symbol for the rape of the nation by Communism and re-enforced anti-Communist stereotypes propagated initially by Goebbels's propaganda ministry. Vociferous anti-Communism was a psychological means of atonement for not having fought vigorously enough against Nazism. Communist Party offices were stormed and ransacked by public mobs,[45] and children of Communist resistance fighters against Nazism suffered maltreatment in schools and abuse from fellow pupils.[46] The FRG had drawn the lessons from the Nazi past by basing its self-understanding on a firm antitotalitarian consensus. The memory of the Nazis served to confirm the evilness of the Communists behind the Iron Curtain. In the 1950s the German parliament debated Nazism firmly within the framework of totalitarianism.[47]

43 Werner Bergmann, *Antisemitismus in öffentlichen Konflikten: Antisemitismus in der politischen Kultur der Bundesrepublik 1949–1989* (Frankfurt/Main, 1997).

44 Frank Stern, *The Whitewashing of the Yellow Badge: Antisemitism and Philosemitism in Postwar Germany* (Oxford, 1992). Also: Jack Zipes and Leslie Morris, eds, *Unlikely History: The Changing German-Jewish Symbiosis, 1945–2000* (Basingstoke, 2002).

45 Patrick Major, *The Death of the KPD: Communism and Anti-Communism in West Germany, 1945–1956* (Oxford, 1997). Also: Klaus Körner, *Die rote Gefahr. Antikommunistische Propaganda in der Bundesrepublik 1950–2000* (Hamburg, 2003).

46 Dieter Nelles, Hartmut Rübner and Heinz Sünker, 'Die "Kinder des Widerstands" – Lebensbedingungen und Sozialisation der Kinder von politisch und religiös Verfolgten des NS-Regimes', *Neue Praxis. Zeitschrift für Sozialarbeit, Sozialpädagogik und Sozialpolitik*, no. 4 (2003).

47 Helmut Dubiel, *Niemand ist frei von der Geschichte: Die nationalsozialistische Herrschaft in den Debatten des Deutschen Bundestages* (Munich, 1999).

Anti-Communism was also crucially important in legitimating the FRG's integration into NATO and the EU. The vast majority of West Germans felt themselves threatened by Soviet Communism.[48] The Berlin blockade of 1948/49, the crushing of the East German rising in 1953, the Berlin ultimatum of 1958, the building of the Berlin Wall in 1961 – all of these events demonstrated to West Germans the aggressive potential of the Soviet Union and strengthened their pro-American and pro-Western attitudes. West Berlin became the self-styled westernmost outpost of liberty, symbolized by the liberty bell in the Rathaus Schöneberg. The Berlin Wall became 'the West's favourite nationalist symbol',[49] because it was widely seen as representative of the barbarity of the dictatorial Communist regime in East Germany which had to imprison its own people. 239 people were killed during the 28 years of its existence. The agonizing death throes, lasting for more than 45 minutes, of one 18-year-old Peter Fechter, shot by East German border guards, was captured live on West German TV cameras in August 1962 and confirmed in many West German minds the need to be vigilant against the Communist east. A wall museum, located at Checkpoint Charlie, documented the many ways in which East Germans attempted to escape the Communist dictatorship.

The increasing division of Germany produced manifold appeals to the integrity of the German cultural nation and its alleged indestructibility. No lesser figure than the first president of the FRG, Theodor Heuss, assigned the task of keeping alive the memory of a united Germany to the Germanic National Museum in Nuremberg in 1952.[50] Specific memorials to German unity were built, like the one in Münster in 1960 ('Indivisible Germany') or the one in the refugee centre Friedland in 1967. Especially the SPD demanded the prioritization of German unity over the CDU/CSU government's policy of Western integration. Where Adenauer argued that West Germany had to join the Western nations in a strong anti-Communist and antitotalitarian alliance which would seek to achieve German reunification from a position of strength, Social Democrats opposed the FRG's entry into the EU and NATO on the grounds that these moves would perpetuate and cement the division of Germany. Kurt Schumacher's angry outburst in parliament, denouncing Adenauer as 'chancellor of the Allies' was representative of a feeling that the chancellor was selling out German national interests in favour of rapid Western integration. But the staunch national position of the SPD was electorally unsuccessful. The national voters supported Adenauer who in turn continued to paint the SPD as an antinational fifth column of Moscow. The 1953 election poster of the CDU read: 'all paths of Marxism lead to Moscow' and the FDP followed this up with 'Where Ollenhauer[51] ploughs, Moscow sows.'

48 The close link between the security consciousness of West Germans and constructions of national identity is emphasized by Joyce Marie Mushaben, *From Post-War to Post-Wall Generations: Changing Attitudes towards the National Question and NATO in the Federal Republic of Germany* (Boulder, 1998).

49 Brian Ladd, *The Ghosts of Berlin: Confronting German History in the Urban Landscape* (Chicago, 1997), p. 30.

50 On Heuss see Christoph Stölzl, ed., *Deutsches Historisches Museum: Ideen—Kontroversen—Perspektiven* (Berlin, 1988), pp. 25ff.

51 Erich Ollenhauer had succeeded Schumacher as chairman of the SPD and was his party's candidate for the chancellorship in 1953.

The 1953 general elections were fought under the impact of the East German rising of 17 June 1953 which had been brutally crushed by Soviet tanks. 17 June subsequently became a national holiday in West Germany and was celebrated as 'Day of National Unity'. A veritable 'cult of the nation' surrounded those celebrations until the mid-1960s.[52] Social Democrats, liberals, the Protestant-national wing of Christian Democracy, trade unionists and representatives of the refugees' organizations attempted to keep 'the flame of national unity' alive through a mass of publications, through festivals, demonstrations and a series of events which often made use of very traditional nationalist rhetoric and symbols. They founded the 'Association for an Indivisible Germany' (*Kuratorium Unteilbares Deutschland*) in June 1954. It presented a wide variety of memories of 17 June 1953. The SPD's interpretation of it as a working-class rising in favour of national unity suited the party's nationalist and class biases. Yet appeals to class and nation did not make the party attractive at election time. Where in 1949 it had been neck and neck with the CDU, in 1953 the Christian Democrats soared ahead. An All-German People's Party (GVP),[53] campaigning primarily on the theme of German unity, fared very badly in 1953, polling only 1.2 per cent of the vote. The fate of East Germany did not win elections in the FRG. Most West Germans remained convinced that Adenauer's policies of non-recognition of Communist East Germany combined with Western integration would be the best way of securing safety and prosperity for West Germany. If it was to prolong German-German divisions, the majority of West Germans were willing to take that risk. It is unclear whether Adenauer himself actually believed in his own policy of strength. He was certainly deeply suspicious of nationalism – a movement he described as the 'cancerous sore of Europe'.[54]

Anchoring the FRG in the emerging EU and in NATO was, for Adenauer, an important means of ensuring that this cancer of nationalism would not return to haunt Germany and Europe. Western integration meant reinventing Germany as a model European country – cosmopolitan, outward-looking and democratic. Anti-Communism facilitated the move from a Nazi Europeanism to a post-war democratic Europeanism. In 1944/45 Nazi propaganda began to emphasize federal concepts of a Europe under German leadership which would defend the European continent against 'Asian Bolshevism'. Many of those engaged in the national-conservative resistance against Nazism had hoped that a post-Hitler Germany would – in alliance with the West – continue to fight the Soviet Union. The merger of anti-Communism and Europeanism thus preceded the proposals for a European Coal and Steel Community. But the success of the reorientation of West Germany towards Europe had more important reasons.

---

52 Edgar Wolfrum, *Geschichtspolitik in der Bundesrepublik Deutschland: Der Weg zur bundesrepublikanischen Erinnerung 1948–1990* (Darmstadt, 1999).

53 It had been founded by among others, Gustav Heinemann, a former interior minister under Adenauer, who had resigned in protest against Adenauer's alleged antinational policies.

54 Konrad Adenauer, *Erinnerungen 1945–1953* (Stuttgart, 1965), Vol. 1, p. 425. See also on this period Hans-Peter Schwarz, *Konrad Adenauer: A German Politician and Statesman in the Period of War, Revolution and Reconstruction*, Vol. 1: *From the German Empire to the Federal Republic, 1876–1952* (Oxford, 1995); Charles Williams, *Adenauer: The Father of the New Germany* (London, 2000).

For the political elites Europe was a means to stabilize the nation state after the upheavals of the Second World War – not just in Germany.[55] It was relatively easy for Germans to be model Europeans, as their economic and political interests were most effectively realized within the framework of the European Union.[56] But it was not just the national interest which led to such a thorough reconfiguration of Germany towards Europe. There was much genuine enthusiasm of the people for closer European integration as a means of overcoming the kind of Europe that had failed to produce security and a minimum of well-being for all its constituent parts in the first half of the twentieth century. European-wide surveys attempting to find out how proud Europeans feel about their nation state have indicated consistently that West Germans were among the least proud and the most willing to endorse a European rather than a national identity since 1945. Arguably the long tradition of German federalism made it easier for Germans to endorse notions of a federal Europe than it was for nations with a strong centralist tradition. Adenauer in particular felt the need to achieve a genuine reconciliation between France and Germany. His embrace of General de Gaulle in the Cathedral of Reims and the Elysée treaties of 1963 signalled such a sea change in the relationship between the two nations. From hereditary enemies they became the motor of European political and economic integration. The new 'Paris–Bonn axis' was to be built on an unprecedented number of exchange programmes, bilateral networks and governmental co-ordination.

Reorienting Germany towards Europe was an important means of reinventing the nation after Nazism. But the idea of a more united Europe was never just a political ploy to a new post-Nazi European order; it was, right from the very start, a tool to improve the economic performance of the European nation states. And if post-war Germans became model Europeans they also built a model economy. The long post-war economic boom marked the dramatic revival of economic fortunes across Western Europe but the change was particularly marked in a Germany which seemed completely destitute in 1945. The FRG rose like a phoenix from the ashes, and, although there was nothing miraculous about it, the 'economic miracle' had a major impact on recasting West German identities. In the 1950s a feeling of 'we can hold our heads high again' (*wir sind wieder wer*) was based first and foremost on economic achievement, although its best known symbol was the 'miracle of Berne', when Germany won the football World Cup against the odds in 1954. Germany's miracles recredited a capitalism which had seemed to have reached the end of the line in 1945. Capitalism seemed guilty of having produced constant economic crises in the inter-war period. It had facilitated the rise of Hitler to power in the early 1930s. The capitalist economic elites were highly discredited, as they, for the most part, co-operated harmoniously with the Nazis during the Third Reich. Initially few economists trusted capitalism to deliver the goods after the Second World War. It was only under the impact of the Pax Americana in the ensuing Cold War that market economists won the upper hand.

55 Alan S. Milward, *The European Rescue of the Nation State* (London, 1992).

56 Werner Bührer, 'Abschied von der Supranationalität: Deutsche Europappolitik und europäische Integration 1958–1972', in A. Schildt, D. Siegfried and K.C. Lammers, eds, *Dynamische Zeiten: Die 60er Jahre in den beiden deutschen Gesellschaften* (Hamburg, 2000), p. 249.

In the FRG it was Ludwig Erhard who more than anyone represented the victory of the market economy over concepts of a socialist planned economy. As economic director of the Anglo-American Bizonia he had been responsible for liberalizing markets in the wake of the currency reform of 1948 which gave to the FRG one of its most enduring and significant symbols: the Deutschmark (DM) – a strong and stable currency which was to become the leading European currency and the arch-symbol of German economic prowess. The currency reform filled the shop windows but it did not decide the success of Erhard's economic reforms. In the short term it increased the divide between the haves and the have nots. One of the most popular carnival songs of 1949 in the Rhineland was sung to the refrain of 'Who shall pay for that? Who has so much money? Who has so much dosh-dosh? Who has so much money?' (*Wer soll das bezahlen? Wer hat soviel Geld? Wer hat soviel Pinke-Pinke? Wer hat soviel Geld?*) When unemployment rose in the late 1940s, many predicted a serious economic crisis. But within the framework of the post-war boom Erhard's policies proved successful. As economics minister and 'father of the economic miracle' he laid the foundation for the long political hegemony of the CDU over West Germany's political system between 1949 and 1966.

Erhard and his advisors did not only recredit capitalism in West Germany; they also gave it a different name. They called it 'social market economy' (*soziale Marktwirtschaft*) which, like the Deutschmark, became one of the cornerstones of West German identity in the post-war world.[57] As the name would suggest, it was a market economy but one with a social conscience. A welfare state would provide a 'social net' through which no one in the FRG should fall: minimum living standards would be guaranteed by the state. 'Rhenish capitalism', as it was sometimes referred to in the English-speaking world, had more than a whiff of corporatism about it. Under the guidance of the state, trade unions and employers' federations worked together for the benefit of the whole economy. Non-adversarial decision-making, a strong currency and fiscal restraint became the hallmarks of West German economic management. After the authoritarian corporatism of the Nazis, it was difficult to sell liberal corporatism after 1945; hence references to the term itself were scarce. But it was alive and kicking and formed yet another important bridge which allowed people to travel the road from the racial *Volksgemeinschaft* to a Westernized parliamentary democracy with remarkable ease.

In the early FRG no politician was as popular as Erhard who, with his big belly and cigars, represented the newfound prosperity of the FRG. His most famous slogans, 'prosperity for all' and 'a refrigerator in every household', promised a mass consumer society which would benefit everyone. It was in effect the same promise that had been made by the Nazis in the 1930s, but where they had failed, West Germany delivered: the label of 'German quality work' became important again in re-establishing the exporting strength of the FRG. In the 1950s many workers still defined themselves through work processes and followed recognizably proletarian lifestyles and leisure-time activities. West Germany was as yet a far cry

[57] A. J. Nicholls, *Freedom with Responsibility: The Social Market Economy in Germany 1918–1963* (Oxford, 1994).

from the 'levelled middle-class society' (*nivellierte Mittelstandsgesellschaft*) propagated by the conservative sociologist Helmut Schelsky. But things began to change and the 1960s saw the definite breakthrough of a consumerist ethos in wider sections of the West German population. Consumer choice and consumer credit now became important anchors of identity.

The misguided idealism of the Nazi years gave way to unashamed consumerism. An uprooted population – every third West German around 1960 had experienced some form of (often enforced) migration – which had gone through more than a decade of deprivation and malnutrition wanted to enjoy itself. Waves of consumption engulfed the fatherland: a food wave, followed by a fashion wave, followed by a travel wave followed by a sex wave.[58] The popularity of international recipes and cook books in the 1950s was an expression of 'German longing for international rapport, for acceptance back into the family of nations. The rhetoric of the recipes was less concerned with practices of preparation than with the stirring of dreams.'[59] Germans acquired all the latest technological gadgets, from Hoovers, electric cookers and washing machines to refrigerators, radios, television sets and the motor car. Listening to the radio and watching television became major family activities, and the craze for consumption generally strengthened the family orientation and the concentration on the private sphere. A nation enjoying itself showed little interest in radical anti-system politics. No other product became more a symbol of the 'economic miracle' than the Volkswagen Beetle – the same car that had inspired the Nazi *Volksgemeinschaft*.[60] Volkswagen itself was not only still a model employer; it also developed a strong corporate image which linked its own success in the 'new' city of Wolfsburg with that of the young FRG. Motorization was nothing if not breathtaking: in 1950 515,600 private cars could be found in the FRG; ten years later that figure had climbed to over 4 million and by 1980 over 23 million cars populated the dense network of *Autobahnen*, itself an important symbol of the new Germany.

Increased opportunities for travel and more leisure time gave rise to a heritage industry which promoted national culture as object of consumption. Museums, landscapes, cities, films and even cuisine were marketed as national in order to attract the growing number of tourists. But the tourist Germany that emerged in the 1950s and 1960s often excluded the most immediate Nazi past. It was one of poetry and philosophy, of magnificent medieval city centres and spectacular castles located in the most romantic of landscapes. Neuschwanstein castle in Bavaria and the Heidelberg castle ruin became two of the most prominent tourist attractions, depicted on endless brochures designed to lure tourists to Germany. Overall, the consumer society brought closer to home the dream of a universalized good life which transcended class boundaries, rural–urban divisions, denominational milieux, occupational differences and other social

[58] Michael Wildt, *Am Beginn der 'Konsumgesellschaft': Mangelerfahrung, Lebenshaltung, Wohlstandshoffnung in Westdeutschland in den fünfziger Jahren* (Hamburg, 1994).

[59] Michael Wildt, 'Plurality of Taste: Food and Consumption in West Germany during the 1950s', *History Workshop Journal*, 39 (1995), p. 34f.

[60] See above, p. 157.

divisions.[61] In other words it recast the dream of the *Volksgemeinschaft* in non-racial, democratic terms.

Women and young people stood at the very heart of this new culture of consumption, which empowered them in a variety of ways. Both as objects and as subjects of consumption their visibility in the public sphere soared. The ideal of the rational housewife, for example, became the symbol of a prudent German nation.[62] The consumption of Americanized forms of mass culture served as prominent positive and negative reference points for the buoyant youth cultures of the 1950s and 1960s, whereas German cultural critics from the right and the left denounced American forms of mass consumption as spelling the end of national culture.[63]

Economic success allowed a consumer society to flourish, in which people defined themselves through denationalized (and often Americanized) consumption patterns. But the success or failure of managing the economy was still linked to national characteristics. In the 1970s West German governments took pride in their successful management of economic crises. The Social Democratic chancellor Helmut Schmidt, nicknamed 'Mr Dynamic' (*Der Macher*), built his reputation on being a level-headed, cool and, above all, a sound crisis manager. His party went into the 1976 election campaign with the slogan 'Model Germany' (*Modell Deutschland*). That model was a socio-economic one. By the 1980s the economic identity of West Germany was so strong that, in the words of economic historian Werner Abelshauer, 'the Federal Republic resembles an economy in search of its political raison d'être'.[64]

Democratizing the state and debating the merits of the nation

The strong economic identity of West Germany was crucially important in allowing Germans to make the transition from the racialized nationalism of the Nazis to a more democratic political self-understanding. This development of a democratic political culture could not be achieved overnight. Hence the 1950s were a transition period in which economics bolstered a yet uncertain political democracy. West Germans were no more convinced democrats in 1949 than they had been in 1919. All surveys clearly demonstrated the widespread scepticism among West Germans towards democracy and politics more generally. Racist and authoritarian viewpoints were widespread, and nationalist rhetoric struck a chord with a majority of Germans.[65] Arguably they needed a longer

[61] Arne Anderson, *Der Traum vom guten Leben: Alltags- und Konsumgeschichte vom Wirtschaftswunder bis heute* (Frankfurt/Main, 1997).

[62] Erica Carter, *How German is She? Postwar West German Reconstruction and the Consuming Woman* (Ann Arbor, 1997).

[63] Axel Schildt, *Zwischen Abendland und Amerika: Studien zur westdeutschen Ideenlandschaft der 50er Jahre* (Munich, 1999).

[64] Werner Abelshauser, *Wirtschaftsgeschichte der Bundesrepublik Deutschland 1945–1980* (Frankfurt/Main, 1983), p. 8.

[65] Elisabeth Noelle-Neumann and Renate Köcher, *Die verletzte Nation: Über den Versuch der Deutschen, ihren Charakter zu ändern* (Stuttgart, 1987).

learning process, which could take place under the conditions of quite exceptional economic growth and under the guidance of the Western allies, who provided the framework for the new democracy and for a more liberal civil society. It was therefore in many respects only during the 1960s that democracy in West Germany came of age.

By the mid-1960s the post-war CDU-led governments had achieved a considerable reinvention of Germany: it was an accepted part of a Western alliance system with a stable democracy and a strong economy. Yet there was throughout the 1960s a growing sense of disillusionment with the status quo represented by the CDU. Much of the Zeitgeist demanded a new beginning, which involved more open discussion of the National Socialist past, the thorough democratization of more areas of public life and a different attitude towards the GDR. The Spiegel affair in 1962 marked the emergence of a strong critical public sphere in West Germany. Following allegations of a betrayal of military secrets, an early morning police raid on the offices of the news magazine *Der Spiegel* reminded many Germans of the methods used by the Gestapo. Leading intellectuals now discovered the merits of pluralism. They called on their fellow citizens to accept and tolerate differences in a highly complex modern society. 'Society' for the first time became more popular than the more traditional idealization of 'community'. The corporatism of 'Rhenish capitalism' came under suspicion because of its inherent antipluralism and denial of interest differences. Ludwig Erhard's concept of an 'organized society' (*formierte Gesellschaft*), which wanted to give society a common aim and unified structure, was rejected as proof of the continued non-acceptance of political conflict as the norm in democratic societies. The Grand Coalition between CDU and SPD between 1966 and 1969 was equally regarded as a sure sign that democracy was underdeveloped in the FRG. The two biggest political parties joined forces to put together one of the most impressive reform programmes in the short history of German parliamentary democracy, but at the same time there were many worries that it might leave the democracy without an effective opposition – a state of affairs which in itself was deeply worrying for democrats.

The student protests between 1967 and 1969 constituted an 'extra-parliamentary opposition', highlighting the deficits of what they perceived as a half-modernized, a half-democratized and a half-liberalized German society which had not properly worked through its Nazi past. What the social-liberal government offered them in 1969 was a 'march through the institutions', i.e. to turn their 'anti-system' protest into a more productive reformist agenda which could be implemented through the system. Some took that gamble and placed their hopes in Brandt's call to 'dare more democracy'. But the anti-terrorist hysteria of the early 1970s, the emergence of a 'surveillance state' (*Überwachungsstaat*) and the rigid exclusion of Communists from all civil service jobs (*Berufsverbote*) disillusioned many who initially supported the Social Democrats' bid for a democratic renewal of the nation.

The productive libertarian potential of the 1968 movement and their imagination of a more tolerant, liberal and democratic Germany remained alive in the vibrant citizens' rights movement, second-wave feminism and the environmental protection movement, which were all heavily engaged in grassroots politics in the 1970s. Their concerns ultimately fed into the formation of the Green Party in 1979/80, which self-consciously continued the struggle for a new politics identified with 1968. Their post-materialist values were rooted in the belief that mass consumption based on the gospel of economic growth would ultimately be self-destructive. Their electoral success among the young in the 1980s made Germany the nation with the strongest ecological consciousness, a kind of Green pathfinder for a more environmentally-conscious Europe. The often violent struggle against nuclear energy in the 1970s was fought against the materialist growth ideology, but it was also fought in the name of *Heimat* and nation. Protesters opposing the building of a nuclear reactor in Whyl near the Franco-German border carried posters which read: 'The *Heimat* is our mother / whoever takes the *Heimat* from us / kills our mother.' And the same protesters reinvented a new version of the famous nineteenth-century nationalist song, 'Keeping guard over the Rhine' (*Die Wacht am Rhein*): 'In Alsace and in Baden poverty ruled for a long time / In wars we shot each other dead for our respective masters / Now we fight for our own interests in Wyhl and Marckolsheim / Together we perform an alternative keeping guard over the Rhine.'[66]

The 1970s and especially the 1980s witnessed a remarkable proliferation of 1968ers, or those who claimed to be 1968ers. They have made 1968 into one of the crucial foundation myths of the Federal Republic – a moment in time when democracy came fully into its own. Imagining a nation in which all spheres of life were democratized and in which there was much greater gender equality was one of the lasting legacies of 1968.[67] The belief that the personal is the political informed cultural practices in a number of ways. The music of 'New German Wave' (*Neue Deutsche Welle*), for example, expressed above all disillusionment with grand political theories and ideas and instead celebrated a new subjectivity.[68] The emphasis on the personal and on the everyday also contributed to a specifically left-wing *Heimat* discourse. It found expression, among other things, in the distinct nostalgia for regional recipes. In the early nineteenth century a *Heimat* cuisine flourished as a middle-class response to aristocratic Francophile tastes. In the 1970s local cuisine was championed as more natural and environmentally friendly.[69]

A left-wing concern with *Heimat* was also at the heart of Edgar Reitz's epic saga *Heimat*, a TV series first released in the summer of 1984. It depicts the everyday life experiences of the Simon family in Schabbach, a small village in the Hunsrück mountains near Koblenz between 1919 and 1982. A family chronicle and a reinvention of the 1950s genre of the *Heimat* film, it attempted to put ordinary people and their experiences centre stage. Reitz's idea of *Heimat* was that of

66 Both quotes in Bernd-A. Rusinek, 'Wyhl', in Etienne François and Hagen S. Schulze, eds, *Deutsche Erinnerungsorte*, 3 vols (Munich, 2001), Vol. 2, p. 660.

67 Geoff Eley, *Forging Democracy: The History of the Left in Europe, 1850–2000* (Oxford, 2002), pp. 341–65.

68 Winfried Longerich, *'Da, Da, Da': Zur Standortbestimmung der Neuen Deutschen Welle* (Pfaffenweiler, 1989).

69 Kirsten Schlegel-Matthies, 'Regionale Speisen in deutschen Kochbüchern des 19. und 20. Jahrhunderts', in Hans-Jürgen Teuteberg, Gerhard Neumann and Alois Wierlacher, eds, *Essen und kulturelle Identität: Europäische Perspektiven* (Berlin, 1997), pp. 212–27.

a tightly knit knowable community, a kind of left-wing antithesis to nationalism.[70] Viewers were invited to identify with the main characters, as they lived their 'normal lives' in the shadow of the swastika. The film was harshly criticized for romanticizing popular memory. Critics asked whether films such as *Heimat* did not reduce the Third Reich to 'a mere backdrop for personal stories held together by such universal themes as love, friendship, family and community'.[71] Did it not marginalize the Holocaust and the political violence in Nazi Germany?

But Reitz's *magnum opus* was clearly not about the Holocaust and politics; it was about everyday experiences of Germans in a rural backwater, and it wanted to raise questions about German identity and twentieth-century German history. A whole string of (largely left of centre) *auteur* film-makers dealt with highly subjective personal encounters of their protagonists with aspects of twentieth-century German history. Rainer Werner Fassbinder's *The Marriage of Maria Braun*, Helga Sanders-Brahms's *Germany, Pale Mother* and Alexander Kluge's *The Patriot* were among the most important contributions to a growing left-wing discourse about German identity.

1968 in no way signalled the left's abandonment of the nation.[72] Dissatisfied with the lofty internationalism of the 1960s, some groups linked their ongoing struggle against what they perceived as American and/or Soviet imperialism with demands for German unity. After the staunch pro-Americanism of virtually all sections of German public opinion in the 1950s, anti-Americanism returned with a vengeance in the 1960s and was linked in particular with protests against the 'imperialist' Vietnam war. But anti-Americanism was also part and parcel of the 'hot autumn' of 1983, when millions of West Germans protested against the stationing of US Cruise and Pershing II missiles on German soil.[73] Sections of the Green party tied 'the German problem' to peace policy in as much as both Germanies were perceived as the first major victims in any armed conflict in Europe. Hence both had a special responsibility for maintaining peace and stability.

But if the national imagination informed some left-wing politics in the 1980s, a far more important trend was the left's movement towards postnationalism. The national principle, representatives of the left argued, had not been the most constructive and fruitful way of imagining Germany. A more critical reassessment of national history took place in the 1960s, which had everything to do with the rediscovery of the Nazi past. Important landmarks for a more vigorous concern with that past included the foundation of the 'Central Office for Solving National Socialist Crimes' in 1958, Theodor Adorno's 1959 radio essay 'What do we mean by "Working Through the Past"?', novels such as Günter Grass's *Tin Drum*, published in 1959, and films such as *Rosen für den Staatsanwalt* (Roses for the State Prosecutor) released in the same year, the spectacular trials

[70] Alon Confino, 'Edgar Reitz's *Heimat* and German Nationhood: Film, Memory, and Understandings of the Past', *German History*, 16 (1998), pp. 185–208.

[71] Sabine Hake, *German National Cinema* (London, 2002), p. 143.

[72] Andrea Ludwig, *Neue oder deutsche Linke? Nation und Nationalismus im Denken von Linken und Grünen* (Opladen, 1995).

[73] Dan Diner, *Verkehrte Welten: Antiamerikanismus in Deutschland: Ein historischer Essay* (Frankfurt/Main, 1993).

of Eichmann in Jerusalem in 1961/62 and the Auschwitz trials in Düsseldorf in 1965, Rolf Hochhuth's drama *The Deputy* of 1963, the photographic exhibitions about the Warsaw Ghetto and Auschwitz in the Paulskirche in 1963 and 1964. Left-of-centre intellectuals began to argue that the Bismarckian Germany amounted to a failed nation state and that the division of Germany had to be accepted as the result of German history in the first half of the twentieth century.

The Fischer controversy in the 1960s was all about such reassessments of national history.[74] The Hamburg-based historian Fritz Fischer interpreted the outbreak of the First World War as the first attempt by Germany's elites to create a German-dominated *Mitteleuropa*. If he was right, Hitler could not any longer be portrayed as the evil exception to an otherwise unblemished national history. On the contrary, the twelve years of National Socialism began to appear as the high point of a continuing German development towards illiberalism and expansionism. A new generation of left-of-centre social historians set about to turn the *Sonderweg* idea on its head: from proud assertion of Germany's differences to the West it became a sad reflection of Germany's aberrations from the West.

Fischer's ideas developed in the context of other criticisms of the old Reich nationalism. A group of Catholic publicists assembled around journals such as *Frankfurter Hefte* and *Neues Abendland* rejected the Prussian myth about German history logically ending in the *Kaiserreich* of 1871. In 1960 the philosopher Karl Jaspers delivered a shattering blow to the national tradition by radically challenging the national orientation of German historiography: 'After all that's happened, the mere fact that this state once existed does not constitute a moral right to its re-erection. On the contrary, in retrospect, a shadow falls on the Bismarckian creation.'[75] On the 100th anniversary of its foundation, in 1971, none other than the president of the FRG, Gustav Heinemann, in a televized speech, drew a straight line from 1871 to 1914, 1939 and 1949. The horrors of two world wars and of the Holocaust were the direct outcome of Germany's peculiar path as a nation state. Heinemann called on his fellow citizens not to look to 1871 as the anchor point of their national identity. Here was a president who had gone on record saying that he could love his wife but not an abstract thing like the nation. The seventy years of a unified German nation state were increasingly seen as the exception rather than the rule. Those decades were no longer perceived as the happiest but as the most catastrophic ones in centuries of German history. As a consequence, liberty and the democratic state order were prioritized over unity: continued adherence to reunification could now be described as the 'self-betrayal' (*Lebenslüge*) of the FRG. In the 1970s the national question was to lose much of the urgency that it had possessed in the 1950s.

It was in this context of an increasingly weaker orientation towards the *Reich* nationalism of old that Willy Brandt's *Ostpolitik* could flourish.[76] For its main

---

74 Stefan Berger, *The Search for Normality: National Identity and Historical Consciousness in Germany since 1800* (Oxford, 1997; pb edn with new foreword, 2003), Chapter 3.

75 Karl Jaspers, 'Freiheit und Wiedervereinigung' (1960), in *idem*, *Hoffnung und Sorge: Schriften zur deutschen Politik, 1945–1965* (Munich, 1965), p. 199.

76 Detlef Nakath, *Deutsch-deutsche Grundlagen: Zur Geschichte der politischen und wirtschaftlichen Beziehungen zwischen der DDR und der Bundesrepublik in den Jahren von 1969 bis 1982* (Schkeuditz, 2002).

protagonists, Brandt and Bahr, *Ostpolitik* was never about accepting the division of Germany. Both wanted to perceive dialogue as a means of reversing the increasing alienation between the two Germanies. A 1963 visit to the GDR of journalists from *Die Zeit* revealed to many West Germans how distant a country the GDR had become.[77] By bringing the people of the two Germanies closer together, the architects of *Ostpolitik* hoped to keep open the German question over the long term. But they, in line with much left-liberal public opinion at the time, moved away from the centredness of the German nation in the Imperial German state. As Brandt once put it: 'Nation is when one sees each other again.' The 1972 election slogan of the SPD was 'Germans, we can be proud of our country'. The Germans who were addressed here were West Germans, and the FRG did indeed acquire more and more characteristics of a nation state. *Ostpolitik* was not only about German-German policy. It was also a major attempt to overcome centuries of anti-Slav sentiments in German nationalism. In particular German-Polish reconciliation in the wake of *Ostpolitik* mirrored the Franco-German reconciliation started two decades earlier. It found expression, for example, in extensive attempts to revise German and Polish schoolbooks so as to end the prevalent national stereotyping of 'the other'.[78]

The acceptance of the post-war territorial borders in east-central Europe and the opening up of a dialogue with Communist East Germany was opposed vigorously by refugees' and expellees' groups and by the CDU/CSU. For many on the centre-right *Ostpolitik* amounted to a national sell-out and Brandt was accused of 'national treason'. By the time a CDU-led government returned to power in 1982, however, most of its leading politicians had de facto accepted *Ostpolitik* and continued the dialogue with the GDR. Demands for reunification became increasingly a 'declaration of belief without need' (*Bekenntnis ohne Bedürfnis*).[79] Officially the FRG remained in favour of reunification, but in reality it became a less and less urgent problem for the majority of West Germans. Knowledge about the GDR and its society decreased substantially. By the late 1980s most younger Germans without relatives in the GDR were far more familiar with French, Italian and British society than with the East German one. The consciousness of belonging to one nation was deteriorating fast. Even in West Berlin people learned to live with the wall. Wall art attracted many tourists, and the wall could even become the scene of rather comical events, such as the first mass exodus of West Germans onto East German territory in July 1988, when the West Berlin police attempted to evacuate a self-made village inhabited by ecologists. The latter climbed the wall and 'fled' eastwards, helped along by East German border guards who later released the 'green fighters' back to the West.

If there was less concern with reunification throughout the 1970s and 1980s, the same cannot be said for questions of national identity. When Helmut Kohl

[77] Marion Gräfin Dönhoff, Rudolf Walter Leonhardt and Theo Sommer, *Reise in ein fernes Land: Bericht über Kultur, Wirtschaft und Politik in der DDR* (Hamburg, 1964).

[78] The Georg-Eckert-Institute for International Research on School Books in Brunswick has minutely documented the many conferences dedicated to this topic from the 1970s onwards.

[79] Lutz Niethammer, *Deutschland danach: Postfaschistische Gesellschaft und nationales Gedächtnis* (Bonn, 1999), p. 118.

became chancellor in 1982 he made heavy weather of what he liked to refer to as a 'spiritual and moral turn' (*geistig-moralische Wende*). It included a greater emphasis on the notion of a good nationalism, often euphemistically referred to as patriotism. The same year that Kohl became chancellor saw heated discussions surrounding what some saw as attempts to revive the corpse of Prussia and Prussian history in the context of the celebrations of the Prussia year. But more importantly the government's concern with boosting an allegedly flagging national identity led to two massive and ongoing debates beginning in the 1980s. The first one concerned multiculturalism and the place of millions of foreign workers and their children in German society. And the second one was about the place of National Socialism and the Holocaust in German historical consciousness.

Foreign, so-called 'guest workers' (*Gastarbeiter*) were recruited by West German industry with the active help of the state after 1955 to overcome acute shortages of manpower.[80] In the 1960s Italians were the biggest national group, but from the 1970s onwards Turks became more numerous with Spaniards, Greeks and Yugoslavs also being heavily represented. The highpoint of recruitment was reached in 1973 when 2.5 million foreign labourers were resident in West Germany. German industrialists, politicians and the wider public perceived their employment as a temporary stop-gap measure, but by the 1980s it was clear for everyone to see that many would not return to their countries of origin. They had effectively become immigrants and their children were growing up in Germany. Their history was one of manifold discriminations and rejections and they were often faced with highly complex processes of renegotiating their own national identities and sense of belonging. West Germans often proved ungrateful to those who had stepped into the breach to work in largely unskilled and low-paid jobs to allow 2.3 million German workers in the 1960s to change from blue-collar to white-collar jobs. Social Democratic governments in the 1970s had substantially restricted their freedom of movement in the FRG, and after 1982 the centre-right governments took a range of measures to make foreign workers leave Germany voluntarily. When increasing numbers of asylum-seekers entered Germany in the 1980s, even leading CDU politicians began to talk about 'the boat being full', adopting the xenophobic rhetoric of the far right.

Racist discourses had always been a subterranean phenomenon in the FRG. A range of neo-Nazi parties scored occasional electoral successes in *Landtag* elections from the 1950s right through to the 1980s. But none of them ever got established in national politics. On 17 June 1981 a range of right-wing intellectuals published the Heidelberg manifesto, which consciously took up the *völkisch* theories of the inter-war period to warn about dangers of Germans being dominated by foreign influences (*Überfremdung*). It was signed not only by extreme right-wing mavericks but also by several reputable university professors and members of the CDU. In the 1980s the far-right wing *Nationalzeitung* sold tens of thousands of copies every week. Representative surveys showed that 10 to 15 per cent of West Germans supported aggressively nationalist and racist

[80] For the following see Ulrich Herbert, *Geschichte der Ausländerpolitik in Deutschland: Saisonarbeiter, Zwangsarbeiter, Gastarbeiter, Flüchtlinge* (Munich, 2001), pp. 192–285.

slogans such as 'Germany to the Germans' and 'Foreigners Out'. Centre-right governments, which made use of populist racist discourses, officially sanctioned racism and prevented moves towards a more proactive immigration policy. The FRG had clearly become an attractive country of immigration for people from many poorer parts of Europe and the wider world, but West German policy refused to accept this fact.

In the meantime millions of foreigners lived among Germans and had a huge impact on everyday national culture: eating habits, for example, changed markedly with what can only be described as the Mediterraneanization of German cuisine. As Germans became more open to the influence of 'foreign' cultures, left-wing intellectuals began to champion ideas of multiculturalism. They envisaged different cultures living harmoniously next to each other, learning from each other and accepting each other. Multiculturalism was meant as an antidote to racism and xenophobia, but it had its downsides too. After all, it encouraged thinking in stable cultural collectives and tended to underestimate the differences within allegedly homogeneous national cultures.

Debates about foreign workers in Germany were always debates about German national identity. The same has been true for debates about German history and architecture. In 1986/87 the so-called historians' controversy (*Historikerstreit*) dealt with attempts to relativize the Holocaust and to remove National Socialism from its position as central stumbling block for the creation of a more positive German historical consciousness.[81] Almost ten years earlier, German modernist architects attacked James Stirling's postmodern design for the Neue Staatsgalerie museum in Stuttgart as fascist, thereby starting a major debate on the aesthetics and politics of Nazi architecture.[82] Historian and advisor to chancellor Kohl, Michael Stürmer, famously argued that positive national identity had to be anchored in positive national traditions. This reflected fears in liberal conservative circles that West Germans were becoming ignorant of their long national history (*geschichtsvergessen*). An alleged over-concentration on the twelve years of National Socialism fostered an entirely negative national identity, they argued. And no nation could build an identity on a history which was exclusively shameful. The result, they feared, would be the acceptance of the division of the German nation and, more importantly, a serious lack of commitment to the West German state. As far back as 1978 a majority of CDU cultural ministers of the *Länder* had recommended new guidelines for school history which were to strengthen feelings of national unity and national identity. The history boom of the 1980s led to a renewed interest in national history – with several multi-volume works on German history reaching the bestseller lists for non-fiction.

Commemorating the fortieth anniversary of the end of the war in May 1985 brought attempts to blur the line between the victors and those who had to be

[81] Richard J. Evans, *In Hitler's Shadow: West German Historians and the Attempt to Escape from the Nazi Past* (London, 1989), and Charles Maier, *The Unmasterable Past: History, Holocaust and German National Identity* (Cambridge, Mass., 1988).

[82] Gavriel D. Rosenfeld, 'The Architects' Debate: Architectural Discourse and the Memory of Nazism in the Federal Republic of Germany 1977–1997', *History and Memory*, 9 (1997), pp. 189–225.

defeated, i.e. the Germans. When Kohl and Reagan visited a military cemetery in Bitburg which also contained graves of members of the Waffen-SS, public protests followed. Bitburg was the most visible reflection of a memory politics which aimed at making all victims of the war equal and downplaying German guilt and German responsibility for war and genocide. The two German wars in the twentieth century were no longer reason enough to say good-bye to the idea of a unified nation state. In October 1987 Helmut Kohl laid the foundations to his pet project: a German historical museum in Berlin, which was to keep the memory of German unity alive. At the same time, however, Kohl also commissioned the building of a museum for the history of the Federal Republic in Bonn, thereby confirming the trend to see West Germany as a nation state in the making.

Left liberals opposed any attempts to sanitize German history. They denied the need for homogeneous national identities in modern states, and remained adamant that Nazism had to remain at the centre of Germany's historical consciousness. It had taken long enough, they argued, to get West Germans to confront that past fully. Indeed, by the 1980s West Germans seemed far more conscious in their dealings with the remnants from the Nazi past than they had been in the 1950s. The concentration camp Dachau, for example, had opened its gates as a memorial to the victims of Nazism in 1965 – after it had been used as an American internment camp and a camp for refugees from the Sudetenland. The memorial had only come about after massive protests of prominent former inmates against plans of the community of Dachau to raze it to the ground. Most of the villagers clearly did not want the world to remember their place as the site of one of the most prominent concentration camps.[83] In Nuremberg, the huge area where the Nazi party conferences were held was left to its own devices after 1945. In the 1960s some of the buildings were demolished, because they were in danger of collapsing. It was only in 1983 that the city of Nuremberg paid half a million Deutschmarks to restore what remained of the central stand and transform it into a documentation centre, which finally opened its gates in the autumn of 2001. In 1982 the former SS cultic centre, the Wewelsburg, was made into a documentation centre, and in 1992 the very Wannsee villa in Berlin which housed the infamous Wannsee conference was turned into a Holocaust memorial centre. Today hundreds of memorials to the National Socialist past constitute a firm framework for German memory culture. Ironically it was an American TV series, *Holocaust*, first shown on German television in 1979, which, for millions of viewers, brought home the full horrors of Nazi genocide. Critics were scathing about the treatment of the Holocaust as a soap opera, but many Germans for the first time identified with the victims – the Jewish family at the centre of the plot.[84]

West Germans had shied away from remembering key aspects of the Nazi past for a long time after 1945, but by the 1980s those who wanted to remember and to memorialize were in the majority. They tended to be the children and sometimes

[83] Harold Marcuse, *Legacies of Dachau: The Uses and Abuses of a Concentration Camp, 1933–2001* (Cambridge, 2001).

[84] Wilhelm van Kampen, *Holocaust: Materialien zu einer amerikanischen Fernsehserie über die Judenverfolgung im 'Dritten Reich'* (Bonn, 1981).

the grandchildren of those with direct experience of the National Socialist regime. Michael Verhoeven's film *The Nasty Girl* (1990) put on screen the real-life story of Anja Rosmus, a schoolgirl from Passau who uncovered – against the massive resistance of most of her fellow citizens – that a number of local dignitaries in her home town had been deeply implicated in the Nazi regime during the Third Reich. 'Dig where you stand' became the motto of a popular History Workshop Movement which spread into almost every part of Germany in the 1970s and 1980s. Lay amateur historians, many of them teachers, trade unionists, youth activists, but also many ordinary citizens, were beginning to study the forgotten groups in history and the forgotten histories. Prominent among their themes were the Nazi years and working-class history. Some groups set up alternative city tours to highlight those places which were not officially commemorated. These groups had a more far-reaching impact on the remaking of German identities in the 1970s and 1980s than professional historians.

In 1985, an unofficial dig of the Berlin History Workshop and the Active Museum of Fascism and Resistance to commemorate the 40th anniversary of the end of the Second World War discovered remains of the cellars of the Gestapo headquarters. In the midst of the vast no man's land between the former Wilhelmstrasse and Prinz-Albrecht-strasse – formerly home to the most terroristic organizations in the Third Reich, the SS, SD, Gestapo, criminal police and the Reich Security Main Office – history workshop groups mounted a major unofficial exhibition to mark the city's 750th year anniversary. Ever since the city has witnessed a long and ongoing battle to find a permanent home for the exhibition and with it for the memorialization of the terror which once emanated from the old and new German capital.[85]

West Germans travelled a long and tortuous path towards a more truthful memory of the National Socialist past. In the 1980s a majority opposed attempts to sideline the Nazi past and return to more conventional forms of national identity. According to Jürgen Habermas and his supporters in the *Historikerstreit*, the real lesson to be drawn from Germany's *Sonderweg* was the cultural and political orientation of Germany to the Western democracies. That had been achieved in the FRG and that should not be given up. Westernization was ultimately more important than national unity. The Federal Republic had become a postnational democracy – a state which had moved beyond nationalism as legitimation for its existence. Many recommended anchoring West German national identity in the set of constitutional values enshrined in the Basic Law. Other nations, notably the US and Switzerland, were held together by common constitutional values rather than by any common history or culture. 'Constitutional patriotism' (*Verfassungspatriotismus*) had been championed by diverse intellectuals, such as Dolf Sternberger, Alexander Schwan, Karl Dietrich Bracher, Kurt Sontheimer and Habermas. Some were liberal conservatives, some were on the left. It was a concept which stressed freedom, parliamentarism and Western values against its enemies from both the right and the left. But many liberal conservatives found 'constitutional patriotism' too bloodless an affair, unable to

[85] Reinhard Rürup, ed., *Topographie des Terrors: Gestapo, SS und Reichssicherheitshauptamt auf dem 'Prinz-Albrecht-Gelände': Eine Dokumentation* (Berlin, 1987).

inspire any real sentiment among ordinary Germans. National identity, they argued, had to be historically rooted. Those arguments were widely perceived to be on the losing side in the second half of the 1980s. The outcome of the *Historikerstreit* seemed to confirm that there was no return to the conventional forms of national identity dreaded by the left-liberal establishment. Even liberal conservatives, such as the FRG's president, Richard von Weizsäcker, shared the firm belief that any German national identity had to work through the darkest years of German history. In a moving and much-acclaimed speech in 1985 which displayed great moral and political sensitivity (and stood in stark contrast to Kohl's and Reagan's visit to Bitburg), Weizsäcker had for the first time fully acknowledged a long list of victims of the National Socialist regime and maintained German responsibility for remembering the Nazi past.

As the history of Nazism remained central to identity politics in the FRG in the 1980s, many West Germans came to believe that the division of Germany was the result of German hubris. If the *Kaiserreich* was not the ultimate endpoint of German national history, but rather the beginning of the slippery slope towards Nazism, who in their right mind would want to recreate such a monster in the middle of Europe? Was it not far better to stick with two German states and accept them as a lesson from history? Had not the Federal Republic in the forty years of its existence acquired all the characteristics of a separate nation state? The preamble of the Basic Law, committing all West German governments to seek reunification, seemed an anachronism to an increasing number of West Germans. Was it not time to accept GDR citizenship and officially recognize a second German state? Was not the FRG one of the most successful reinventions of Germany ever? Were West Germans not proud first and foremost of what they had achieved after 1945? Was not the memory of a united Germany an increasingly distant, and what is more, unpalatable memory? West Germany was well on its way towards accepting itself and its own nationhood,[86] when events in the other Germany ultimately led to a (brief) surge of national feeling on both sides of the inner-German border. Reunification in 1990 turned on its head the idea that Germany's division was the logical conclusion of German history in the first half of the twentieth century. Yet another reinvention of the nation was on the cards.

86 Axel Schildt, *Ankunft im Westen: Ein Essay zur Erfolgsgeschichte der Bundesrepublik* (Frankfurt/Main, 1999).

7

The failure of a 'socialist nation': the German Democratic Republic, 1945–1990

In January 1967 *Neues Deutschland*, the daily newspaper of the ruling Communist party of the GDR, the Socialist Unity party (SED), began publishing a flood of letters and articles 'discussing' the question of whether Germany or the GDR was the fatherland of East Germans. Similar 'debates' took place on East German television, radio and in all other print media. Most of the letter writers and discussants repeated time and again their deep commitment and spontaneous solidarity to the GDR. Key slogans emerging from the debate and reproduced on innumerable billboards across the republic included: 'Everything binds us to our socialist fatherland – nothing to imperialist West Germany', and 'The love and faithfulness of youth belongs to the socialist GDR'.

On 19 March 1970 the chancellor of the FRG, Willy Brandt, visited the East German town of Erfurt to attend the first-ever German-German meeting of heads of government. On the East German side of the border, Brandt's special train was greeted by crowds of waving East German citizens. Many of the houses close to the railway line displayed large banners with a big Y – a synonym for Willy Brandt. In Erfurt itself, the GDR government had barred anyone from taking holidays on that particular day and it kept school children in school longer than usual. The square in front of the railway station was blocked off by police. And yet, despite all precautionary measures, about 2000 citizens of the GDR broke through the police cordon shouting 'Willy, Willy'. The tumultuous scenes continued after Brandt had entered his hotel. Crowds of people continued to shout his name and demand freedom of opinion, free elections and an end to travel restrictions.

In December 1981 another Social Democratic chancellor of the FRG, Helmut Schmidt, visited the GDR. The Communist authorities were determined that scenes like the ones in Erfurt should not occur again. When Schmidt visited the small town of Güstrow in Mecklenburg, the East German secret police, the Stasi, turned it into a Potemkin village. Those citizens deemed 'politically unreliable' were warned beforehand to stay inside their houses. All roads leading into the town were blocked off. A heavy police presence ensured that ordinary citizens of Güstrow did not disrupt the carefully stage-managed event. Busloads of reliable Communist comrades were offloaded in the town centre where they pretended to be ordinary inhabitants of Güstrow, cheering the GDR leaders accompanying Schmidt on his walk around the Güstrow Christmas market.

These three scenes from the life of the GDR demonstrate the gulf which lay between its claims to have created a 'socialist nation' and the reality. This chapter seeks to explore what the socialist reinvention of the nation in the GDR consisted of and why it eventually failed so spectacularly in 1989 – almost exactly forty years after its foundation. It will first discuss the two crucial pillars on which the 'socialist nation' was founded: antifascism and friendship with the Soviet Union. Subsequently it will explore how the attempt to invent a socialist nation in the GDR remained inextricably linked with developments in the FRG. Furthermore the changing constructs of national identity put forward by the ruling Communists will be examined. If initially they propagated a unified socialist Germany, from the mid-1960s they moved to the idea of two separate German nations developing in the FRG and the GDR. Finally, this chapter will ask why the opposition to the SED found it so difficult to harness the concept of the nation for its own cause. In 1951 the general secretary of the SED, Walter Ulbricht, declared that the building of a new Germany was under way: 'The symbols of the old Germany ... were destroyed in the Second World War. The men and women of the new Germany are clearing away the ruins of the old Imperial Germany. From the ruins of the old Germany a new one arises.'[1] What then was new about that latest reinvention of the German nation?

Antifascism, ethnic minorities and Communist internationalism

Official histories of the GDR referred to the period from 1945 to 1949 as 'antifascist-democratic transformation', indicating the crucial importance of antifascism in legitimating the existence of the GDR. The state founded in 1949 presented itself, first and foremost, as an antifascist state. The Communists prolonged their popular front policies of the 1930s into the post-war period and presented themselves as uniting and leading all antifascist forces in German society. The foundation of a socialist GDR, they argued, counterbalanced the catastrophic defeat of the German working class in 1933. Communists, through long years of bitter sacrifices in the antifascist struggle, had finally succeeded and the Marxist promise of a socialist future seemed to come true at last. Many of those leading the new state had indeed been persecuted and incarcerated by the Nazis. Others had fled Nazi Germany and survived in exile. Now their time had come, and they did not shy away from using their antifascist credentials to quell any kind of opposition to the emerging Communist dictatorship. Their enemies were routinely denounced as 'fascists'. But for many Communists antifascism was not just a mere propaganda instrument to

[1] Walter Ulbricht, *Zur Geschichte der deutschen Arbeiterbewegung: Aus Reden und Aufsätzen* (Berlin, 1958), p. 299f.

legitimate the GDR. It was part and parcel of their lived experience, and they wanted to make that experience the anchor point of the new state. The lessons of their antifascist struggle were to inform the attempt to create a better, a socialist future.

Antifascism became one of the most important building blocks of the official GDR identity. Its most potent symbol was the former concentration camp of Buchenwald. Here, the leader of the Weimar KPD, Ernst Thälmann, had been murdered by the Nazis. Here, antifascist prisoners had staged a successful uprising in the dying days of the Nazi regime. And here Communists and Social Democrats had sworn themselves to overcome the fatal division of the working-class parties, which they held in large measure responsible for the victory of fascism. The SED, the result of an enforced merger between KPD and SPD in the Soviet zone of occupation in 1946, portrayed itself as having learnt the lessons of the antifascist struggle of the Buchenwald prisoners and framed their story around a heroic narrative of resistance and eventual victory. The official monument, designed by Fritz Cremer and erected just outside the entrance to Buchenwald in 1958, did not depict the emaciated and desperate victims of the Nazi concentration camps. Instead it showed hardened fighters, with rifles and flags in their hands, fists clenched to give the Communist salute, marching into a better future (represented by the figure of a child in the group). Millions of GDR school children and citizens swore the oath of Buchenwald when visiting the camp (an almost obligatory part of the GDR's school curriculum): 'On this parade-ground that has seen the horrors of fascism, we swear to all humanity that our fight will not be over until the people of the world have called each and every one of these criminals to justice! Our quest is to tear out the Nazi evil by its roots. Our goal is a new world of peace and freedom.'[2] It committed those visiting the memorial to learn the lessons of the past and support the socialist nation – the only true heir to the legacy of the antifascist struggle.

The 1 per cent active anti-Nazi fighters in the GDR were well aware that many ordinary Germans had either actively supported or at least willingly endured the Nazi regime. By inviting them to endorse, with hindsight, the Communist struggle against the Nazis, they were at the same time promising them not to ask any searching questions about their own loyalties during the Nazi years. Communist ideology laid the blame for Nazism firmly at the door of capitalists and imperialists, thereby exonerating the German people. The famous GDR documentary film, *You and Many Comrades* (*Du und mancher Kamerad*), for example, relentlessly emphasized the link between capitalism and fascism. Active Communist antifascists were not haunted by feelings of guilt about their own past, and they were now embarking on the task of converting the German people, or at least those resident in the GDR to the values and ideas of antifascism. As long as the people were willing to endorse the antifascist state ideology and draw the same lessons from it as the ruling Communist party, the past remained trouble-free territory. Unlike the FRG which had to undergo a painful process of a belated working through of the National Socialist past, which involved confronting its own demons, the GDR's antifascism ironically made the fascist past much less troublesome.[3]

2 Cited in Rudy Koshar, *From Monuments to Traces: Artifacts of German Memory, 1870–1990* (Berkeley, 2000), p. 209.

3 Mary Fulbrook, *German National Identity after the Holocaust* (Cambridge, 1999).

Working through the past, GDR-style, often remained a formulaic and shambolic act, ordered from above, which remained without much meaning especially for younger Germans. Oral interviews carried out in the 1980s with GDR citizens who had been young adults under Nazism revealed a large-scale absence of any feelings of guilt or shame.[4]

The GDR in fact did not portray National Socialism as a part of its own history. Unlike the FRG, the GDR never claimed to be a successor state of the German *Reich*. Instead it propagated a clean break with the past. National Socialism was the problem of the capitalist FRG. There, Communists insisted, it was still virulent. After all, as the GDR did not tire of pointing out, former Nazis continued to occupy important positions in the higher echelons of West German society. In the GDR, by contrast, antifascism had won the day. And indeed, the GDR could point out that, with the help of the Soviets, denazification had been a far more thorough affair in the Soviet zone of occupation than in the West. More than half a million former members of the NSDAP were removed from their positions and replaced with those whom the regime deemed politically reliable. Especially in education, the legal profession, the economy and the civil service a thorough change of elites took place which had no parallel in the FRG. But at the same time, the Soviets, like their American counterparts, were keen to make use of the expertise of those Nazis who had useful specialist knowledge. Thus, some Nazis, provided they supported the Communist state, continued their careers even in the antifascist GDR.[5]

The GDR's antifascism was highly selective. It celebrated, above all, the Communist struggle. Communist martyrs were hailed as 'founding fathers' of the GDR. Socialists and other antifascists were acknowledged as long as they, if they were still alive, supported the SED and the GDR. Heroically fighting and dying males dominated the Communist pantheon of the resistance to Nazism. Women, by contrast, were mostly depicted as passive victims and survivors.[6] Those antifascists who did not fit the Communist tale of betrayal and redemption were excluded from the official memory altogether. Thus, for example, some victim groups, such as homosexuals and lesbians, were hardly talked about at all in the homophobic GDR. Even the memory of the Holocaust had to take a back seat in comparison to the memory of the heroic Communist resistance.

Revelations about the Holocaust at the end of the Second World War had dented the Communist certainties about fascism being a nasty way of propping up capitalism. But National Socialism was still primarily interpreted as a regime defending capitalist interests against the working class. The centrality of the idea of the 'racial nation' to any understanding of National Socialism escaped Communist theories of fascism. Nevertheless a Holocaust discourse was maintained in the GDR

4 Lutz Niethammer, Dorothee Wierling and Alexander von Plato, *Die volkseigene Erfahrung* (Berlin, 1991).

5 Norman Naimark, *The Russians in Germany: A History of the Soviet Zone of Occupation, 1945–1949* (Cambridge, Mass., 1995); Jürgen Danyel, ed., *Die geteilte Vergangenheit: Zum Umgang mit dem Nationalsozialismus in den beiden deutschen Staaten* (Berlin, 1995).

6 Claudia Koonz, 'Between Memory and Oblivion: Concentration Camps in German Memory', in John Gillis, ed., *Commemorations: The Politics of National Identity* (Princeton, 1994), pp. 258–80.

from the beginning, although it was one which had many uncharted areas.[7] It became a major topic of historical research only in the 1980s, when it reflected the SED's greater willingness to confront the legacy of the Holocaust. The GDR made strenuous efforts to commemorate the 50th anniversary of the Night of Broken Glass in November 1988 and announced plans to rebuild the main Berlin synagogue at Oranienburgerstraße (completed in 1991). The general secretary of the SED, Erich Honecker, also signalled that the GDR was at long last willing to compensate Jewish victims of Nazism.

Back in the early 1950s less than 2000 Jews living on the territory of the GDR were shocked by the nasty antisemitic campaigns which raged through Communist Eastern Europe. The member of the SED's politburo, Paul Merker, was its most prominent victim in East Germany. A champion of Jewish emigration to Palestine in the early 1940s, he was now accused of being 'in the pay of Zionist monopoly capitalists'. Anti-Zionism remained a prominent feature of Eastern European Communist regimes, even after the overtly antisemitic campaigns subsided. Although Marxists could look back on a proud record of denouncing and fighting antisemitism, the left had also been influenced by long-standing antisemitic tendencies.[8] The GDR's media were certainly full of anti-Israeli statements which made use of antisemitic stereotypes. In the 1980s the small right-wing skinhead counter-culture, existing on the margins of GDR society, adapted such official antisemitism for their own purposes. The churches in the GDR had already warned of a rise of antisemitic incidents in 1978. By that time, however, the official GDR had learnt to live with its tiny Jewish communities, numbering hardly more than 400 people. Levels of antisemitism were lower than in the FRG, and the eight Jewish communities received generous financial support from the state. In some respects they had become a 'privileged minority',[9] albeit one which was not allowed an independent political voice.

If the socialist nation had at times a problematic relationship with its Jewish citizens, it also had problems with a small Slav national minority, the Sorbs. Unlike the Nazis, the SED did not repress them as racial 'others'. Quite the contrary, the approximately 50,000 people living around Bautzen, Hoyerswerda and the Spreewald enjoyed a considerable amount of cultural protection. The SED allowed them their own representative institution, the Domowina. It encouraged Sorb folklore festivals and the use of the Sorb's own language, Wendish. It even paid for the upkeep of newspapers in Wendish. As long as the Sorbs were willing to accept the leading role of the SED, they were, not unlike the Jews, treated as a privileged minority. However, problems arose over the GDR's policies of industrialization and in particular its ruthless exploitation of brown coal in opencast mining which lay in precisely those areas where the Sorb villages and towns were located. Hence, where the GDR's cultural policy attempted to encourage a

7 Karin Hartewig, ' "Proben des Abgrunds, über welchem unsere Zivilisation wie eine Brücke schwebt": Der Holocaust in der Publizistik der SBZ/DDR', in Norbert Frei and Sybille Steinbacher, eds, *Beschweigen und Bekennen: Die deutsche Nachkriegsgesellschaft und der Holocaust* (Göttingen, 2001), pp. 35–50.

8 Thomas Haury, *Antisemitismus von links* (Hamburg, 2003).

9 Robin Ostow, *Jews in Contemporary East Germany: The Children of Moses in the Land of Marx* (London, 1989).

sense of Sorbian identity, its economic policies destroyed and uprooted the very communities whose culture it sought to protect.[10]

Jewish and Slav minorities were citizens of the GDR. What about the socialist nation's treatment of foreigners? In 1989 about 190,000 foreigners lived on the territory of the GDR. Some were political refugees. The GDR demonstrated its international solidarity by allowing Communist refugees (for example from Greece or Chile) to settle in the GDR. Many foreigners, about 91,000 in 1989, were workers who had come to the GDR as the result of bilateral treaties with other Communist countries. The first of these had been signed with Poland and Hungary in the early 1960s. From the 1970s onwards an increasing number of workers, mostly single men between the ages of 18 and 35, came from the developing world, e.g. from Vietnam, Mozambique, Algeria and Cuba. In line with the official Marxist internationalism their employment was often depicted as a kind of development aid for socialist 'brother countries'. In reality, however, these workers were desperately needed to make up for the severe labour shortage in the factories. They were artificially ghettoized and isolated. Housing provided by the state was often poor and the authorities eyed foreign workers with suspicion. They were widely viewed as temporary 'guests' who had to behave 'properly'. Contact with GDR citizens was discouraged. In fact, GDR citizens had to report any such contact to the authorities who kept a file on every single foreigner. Cultural prejudices and the completely untenable assumption that foreign workers bought up GDR goods and thereby contributed to the less than satisfactory provision of consumer goods led to a number of xenophobic incidents. Little wonder then that many foreign workers were disappointed about their experiences with the socialist Germany and often returned to their countries of origin early. But many also attempted to negotiate their position in GDR society both vis-à-vis the authorities and their German work colleagues. Apart from workers, the GDR invited tens of thousands of foreign students, again mainly from socialist countries of the developing world, to study at universities and obtain skills which were badly needed in their native countries. Here the claim of the GDR to provide developmental aid was more justified. The universities also made more substantial efforts to integrate foreign students into the indigenous student body, although the official emphasis on discipline and control was still paramount. The formal commitment of the GDR to internationalist solidarity between socialist peoples did not necessarily stamp out racism in the wider population.[11]

Friendship with the Soviet Union and Sovietization

If antifascism was one leg on which the socialist nation in the GDR came to stand, the other was its friendship and solidarity with the 'motherland of the

[10] Peter Barker, *Slavs in Germany: the Sorbian Minority and the German States since 1945* (Lampeter, 2000).

[11] On foreigners in the GDR see the forthcoming University of London PhD thesis by Damian Mac Con Uladh. I am grateful to him for letting me see parts of his thesis and discussing the topic with me.

proletariat', the Soviet Union. The Soviet army was described as liberator of German workers and peasants oppressed by the Nazis. Memorials to the Soviet liberators dotted the official memory landscape. The most monumental display of Soviet heroism could be found in Berlin Treptow: the monument for the fallen Soviet soldiers was commissioned in 1946 and opened in 1949. Its central statue depicted a kneeling Soviet soldier, 11.6 metres high, holding a German child by the hand, sword in his other hand, a broken swastika at his feet.

A poem written by pupils at the youth high school of the SED's youth organization, the Free German Youth (FDJ), brought out another aspect of that liberation: the Soviets were helping the liberated German people to build socialism:

Free became the peasant on his own soil	Frei ward der Bauer auf eigenem Grund,
Thanks to you, Soviet soldiers.	Dank euch, ihr Sowjetsoldaten.
Allied to the liberated proletarian	Mit dem befreiten Proleten im Bund
He works with plough and spade.	Schafft er mit Pflug und Spaten.
Because all hatred, all misery was	Denn allen Hass, alle Not überwand
Conquered gloriously by the Soviet Union	Siegreich die Sowjetunion.
As brothers they lend a helping hand	Brüderlich reicht sie helfend die Hand
Also to our German nation.	Auch unser deutschen Nation.[12]

The German–Soviet friendship society boasted a mass membership organized in local branches stretching across the country. Special weeks of German–Soviet friendship were organized, which included numerous cultural events and a regular exchange of delegations. Many East Germans travelled to the Soviet Union and forged personal friendships with Soviet citizens. East Germans had a much greater appreciation of the suffering of the Soviet people in the Second World War than their West German counterparts. Article 6 of the 1974 constitution of the GDR described the socialist nation as 'forever and irrevocably allied to the Union of Socialist Soviet Republics'. Previous alliances between Russia and the German lands, such as the anti-Napoleon coalition in the early nineteenth century, were celebrated as precursors of the contemporary alliance between the Soviet Union and the GDR. The 140th anniversary of the Battle of Leipzig in 1953 was commemorated with great aplomb, and the Leipzig monument, dedicated to this battle, was made into a symbol of amicable German–Soviet relations. By contrast, a strict silence was observed on all those aspects of German–Soviet relations, which did not fit, such as the Hitler–Stalin pact of 1939.

Initially, friendship with the Soviet Union did not imply slavishly following a Soviet model. Anton Ackermann put forward the notion of a 'German road to socialism': Germany, he argued, was much more industrialized and proletarianized than Russia had been in 1917. Hence socialism would come to it more easily and would not have to take recourse to the stringent dictatorial measures employed in the Soviet Union. The 'dictatorship of the proletariat' would not have to be as harsh. However, following the break between the Soviet and the Yugoslav Communist parties in 1946, all national roads to socialism smacked of 'Titoism'. What followed was the thorough Sovietization of Communist Eastern

[12] *Leben, Singen, Kämpfen. Liederbuch der FDJ* (Berlin, 1952), p. 42f.

Europe, including the GDR.[13] One of the key slogans in the GDR throughout the 1950s was: 'To learn from the Soviet people means to learn victory'. Politically, the SED became obsessed with controlling all aspects of the GDR's society. The heavy hand of the socialist state attempted to stamp out all autonomous spheres in society. The federal political system, initially reconstituted in the form of five *Länder*, was replaced in 1952 with 14 *Bezirke* which were far more tightly controlled from the centre. Regionalism and a sense of *Heimat* were, however, maintained in the GDR, but only where they did not challenge the authority of the SED and instead promised to encourage a GDR identity.[14]

The SED purged itself several times in the late 1940s and early 1950s, removing from power in particular former Social Democrats and those Communists who had spent their years of exile in Western countries rather than the Soviet Union. Soviet symbols and rituals were taken over to represent party, state and diverse social groups in the GDR. The Stalin cult was adopted and GDR strongman Walter Ulbricht initiated a similar cult around his personality. Johannes R. Becher, culture minister in the GDR, wrote one of innumerable poems on the 'great Stalin': 'When happiness colours the cheeks in red / One gives thanks to you, Stalin, and says nothing but "You"! / A pauper whispers "Stalin" even whilst dying / And Stalin closes his eyes.' ('Wenn sich vor Freude rot die Wangen färben / Dankt man Dir, Stalin, und sagt nichts als "Du"! / Ein Armer flüstert "Stalin" noch im Sterben / Und Stalins Hand drückt ihm die Augen zu.')[15] Stalin's works had to be read in every 'work collective' up and down the land, and the first road which was rebuilt in East Berlin after the war was named after the Soviet dictator. The seven-kilometre long project was a straight copy of Soviet architectural models.

Political Sovietization was accompanied by social and economic Sovietization. With the help of the Soviets, German Communists unleashed nothing short of a social revolution on the territory of the Soviet zone of occupation: land reform, nationalization of major industries and the implementation of policies of positive discrimination to educate its own working-class elite. From a Marxist perspective a socialist nation had to be created from the economic foundations upwards. Economic management and planning, the collectivization of agriculture, and cultural policies all followed closely Soviet models. Was the GDR then, as is sometimes alleged, simply a Soviet puppet state, a kind of Russian *homunculus*? Certainly, the continued support of the Soviet Union was crucial for the existence of the GDR, which always lacked democratic legitimacy. When the Soviet Union withdrew its guarantees for a Communist GDR in the late 1980s, it duly collapsed.

But the GDR was more than a Soviet concoction or implant. Many specifically German traditions went into the reinvention of a socialist Germany, especially traditions of the German labour movement and of the KPD in the inter-war

13 Konrad Jarausch and Hannes Siegrist, eds, *Amerikanisierung und Sowjetisierung in Deutschland 1945–1970* (Frankfurt/Main, 1997).

14 Mary Fulbrook, 'Democratic Centralism and Regionalism in the GDR', in Maiken Umbach, ed., *German Federalism: Past, Present, Future* (London, 2002), pp. 146–71.

15 Cited in Günter Kunert, 'Ein Armer flüstert "Stalin" noch im Sterben', *Die Welt*, 5 March 2003. On the Ulbricht years in the GDR generally see Patrick Major and Jonathan Osmond, eds, *The Workers' and Peasants' State: Communism and Society in East Germany under Ulbricht, 1945–71* (Manchester, 2002).

period.[16] The GDR presented itself as the result of a long history of class struggles in Germany. The forward march of the long-suffering masses to emancipation and freedom culminated in the development of a socialist society in the GDR. However, until the mid-1950s the SED leadership was deeply worried that the Soviets might use the GDR as a pawn in a greater game of international Cold War diplomacy. Stalin, after all, repeatedly offered a unified and neutral Germany which might not turn out to be Communist. Hence German Communists rather than their Soviet allies were forcefully pursuing radical social and political change, which would be difficult to undo in the foreseeable future. They had a direct interest in deepening the differences with the FRG and making reunification a less likely option. The driving force behind the Sovietization of East Germany and the Stalinization of the SED therefore were German Communists rather than the Soviet military authorities.[17] The building of the Berlin Wall in 1961 was again in no small measure due to pressure brought to bear by the East German leadership on the Soviets. And in the 1980s, Honecker and his gerontocracy decided against their Soviet allies that Gorbachev's brand of reform communism would not provide an acceptable model for developments in the GDR.

Sovietization shaped the face and outlook of the GDR to a considerable extent despite the fact that large sections of the population continued to reject it. There was no 'Easternization' of East Germans in the same way that one can speak about a 'Westernization' of West Germans after 1945.[18] The very idea of an eternal German-Soviet friendship never took hold of the popular imagination the way that pro-Americanism did in the West. It always retained something of a stage-managed affair. For a start, the portrayal of Soviet soldiers as liberators did not square with the experience of millions of Germans. Goebbels's propaganda ministry had told them for years to think of Slavs and Russians in particular as savage subhumans. German men had fought a war of annihilation against the Soviets, and had been involved in some of the most gruesome atrocities of the Second World War. The barbarization of warfare in the East, for which the *Wehrmacht* had been responsible, had produced Soviet revenge atrocities. Hundreds of thousands of German women had been raped by Soviet soldiers. Hundreds of thousands of German ex-prisoners of war found it difficult to forget the atrocious conditions they had suffered in the Soviet camps. The GDR welcomed them back as heroes who had performed a 'national duty' in the Soviet Union and made good some of the horrors that the Nazis had left behind. They were celebrated as ambassadors of the new socialist Germany who had played an important part in the ongoing reconciliation process. The GDR, in other words, tried hard to make former prisoners of war loyal citizens of the socialist nation. But in the process they more often than not treated them and the wider population

16 Michael Lemke, ed., *Sowjetisierung und Eigenständigkeit in der SBZ/DDR (1945–1953)* (Cologne, 1999).

17 Corey Ross, *The East German Dictatorship: Problems and Perspectives in the Interpretation of the GDR* (London, 2002), p. 164. On the making of the GDR and its many continuities to German history see also Gareth Pritchard, *The Making of the GDR 1945–53: From Antifascism to Stalinism* (Manchester, 2000).

18 See above, Chapter 6.

like children who had to be converted to antifascism and German–Soviet friendship.[19] The recipients of these doses of re-education were on the whole somewhat reluctant to follow where the SED led.

The Soviets were seen by many as unwelcome occupiers who backed up an unwelcome political regime. Russian became the compulsory first foreign language in GDR schools, but it remained unpopular with many East German pupils. The SED was widely known as 'party of Russians' (*Russenpartei*), and deeply embedded negative stereotypes of Russians continued to be active among wider sections of the East German population. Millions of refugees and expellees from the 'German east' were not allowed to build up their own interest organizations and were prevented from voicing any criticism of the enforced population movements at the end of the Second World War. The GDR officially accepted the new boundaries of Germany and celebrated comradely relations with the very people's republics who had ordered the expulsion of its German minorities. Hence the GDR disallowed any official memory of the 'German east' and instead sought to integrate the so-called 'resettlers' (*Umsiedler*) into East German society. They were given rapid and unbureaucratic help. Where they had been farmers they were provided with land and encouraged to build up a new existence as farmers.[20] But the enforced collectivization of agriculture, which gathered pace in the late 1950s, had truly disastrous results on the long-term loyalty of many formerly independent farmers to the GDR. Those who did not go West were often permanently alienated, harbouring their bitter private memories which could not be squared with the official celebrations of co-operative farming.[21]

If, on the whole, the East German population proved to be reluctant converts to Sovietization, this only doubled the Communists' zeal in educating them to see the light. The GDR is frequently described as an 'educative dictatorship' (*Erziehungsdiktatur*), and, indeed, the education of the young in particular was taken very seriously by the SED. Young Pioneers and the FDJ organized children from an early age. The party's youth groups organized leisure-time activities. In the schools the young were educated to become loyal citizens of the socialist nation and to hate the class enemy who resided in the FRG.[22] The problem was that many of the emancipatory and libertarian norms and values of socialism were difficult to reconcile with the reality of a kind of musty authoritarianism in the GDR. The difference between the claims of socialism and its 'actually-existing' variant produced disillusionment and crises of confidence which resulted, time and again, in generational conflict. Young people did not always take the socialist identity that was on offer. Those born between 1945 and 1955, raised entirely

[19] Frank Biess, ' "Pioneers of a New Germany": Returning POWs from the Soviet Union and the Making of East German Citizens', *Central European History*, 32 (1999), pp. 143–80.

[20] Philipp Ther, *Deutsche und polnische Vertriebene: Gesellschaft und Vertriebenenpolitik in der SBZ/DDR und in Polen 1945–1956* (Göttingen, 1999).

[21] Arnd Bauerkämper, 'Collectivisation and Memory: Views of the Past and the Transformation of Rural Society in the GDR from 1952 to the early 1960s', *German Studies Review*, 25 (2002), pp. 213–25.

[22] On the importance of schooling for the GDR's attempt to create a new Marxist nation see John G. Rodden, *Repainting the Little Red Schoolhouse: A History of Eastern German Education 1945–1995* (Oxford, 2002).

in the GDR, did not become prototypes of the new socialist Germany that the SED wanted to create.[23]

Communists constantly sought to mobilize and politicize the whole of the population. Whereas the conservative governments in the early FRG had encouraged the depoliticization and family orientation of West Germans after Nazism, the GDR did precisely the opposite. It sought to convert Germans to a new anti-fascist and Communist political order. It wanted them to transfer their energies from building the Nazi *Volksgemeinschaft* to constructing a new socialist Germany. What the SED failed to recognize was that, after total war and total defeat, the majority of Germans, East and West, had little appetite for resuming highly politicized struggles. They instead concentrated on their immediate surroundings of family, neighbours and friends. It was in these 'private' circles that much of the notorious bartering went on which characterized the GDR economy and compensated for the lack of a working market. GDR citizens attempted to pursue their common interests outside of the highly regulated public sphere. They sought to create a 'niche society' (*Nischengesellschaft*)[24] in the face of determined attempts by the SED to politicize them. There always was, of course, considerable overlap and interaction between the public and the private spheres, as the powerful representatives of the SED and the many citizens of the GDR sought to negotiate where Communist control was to end in the socialist nation.[25]

It would be mistaken to portray the invention of a socialist nation as nothing but the Soviet-backed dictatorship of a minority of German Communists over a long-suffering majority. After all, conformity with the SED regime was widespread. Millions actively and willingly took part in the socialist remaking of Germany. The SED had almost 2 million members by the 1980s. Millions more were members of SED-sponsored mass organizations. Much of that conformity was, of course, bound up with career prospects and other tangible benefits, but it was also the result of people trying to reorganize and readjust their lives and beliefs after 1945. Many of those born into the GDR were at least partially affected by their constant bombardment with slogans and ideas underpinning the socialist identity of the GDR. And for many of those socialized under Nazism, the authoritarianism of the SED state offered a relatively easy way of accommodating their authoritarian socialization received under an altogether different reinvention of the nation. As Lutz Niethammer remarked, 'the SED inherited a people, of which about one tenth refused to join in, but which on the whole was well trained in its secondary national virtues and which knew how to raise the arm and keep the fist in the pocket'.[26] In fact, conformity to authoritarianism had, as we have seen, a long tradition in the various reinventions of the nation in the German lands. The GDR carried on some of the traditions of German statism

[23] Dorothee Wierling, *Geboren im Jahr Eins: Der Jahrgang 1949 in der DDR und seine historischen Erfahrungen* (Berlin, 2002).

[24] Günter Gaus, *Wo Deutschland liegt* (Munich, 1983).

[25] Thomas Lindenberger, ed., *Herrschaft und Eigen-Sinn in der Diktatur: Studien zur Gesellschaftsgeschichte der DDR* (Cologne, 1999); Richard Bessel and Ralph Jessen, eds, *Die Grenzen der Diktatur: Staat und Gesellschaft in der SBZ/DDR* (Göttingen, 1996).

[26] Lutz Niethammer, *Deutschland danach: Postfaschistiche Gesellschaft und nationales Gedächtnis* (Bonn, 1999), p. 174.

and authoritarianism. It was a heavily bureaucratic system which emphasized control (through an intricate web of surveillance of the entire population spun by the notorious secret police, the Stasi) and mobilization (through propaganda). The highly bureaucratic, impersonal and officious language of officialdom in the GDR was reminiscent of Imperial Germany, as was the authority invested in representatives of the state. Other continuities to a more traditional Germanness in the GDR included anti-Western thought, anticapitalism, and a strong emphasis on the importance of intellectuals in bringing about the new nation.

East Germany remained more recognizably German than West Germany. It was a more heavily militarized society. Not for nothing was it nicknamed 'Red Prussia'. The image of goose-stepping East German soldiers parading every 1 May in front of the entire leadership of the GDR was a constant reminder of the traditions of the Prussian army. Serving in the army was portrayed as fulfilling one's national duty in the GDR. School children underwent 'premilitary education' which involved scouting games but also shooting practice. Paramilitary 'fighting groups' (*Kampfgruppen*) sought to mobilize the entire workforce of the GDR. In the early 1950s the paramilitary Society for Sport and Technology (GST) sought to attract members with the slogan: 'Whoever loves peace, *Heimat* and life joins the GST and practices'.[27] Ten per cent of the GDR's total population were active members of some form of military or paramilitary organization. Military metaphors abounded in the official language of the GDR. Uniforms were everywhere. Not having served in the army or refusing to join one of the numerous paramilitary organizations could have serious consequences for career prospects. A form of conscientious objection was introduced in 1964, following a long campaign by the East German churches. But enlisting as a 'construction soldier' (*Bausoldat*) meant facing abysmal treatment and ruined future prospects. Ironically a highly militarized socialist nation presented itself constantly as the German 'peace state' (*Friedensstaat*). Constant vigilance was necessary, the SED argued, because of the imperialist ambitions and the aggressive potential of West Germany and NATO.[28]

Looking West: the 'workers' state' and the FRG

The main 'other' of the East German socialist nation was no longer an ethnic one, but a class one. It was the potentially fascist bourgeoisie ruling in West Germany, allied to the imperialist USA, and seeking to overpower the socialist GDR. The GDR put major resources into overcoming the continued non-recognition of the socialist Germany by most Western and developing nations. Its very existence, GDR representatives argued, proved how unrealistic the policy of continued non-recognition by the 'West German imperialists' was. The tenth anniversary of the

27 'Schüsse auf Pappkameraden', *Der Spiegel*, 19 May 1953.

28 Corey Ross, 'Protecting the Accomplishments of Socialism? The (Re)Militarization of Life in the German Democratic Republic', in Major and Osmond, eds, *The Workers' and Peasants' State*, pp. 78–93 (as note 15).

GDR was celebrated as a severe setback for the FRG. Yet, until the advent of *Ostpolitik*, West Germany was highly successful in preventing the international recognition of what in West German official language remained 'the zone' or 'the so-called GDR'.

Language emerged as a key battlefield in the GDR's struggle for legitimacy.[29] It was only in the 1970s that official circles in West Germany began to refer to the GDR by its official name: Deutsche Demokratische Republik or DDR. Even thereafter conservative newspapers, such as the tabloid *Bild*, used the acronym 'DDR' only in inverted commas to indicate that it was not a legitimate state. Officials in West Germany referred to the FRG itself simply as 'Deutschland' to underline its claim to represent the whole of Germany. The term Bundesrepublik or worse, the acronym BRD, was used in turn by the GDR to indicate its own difference. The FRG promptly retaliated by proscribing the use of these terms. In the 1950s West German linguists complained about the manipulation and misuse of the German language in the GDR, bemoaning the emergence of a 'Soviet German' (*Sowjetdeutsch*). While such value-judgements were clearly ideological in nature, substantial linguistic differences did indeed develop during the forty years of separation. Sometimes the same word had different meanings. Brigade, for example, was an army unit in West German while it referred to a work unit in a factory in East German. The same word could have very different connotations: comrade and communist, for example, carried positive connotations in the GDR and negative ones in the FRG. In both countries different words were used to express one and the same thing. A West German 'employer', for example, became a 'capitalist' in East German. West German 'release of workers' translated as 'mass redundancies' in East German. Conceptual terms signifying whole ideologies such as 'class war' or 'social partnership' were used very differently in the two Germanies. There were also, of course, a range of different neologisms. In West Germany the influx of a deluge of English words transformed the German language to a considerable extent. For East Germans the Anglicization of the German language was a sure sign that Anglo-American capitalism had the FRG firmly under its thumb.

The GDR portrayed an Americanized West Germany as un-German. It opposed Americanized popular culture such as jazz and later, rock and roll. Expressions of 'Western decadence', they reflected the 'anarchism of capitalist society'.[30] They threatened to lure the GDR youth away from socialist ethics, as laid down in the 'Ten Principles of Socialist Ethics and Morality' put forward by the 1958 SED congress. This crackdown on American popular culture led to direct confrontation with East German youth, whose musical tastes were turned into a highly political affair by the Communist state. Official attempts to promote a popular music and culture which would transport politically correct messages and enhance socialist consciousness was often a non-starter with the consumers of popular

[29] Michael Townson, *Mother-tongue and Fatherland: Language and Politics in Germany* (Manchester, 1992), pp. 178–92. Also on the differences between the German language East and West see Patrick Stevenson, *Language and German Disunity: A Sociolinguistic History of East and West in Germany, 1945–2000* (Oxford, 2002).

[30] Uta G. Poiger, *Jazz, Rock and Rebels: Cold War Politics and American Culture in a Divided Germany* (Berkeley, 2000).

music. Who, after all, would want to listen to songs entitled 'Our agricultural co-operative owns one hundred geese' (*Unsere LPG hat hundert Gänse*)?

The anti-Western impetus of the socialist nation was obvious in the Communists' functionalization of the Allied bombing of Dresden in the Second World War. On 13 February 1945 Dresden, overcrowded with refugees, was almost completely destroyed in a night of relentless bombing. Incendiary devices caused a five-day long firestorm. 35,000 people died. The GDR identified the horrors of the bombing war with imperialist barbarity and aggression of the American and British forces, which, according to the ruling Communists, could strike again at any time.

Anti-Western sentiments were combined with the SED's constant portrayal of the GDR as the better Germany. It was more antifascist and had learnt the lessons of the past more thoroughly than the FRG. It was a 'workers' and farmers' state' (*Arbeiter- und Bauernstaat*) in which the working people were no longer exploited. Instead the SED as the party of the working class led the state to serve the interests of the people – guided by the principles of Marxism–Leninism. Working-class history and the history of class struggles and the labour movement was prioritized over any other kind of history in the official memory of the socialist nation. The working class itself was artificially preserved and put on constant display.[31] It was put on stage because workers were at the very heart of the SED's claim to legitimacy. Skilled workers were courted by the regime which advertised itself on job security, the constitutionally guaranteed right to work, social security, an egalitarian wage system, low rents, subsidized basic food products and better opportunities for working-class children in the educational system. A cult of the worker developed which depicted workers as the rock on which the new nation was being built. Kindergarten children were taught to respect and love workers. The 1967 Law on Citizenship emphasized the elevated position of the working class in the socialist nation: 'The citizenship of the German Democratic Republic is membership of its residents in the first peace-loving, democratic and socialist German state, in which the working class exercises political power in alliance with the farmers' co-operative class, the socialist intelligentsia and other labouring people.'[32]

One of the most potent symbols of this nation based on working-class power was the newly built city of Eisenhüttenstadt (named Stalinstadt for a brief period before deStalinization), the East German equivalent of Wolfsburg in the West.[33] Planned around the construction of a massive steel industry, it attracted workers because wages were higher and consumer goods were more readily available. It was also easier to get one of the sought-after modern flats. Chances for social mobility were higher. Interviews with workers who had lived and worked in Eisenhüttenstadt revealed their highly positive evaluation of their own life experiences which they saw characterized by increasing prosperity and high levels of social security. They emphasized as extremely positive the camaraderie and

[31] Christoph Klessmann, 'Workers in the Workers' State: German Traditions, the Soviet Model and the Magnetic Attraction of West Germany', in *idem*, ed., *The Divided Past: Re-writing Post War German History* (Oxford, 2001), pp. 11–41.

[32] Carl-Christoph Schweitzer et al., *Politics and Government in Germany 1944–1994: Basic Documents* (Oxford, 1995), pp. 379ff.

[33] See above, p. 186.

solidarity of a strong work-based culture.[34] The GDR can indeed be described as a workplace society. People identified with their place of work more than was the case in the FRG. A much greater share of the lives of East Germans was centred on the workplace. Many East Germans felt 'at home' in their work collective and forged very strong workplace identities. Workers enjoyed considerable protection against arbitrary dismissal. Trade unions and workers' brigades were given substantial means to ensure that workers received continuous training and to provide for leisure activities, sick pay and the allocation of holiday places. Enterprises offered a wide range of educational and social amenities from libraries to crèches. The SED not only used material incentives to woo workers: not unlike the Nazis, the Communists appealed to the workers' pride in 'their' products and attempted to link the propagation of German 'quality work' to the development of class consciousness and the raising of productivity rates.

Given that the SED built its invention of a socialist nation on the construction of images of a working-class state, it must have come as a huge shock when the workers turned against 'their' nation in the spring of 1953. Increases in work norms and prices led to a spontaneous strike wave in factories across the GDR. On 16 and 17 June strikes were recorded in 560 cities and towns across the GDR. Huge public demonstrations demanded an end to SED rule, free elections and reunification with West Germany. Building workers led the demonstrations in East Berlin. With the help of Soviet tanks the rising was quickly repressed. Several dozen people were killed on the streets and 1600 protesters were sentenced to often long jail sentences in the aftermath of the rising. Brecht's ironic comment, unpublished at the time, was that the government of the GDR should perhaps dissolve its people and elect another. Officially the SED portrayed the rising as 'fascist provocation' masterminded in Bonn and Washington.

But they knew better and after 1953 the SED was even more cautious in ensuring the accommodation of working-class interests. Many workers, however, remained reluctant converts to the 'workers' state'. When the Communists sought to raise productivity through the creation of 'socialist heroes of work', the 'master hero', the miner Adolf Hennecke, received an anonymous letter addressing him as 'pimp of Soviet exploitation of German workers'.[35] Communist appeals to 'German quality work' and 'honour of labour' were not always gratefully received by workers.[36] They often used their work collectives, the brigades, to represent their own interests at factory level. Struggles over pay, work norms, paid vacations and work safety were common, and informal strikes and work stoppages happened throughout the existence of the GDR. Management tended to give in to working-class demands wherever possible. After all, the GDR was supposed to be a working-class state. Hence workers' interests were placated even where it was

[34] Rosemarie Beier ed., *Aufbau West – Aufbau Ost: Die Planstädte Wolfsburg und Eisenhüttenstadt in der Nachkriegszeit* (Berlin, 1997); Dagmar Semmelmann, Gudrun Prengel and Ursula Krüger, eds, *Eisenhüttenstädter Lesebuch* (Berlin, 2000).

[35] Corey Ross, *Constructing Socialism at the Grass-Roots: The Transformation of East Germany, 1945–1965* (London, 2000), p. 45.

[36] Alf Lüdtke, ' "Helden der Arbeit" – Mühe beim Arbeiten. Zur mißmutigen Loyalität von Industriearbeitern in der DDR', in Hartmut Kaelble *et al.*, eds, *Sozialgeschichte der DDR* (Stuttgart, 1994).

obviously detrimental to the GDR's economic interests. The most famous example was the notorious over-employment which was maintained to justify the proud claim that in the GDR every citizen had a 'right to work'. Unemployment was the scourge of the capitalist West. Another example was the introduction of the five-day working week in the GDR in 1967, in direct response to a similar measure in the FRG. It was done despite the fact that it would lower productivity even more.

The workers' reluctance to endorse the reinvention of a socialist Germany was in many respects central to the eventual demise of the GDR.[37] The resistance of 'really existing workers' to 'really existing socialism' was made a topic in Frank Beyer's celebrated film *Spur der Steine* (*Traces of Stones*) (1966). The main protagonist of the film, the leader of a building brigade in a chemical factory, Balla, is deeply suspicious of SED propaganda. In a scene where he listens to a SED official promising the workers a glorious future in the socialist nation, Balla remarks to his fellow workers: 'They promise you the future like the priests promise you an after-life, and before you know it, you are dead.' In the film Balla undergoes a conversion process and ultimately accepts the higher authority of the SED.[38] Beyer, like many left-of-centre intellectuals, was broadly supportive of the attempt to reinvent a socialist nation. In fact, the SED could initially draw on the resourcefulness of the socialist cultural movement of the Weimar Republic which it sought to recreate. Many writers and intellectuals who had been exiled by the Nazis returned to the Soviet zone of occupation in the hope that it was here that a new and better Germany would emerge. They were fascinated by the wide-reaching attempt to remake German society. But the SED squandered this cultural capital through its own preoccupation with control and censorship. As the case of Beyer illustrates, even the most loyal criticism was still unwelcome: his film could not be shown in the GDR. Time and again SED officials disappointed and frustrated precisely those intellectuals who were most willing to support an audacious reinvention of the German nation.

By contrast, workers remained far more sceptical than intellectuals about the kind of heavy-handed social engineering attempted by the SED. Their mistrust was heightened by the fact that the SED, far from celebrating proletarians as they were, sought to mould German workers in the labour movement image. In line with a strong tradition in labour movement culture they wanted to educate workers and lead them to appreciate 'true' culture, which often meant middle-class culture.[39] Thus, for example, the GDR put considerable energies into creating a 'national opera', which was supposed to demonstrate the cultural superiority of the socialist nation to its capitalist rival in the West.[40] Bettering the

[37] Jeffrey Kopstein, 'Chipping Away at the State: Workers' Resistance and the Demise of East Germany', *World Politics*, 48 (1996), pp. 391–423.

[38] Joshua Feinstein, '*Spur der Steine*: Zum Verhältnis von Gegenwart und Geschichte im DEFA-Spielfilm der sechziger Jahre', in Martin Sabrow, ed., *Verwaltete Vergangenheit: Geschichtskultur und Herrschaftslegitimation in der DDR* (Leipzig, 1997), pp. 217–36.

[39] Anna-Sabine Ernst, 'The Politics of Culture and the Culture of Everyday Life in the GDR in the 1950s', in David E. Barclay and Eric D. Weitz, eds, *Between Reform and Revolution: German Socialism and Communism from 1840 to 1990* (Oxford, 1998), pp. 489–506.

[40] Joy Haslam Calico, ' "Für eine deutsche Nationaloper": Opera in the Discourses of Unification and Legitimation in the German Democratic Republic', in Celia Applegate and Pamela Potter, eds, *Music and German National Identity* (Chicago, 2002), pp. 190–204, quote on p. 191.

workers' tastes and morality did often increase the gulf between workers and the representatives of the socialist nation. The SED was, however, not completely unsuccessful in reaching a tenuous and always fragile *modus vivendi* with the workers. Both workers and government could unite around a basic consensus which incorporated a promise of social security, work, egalitarianism and slowly growing prosperity. The Communists' accommodation of working-class interests goes some way towards explaining why there were few public challenges to the SED regime, let alone the foundation of popular opposition movements like the independent trade union Solidarność in Poland. Yet the GDR's claim that only the socialist nation had liberated the masses of workers, whereas the capitalist West continued to exploit working people rang hollow in the ears of many East Germans.

This was true also for East German women, despite the fact that the GDR boasted a greater degree of gender equality than West Germany. It provided all sorts of incentives for women to educate themselves and receive better training and more qualifications. The image of women as 'capable tractor drivers' was a popular one in the early GDR. Women, that was the message, were able to take over even the most manly of jobs. They could rely on the state to provide facilities for childcare thus making it easier to combine having children with pursuing a career. The 1950 Law for the Protection of Mother and Child and the Rights of Women gave pregnant women generous leave and guaranteed job protection. Antenatal and postnatal care were exemplary, and the state paid out generous sums to mothers of three or more children. In the 1980s women's employment rates stood at a staggering 80–90 per cent. Already by the mid-1970s 60 per cent of all students at universities were women.

The socialist nation promised women's liberation, but it also continued to discriminate against women in a variety of ways. The SED remained primarily focussed on the interests of male skilled workers and pushed the issue of gender equality into the background.[41] Few of the top jobs in any area of employment went to women, who were also largely left with the double burden of working and home-making. Employed women could take off one day a month as 'household day'. Men were not allowed the same 'privilege' – a sure sign that housework was still regarded as a woman's duty.[42] Although gendered pay differentials were lower than in the FRG, they did exist. Tempting women into the labour market was not just a means to liberate them but also an important way of overcoming the continued acute labour shortage. Traces of a very traditional proletarian antifeminism could be found everywhere in the workplace culture of the GDR. The SED did not tolerate any autonomous representation of women's interests. The German Women's Association (DFB) was a mass organization with over 1 million members, but it acted, like the trade unions and other mass organizations, primarily as a transmitter of official directives from the SED. Hence many women, like their male colleagues, remained highly sceptical about the

[41] Donna Harsch, 'Approach/Avoidance: Communists and Women in East Germany, 1945–1949', *Social History*, 25 (2000), pp. 156–82.

[42] Heike Trappe, *Emanzipation oder Zwang? Frauen in der DDR zwischen Beruf, Familie und Sozialpolitik* (Berlin, 1995).

proud claims of the SED that the socialist nation had, for the first time in German history, brought true emancipation for male and female workers.

The 'workers' state' continued to be unattractive to many of its citizens, because it failed to address them as consumers. For sure, many East Germans were proud of their economic achievements and happy with high levels of social security. If West Germany became a showcase for Western capitalism, so the GDR was often seen as a showcase for East-European Communism. Germans, it seemed, could even make Communism work. By the 1980s many Western observers believed the GDR to be among the top ten industrialized nations of the world. If it always remained behind its West German counterpart, East Germans could point out that the GDR had a far more difficult start. No Marshall Plan aid helped its economy along. Instead it continued to pay heavy reparations to the Soviet Union at a time when all such payments had ceased in the FRG. For a while the GDR government had propagated the idea of catching up and overtaking West Germany economically. When that proved illusory, the SED fell back on the idea of emphasizing the close links between economic and social policies and attacking West Germany for leaving many workers exposed to the vagaries of the market. Rising social inequalities in the West were juxtaposed with the egalitarian policies pursued by the SED. The 'welfare dictatorship'[43] of the GDR promised greater social equality and committed the government to delivering higher living standards and growing prosperity. Hence the socialist GDR ultimately oriented itself towards very similar goals to the ones pursued by the capitalist FRG. There were hardly any attempts to define specifically socialist lifestyles and consumption patterns. Instead the GDR followed the West in propagating economic growth as the basis for 'prosperity for all'. But it could never hope to keep up with the consumer revolution in the FRG. Pictures of higher living standards and greater availability consumer goods were readily available in every household of the GDR through West German television. Images of the 'golden West' were transmitted through contacts with relatives in West Germany. Western clothing and music lost nothing of their appeal to the young. The West German Deutschmark was effectively a second currency in the GDR which provided access to goods and services not otherwise available.[44]

Despite experimenting with a more flexible economic system in the 1960s, the GDR economy never took off in the same way as the West German one did in the 1950s. Trade deficits grew throughout the 1970s. The economy stagnated and declined with deficits spiralling out of control in the 1980s. The socialist nation, built on the idea of a different economic system, failed, first and foremost, economically. It could not keep up with the economic standards set by capitalist West Germany. The GDR's constant self-portrayal as the better Germany in the end rang hollow with the majority of its citizens, who opted for reunification

43 Konrad Jarausch, 'Care and Coercion: The GDR as Welfare Dictatorship', in *idem*, ed., *Dictatorship as Experience: Towards a Socio-Cultural History of the GDR* (Oxford, 1999), pp. 47–69.

44 Katherine Pence, ' "You as a Woman will Understand": Consumption, Gender and the Relationship between State and Citizenry in the GDR's Crisis of 17 June 1953', *German History*, 19 (2001), pp. 218–52; Ina Merkel, *Utopie und Bedürfnis: Die Geschichte der Konsumkultur in der DDR* (Cologne, 1999).

with the 'golden West' which, they hoped, would bring, at long last, access to the consumer revolution they hoped to share with their West German relatives.

From the goal of a unified socialist Germany to the theory of two Germanies

Immediately after 1945, Communists, following an influential publication by Alexander Abusch,[45] tended to describe the whole of German history as a succession of major disasters. However, as the SED quickly realized, it was impossible to build a new socialist identity of the nation on an entirely negative view of national history. Hence Abusch's interpretation was dubbed 'misery theory' and dropped. Instead the East German Communists began to refer back to ideas which had already been prominent among representatives of the Moscow-based National Committte for a Free Germany. The Committee was largely engaged on propaganda work among German prisoners of war in the Soviet Union. Talking to Nazified German soldiers, its instructors emphasized the difference between a good nationalism, based on pride in the achievements of the German people, and the bad nationalism of the Nazis. In 1952 Albert Norden explicitly called for the development of a concept of national history which would distinguish between the 'progressive' and the 'reactionary' class line in German history.[46] The 'class theory of the nation' neatly divided German history into a progressive and a reactionary line. The progressive line went from Thomas Müntzer and the peasant rebellions of the sixteenth century, to the 1848 revolutionaries, to Marx and the early labour movement, to the KPD and eventually the foundation of the GDR in 1949. The reactionary class line incorporated Luther, feudalism, the Prussian Junkers, militarism, capitalism, the reformist wing of the Social Democratic Party and National Socialism. It eventually culminated in the foundation of the FRG.

As Prussia was perceived as a part of the reactionary class line, the early GDR committed a number of spectacular incidents of iconoclasticism – none more so than the dynamiting of the Hohenzollern palace in the centre of Berlin. Dozens of East Elbian manorhouses, left behind after their former owners had fled to the West, were razed to the ground. But such symbolic distancing of the new Germany from its Prussian heritage was short-lived. The GDR's 1952 Decree on Maintaining National Cultural Monuments made it the state's responsibility to take care of the whole of the national heritage. National landmarks were not dynamited any longer but appropriated to the GDR's own reading of national history, as the example of the Leipzig memorial to the Battle of Nations demonstrates.[47] The official version of national history was worked out by historians close to the SED and sanctioned by the politburo of the ruling party. In 1952 it was put on display in the Museum of German History which opened its doors in East Berlin. It presented the trinity of capitalism, imperialism and militarism as the enemy of the working people, whose struggle against them was documented

45 Alexander Abusch, *Der Irrweg einer Nation* (Berlin, 1946); the book was first published in Mexico in 1945, where Abusch had fled from the Nazis.

46 Albert Norden, *Kampf um die Nation* (Berlin, 1952).

47 See above, p. 205.

and displayed through the centuries culminating in the foundation of the first socialist state on German soil.[48]

The socialist nation was busy creating its own pantheon of national heroes. In particular representatives of liberal nationalism in the first half of the nineteenth century were now discovered as precursors of a nation committed to social egalitarianism. The national heroes of the past stood alongside the socialist heroes of the present. The making of socialist heroes followed a rather stereotypical fashion. They had to be ordinary people, mostly from the working class who had shown great potential from an early age. They had matured under the leadership of the Communist party and had risen to a major challenge. They led morally clean lives, were lifestyle gurus to others and useful members of society whose deeds benefited the whole. The socialist hero was the person next door whom one could trust. The underlying message of those hero narratives was, of course, that readers could become socialist heroes themselves.[49]

The official reading of national history, which was supposed to contribute to the construction of a positive socialist national identity, was put on display in a dense network of national days celebrated annually in the GDR.[50] On 15 January, the GDR commemorated the violent death of two of its arch-martyrs, the founders of the KPD, Rosa Luxemburg and Karl Liebknecht, who had been murdered by right-wing paramilitaries in 1919. Hundreds of thousands of people, headed by the politburo of the SED marched to their graves in the cemetery in Friedrichsfelde. In 1951 a monumental porphyry cube carrying the inscription 'The dead are a constant reminder' was placed next to the graves. The saints of the communist movement were supposed to remind the people that it was the GDR which was fulfilling their legacies and building the socialist German nation. But those critical of the GDR also referred back to Luxemburg, who had been a prominent critic of Leninism. In 1988 political dissenters unrolled a banner at the Liebknecht–Luxemburg demonstration, displaying one of Luxemburg's most famous sentences: 'Freedom is always the freedom of those who have a different opinion.' (*Freiheit ist immer die Freiheit der Andersdenkenden*) They were immediately arrested, but once again, the more emancipatory and liberating side of Marxist political thinking had been used against the very regime which pretended to be the heir to the Marxist legacy.

The annual calendar of festivities continued on 21 April with the foundation day of the SED. This was quickly followed by 1 May, International Labour Day, which was regularly celebrated with a martial display of military hardware. 8 May, the end of the Second World War in Europe, was commemorated as liberation from fascism. Through the heroic struggle of the Soviet Union, supported by German Communists, the defeat of 15 January was transformed into a belated victory. In September the memorial day for the victims of fascism underlined this

[48] H. Glenn Penny III, 'The Museum für deutsche Geschichte and German National Identity', *Central European History*, 28 (1995), p. 343.

[49] Silke Satjukow and Rainer Gries, eds, *Sozialistische Helden: Eine Kulturgeschichte von Propagandafiguren in Osteuropa und der DDR* (Berlin, 2002).

[50] Monika Gibas, ' "Auferstanden aus Ruinen und der Zukunft zugewandt!" Politische Feier- und Gedenktage der DDR', in Sabine Behrenbeck and Alexander Nützenadel, eds, *Inszenierungen des Nationalstaats: Politische Feiern in Italien und Deutschland seit 1860/71* (Cologne, 2000), pp. 191–220, quote on p. 193.

message. 7 October, the 'Day of the Republic', when the GDR had been founded, was celebrated in every town and village. The central festivities in Berlin were televised live and broadcast on radio. Commemorating the foundation of the first socialist state on German soil was a ritual which was meant to strengthen the commitment of the people to the 'workers' and farmers' state'. Finally, 7 November marked the day on which the victory of the Bolsheviks in the Soviet Union in 1917 was remembered as the starting point of a worldwide liberation of the people from the 'yoke of capitalism'. Each of these dates mobilized hundreds of thousands of people in carefully stage-managed mass demonstrations. Uniformed citizens, mostly younger ones, swore oaths of allegiance to the socialist nation. Military parades and torchlit processions, the laying of wreaths, commemorative speeches and the masses marching past the leadership of the Communist party waving down on their people – all of this belonged firmly to the stale and formulaic rituals attempting to boost national identity. Some of those who marched undoubtedly believed in the slogans and ideas presented at these celebrations, but many also privatized this unsparing official memorial culture. They turned it into a kind of Sunday entertainment and celebrated it, not as a visible sign of their commitment to the GDR, but as a nice day out with family and friends.

After 1949 the GDR portrayed itself as genuinely seeking the socialist unity of the nation. Not unlike the FRG they saw in Imperial Germany the basic territorial framework for a nation state, but they, very unlike the FRG, insisted that it had to be reconstituted along socialist lines. The policies of Western integration pursued by Adenauer in the FRG were attacked as divisive. An article in a journal for young East Germans put it thus:

> Our fatherland is the [GDR]. For the first time in German history the working people exercise power in this republic. [...] This fatherland is the future for the whole of Germany, the one and indivisible German nation. To love one's fatherland therefore means to love the [GDR] with all its progressive achievements [...] We have to defend the fatherland of the German workers against all impudent demands of the West German imperialists. [...] We German patriots will defeat the enemies of our fatherland, and against the power of West German monopolists and big landowners we shall make the whole of Germany a country for the working people. Our energies to accomplish this task will feed themselves on our burning hatred against its Junker and imperialist enemies.[51]

In the 1950s the 'Germany Meetings of Youth' were organized by the SED to portray itself as the only true national force in the whole of Germany. The 'basic national concept' (*nationale Grundkonzeption*) of the SED sought to portray the revolutionary German labour movement as representing the true national interests of the German people throughout the nineteenth and twentieth centuries. Class replaced categories such as 'culture', 'language' and 'race' as guiding principle of narrating the story of the German nation. However, such a class-based progressive national paradigm transported many traditional nationalist assumptions.[52]

---

51 'Wer ist ein Patriot?' *Junge Generation*, 12 (1955), reprinted in Matthias Judt, ed., *DDR-Geschichte in Dokumenten: Beschlüsse, Berichte, interne Materialien und Alltagszeugnisse* (Berlin, 1997), p. 512f.

52 Klaus Erdmann, *Der gescheiterte Nationalstaat: Die Interdependenz von Nations- und Geschichtsverständnis im politischen Bedingungsgefüge der DDR* (Frankfurt/Main, 1996).

It read German national history back into the dark Middle Ages; it preferred strong centralist movements and condemned particularism as weakening the German nation; and it celebrated the national struggle against Napoleon as justified resistance to the oppression of the nation state. The GDR, in short, was presented as culmination of all that was good in German national history. As Albert Norden put it in 1967: 'The flag and the leadership of the nation today lies in the hands of the German working class.'[53]

All of these claims were, of course, nothing but shadow-boxing. The SED knew full well that it lacked legitimacy in its own country and that no serious political force in the FRG supported its particular reinvention of the German nation. The GDR elites were terrified that the Soviet Union might bargain away the 'socialist achievements' in the GDR in return for a non-socialist but neutral Germany. They relaxed a little only after the Stalin notes of 1952 had been rejected by the West and the GDR was rapidly integrated into the community of East European Communist states. But they were still facing a daily plebiscite of East Germans who left the country in droves. 3.8 million East Germans fled the GDR before 1961. By the time the building of the Berlin Wall closed the last hole in the Iron Curtain, one in six had turned their back on the 'workers' and farmers' state'.[54] These millions were not just political dissidents and what the SED quickly dubbed 'bourgeois class enemies', i.e. industrialists, large landowners and members of the professional middle classes. They also included hundreds of thousands of workers and small farmers tempted by the promises of a better life in the West. The SED portrayed the wall as an 'antifascist protective wall' and argued that warmongers in the West had been stopped in their attempts to undermine the socialist regime in the GDR. The cynical attempt to portray the imprisonment of its own population as a measure to keep the peace in Europe was believed by hardly anyone. The wall was the only way of stopping millions of East Germans from going where they saw a better future for themselves, but it was also a clear declaration of bankruptcy for the claims of the GDR to represent the true interests of the nation. The SED's constant emphasis on the unity of the masses and their political leadership had an even hollower sound after 13 August 1961.

Ironically it was in the decade and a half after the building of the Berlin Wall that, if one is to believe the secret popular opinion research conducted by the SED, an increasing number of East Germans seemed to accept the GDR, including the leading role of the SED in state and society.[55] But perhaps, as Mark Allinson has argued, apathy and lethargy describe the position of the majority of the population better than active support.[56] People saw no alternative to accommodating themselves to a regime which looked as though it was here to stay. Even if they found things to praise about the GDR, they remained dissatisfied about other aspects

[53] Albert Norden, 'Die DDR weist den sozialistischen Weg der Nation', *Zeitschrift für Geschichtswissenschaft*, 15 (1967), p. 1141.

[54] Helge Heydemeyer, *Flucht und Zuwanderung aus der SBZ-DDR 1945/49–1961: Die Flüchtlingspolitik der Bundesrepublik Deutschland bis zum Bau der Mauer* (Düsseldorf, 1994).

[55] Heinz Niemann, *Hinterm Zaun: Politische Kultur und Meinungsforschung in der DDR – die geheimen Berichte an das Politbüro der SED* (Berlin, 1995).

[56] Mark Allinson, *Politics and Popular Opinion in East Germany 1945–1968* (Manchester, 2000).

and were, on the whole, more resigned to than enthused about SED rule. Passive toleration of the regime was widespread, but this remained a far cry from the kind of positive endorsement of SED rule that Communists were looking for. What was, however, increasingly obvious was that decades of division had made East Germans different from West Germans. Language, patterns of behaviour, values, they all began to develop differently, but such slow estrangement between East and West did not necessarily endear East Germans any more to their Communist rulers.

The GDR continued until the advent of *Ostpolitik* to pronounce its (entirely shambolic) desire to see the emergence of a united socialist Germany. As late as 1968 the revamped constitution of the GDR called for the rebuilding of the unity of the nation 'on the basis of democracy and socialism'. But when the FRG moved towards propagating 'change through rapprochement', the SED felt threatened by such overtures. It reacted by declaring the death of the unified German nation. Demands for a unified socialist Germany were dropped. Instead GDR representatives proclaimed the theory of the long-term peaceful co-existence of two nations, a capitalist Federal Republic and a socialist GDR. In 1971 the 8th party conference of the SED made it official: like Switzerland and Austria before, the GDR was on its way to develop into a separate German nation.[57] The aborted 'national dialogue' between SPD and SED in 1966 had been a first sign that German-German relations were about to change. Reacting to a letter from the central committee of the SED suggesting an exchange of opinion about basic questions to do with German unity, the SPD agreed for the first time ever to exchange speakers. In the end it all came to nothing, but four years later Brandt's visit to Erfurt accelerated the SED's move away from the rhetoric of national unity. The 1974 GDR constitution dropped any reference to Germany and described the GDR merely as a 'socialist state of workers and peasants'. The acronym GDR was no longer spelt out in full. The text of the GDR national anthem with its explicit reference to German unity was not sung any more. The radio station *Deutschlandsender* was renamed *Stimme der DDR*. The Hotel German in Leipzig became the Hotel am Ring. The German Writers' Assocation became the Writers Association of the GDR'. Handwritten notes of Erich Honecker for a talk with Leonid Brezhnev in August 1970 could not be clearer: 'Germany has ceased to exist. There is the socialist GDR and the capitalist Federal Republic.'[58]

The proclamation of the socialist nation went hand in hand with a rigorous policy of demarcation from the FRG. After 1967 the SED started several consecutive campaigns against 'all-German illusions'. The two nations theory was part of a defensive strategy of the SED. It feared that too much dialogue between East and West would give new nourishment to hopes for reunification among GDR citizens. *Ostpolitik* was eyed suspiciously as a means with which to undermine Communism. It reflected the beleaguered mentality of the SED which had grown so used to perceiving the FRG as a constant threat to its stability and legitimacy.

[57] Walter Schmidt, 'Das Zwei-Nationen-Konzept der SED und sein Scheitern', *Beiträge zur Geschichte der Arbeiterbewegung*, 38 (1996), pp. 3–35; Gerhard Naumann and Eckhard Trümpler, *Der Flop mit der DDR-Nation 1971* (Berlin, 1991).

[58] Reprinted in Judt, ed., *DDR-Geschichte*, p. 516 (as note 51).

In 1972 the Basic Treaty between FRG and GDR contributed to the normalization of relations between the two Germanies. It was to bring the GDR the long-sought international recognition and UN membership. It now appeared a fully paid up and respected member of the international community of states. But in inner-German relations the SED was keen to take things one step further. It wanted the FRG to recognize GDR citizenship and did everything to treat West Germany just like any other capitalist foreign country. Of course, it knew full well that it was anything but that: after all, the central committee of the SED had one full department exclusively concerned with developments in and relations with the FRG. But it wanted to do everything to stress the lacuna that separated the 'humanistic-socialist culture' of the GDR from the degenerate and vacuous 'capitalist culture' of the FRG.

The GDR had always taken great care to portray itself as heir to the proud cultural heritage of the German nation. Within its first ten years the anniversaries of Goethe (1949), Bach (1950), Beethoven (1952), Schiller and Händel (both in 1959) were commemorated with great aplomb. The rebuilding of the Weimar national theatre in 1949 specifically claimed Goethe and Schiller as founding fathers of the GDR's 'humanistic culture'. The SED also made extensive use of the *Heimat* discourse to underpin notions of a separate socialist nation. Postcards of schools, holiday homes, motorways, shopping centres, hospitals, nature parks and newly built residential areas were all meant as pictorial representations of the 'socialist achievements' of the GDR. They called on the people to identify with the nation which had achieved so much for its population.[59] When 'cosmonaut' (the West German word would have been 'astronaut') Sigmund Jähn travelled into space in a Soviet spaceship, *Neues Deutschland* created the headline: 'The first German in space – a citizen of the GDR'.[60]

In the 1980s a separate socialist nation attempted self-confidently to appropriate the whole of German history in order to harness its claim to national independence. Historians now placed the concept of 'heritage' (*Erbe*) next to the concept of 'tradition' (*Tradition*). Whereas the latter described those progressive forces, events and developments which could be claimed for the GDR, the former was used to justify research into areas of German history which had been neglected in the past. Territorially, the formerly excluded areas like Prussia, Silesia and all those which had been incorporated into different East European states after 1945, were to be given new attention. Chronologically, the concentration on certain key periods of German history was to be given up. And socially, the emphasis on working-class history was to be supplemented by incorporating more research on other classes and their interest organizations.[61] In 1980 the statue of Frederick II was returned to the Unter den Linden in East Berlin from where the former 'arch villain' – symbol of an expansionist German policy in Eastern Europe – had been removed in 1950. In 1983 the Luther year saw the restoration of the Luther museum in Wittenberg. Once denounced as 'traitor of the German peasants',

59 Erasmus Schröter, ed., *Bild der Heimat. Die Echt-Foto-Postkarten aus der DDR* (Berlin, 2002).

60 *Neues Deutschland*, 27 August 1978.

61 Helmut Meier and Walter Schmidt, eds, *Erbe und Tradition in der DDR: Die Debatte der Historiker* (Berlin, 1988).

Luther was now hailed as a major German humanist. In 1985 a celebrated biography of Otto von Bismarck by leading GDR historian Ernst Engelberg revised the entirely negative view of the 'iron chancellor' which had prevailed in GDR historiography. On the occasion of the 750th anniversary of Berlin, the Nikolai quarter was recreated near the centre of town in historist architectural mode. About 800 buildings in total grouped around the reconstructed Nikolai church, the oldest parish church in Berlin, were fitted with historical façades and marketed as a major tourist attraction. Overall the 1980s saw a coherent attempt to adapt Prussian and national history in order to foster a sense of the deep historical roots of the socialist GDR nation. Ironically, that emphasis on national history might in the end have contributed to a renewed sense of a common German past among citizens of the GDR.[62]

However much the SED attempted to portray the GDR as a separate German nation, the idea remained an ideological construct. Marxism saw nations being built on economic foundations. As those were fundamentally different in the FRG and the GDR, the SED concluded that two nations were developing in Germany. But the socio-economic differences between the two states did not constitute them as two separate nations. Undoubtedly East Germans took pride in the economic, sporting and cultural achievements of the GDR. East and West Germans moved apart in many respects over forty years of separation. Many West Germans lost interest in an often unknown GDR. But the West continued to act as a magnet for the political and economic hopes and desires of many East Germans. The GDR appeared outwardly stable and tranquil after June 1953, but the lack of legitimacy always remained an issue which made the SED extremely sensitive to any kind of criticism. And the history of the GDR was littered with the history of dissenting voices. After 1945 much fundamental opposition to the setting up of a socialist state in the Soviet zone of occupation was brutally repressed by the SED, backed up by the Soviet occupiers. Campaigns against the churches and Social Democracy were particularly long-lasting and nasty, as both were seen as political forces with broad popular appeal which continued to maintain the idea of national unity. Thousands of opponents of the SED regime vanished in the Soviet gulags, many more were imprisoned in the GDR and tens of thousands opted to leave for West Germany. By the time the Berlin wall was built in 1961, many of those who had fundamental political reservations about SED rule had left.

What remained was internal opposition from within the SED by those who wanted to reform the rigid authoritarian Communism of East Germany. Theirs tended to be a different, more democratic vision of Communism. Wolf Biermann, Rudolf Bahro and Robert Havemann are examples of prominent dissidents in the GDR who all regarded themselves as Communists. They rarely invoked the goal of reunification with the FRG and hardly ever used the rhetoric of the nation when pursuing their political goals. There were exceptions, such as Wolfgang Harich, who combined an undogmatic communism with a deep concern for national unity. But in the 1970s and 1980s much of this internal dissent came from people who identified more with the GDR than with any idea of a unified

[62] Jan Brinks, *Die DDR-Geschichtswissenschaft auf dem Weg zur deutschen Einheit: Luther, Friedrich II und Bismarck als Paradigmen politischen Wandels* (Frankfurt/Main, 1992).

German nation state. The SED leadership, however, proved incapable of entering a dialogue even with the most loyal of dissenters. It feared that any move towards a reformed communism might contribute to the loss of the party's authority and lead the GDR onto the slippery slope of reunification on Western terms. Hence it strongly backed both military action to end the Prague Spring in 1968 and the repression of the independent trade union movement Solidarność in Poland in 1981. In the late 1980s the SED leadership distanced itself from the kind of reforms attempted by Gorbachev in the Soviet Union. Anti-Stalinist films like Tengis Abuladse's *Repentance* could not be shown in the GDR, and an issue of the Soviet magazine *Sputnik*, largely read by the SED faithful(!), was banned in 1988. The SED was quick to declare its solidarity with the Communist party of China after the latter had brutally repressed the democracy movement in 1989.

By that time a strong citizens' movement expressed its desire for a 'different GDR'.[63] When Hungary opened its borders with the West and the iron curtain was breached for the first time since 1961, tens of thousands of East Germans fled their country, revealing the continued lack of legitimacy of SED rule. For those people who took to the streets in 1989 and shouted 'We stay here', and for those intellectuals who, on 4 November, published a manifesto entitled *For our Country* (meaning the GDR), the protest was still about changing the GDR. But increasingly the mood on the streets of East Germany changed. The slogans of the protesters reflected this: 'We are the people' changed to 'We are one people'. The economic and political appeal of the FRG turned out to be stronger than all promises of a reformed socialism in the GDR. The SED lacked the willpower to defend its crumbling rule, and when it decided to open the Berlin Wall on 9 November 1989, the GDR's vision of an altogether different German nation was about to draw to a close.[64] The attempt to build a German identity on antifascism, the traditions of the Marxist labour movement and the history of all 'progressive forces' in German history had ended in failure. A reunified Germany would have to reinvent, once again, the nation in the changed circumstances of a post-Cold War political world.

[63] C. Joppke, *East German Dissidents and the Revolution of 1989: Social Movement in a Leninist Regime* (Basingstoke, 1995).

[64] Charles Maier, *Dissolution: The Crisis of Communism and the End of East Germany* (Princeton, 1997); also: Hartmut Zwahr, *Ende einer Selbstzerstörung: Leipzig und die Revolution in der DDR*, 2nd edn (Göttingen, 1993).

8

Quo vadis *Germany? National identity debates after reunification*

In March 2001 the general secretary of the CDU, Laurenz Meyer, kicked off a major public debate by stating that he was proud of being a German. When the Green Party minister for the environment Jürgen Trittin likened him to a 'skinhead' in physique and mentality, Christian Democrats called for Trittin's resignation. Even the president, Johannes Rau, was subsequently dragged into the heated 'national pride debate' (*Nationalstolzdebatte*). He had voiced his own difficulties with feeling proud of Germany which made CDU politicians question his credentials for occupying the highest office in the state. Public opinion surveys were published which showed that 60 per cent of Germans were proud of their country. A staggering 94 per cent of Germans had positive connotations with the term *Heimat*, and 81 per cent thought that the government should insist more on pushing through German interests in multinational organizations such as the EU.[1] For weeks the columns of the newspapers were full of arguments why Germans should or should not be proud of their nation, which aspects they had reason to be proud of and why national pride was a dangerous thing. On one level the whole debate was an exaggerated party political squabble. Politicians, finding it increasingly difficult to bring across to the voters highly complex and technical policy options, chose the emotive field of national identity to score points. The affair seemed to underline the philosopher Peter Sloterdijk's satirical description of the nation as 'stress community'. For Sloterdijk nations are communities of excitable people who keep themselves entertained through media-induced hysterics and panics surrounding the topic of national identity. By doing this they keep avoiding the real questions about the need for political and social change.[2]

On another level, however, the 'national pride debate' signified just how contested and emotional the issue of national identity was in the reunified Germany. After all, which French or British politician could kick off a major public debate

[1] Klaus-Peter Schöppner, 'Die meisten Deutschen sind stolz auf ihr Vaterland', *Die Welt*, 3 April 2001.

[2] Peter Sloterdijk, 'Der starke Grund, zusammen zu sein', *Die Zeit*, 2 January 1998.

by simply stating that they were proud of their nation. The years after 1990 have indeed seen a phenomenal number of (ongoing) debates on the meaning and position of national identity in the new Germany.[3] Public intellectuals have fanned the flames of the debate and put forward diverse constructions of national identity and different readings of the German past.[4] Several commentators, mainly on the left, preferred to use the term 'unification' to 'reunification' to indicate that what was in the making was not something that had existed previously, least of all a reincarnation of Bismarckian Prussian Germany. Fears on the far left and among some foreign commentators of the emergence of a 'Fourth Reich' soon proved unfounded. As the celebrations of East and West Germans on top of the Berlin Wall gave way to feelings of estrangement and division between the 'Ossis' and the 'Wessis', popular national sentiment evaporated. Subsequently politicians and intellectuals, mainly on the centre-right, demanded measures which would foster a greater sense of national cohesion, a kind of official nationalism to overcome what many perceived as a 'unification crisis'.[5] In 1994 prominent public figures founded the association 'We for Germany' which initiated a massive advertising campaign aimed at strengthening the national self-confidence of Germans. However, this campaign, as all other debates surrounding the issue of national identity, rather than uniting Germans, caused more controversy and division. In this chapter I would like to explore some of these debates. First of all, I will trace the elusive search for national 'normality' in the reunified Germany, analysing very different attempts to recast Germanness after 1990 and discussing the renaissance of a politics of national symbols. Subsequently I will look at German identity debates in the context of the changing position of Germany in international politics. Both the National Socialist and the Communist pasts have been central to identity discourses after 1990 and will be reviewed in a third section here. Finally I will comment on the rediscovery of a discourse of German victimhood in the early 2000s.

The search for national normality

In 1990 the influential publicist Karl Heinz Bohrer described the old FRG as the epitomy of provincialism and expressed his hope that the new Germany would abandon the alleged postnational *Sonderweg* of the FRG. The creation of a new metropolitan centre, preferably in Berlin, and the return of the nation to power politics, he argued, would be an opportunity to build a different, less provincial republic.[6] The rediscovery of national history played a major part in Bohrer's plans for a recast German identity. In 2001, when giving the first Gadamer lectures at the University of Heidelberg, he castigated his fellow Germans for having a 'non-relation to German history'. He attacked left-liberal historians for reducing German

3 Stefan Berger, *The Search for Normality: National Identity and Historical Consciousness in Germany since 1800* (Oxford, 1997; pb edn with new foreword, 2003), Part 2, on the debates surrounding German history after 1989/90.

4 Michael Geyer, ed., *The Power of Intellectuals in Contemporary Germany* (Chicago, 2001).

5 On diverse aspects of this crisis see Jürgen Kocka, *Vereinigungskrise. Zur Geschichte der Gegenwart* (Göttingen, 1995).

6 Karl Heinz Bohrer, 'Provinzialismus', *Merkur*, 44 (1990), pp. 1096–112; 45 (1991), pp. 255–66; 46 (1992), pp. 88–90.

history to the twelve years of National Socialism and turning the entire nineteenth century into the prehistory of the Third Reich. Having annihilated German national history this left-wing *juste milieu*, according to Bohrer, championed a deeply unhistorical and bloodless constitutional patriotism. It would be impossible to build the nation anew, he predicted, if this fear of anchoring identity in history was to continue.[7]

Bohrer was not alone in putting forward the idea that, somehow, the old Federal Republic was in need of reinvention. National self-deprecation, one could now read frequently, would only lead to self-paralysis and self-destruction. Positive national identity needed to be fostered if the nation state was to be sustained. The former editor of the influential *FAZ*, Joachim Fest, for example, criticized the country's 'curiously dreamlike existence, untragic, even a bit happy in the depth of consumerism and leisure-time worlds.' And historian Christian Meier, writing in Bohrer's monthly journal, found that 'the FRG was worthy, successful and sometimes even endearing, and yet at the same time it was narrow, all too abstract in its public thought and last but not least also extremely tense ... Is it fair to say that it had no authenticity and originality?'[8]

Major public debates about history, which until the 1990s had been focussed exclusively on the Nazi years, were now incorporating the Federal Republic. In 1998 the student revolt of 1968 took centre stage. On the right some commentators argued that the legacy of 1968 and its impact on West German society needed to be overcome before the reunified Germany could return to national normality. The 1968ers' excessive public breast-beating about the Nazi past, they alleged, had produced a neurotic guilt complex which was preventing the new Germany from finding a more balanced relationship to its past. Throughout the 1990s calls for recasting the image of Germany involved criticism of the model set by the post-68 FRG.

Conservatives viewed with scepticism the liberalization, pluralization and Westernization of the Federal Republic since the 1960s. Where left liberals had come to view 1968 as the *annus mirabilis* signalling a major transformation of the FRG towards a more liberal, plural and Western society, liberal conservatives disliked what they referred to as the hedonism, egalitarianism, libertarianism and 'everything goes' mentality of the 1968ers. In 2001 allegations against the foreign minister and vice-chancellor Joschka Fischer that he had harboured sympathies for left-wing terrorism in the 1970s renewed the debate. Fischer agreed to appear as a character witness for former terrorist Hans-Joachim Klein who was put on trial for the kidnapping and murder of three people in 1975. The press published photographs showing Fischer, disguised under a motorcycle helmet, beating a policeman during the 'Kettenhof riots' against housing speculators in Frankfurt's Westend in April 1973. During the trial Fischer insisted that he had always distanced himself from left-wing terrorism and that his own use of violence had always been in self-defence. However, he also gave an unapologetic account of his activities around 1968, claiming that what he and others like him had been doing was attempting to create a counter-culture to the stifling

[7] Arno Orzessek, 'Jenseits des Holocaust', *Süddeutsche Zeitung*, 1 June 2001.

[8] Joachim Fest, 'Nicht wie alle Welt', *FAZ*, 13 June 1992; Christian Meier, 'Am Ende der alten Bundesrepublik', *Merkur*, 48 (1994), pp. 561–72.

bourgeois consensus culture at the time. Thereby, he insisted, 1968 had contributed to a more pluralistic and ultimately more liberal society emerging in the FRG. The centre-right attacked him for not sufficiently distancing himself from his own militant past, but left-liberal public opinion celebrated the career of Fischer from street fighter to vice-chancellor as living proof of the fundamental change of a liberalized West German state which had been capable of integrating the youth protest of the late 1960s.[9]

Apart from 1968, which had been the wrong turn for many liberal conservatives, the other favourite topic with which to criticize what was frequently referred to as the left-liberal establishment was *Ostpolitik*. Ignoring the fact that conservatives had continued *Ostpolitik* after 1982, the Social Democrats were accused of selling out the nation and accommodating themselves with the peaceful co-existence of two Germanies. They, according to conservative critics in the 1990s, struck up a close and cosy relationship with representatives of a vile Communist dictatorship. *Ostpolitik* and its advocates had pushed to the sidelines the national question and stabilized the GDR. In the name of peace and co-existence an inhumane dictatorship had been given legitimacy.[10] In 2000 the CDU celebrated Helmut Kohl as 'chancellor of unity' and contrasted this with the dubious national credentials of the SPD. However, as with the debate on 1968, conservatives faced considerable resistance. Several commentators pointed out that *Ostpolitik*, far from stabilizing the GDR, softened up the Communist dictatorship, eroded its legitimacy and paved the way to the successful revolution of 1989.[11] Overall, debates about 1968, *Ostpolitik* and the legacy of the old FRG ended inconclusively. If anything, left-liberal positions seemed to defend themselves well against conservative attempts to push the national agenda further.

On the left the revival of a national discourse often brought fears about the future of what was perceived as the hard-won Western civility of the old FRG.[12] On balance the West German left had been sceptical of reunification. Prominent critics included the leader of the SPD in 1990, Oskar Lafontaine, and one of the literary giants of the FRG, the novelist Günter Grass who received the Nobel Prize for Literature in 1999. Lafontaine refused to play the national card throughout the election campaign of 1990. Instead he warned of dire economic consequences of an all-too-rapid unification process. His stance was seen as representative of the postnational outlook on the left of his generation which had few emotional ties to East Germany. In the circumstances Chancellor Kohl, who promised 'flowering industrial landscapes' within four years, won the elections handsomely in the east. Lafontaine was widely perceived as the loser who had misread the political mood in the country.

9 Kay Schiller, 'Political Militancy and Generation Conflict in West Germany during the "Red Decade" ', *Debatte*, 11:1 (2003), pp. 19–38.

10 All of the standard arguments are rehearsed in Konrad Löw, ... *bis zum Verrat der Freiheit. Die Gesellschaft der Bundesrepublik und die 'DDR'* , 2nd edn (Munich, 1994); Jens Hacker, *Deutsche Irrtümer: Schönfärber und Helfershelfer der SED-Diktatur im Westen* (Frankfurt/Main, 1992).

11 A concise summary of these arguments can be found in Peter Bender, 'Der goldene Angelhaken: Entspannungspolitik und Systemwandel', *aus politik und zeitgeschichte*, 8 April 1994, pp. 11–15.

12 Generally on intellectuals and their stance towards reunification see Jan Werner Müller, *Another Country. German Intellectuals: Unification and National Identity* (New Haven, 2000).

Grass's critique of reunification was even more fundamental. As a West German Social Democrat with close ties to former chancellor Willy Brandt he had no sympathy for the SED regime in the GDR. German history was one of the great themes of his literary oeuvre. His rejection of reunification was rooted in his interpretation of the past and his fears about the future. According to Grass, the division of Germany was the logical outcome of and atonement for the Holocaust: 'Who currently thinks about Germany and looks for answers to the German question has to reflect on the meaning of Auschwitz. The place of terror, symbol for the lasting trauma, excludes a future united Germany. If, what stands to be feared, such a united state will nevertheless be enforced, its failure will be predetermined.'[13] A reunified Germany, Grass feared, would be too powerful. Sooner or later it would fall back onto the path which had led to disaster between 1933 and 1945. Germany, he argued, could only exist as a cultural nation, not as a state nation. His celebrated unification novel *Ein weites Feld*, published in 1995, carried a strong anti-unification subtext.

Having failed to halt the unification process, some sceptics on the left were adamant that any recasting of the West German identity post-1990 should be kept to the absolute minimum. What was needed, they argued, was the rapid modernization of East Germany to bring the new *Länder* up to the level of the old ones, but otherwise they declared business as usual. The most prominent representative of such a position was the philosopher Jürgen Habermas. In 1990 he was fearful that the Westernization of the FRG might not have gone deep enough. Germans, under the impact of unification, might reveal themselves as shallow Westerners and return to more traditional forms of German nationalism. 'Deutschmark nationalism' seemed to threaten the constitutional patriotism championed by Habermas.[14] East Germans, blinded by the promises of the Deutschmark, had, he argued, abandoned the democratic potentials of their revolution and opted for national unity. But even the democratic revolution was seen by Habermas only in terms of a 'catching up revolution', i.e. East Germans catching up with the levels of modernization and Westernization already achieved by their West German cousins. Habermas's standards were Western ones, and his scepticism derived from his fears that the rush towards unity endangered the Westernization of Germany.

Yet the sceptics, including Lafontaine, Grass and Habermas, increasingly found themselves in a minority – even among the left. As far back as 1990 Brandt, generationally far more attuned to the issue of national unity than Lafontaine, had taken a markedly national position, famously pronouncing: 'Now grows together what belongs together.' Subsequently the refounded Hofgeismar circle in the SPD pleaded for a return of the party to the idea of the nation. Many left liberals now began to argue that the democratic revolution of 1989 should not be perceived primarily as a threat to the Westernization of the FRG but rather an opportunity to recapture the national idea from the political right and fuse nationalism with liberty and democracy. For the first time since 1848 demands

13 Günter Grass, 'Kurze Rede eines vaterlandslosen Gesellen', *Die Zeit*, 9 February 1990. See also *idem*, *Two States – One Nation? The Case Against German Reunification* (London, 1990).

14 Jürgen Habermas, 'Yet Again: German Identity – A Unified Nation of Angry DM-Burghers', *New German Critique*, 52 (1991), pp. 84–101.

for freedom had coincided with demands for national unity. 1989 thus offered the opportunity to fuse the democratic and Westernized political culture with the national principle. An 'enlightened German patriotism' would finally end all German *Sonderwege* and bring the country in line with the 'normal' patriotism of other West European countries such as France and Britain.[15]

Historian Heinrich August Winkler formulated the idea of the long journey of Germany towards Western values and ideas in a two-volume national history, which was published to much acclaim in 2000.[16] Some time, and the exact time remained the object of much controversy, between 1949 and 1989 the FRG had finally arrived in the West, and the revolution of 1989, with its democratic practices and insistence on popular sovereignty, strengthened the commitment of the newly reunified nation to the West. Germany was a nation state again. The post-national *Sonderweg* of the old FRG had been abandoned. But the new Germany was presented as a 'post-classical' nation state which differed from the autonomous nation state of the nineteenth century in several important ways, not the least through its commitment to Western ideals and its firm integration in supranational organizations.[17] Winkler's was a history culminating in the success story of the FRG which crowned a history of great potential in the nineteenth century and even greater disasters in the first half of the twentieth. A major exhibition entitled '50 Years of Unity, Rule of Law and Liberty: Paths of the Germans, 1949–1999' celebrated the democratic revolution in the GDR but hailed as the cornerstones of a happy national future the successes of West Germany, in particular its federal system, its social market economy and its constitution.

Many commentators argued that the FRG had become less German and more European: 'The normalization and Westernization of Germany shows not the least in a gradual and slow change of climate: the country has become more Mediterranean and more British at the same time, a little bit lighter and more full of life, but also more sober and less excited.'[18] Fritz Stern, renowned American historian of German-Jewish origins, argued that the renewed ascendancy of Germany, based on its economic, technological and human capabilities, might mean a 'second chance' for the nation to use its strengths, this time for the good of Europe and the wider world.[19] The return to the nation would not automatically lead to a repeat of the disastrous German history during the first half of the twentieth century. Ralf Dahrendorf, renowned sociologist and himself a bridge-builder between British and German political cultures, reminded Germans of the need for nation states. They were, after all, through their institutions and constitutions, the only reliable guarantors of civic liberties in Europe. Hence he pleaded for an alliance of self-confident nation states in a co-operative Europe.[20]

15 Heinrich August Winkler, 'Ende aller Sonderwege', *Der Spiegel*, 11 June 2001.
16 *Idem, Der lange Weg nach Westen*, 2 vols (Munich, 2000).
17 *Idem*, 'Abschied von einem deutschen Sonderweg: Wider die postnationale Nostalgie', *Die Neue Gesellschaft/Frankfurter*, 40 (1993), pp. 633–6.
18 Reinhard Mohr, 'Deutsch, aber glücklich', *Der Spiegel*, 20 October 1997.
19 Fritz Stern, 'Deutschland um 1900 – und eine zweite Chance', in Wolfgang Hardtwig and Harm-Hinrich Brandt, eds, *Deutschlands Weg in die Moderne: Politik, Gesellschaft und Kultur im 19. Jahrhundert* (Munich, 1993), pp. 32–44.
20 Ralf Dahrendorf, 'Die Sache mit der Nation', *Merkur*, 44 (1990), pp. 823–34.

Richard Schröder, pastor in the GDR, prominent SPD leader after 1990 and professor of theology and philosophy in Berlin, in a series of well-received essays, argued for the need to be critical of the German past but also self-confident about the democratic achievements of Germany:

> When I say: Germany is what I like best (not necessarily the most convenient), this is not nationalism which discriminates against anyone, because everyone should be able to love his country. After all, I do not discriminate against someone who says: My children are the children I love best ... It is completely OK that it is this country and its problems which are more important, more serious and closer to me than those of other countries, and it is equally completely OK that I am not indifferent to the problems of the rest of the world.[21]

For students of nationalism this was, of course, an all-too-familiar argument: once more the nation was imagined as family, thus making it part of an alleged 'natural' order of things. Former SPD chancellor Helmut Schmidt helped to launch a German national foundation in Weimar in April 1994 with the explicit aim of overcoming the alleged lack of national identity in the reunified Germany.

Such positive reassessments of the nation and the national principle among wide sections of left-liberal intellectuals were, however, not enough for many among the liberal-conservative spectrum of the new Germany. The charge of antinationalism was too convenient a stick with which to beat the left. And reunification, thus voices on the centre-right argued, needed a more wholehearted return to the nation and a more decisive break with the postnationalism of the old FRG. Thus, for example, in 1994 one of the leading politicians of the CDU, Wolfgang Schäuble, widely regarded as heir in waiting of Chancellor Kohl, spelt out the new focus on the nation in book-length form.[22] Schäuble's plea for a strengthening of national identity found an echo in the activities of the Germany Forum (*Deutschlandforum*) of the CDU, founded in 1992. When, in 1995, the conservative publicist Johannes Gross, in line with Schäuble's argument a year earlier, put forward the idea that, after a brief interregnum between 1945 and 1990 Germany was returning to national normality, Habermas warned not to fall back on false continuities.[23] Given that before 1945 Germans experienced National Socialism, an unstable and unloved republic and an authoritarian semi-constitutional system, one might indeed wonder which normality Gross was thinking of. But conservatives like Gross were intent on filling the new German identity with slightly different ingredients from the ones that had dominated West German identity discourses post-1968.

The challenge of the new right and neo-Nazism

A self-styled new right sought to ally itself to more traditional liberal-conservative forces in the new Germany in the first half of the 1990s, and there was considerable overlap between the new right and traditional conservative discourses on the

[21] Richard Schröder, *Deutschland, schwierig Vaterland: Für eine neue politische Kultur* (Freiburg, 1993), p. 23.

[22] Wolfgang Schäuble, *Und der Zukunft zugewandt* (Berlin, 1994).

[23] Johannes Gross, *Begründung der Berliner Republik: Deutschland am Ende des 20. Jahrhunderts* (Berlin, 1995); Jürgen Habermas, *Die Normalität einer Berliner Republik* (Frankfurt/Main, 1995).

nation. In June 2000 the Germany Foundation awarded the Konrad Adenauer Prize for Research Achievements to one of the doyens of the new right, Ernst Nolte. Nolte's continued attempts to relativize the Holocaust had made him a pariah among wide sections of the historical community. Hence it came as a surprise when the conservative director of the prestigious Munich-based Institute of Contemporary History, Horst Möller, agreed to give the encomium on Nolte. Other historians demanded Möller's resignation because of his fraternization with Nolte. The overwhelming reaction in the media to the award and Möller's decision to back Nolte was negative. Even the CDU's chairwoman Angela Merkel distanced herself from the Germany Foundation. Moderate conservatives were careful not to be associated with representatives of the new right. But who was the new right and what did their constructions of the nation amount to?

Those who rallied to the banner of a 'new right' included a motley crew of novelists, such as Botho Strauß; historians, such as Nolte, Rainer Zitelmann and Karlheinz Weißmann; publicists and journalists, such as Ansgar Graw, Heimo Schwilk and Ulrich Schacht; and nationalist politicians on the right wing of the CDU, such as the Germany Forum, and of the FDP, such as former general state attorney Alexander von Stahl and the members of the so-called Stresemann Club in Dresden. It was also heavily supported by the right-wing weekly *Junge Freiheit* (circulation: about 35,000 copies). Two key texts, published by the new right, called for the creation of a more 'self-confident nation' and an end to the allegedly totalitarian ideology of Westernization.[24] Many of the new right's ideas harked back to the conservative revolution of the inter-war period: a tragic view of history combined with doses of xenophobia and a strong emphasis on traditional German values such as duty, asceticism, idealization of leadership and the sacralization of the nation. It presented itself as heir to the statist and antidemocratic political thought of Carl Schmit. The old FRG was taken to account for its alleged antinationalism (especially among the left liberal mainstream), its shyness about power politics and its adoption of a Western political culture. The main stumbling block for the emergence of a more positive national identity, National Socialism, was reinterpreted as a modernizing dictatorship. The new right's attempts to portray the Nazis as conscious modernizers and revolutionaries producing an 'economic miracle' and a developed consumer society as well as planning a comprehensive welfare state was an attempt to make the National Socialist past more palatable to German historical memory. The horrific impact of 'racial nationalism' was marginalized. As representatives of the new right were heavily anti-Communist they argued that a second 'coming-to-terms with the past', the Communist past of East Germany, was on the cards. It would shift the Holocaust and Nazism from its central place in German identity debates and discredit those West German forces whose 'anti-anti-Communism' had allegedly blinded them to the realities of the Communist dictatorship.[25]

24 Heimo Schwilk and Ulrich Schacht, eds, *Die selbstbewusste Nation: 'Anschwellender Bocksgesang' und weitere Beiträge zu einer deutschen Debatte* (Frankfurt/Main, 1994); Rainer Zitelmann, Karlheinz Weißmann and Michael Grossheim, eds, *Westbindung: Chancen und Risiken für Deutschland* (Frankfurt/Main, 1993).

25 For detailed analyses of the new right see Johannes Klotz and Ulrich Schneider, eds, *Die selbstbewusste Nation und ihr Geschichtsbild: Geschichtslegenden der Neuen Rechten* (Cologne,

The borderline between the new right and more mainstream liberal conservatism at times became blurred. After all, conservatives also wanted to move away from the post-68 self-definitions of the FRG. They equally subscribed to the notion of a newfound national normality, and they endorsed the idea of national revival. Finally they had been concerned about an entirely negative historical consciousness focussed on the history of the Holocaust, and they were heavily anti-Communist. However, where mainstream liberal conservatives tended to draw the line was the relativization of the criminal energies of National Socialism and the return to ideas of the 'conservative revolution' of the inter-war period. Mainstream conservatives, it turned out after 1990, had become Westernized to such a degree that they found it difficult to return to a deliberate anti-Western political culture championed by the new right.

On 8 May 1995, on the occasion of the fiftieth anniversary of the end of the Second World War in Europe, key representatives of the new right published a 'call against forgetting' in the *FAZ*. Denouncing the view that 8 May should be celebrated primarily as liberation from Nazi tyranny, they put forward an alternative reading according to which 8 May should be remembered as the beginning of the division of Germany and the beginning of the 'expulsion terror' against Germans in the 'German east'. The initiative, however, turned out a complete failure and underlined the limited appeal of the new right in the new Germany. After 1995 key representatives of the new right returned to the margins of the intellectual debate. Their extremist views had failed to enter the mainstream. In the second half of the 1990s these ideas returned to the neo-Nazi scene, where they always had their most ardent supporters.

For decades extremist right-wing parties, such as the DVU, the Republicans or the NPD, occasionally mobilized enough support at regional elections to enter state parliaments – usually on a ticket of xenophobia and blatant nationalism. Support of political extremism cannot be dismissed as a protest vote, as most supporters of far right-wing parties have relatively consistent extremist worldviews.[26] However, throughout the 1990s levels of xenophobic nationalism in Germany lay consistently between 10 and 15 per cent, which is no higher than in other West European countries. The share of the vote of extremist parties in elections remained regularly below these figures.

The degree to which neo-Nazism established itself amongst East German youth culture in the 1990s has been more worrying than the occasional electoral success of extreme right-wing parties.[27] The new Nazis appealed especially to young males with little education. They have been responsible for the steep increase in the number of racially motivated crimes. It was only in 1992 that the category 'crime against foreigners' had to be introduced in the German penal code. The pogroms of Hoyerswerda (1991) and Rostock-Lichtenhagen (1992) brought images of hundreds of neo-Nazi skinhead youths burning down homes for asylum

1997); Gerd Wiegel, *Die Zukunft der Vergangenheit: Konservativer Geschichtsdiskurs und kulturelle Hegemonie* (Cologne, 2001).

26 Jürgen W. Falter, *Wer wählt rechts? Die Wähler und Anhänger rechtsextremistischer Parteien im vereinigten Deutschland* (Munich, 1994).

27 Toralf Staud, 'Nazis sind chic', *Die Zeit*, 18 February 2001.

seekers, egged on by 'ordinary' onlookers.[28] The appeal of xenophobia in the East has been related to the GDR's policies of ghettoizing and isolating foreigners who were, in the minds of many East Germans, closely related to the interests of the hated SED-regime.[29] However, attacks against foreigners, especially non-white and non-European foreigners, were by no means restricted to the East. Repeated surveys among East and West Germans did not reveal significantly higher levels of xenophobia in East Germany. The response against neo-Nazi violence was also overwhelming in both East and West Germany: anti-Nazi citizens' initiatives sprang up across the country, and tens of thousands of ordinary citizens organized anti-Nazi vigils, lighting rows of burning candles (*Lichterketten*) to declare their solidarity with foreigners living in Germany.

Between 1990 and 2000 the Society for the German Language, which runs an annual competition for the 'non-word' (*Unwort*) of the year, chose three terms which all have to do with xenophobia. In 1991 'free of foreigners' (*ausländerfrei*) was chosen. It had become famous through the demands of the neo-Nazi youth to keep their towns '*ausländerfrei*'. It was also strongly reminiscent of the Nazi term 'free of Jews' (*judenfrei*). In 1993 'domination by foreign influences' (*Überfremdung*) made the running – a term already used by the Nazis and returning to the German language in connection with the debates about a reform of the country's liberal asylum laws. Finally, in 2000 'nationally liberated zones' (*national befreite Zonen*) was picked up as a term used by right-wing extremists to indicate those areas where their terror led to the removal of all foreigners.

Politicians across the party-political spectrum denounced the far right-wing violence, but they were not completely without responsibility for its spread during the first half of the 1990s. Despite the fact that the vast majority of migrants came from within the EU, the CDU started a campaign to change the asylum laws in Germany which made use of crude xenophobic statements. They presented asylum seekers as swindlers and crooks intent on exploiting the social support and medical care available to them in Germany. The conservative print media assisted them in such negative stereotyping and stirred up hatred against asylum seekers. When, in December 1992, the SPD accepted the argument about restricting the numbers of asylum seekers by automatically sending back all those who had entered Germany via another safe country (*Drittstaatenregelung*), the numbers of asylum seekers dropped sharply. But foreigners remained the focus of a heated public debate, as the discussion turned to the need for a new immigration law. Faced with predictions of significant labour shortages in certain areas of the labour market, an increasing number of experts and politicians (mostly from he left) argued that Germany had long become a country of immigration. Like other traditional immigration countries, such as the USA, Germany therefore should adopt a more proactive immigration policy.

These debates about immigration were closely connected to arguments which either favoured or rejected notions of a multicultural society. On the left the champions of multiculturalism used the term largely to foster a greater acceptance of

[28] Hajo Funke, *Brandstifter* (Göttingen, 1993).

[29] Jan C. Behrends, Dennis Kuck and Patrice G. Poutrous, 'Historische Ursachen der Fremdenfeindlichkeit in den Neuen Bundesländern', *H-Soz-u-Kult*, 10 August 2000.

foreign cultures in Germany. On the right, the term raised anxieties about foreigners pushing to the sideline an indigenous German culture and making Germans a minority among others in their own country. *Völkisch* ideas of the nation raised their head again in the context of this debate, but proved to be not acceptable among the political and intellectual mainstream. The CDU argued for retaining German culture as the 'lead culture' (*Leitkultur*) in Germany. When, after 1998, the centre-left government announced plans to change the 1913 citizenship law, its plans to allow dual citizenship were criticized by the centre-right. According to their arguments, one national identity had to take precedence over the other; any one individual could not feel the same kind of loyalty to two different nation states. On the left, by contrast, dual citizenship was seen as a pragmatic solution to the problem of how best to integrate the millions of 'foreigners', many of whom had been born in the country or lived in it for decades. An increasing number of people, the left argued, did not have clear-cut national identities. Hybrid or patchwork identities were becoming more common. In 1999 a populist xenophobic campaign of the CDU against dual citizenship in Hesse was highly successful in ensuring a crushing election defeat for the SPD in this former stronghold of Social Democracy. It forced the government to introduce a less generous reform of the citizenship law the same year, which only allowed dual citizenship up to the age of 23. But the reform itself was still a major watershed. It brought Germany away from its adherence to blood and descent as determining factors of citizenship and adopted the Western territorial principle: those born in the country would henceforth have an automatic right to obtain German citizenship. The law was widely accepted in Germany. Another xenophobic campaign of the CDU (focussed on the slogan 'More children rather than more people from India' (*Kinder statt Inder*), which coincided with the *Land* elections in North-Rhine Westphalia in 2000, failed miserably to generate a rise in the party's election ratings.[30] The centre-left, it would appear, has successfully reformed German citizenship in line with its staunchly pro-Western reconstruction of German national identity after 1990.

Representing the nation: debates surrounding national symbols and international politics

The defeat of the new right's reinvention of Germany took place against the background of a strong revival of political debates surrounding national symbols and national history. The history boom of the 1990s was reflected in the high ratings for television history, excellent sales figures for history books and the many historical anniversaries which received considerable attention in the German media. The television history of Guido Knopp in particular attracted millions of viewers on primetime television.[31] Many of his series focussed on the

[30] Ulrich Herbert, *Geschichte der Ausländerpolitik in Deutschland: Saisonarbeiter, Zwangsarbeiter, Gastarbeiter, Flüchtlinge* (Munich, 2001), pp. 286–334.

[31] Wulf Kansteiner, 'The Radicalisation of German Memory in the Age of its Commercial Reproduction: Hitler and the Third Reich in the TV Documentaries of Guido Knopp', in Norbert Finzsch and Ursula Lehmkuhl, eds, *Atlantic Communications: The Media in American and German History from the Seventeenth to the Twentieth Century* (Oxford, 2004), pp. 335–72.

Nazi period, with a particularly celebrated one on the 'Holokaust'. Knopp insisted on the unusual spelling, which, he argued, put a greater emphasis on the German responsibility for the murder of European Jewry. Knopp's television history has, however, been controversial. He has been accused of adopting National Socialist aesthetics in some of his series and of focussing too much on Hitler and the top brass of the Nazi elite. The 'Knopp phenomenon' became part of a wider debate about national history and national symbols which was nowhere more intense than in the new capital of Germany, Berlin.[32]

It was by no means a foregone conclusion that Berlin would become the new capital city. Considerable cross-party resistance to such a move was based on fear that it might send the wrong kind of signal to the world about Germany returning to its Bismarckian past. Ultimately, it was the successor party to the SED, the Party of Democratic Socialism (PDS), which, in a free vote, swayed the decision in favour of Berlin. Had it been up to the West German parties, a majority would have opted for Bonn. Undoubtedly some on the centre-right opted for Berlin, because they deplored Bonn as the very symbol of the FRG's provinciality and lack of national pride. But on the centre-left one could also hear the argument that Berlin was the best place for the new Germany to confront head-on the demons of its past. The much-celebrated Jewish museum in Berlin, the planned 'Topography of Terror' documentation centre of those institutions which were at the very heart of the National Socialist terror regime, and, above all, the planned Holocaust memorial in the centre of Berlin, right between the Reichstag and the Potsdamer Platz, would be powerful reminders of National Socialism.[33] Almost two decades of controversial debates surrounding these memorial places have anchored the memory of National Socialism more firmly in the collective consciousness. Predictably there have been voices who argued that the new Germany could not build its national identity on the memory of Nazi terror and the Holocaust. Wolf-Jobst Siedler, conservative publisher and publicist, for example, accused his fellow countrymen of megalomania when it came to memorializing German shame and guilt.[34] And architecturally, the new Berlin would be a testimony to 'the successful rehabilitation of once stigmatized traditions'.[35] Architectural forms that were once taboo as fascist, have been successfully revived under the label of postmodernism across Germany.

Siedler, incidentally, has also been one of the foremost supporters of the idea that the old Hohenzollern palace should be rebuilt in the middle of Berlin. Dynamited by the GDR in 1950 it was resurrected as a decorated scaffold in 1993/94. The then director of the Berlin Historical Museum and later minister for culture in Berlin, Christoph Stölzl, described the project as the most fitting symbol for the newfound national unity.[36] Opposition to the project came from those on the left

32 Cornelia Siebeck, 'Inszenierung von Geschichte in der "Berliner Republik"', *WerkstattGeschichte*, 33 (2002), pp. 45–58.

33 Jan-Holger Kirsch, *Nationaler Mythos oder historische Trauer? Der Streit um ein zentrales 'Holocaust-Mahnmal' für die Berliner Republik* (Cologne, 2003).

34 See, for example, Wolf Jobst Siedler, 'Die Hoffahrt der Bußfertigen', *Süddeutsche Zeitung*, 29 April 2001.

35 Gavriel D. Rosenfeld, 'The Architects' Debate: Architectural Discourse and the Memory of Nazism in the Federal Republic of Germany 1977–1997; *History and Memory*, 9 (1997), p. 215.

36 'Das Schloss der Republik: Menschen brauchen Visionen', *Die Welt*, 15 May 1993.

who feared a revival of Prussianism in the new Germany but, above all, from East Germans who wanted to retain the GDR's 'Palace of the Republic', home to the GDR's *Volkskammer*, which stood on the site of the former Hohenzollern palace. When the red-green government came to power in 1998, some commentators were alarmed by Chancellor Schröder's support for rebuilding the palace and feared a 'left-wing Wilhelminism'. It was indeed an important signal that the new centre-left government was intent on using a politics of national symbols to its advantage. It wanted to signal a kind of 'national normality' of its own in an eclectic mix of new and old: thus, the Hohenzollern palace could be restored, but at the same time the citizenship law had to be reformed and the Holocaust memorial had to be built.

Fears of a revival of Prussian sentiments had been fostered by some heavy political symbolism in the early 1990s. The coffins of Frederick Wilhelm and Frederick II were taken to Potsdam in 1991 with great pomp and reburied in a midnight ceremony attended by, among other dignitaries, Chancellor Kohl. The Quadriga was restored on top of the Brandenburg gate the same year. Hence it was with some trepidation that commentators on the left looked toward the 300th anniversary of the crowning of the first Prussian king in 2001. Another Prussia year, right at the beginning of the new millenium, brought an outpouring of books on Prussia, several major exhibitions and hundreds of thousands of visitors to Berlin and Potsdam. In the media Prussian virtues and the positive legacies of Prussia were emphasized more than ever before. When historians and politicians praised Prussian commitment to achievement and duty, tolerance, reform and modesty, and when they spoke of Prussia's enlightened absolutism and adherence to the rule of law few people protested as they had done back in 1982.[37] The old Prussia, one now heard more often, was dead and gone, and this allowed Germans a more balanced look at this state's legacy. A brief debate following suggestions about resurrecting a kind of rump Prussia through a merger between Berlin and Brandenburg came to nothing. Overall the Prussia year of 2001 became more renowned for its tourism than for its identity debates. But tourism, as we have emphasized in previous chapters, has long been an important site of identity creation and should therefore not be underestimated. History, memory and national identity have all become part and parcel of the entertainment industry, but commercialization does not prevent or counter the political functionalization of the past. A documentary about Wilhelm II, portraying him in a very positive light, premiered late in 2000 with much media attention and the *crème de la crème* of the German aristocracy in attendance, but then again it hardly signalled the return of the German movie industry to the kind of nationalist staple diet which had characterized it in the inter-war period, or even in the 1950s. The launching of a publicly financed Otto von Bismarck Foundation in the summer of 1997 raised fears of another Bismarck cult, but the foundation has established itself as a sober research institute rather than a propagandistic instrument of official nationalism.[38]

37 See above, p. 193.

38 http://www.bismarck-stiftung.de/frameset_intern.htm. On the history of the foundation, see also Michael Epkenhans, *Die Otto-von-Bismarck-Stiftung 1996–2000* (Friedrichsruh, 2000).

There are few signs that the official Germany is intent on self-consciously returning to Prussian traditions.

More sinister however, were private attempts to rebuild the Potsdam *Garnisonskirche*.[39] The church was the military temple of the Hohenzollern dynasty, and the place where Hindenburg and Hitler shook hands in 1933. Frederick Wilhelm I had built the church for his soldiers and it boasted a wide collection of Prussian army standards. In the 1980s a conservative association, headed by the retired army officer Max Klaar, collected enough money to restore the famous chimes of the church. They were placed in Iserlohn and were supposed to move back to Potsdam after reunification. In the 1980s this initiative seemed ludicrously anachronistic to many in West Germany. But when reunification came about, the chimes did move east and the association continued to collect money. They are now in a position to start the building work and restore what can only be construed as a memorial shrine to the old Prussia and its norms and values. However, the conservative association finds itself at loggerheads with the Protestant church, which wants the church rebuilt only as a centre for reconciliation – a kind of German equivalent of Coventry cathedral. In marked contrast to their positioning before 1945 the Protestant church has been careful to prevent any instrumentalization of religion for national purposes. Thus, for example, they refused suggestions by the government to ring the church bells on the occasion of German reunification on 3 October 1990. They did organize special church services on the day, but the bells would only ring to call the community of believers and not to celebrate national unity.

In 1993 the problem of creating national memorials in Germany was highlighted by the decision of the Kohl government to transform Schinkel's Neue Wache on the Berlin boulevard Unter den Linden into the new central national memorial. The location, the artistic and aesthetic arrangements and the inscription were all the subject of an extensive debate in the media. In particular the enlarged Pietà figure by Käthe Kollwitz of a mother bemoaning the death of her soldier son has drawn strong criticism. Being in a Christian tradition it completely ignored antisemitism, the Holocaust and German responsibility for two world wars, and instead foregrounded a notion of universal suffering.

It is difficult to see how former sites of Hohenzollern glory can become fitting national memorials for a democratic Germany today. Other architectural landmarks seem more suited to this purpose, perhaps none more so than the Reichstag. The new parliament building has received its fair share of public attention and debate. When Bulgarian-born artists Christo and Jean-Claude wrapped up the Reichstag for ten days in the summer of 1995, conservatives raised concerns that it might damage the dignity of the parliament building. But 5 million visitors ensured that the building was discussed and noticed by Germans as never before. Christo himself described his project in terms of fitting out the Germans with a 'lighter' national identity. Some years later the British architect Sir Norman Foster refused to reconstruct a historical copy of the Reichstag cupola and insisted on building a glass cupola – a symbol for the openness and transparency of the

[39] Frank Pergande, 'Das umstrittene Erbe des Soldatenkönigs', *FAZ*, 4 December 2001.

democratic politics in the new Germany[40] [Figure 8.1]. The cupola has become one of the main tourist attractions in the new Berlin. Overall, the many debates about national symbols and symbolic politics have been far more important than the national symbols themselves. Attempts to steer the symbolic politics of the new Germany away from the National Socialist past and towards a more positive (and more traditional) national memory culture have not been too successful. Instead, the reunified Germany has shown a remarkable capacity to encourage a (self-)critical rather than affirmative perspective on the national past. The many ghosts of German history will not easily be laid to rest – especially not in Berlin.

When the decision had been taken to move the capital from Bonn to Berlin a lead editorial in the flagship of the liberal conservative print media, the *FAZ*, argued: 'the new Germany has signalled its readiness to shed its semi-sovereign past and take on a new role which will be better matched to its changed position in the world. It is no longer possible to have the lowest possible profile internationally, only to whisper the word nation and to let others in this tension-ridden world pull the chestnuts out of the fire – as has happened most recently in the Gulf.'[41] Many on the centre-right followed suit and proclaimed the German return to power politics. Some, like Hans-Peter Schwarz, a historian close to the CDU, had already lamented the German inability to return to power politics in the 1980s.[42] After 1990 he returned to this theme with a vengeance. The new Germany, he argued, was best described as 'Europe's central power' (*Zentralmacht Europas*), which signalled both the recasting of Germany as a major European power and the revival of *Mittellage* ideology, i.e. the belief that Germany's geographical position in the middle of Europe was Germany's foreign policy destiny, past and present.[43]

A more self-confident pursuit of national interests was now demanded with increasing regularity and frequency. Conservative historians blamed Germany's *Mittellage* for all of the nation's catastrophes, from the Thirty Years' War to the First World War and the nationalist hubris of Hitler's 'Thousand Year *Reich*'. The *Mittellage* had made Imperial Germany unsuitable for more democratic and participatory forms of government and it had produced the restlessness and the demands for expansion and hegemony during the first half of the twentieth century. *Mittellage* also occasionally led to dreams of a renewed German hegemony over the countries of 'central Europe' (*Mitteleuropa*) and calls for a more important world political role in the light of Germany's alleged superpower status.[44] Most recently Gregor Schöllgen, Professor of History at Erlangen University, who also

40 Norman Foster, 'Ein optimistisches Zeichen für ein modernes Deutschland: Der Bundestag in Berlin', in Heinrich Wefing, ed., *'Dem Deutschen Volke': Der Bundestag im Berliner Reichstagsgebäude* (Berlin, 1999), pp. 180–91.

41 *FAZ*, 21 June 1991.

42 Hans-Peter Schwarz, *Die gezähmten Deutschen: Von der Machtbesessenheit zur Machtvergessenheit* (Stuttgart, 1985).

43 *Idem*, *Die Zentralmacht Europas: Deutschlands Rückkehr auf die Weltbühne* (Berlin, 1994).

44 The revival of *Mitte* ideology can be found in particular in Klaus Hildebrand, *Das vergangene Reich*; Gregor Schöllgen, *Die Macht in der Mitte Europas: Stationen deutscher Außenpolitik von Friedrich dem Großen bis zur Gegenwart* (Munich, 1992); Michael Stürmer, *Die Grenzen der Macht: Begegnung der Deutschen mit der Geschichte* (Berlin, 1990); Christian Hacke, *Weltmacht wider Willen: Die Außenpolitik der Bundesrepublik Deutschland*, 2nd rev. edn (Frankfurt/Main, 1993); Gregor Schöllgen, *Angst vor der Macht: Die Deutschen und ihre Außenpolitik* (Berlin, 1993).

Figure 8.1 Reichstag with glass cupola by Sir Norman Foster, © Dieter E. Hoppe.

teaches future German diplomats at the Foreign Office, has celebrated Germany's return to the 'world stage' and to power politics. He approves of Chancellor Schröder's words that Germany's foreign policy would be made in Berlin and nowhere else, and he applauds Germany's act of emancipation from its American ally over the second Gulf War. According to Schöllgen, the transatlantic age is drawing to a close and the 'normal nation state with the potential of becoming a European great power' would have to find its own 'German way'.[45]

Among left-liberal intellectuals and politicians scepticism about any such German return to independent power politics and the 'world stage' has remained strong. Instead they tended to advocate continuing partnership with all neighbouring states and as many European economic, political and intellectual links as possible. Continuity in domestic politics was to be combined with continuity in foreign policy. Chancellor Schröder himself emphasized those sentiments when he wrote in the magazine *Stern* about 'My Berlin Republic': 'What matters now is to continue the democratic project in Berlin. To continue with a successful democracy, a stable federalism, a policy of good neighbourly relations, a strong commitment to Europe and to the atlantic alliance. All this is now part of our baggage which we take to Berlin.'[46]

The second Gulf War has not changed this basic longing for continuity. In line with the French political class and supported by much of European public opinion, the German government decided to disagree with its American ally, but it has always insisted that it was a disagreement among friends. Continuity had, of course, already been the overwhelming message of German foreign policy under the centre-right government of Helmut Kohl. It had, after all, accepted the existing state borders of Germany, forgoing all claims of territories belonging to neighbouring states since 1945. Whilst some refugees' and expellees' organizations still uphold their right to return to what they regard as their *Heimat*, most Germans today have no problem with their nation's borders. The question of compensation payments to the Sudeten Germans continues to sour German–Czech relations, and there have been attempts of the shadowy Association for Germandom Abroad (VDA) to 're-Germanize' Kaliningrad (the former Königsberg).[47] Some maverick historians such as Arnulf Baring may have speculated about a new 'Eastern settlement movement' (*Ostsiedlung*) of the Germans. He called on his countrymen to think more about their 'lost territories' in the east.[48] But the overwhelming emphasis both of official policies and intellectual discourse has been on reconciliation and partnership with Germany's Eastern European neighbours to complement the excellent relations the FRG already enjoyed along its Western borders. One symbol of such reconciliation and dialogue has been the newly created university of Frankfurt/Oder – a city divided by the German-Polish border.

45 Gregor Schöllgen, *Der Auftritt: Deutschlands Rückkehr auf die Weltbühne* (Berlin, 2003).

46 Gerhard Schröder, 'Meine Berliner Republik', *Stern*, 2 September 1999.

47 J.H. Brinks, 'Political Geography of Contemporary Affairs: The Miraculous Resurrection of Immanuel Kant. Germany's Breakthrough to Former East Prussia', *Political Geography* 17 (1998), pp. 611–15; Christian Wellmann, 'Recognising Borders: Coping with Historically Contested Territory', in Hanne-Margret Birckenbach and Christian Wellmann, eds, *The Kaliningrad Challenge: Options and Recommendations* (Münster, 2003), pp. 1–21.

48 Arnulf Baring, *Deutschland, was nun?* (Berlin, 1991).

The university has sites on both sides of the border, and it attracts students from both countries, with courses being held in German and Polish.[49]

The foreign policy of pre- and post-reunification German governments has been grounded in the willingness to forge good neighbourly relations within an increasingly integrated and united European Union. Reunification, many politicians argued, made the success of Europe even more urgent. The political elite of the country views further European integration as central to the long-term success of German reunification. Europe has become a widely accepted symbol for overcoming the nationalist conflicts and wars which characterized the first half of the twentieth century. Europe has come to stand for common prosperity, welfare and democracy. The mass tourism of Germans in Europe has strengthened the feeling of a common cultural space. Despite the success of the Deutschmark and the currency's importance for German identity, the political elite was united in favouring the introduction of the Euro in 2002.

Of course, there have been problems with the European identity of Germany as well. The introduction of the Euro showed clearly the danger of Europe becoming an elite project without majority support in the broader population. If there had been a referendum, the majority of Germans would have voted against the introduction of the Euro. Europe lacks the powerful myths of origin and the historical mythologies more generally that have been so characteristic of European nation states.[50] Notions of a Christian Europe may exclude countries, like Turkey, from the EU and strengthen an already vibrant anti-Islamic discourse across Europe. Federalism is pushed not least by the German governments as a model for the future organization of Europe, but a 'Europe of the regions' is greeted with considerable scepticism in those nation states with a strong tradition of central government. Last but not least, divisions within Europe can be subtly exploited by non-European powers, as recently demonstrated by the US foreign policy in the second Iraq war, when the US foreign secretary, Donald Rumsfeld, made a pointed distinction between 'new' and 'old Europe'. However many difficulties and problems there are with Europe and a European identity, it still remains the case that German foreign policy today no longer seeks the creation of a 'Germanic Europe', but rather pursues the notion of a 'Europeanized Germany' – sometimes against the wishes of a majority within its own population.[51]

One crucial difference to the pre-1990 West German Europeanism, however, is the greater involvement of the reunified Germany in the management of international crises. This includes a greater military role for Germany. In 1991 the debates about the first Gulf War saw almost the entire left opposed to German military participation in the war. Over the past forty years the Bundeswehr had become more a social than a military institution. German citizens got used to seeing German soldiers on TV helping to defend the German coastline against the

[49] Gesine Schwan, 'Vom Weimarer Dreieck zum geeinten Kontinent: Die Rolle der Europa-Universität Viadrina im Einigungsprozess der EU', *Vorgänge*, 16:2 (2003), pp. 36–40.

[50] Wolfgang Schmale, *Scheitert Europa an seinem Mythendefizit?* (Bochum, 1997).

[51] Willfried Spohn, 'Continuities and Changes of Europe in German National Identity', in Mikael af Malmborg and Bo Strath, eds, *The Meaning of Europe* (Oxford, 2002), p. 306.

raging sea, or trying to prevent German rivers flooding towns and villages. But seeing German soldiers fight wars abroad was something that most Germans were not used to any more. In the 1990s this changed, and once again it was the red-green government which contributed vitally to this change. For the first time after 1945 it sent German troops to participate in the NATO war against Yugoslavia in 1999.[52] Many Yugoslavs still remembered the terror rule of the Wehrmacht after 1941. Hence the past should have been deeply problematic for any German military involvement in the Balkans. But, in fact, the Green foreign minister, Fischer, and the entire government argued precisely on historical grounds for German military interventionism. The Yugoslav leadership under its president, Milosevic, was depicted as a fascist regime. Comparisons between Milosevic and Hitler abounded in the media. The Serbian acts of ethnic cleansing in Kosovo were compared to Auschwitz. It was therefore precisely because of the lessons that Germany had learnt out of its own National Socialist past that it participated in the war to stop acts of genocide elsewhere in Europe.

When a German judge was appointed to the international Yugoslavia war crimes tribunal in The Hague, it was a powerful gesture that Germany had stopped being the accused – a role it had occupied so prominently in Nuremberg in 1946. Fifty years later the international community had finally allowed it to change sides. It had stopped being the accused and was now sitting among the judges. In a similar vein Germany for the first time was allowed a non-permanent seat on the UN Security Council in January 2003. However, with the exception of right-wing fringe parties and their supporters, few would dream of Germany flexing its military muscle outside international organizations, such as the UN or NATO. The new military role of Germany has not been accompanied by a resurgence of militarism. The German army does not comprise more than 350,000 soldiers and is suffering from budget cuts. Among young men, conscientious objection and the alternative 'civic service' is as popular as military service. Even among those 50 per cent of young males who opt for the military the army is rarely seen as a school of manliness. As gender roles have become increasingly fuzzy over the last thirty years, fewer and fewer people have clung to the ideal of the army as school of the nation (or at least the male part of the nation). The 1990s saw a debate about whether military service was to be retained at all. Many voices in Germany today argue for a small and highly professional army. Militarism is no longer a significant part of constructing German national identity in the twenty-first century.

A past that truly will not go away: debates about National Socialism

The well-known writer and novelist Martin Walser became the most outspoken advocate for ending what he described as constant public breast-beating over

[52] German aeroplanes had already been used in the 1995 NATO action in Bosnia, after the supreme court had approved the constitutionality of such 'out of area' actions of the Bundeswehr in 1994.

Germany's Nazi past.[53] Walser was in some respect similar to Grass, as the themes of national identity and national history ran consistently through his literary work. In 1998, in his acceptance speech of the Peace Prize of the German Book Trade, one of the country's most prestigious literary awards, he attacked the 'national masochism' of the country's media and of its public intellectuals such as Grass and Habermas. Constantly putting 'German shame' on display, he argued, only gave rise to neo-Nazism and contributed to the neglect of the national theme in Germany. Those who listened to Walser's speech in Frankfurt's Paulskirche, among them many of the great and the good of Germany's political and intellectual establishment, gave him a standing ovation at the end of it. Next day many commentators in the newspapers thought that Walser was only saying aloud what many Germans were already thinking. And the novelist himself subsequently emphasized that he saw himself as the mouthpiece of the silent majority in Germany.

However, one of the few who had not cheered Walser inside the Paulskirche, was the chairman of the Central Council of Jews in Germany, Ignatz Bubis. Bubis publicly denounced Walser as an 'intellectual arsonist'. He accused the novelist of wanting to draw a line under the National Socialist past so as to make it easier to propagate a renewed nationalism in Germany. The attack rapidly divided the German public. Several influential opinion-makers, including the editor of the left-liberal *Der Spiegel* magazine, Rudolf Augstein, defended Walser and in turn attacked Bubis for wanting to turn the memory of Auschwitz into a perennial weapon to be used against Germany. Even Chancellor Schröder intervened in the debate with the somewhat cryptic remark that a writer had to be allowed to say these things. It was the same chancellor who in fact invited Walser to join him in a public discussion about the significance of 8 May (the end of the Second World War in Europe) in 2002. Walser said little new on the occasion. He reiterated his emotional commitment to the German nation,[54] but it was a powerful message sent out by Schröder that Germans could now publicly discuss the issues of national pride and self-confidence.

Public opinion surveys, which demonstrate a steep decline in knowledge about National Socialism, demonstrate that many, in particular younger Germans, do not want to be bothered with the Nazi past any more.[55] Lack of knowledge about Nazism goes hand in hand with a rise in antisemitic stereotypes.[56] A new intellectual antisemitism has been spreading in the reunified Germany.[57] The Holocaust

[53] Micha Brumlik, Hajo Funke and Lars Rensmann, *Umkämpftes Vergessen: Walser-Debatte, Holocaust-Mahnmal und neuere deutsche Geschichtspolitik* (Berlin, 2000). A much more upbeat assessment of how the united Germany has attempted to face the Nazi past during the 1990s can be found in Bill Niven, *Facing the Nazi Past: United Germany and the Legacy of the Third Reich* (London, 2001).

[54] Martin Walser, 'Über ein Geschichtsgefühl', *FAZ*, 10 May 2002.

[55] 'Schluss mit dem Holocaust', *Süddeutsche Zeitung*, 4 November 2002; 'Zwei von drei Jugendlichen kennen den Begriff Holocaust nicht', *Berliner Morgenpost*, 10 August 2000.

[56] Uwe Bahnsen, 'Vergangenheit bewältigen und die Zukunft nicht ausblenden', *Die Welt* 13 November 2000; Julia Brunner, 'Studie: Zwei Drittel der Jugendlichen denken antisemitisch', *Die Welt*, 8 September 2000.

[57] Dan Diner, 'Es redet aus ihnen heraus', *Die Welt*, 15 June 2002.

has never been part of the private memory of people in the nation of perpetrators.[58] And as the personal memory of the Holocaust gives way to historical memory, the Holocaust is beginning to lose its spell over German history. It has become a history which is being successfully Europeanized and globalized as a parable of evil in history – a narrative for a cultural memory no longer linked to a specific time and place.[59] 27 January, the day Auschwitz was liberated, after all, has been commemorated as Holocaust Day across Europe and the wider world since 1996.

And yet millions of Germans saw one of the major film sensations of the 1990s: Steven Spielberg's *Schindler's List* (1993). It was very positively reviewed in the German media. One of the major publishing sensations of the 1990s was the diary of Viktor Klemperer, a Jewish professor of Romance philology at Dresden, who, throughout the Nazi years, gave an authentic record of daily life and daily discrimination against the Jews. The hero in Spielberg's film was a German, and Klemperer affirmed his own Germanness throughout the diary, but the impact of both film and diary nevertheless showed that the German public remained deeply fascinated with the Nazi years.

The Goldhagen debate, which raged through Germany in 1996, was another indicator that it would not be easy to push the Holocaust away from its central position in German identity politics.[60] Daniel J. Goldhagen's thesis about the Holocaust as a national project of the Germans driven forward by a collective 'eliminationist mindset' was rejected by the entire historical establishment. However, when Goldhagen toured Germany, mass audiences of overwhelmingly younger Germans supported the American assistant professor against his mostly elderly and slightly aloof professorial German counterparts. Certainly the question that Goldhagen set out to answer, namely why the Holocaust could happen in Germany, does not seem to have lost any of its fascination after reunification.

The opening of the Jewish Museum in September 2001 was widely welcomed as another sign that the new Germany is taking seriously German-Jewish history and culture. Even one of the most consistent critics of German attempts to come to terms with the National Socialist past, the Jewish publicist Ralph Giordano, did not hesitate to link his own identity firmly to notions of Germanness. He called on the millions of Germans who thought like him, not to give right-wing extremism and antisemitism another chance: 'Let's not leave Germany once again to those who will potentially ruin it. Instead let us protect, guard and defend this democratic republic! Firmly anchored in Europe, she is also – I dare use the

58 Thomas Wild, 'Für Opas Gedächtnislücken ist uns das Beste gerade gut genug', *Berliner Zeitung*, 8 July 2002.

59 Michael Jeismann, *Auf Wiedersehen Gestern: Die deutsche Vergangenheit und die Politik von morgen* (Stuttgart, 2001).

60 Daniel Jonah Goldhagen, *Hitler's Willing Executioners: Ordinary Germans and the Holocaust* (New York, 1996), provoked a controversy before it was even translated into German. The debate was started by Volker Ullrich, 'Hitlers willige Mordgesellen', *Die Zeit*, 12 April 1996, who predicted that this book would lead to a new *Historikerstreit*. The intellectual standing of this weekly in Germany almost ensured that his prediction was a self-fulfilling prophecy. See Julius H. Schoeps, ed., *Ein Volk von Mördern? Die Dokumentation zur Goldhagen Kontroverse um die Rolle der Deutschen im Holocaust* (Hamburg, 1996).

old-fashioned term – our fatherland.'[61] Was this the return of dreams of a 'German-Jewish symbiosis'? As Salomon Korn, chair of the Jewish community in Frankfurt/ Main, reminded his fellow Germans, any talk about a 'German-Jewish culture' or 'German-Jewish symbiosis' remained deeply problematical in a post-Holocaust Germany.[62]

The National Socialist past has retained its crucial significance for German identity debates in other respects too. After a long campaign the red-green government finally gave an official rehabilitation to those soldiers of the Wehrmacht who had been court-martialled and executed as deserters.[63] The involvement of the Wehrmacht in the Holocaust (something known to experts for decades) came under public scrutiny in a major exhibition which began to tour Germany in 1995. Organized by the Hamburg-based Institute for Social Research, it has been seen by over 1 million people. Right-wing protests about this alleged attempt to smear the 'clean' German soldiers were met with more public interest. The exhibition had to be withdrawn and reworked, because some of the photos did not show victims of the Wehrmacht but of the Soviet secret police. But when it reopened it still pulled in the crowds. Finally, the long debate concerning compensation payments for slave labourers in the Third Reich culminated in August 2000 in the creation of a national foundation: 'Compensation, Responsibility and the Future'. One year earlier, the president, Johannes Rau, in a widely reported speech before parliament, had asked former slave labourers for forgiveness in the name of the German people. From 2001 billions of Euros were made available to compensate former slave labourers who individually have been receiving sums between £1,700 and £5,000.[64] The money was paid out largely by German companies fearful that their global business interests might be negatively affected by threats by Holocaust survivors and non-Jewish slave labourers to sue the companies which had employed slave labour during the Third Reich. Still, the existence of the foundation is the most recent sign that the reunified Germany will not forget about its Nazi past.

Many local history workshop-type grassroots activities also continue to make the National Socialist past an important topic for public debate. Some commentators have even argued that the German people, not unlike the Jewish people, have become a 'symbolical people', representing the incarnation of evil in a post-Holocaust world.[65] Any search for normality that seeks to sideline the memory of the Holocaust and of National Socialism seems doomed to failure from the start. However, normalization no longer entails denial of the past but has in fact endorsed the Nazi past. Representatives of the new Germany readily admit German guilt and they do not deny the more gruesome aspects of German history in the first half of the twentieth century. But at the same time they insist that Germany has learnt its lessons. German history post-1945 is presented as living

[61] Ralph Giordano, 'Die Last, Deutscher zu sein', *Die Welt*, 1 April 2001.

[62] Salomon Korn, 'Im Transitraum der Weltgeschichte', *Süddeutsche Zeitung*, 4 June 2003.

[63] Wolfram Wette, ed., *Deserteure der Wehrmacht: Feiglinge–Opfer–Hoffnungsträger? Dokumentaion eines Meinungswandels* (Essen, 1995).

[64] Mattias Arning, *Späte Abrechnung: Über Zwangsarbeiter, Schlußstriche und Berliner Verständigungen* (Frankfurt/Main, 2001).

[65] C.K. Williams, 'Das symbolische Volk der Täter', *Die Zeit*, 7 November 2002.

proof that the nation has finally taken its side next to and in the midst of the Western community of 'civilized' and democratic nation states. It was precisely on this basis that Chancellor Schröder's first state-of-the-nation address in 1998 could argue that Germans were building a 'self-confident nation' in line with levels of national pride to be found elsewhere in Western Europe.

Perspectives on the GDR

The only problem with such a national past is that it is necessarily one which relies heavily on the West German success story after 1945. What about East Germany, one is tempted to ask. How do they fit into this emerging national narrative of the reunified Germany? The simple answer is: not very well. Anti-Communism was an important ingredient of the West German identity before 1990.[66] Ironically, the years following the demise of Communism across Eastern Europe saw anti-Communism in the West increase.[67] On the right many commentators highlighted the horrors of Communism, sometimes with the deliberate aim of dislocating the National Socialist past from its central place in German identity debates and making the Communist past the new focus of attention. The red dictatorship was presented as at least as bad (if not worse) than the brown dictatorship. After all, it was argued, it went on for much longer and corrupted society far more thoroughly than the twelve years of National Socialism. The antifascism of the Communist GDR was denounced as nothing more than a propaganda tool of the SED. When it was discovered that the Buchenwald concentration camp – the most sacred territory of the cult of antifascism in the old GDR[68] – had also been used by the Soviets after 1945 to imprison about 28,000 former Nazis and opponents of Stalinism, sensationalist newspaper reports in the yellow press presented the Communist 'concentration' camp in the same light as the Nazi one. Making Buchenwald a site which remembered both the victims of Nazism and Stalinism was one of the most difficult tasks in the minefields of German memory politics in the 1990s.[69]

The publication of the *Black Book of Communism* in 1997 (first in French) fanned the flames of anti-Communism in the West.[70] Unfortunately, for its German admirers, it did not include a chapter on the GDR, but the foreword to the German edition sought to rectify this 'omission'. Subsequently a range of other publications have sought to present the SED regime and Communism in general in the darkest colours, highlighting one-sidedly their criminal energies.[71] Throughout the

---

66 See above, p. 181f.

67 Stefan Berger, 'Anti-Communism after the Fall of Communism? The Anti-Left Syndrome of the SPD and its Impact on Contemporary German Politics', *Debatte*, 3:1 (1995), pp. 66–97; 3:2 (1995), pp. 103ff.

68 See above, p. 201.

69 Hasko Zimmer, *Der Buchenwald-Konflikt: Zum Streit um Geschichte und Erinnerung im Kontext der deutschen Vereinigung* (Münster, 1999).

70 Stéphane Courtois *et al.* eds, *Black Book of Communism: Crimes, Terror, Repression* (Harvard, 1999).

71 One recent example is Uwe Backes and Stéphane Courtois, eds, *'Ein Gespenst geht um in Europa': Das Erbe kommunistischer Ideologien* (Cologne, 2002).

first half of the 1990s attempts were made to remove the portrayal of the Communist resistance to National Socialism from the permanent public exhibition on the resistance in Berlin.[72] Campaigns were started to rename East Berlin streets named after well-known Communists. Much public attention was focussed on the criminal activities of the SED regime. The Berlin-based Office for Governmental and Unification Criminality investigated – throughout the nine years of its existence – more than 20,000 cases of criminal GDR activities ranging from the violent deaths of those attempting to flee the GDR to sport doping.[73]

Mary Fulbrook has described the strong vilification of GDR history in the German memory culture of the 1990s as 'Checkpoint Charlie approach to German history'.[74] But the attempt to make a blatant and simplistic anti-Communism the foundation myth of the reunified Germany ultimately had only limited success. For a start, the booming historical research on GDR history has been varied. A plurality of research methods and agendas has been developed at a great number of research institutes and university departments. Many historians have emphasized that it is insufficient to reduce the GDR to its dictatorial aspects and instead have sought to understand and analyse the complex interplay between state and society in the GDR. Two official parliamentary commissions on GDR history produced much debate and a considerable amount of mud-slinging between government and opposition over the question of which West German party had supported the 'evil machinations' of the 'Stasi regime' most. But they also revealed how difficult it was to see the GDR simply in terms of a dictatorship. A number of East German social scientists and historians, many of them unemployed after 1990, set up an alternative commission and produced a steady stream of publications seeking to counter what they perceived as the one-sided public denunciation of the GDR after 1990.[75]

Debates about the impact of the secret police, the Stasi, on East German society haunted public debates throughout the 1990s and contributed in a major way to presenting the GDR primarily as a system of coercion and terror. As early as 1990 a formidable witch hunt focussed on the prominent East German novelist Christa Wolf. An SED member to the end of the GDR, she only revealed her own harassment by the Stasi in a novella published after the fall of the GDR. Immediately questions were asked why she presented herself as a victim of the SED regime only after its demise. One year later, in 1991, two key representatives of the literary East Berlin-based counter-culture, Sascha Anderson and Rainer Schedlinski, were 'outed' as Stasi informants. Subsequently many other former

[72] Peter Steinbach, 'Teufel Hitler – Beelzebub Stalin? Zur Kontroverse um die Darstellung des Nationalkomitees Freies Deutschland in der ständigen Ausstellung "Widerstand gegen den Nationalsozialismus" in der Gedenkstätte Deutscher Widerstand', in *Zeitschrift für Geschichtswissenschaft* 42 (1994), pp. 651–62.

[73] Claudia Roth, 'Die "bewaffneten Historiker" treten ab', *Die Welt*, 29 December 2000.

[74] Mary Fulbrook, 'Reckoning with the Past: Heroes, Victims, and Villains in the History of the German Democratic Republic', in Reinhard Alter and Peter Monteath, eds, *Rewriting the German Past: History and Identity in the New Germany* (Atlantic Highlands, 1997), pp. 175–196.

[75] Stefan Berger, 'Former GDR Historians in the Reunified Germany: An Alternative Historical Culture and its Attempts to Come to Terms with the GDR Past', *Journal of Contemporary History*, 38 (2003), pp. 63–83.

GDR notables, including many former dissidents, were accused of having been in the pay of the Stasi. The Stasi debates undoubtedly revealed a frightening level of surveillance of every aspect and every niche of East German society. But there were also an increasing number of voices insisting that any one-sided concentration on the Stasi and the SED as central institutions in the GDR would reveal very little about how East German society actually functioned.[76]

The mountains of files left by the Stasi were a valuable, if somewhat problematic, historical source, revealing a great deal about diverse aspects of the GDR. They also served as the basis on which all East German employees in public services were screened for former Stasi connections. If the screening revealed Stasi activities, they often lost their jobs. In fact about 70 per cent of the former East German elites were replaced by West Germans after 1990. Such radical elite change, almost total in some areas and institutions, stood in marked contrast to the continuities between Nazi and West German elites after 1945 and created much bitterness among former supporters of the SED regime. Such heavy-handed Western interventionism was a consequence of Western concerns not to repeat the haphazard and half-hearted coming-to-terms with the Nazi past which had been characteristic of West Germany in the 1950s. Once again the reunified Germany, or more precisely its Western elites, were intent on demonstrating that they had learned the lessons of the Nazi past and its aftermath. But the radical removal of former GDR elites accompanied by rapid and deep social change affecting the whole of East German society deepened the gulf between East and West Germans. East Germans now accused their Western cousins of selling them short and colonizing the East. The East German image of the arrogant 'Wessi' was matched by the West German image of the lazy 'Ossi' relying on massive financial help from the West to get out of the mess created by forty years of 'actually existing socialism'.[77] The Berlin Wall was gone, but, so it seemed to many, the wall in the heads of Germans East and West was growing higher every year. Nine years after reunification, East and West Germans still had completely different and mutually incompatible outlooks on life, politics and what the future might bring.[78]

Was there anything worth preserving of the GDR in the reunified Germany? Former supporters of the SED regime remained convinced that at least the basis for a non-capitalist economy had been laid in the GDR. A socialist Germany had failed because it could not find a more democratic way of organizing its society. Hence, among the far left, the search for democratic socialist alternatives to the restoration of capitalism was on. Some commentators pointed to a much stronger work culture in which people identified more with their places of work. East German women in particular have argued that they had achieved greater levels

[76] Reinhard Alter, 'Cultural Modernity and Political Identity: from the Historians' Dispute to the Literature Dispute', in Alter and Monteath, eds, *Rewriting*, pp. 152–74 (see note 74).

[77] More than a third of per capita income in the East German *Länder* has been transferred from West to East after 1990.

[78] Elmar Brähler and Horst-Eberhard Richter, 'Deutsche – zehn Jahre nach der Wende: Ergebnisse einer vergleichenden Ost–West Untersuchung', in *aus politik und zeitgeschichte*, 5 November 1999, pp. 24–31.

of de facto emancipation than their feminist counterparts in the West.[79] Others have argued that the 1989 revolution should bolster concepts of active citizenship and a stronger civil society in the reunified Germany. As the world of East Germans was turned upside down in the reunification process they tended to cling to the recognizable symbols of the world they had known. Thus, for example, they campaigned heavily to retain the traffic light figure at GDR city crosswalks (*Ampelmännchen*), and the *Jugendweihe*[80] remains highly popular in East Germany.

A veritable 'ostalgia' (*Ostalgie*) took hold of East Germans in the 1990s. Consumer goods closely associated with the former GDR, from Trabant motor cars to Rotkäppchen sparkling wine became markers of identity, as East Germans craved for a vanished material culture which seemed symbolical of their vanished former lifeworld.[81] The GDR might seem an unlikely object for nostalgic backward gazing, but the success of 'ostalgia', carefully nurtured by diverse commercial interests, ultimately rests on feelings of humiliation and alienation. It is a sure sign that many East Germans have not yet fully arrived in the reunified country. Eight years after reunification a publication entitled *The GDR Turns Fifty* could still appear indicating that, in the heads of some East Germans at least, their former state had refused to die.[82] Popular films such as *Good-bye Lenin* looked back lightheartedly on the cosy provincialism of the GDR, and German television is broadcasting TV shows commemorating the GDR and its 'heroes'.

The PDS successfully established itself as a regional political party in East Germany by presenting itself as the most creditable alternative to the 'colonizing' and 'alien' Western party political imports.[83] Most East Germans, however, would readily admit that many things changed for the better after 1990, but they still have been suffering from an often difficult and painful adaptation to completely changed circumstances. What happened to them was what Hannah Arendt described as 'loss of world'.[84] Few wanted the old SED regime back, but the new Germany was all-too-strange, and, what is more, it was often experienced as unwelcoming and humiliating. Walter Schmidt, former head of the Institute of Historical Research at the old GDR Academy of Sciences, talked about his own difficulties of settling in a post-reunification Germany which one-sidedly consigned the GDR to the dustbin of history:

> The identity of all those who have worked here [in the GDR] cannot be maintained if everything that has been done and achieved in more than four decades is simply invalidated and declared useless. My identity is incomprehensible without the GDR,

---

79 For the debate between East German 'Muttis' and West German 'Emanzen' see Heike Ellermann and Katrin Klatt, *Bundesdeutsche Hausfrau? – Nie im Leben! Eine Studie zum Selbstverständnis von Frauen in Ost und West* (Berlin, 1995).

80 A rites of passage celebration at the age of 14, initially propagated by the SED to rival the Christian confirmation.

81 Paul Betts, 'The Twilight of the Idols: East German Memory and Material Culture', *Journal of Modern History*, 72 (2000), pp. 731–65.

82 Volker Handloik and Harald Hauswird, eds, *Die DDR wird 50* (Berlin, 1998).

83 Eric Canepa, 'Germany's Party of Democratic Socialism', *Socialist Register* (1994), pp. 312–41.

84 Hannah Arendt, *The Human Condition* (Chicago, 1958).

its hopes and disappointments, its achievements and errors, its expectations and its ultimate failure.[85]

Two often mutually incompatible historical memories are still underpinning different identity constructions in East and West Germany at the beginning of the twenty-first century. Take, for example, the 150th anniversary of the German revolution of 1848, which was a major event in both parts of Germany throughout 1998. But where the West primarily commemorated the parliamentary movement focussed on the Paulskirche, the East remembered the social revolution and the fights on the barricades.[86]

In 1999 psychologists alleged that authoritarian personalities had been produced by the GDR-specific socialization in nurseries and kindergardens. Submissiveness, conformity and compliance were rooted in the GDR educational system and allegedly explained the rise of neo-Nazism in East Germany as well as the negative attitudes of many East Germans to parliamentary democracy. Simplistic psychological arguments are, however, as Arnd Bauerkämper has pointed out, a poor replacement for historical analysis. State paternalism in the GDR put a premium on values oriented towards consensus, social harmony and state regulation. Its strength helps to explain the difficulties of East Germans with adapting to the more pluralist, conflictual and liberal character of West German democracy.[87]

Such problems were exacerbated by a reunification process which gave East Germans few opportunities to contribute to the making of a constitutional framework for the new Germany. The new East German *Länder* simply joined the old West German *Länder* and took over the constitution of the old FRG. In 1990 Habermas, among others, argued for a different path towards reunification. He wanted to build the new nation on a new constitution, but the clear majority of those involved in the public debate favoured accession of the GDR to the old FRG. The *Grundgesetz* had, they argued, withstood the test of time and that little could be gained in replacing it with another constitution. That might indeed have been the case, but it left many East Germans feeling as though they had to fit into a cast provided by West Germans. Subsequent problems with system transfer, including an underperforming economy and massive unemployment, could therefore easily translate into anti-Western feeling.[88] But in the medium to long term the chances for a successful integration of East and West Germans still remain good. From the evidence we have surveyed here it seems unlikely that the

[85] Walter Schmidt, 'DDR Geschichtswissenschaft im Umbruch. Leistungen–Grenzen – Probleme', in Rainer Eckert, Wolfgang Küttler and Gustav Seeber, eds, *Krise–Umbruch–Neubeginn. Eine kritische und selbstkritische Dokumentation der DDR-Geschichtswissenschaft 1989/90* (Stuttgart, 1992), p. 175.

[86] Manfred Hettling, 'Die Jagd nach dem demokratischen Anfang: Rückblick auf das Jubiläumsjahr zu 1848', *Geschichte in Wissenschaft und Unterricht*, 51 (2000), pp. 302–12.

[87] Arnd Bauerkämper, 'The Incorporation of a Fragmented Society: Historical Roots of Values in Individuals' Choices after 1989', in Jörn Leonhard and Lothar Funk, eds, *Ten Years of German Unification: Transfer, Transformation, Incorporation?* (Birmingham, 2002), pp. 81–97.

[88] Chris Flockton and Eva Kolinsky, eds, *Recasting East Germany: Social Transformation after the GDR* (London, 1999).

GDR will be reduced to a dirty footnote in German history, as some observers had feared after 1990. It also seems unlikely that the GDR will become the new villain in German history, replacing the National Socialist years in the memory culture of the reunified Germany. A more differentiated approach to the history of the GDR alongside generational change and the increasing bringing into line of living standards in East and West will chip away at the wall in the heads of Germans and contribute to the making of a less divided nation.

The rediscovery of the discourse of victimhood

Germans have not only highlighted their roles as perpetrators of crimes against humanity; they have also rediscovered themselves as victims in their twentieth-century history. If the GDR was effectively a Soviet *homunculus* which only lived through the grace of the Soviet occupying forces and had no deep roots in German history, then the overwhelming majority of East Germans can be presented as victims of a Communist dictatorship alien to indigenous German traditions. Such a perspective is, however, unlikely to gain significant support. The deep involvement of millions of East Germans with the GDR has been too obvious and the continuities of the GDR with some traditions of the German labour movements is too visible. More promising have been renewed attempts to present Germans as victims of total war and its aftermath between 1941 and 1946. In 1992 Joseph Vilsmeier adopted the perspective of the honest, decent, heroic and suffering German soldier in his epic war film, *Stalingrad*. It was a perspective easily recognizable to those familiar with the German war films of the 1950s. The VE day celebrations in 1995 saw the familiar urge of German politicians to present themselves as part of a Germany which had been liberated from Nazism. While Germans may speak of liberation in the sense that it allowed them to develop, over the long term, the kind of civic political culture which resembled the one more deeply rooted in the British and French democracies, the discourse on liberation has to be treated with caution when it deteriorates into a claim that the Germans had been oppressed by the Nazis.

Most recently, the Germans have been imagined as victims of fascism and total war, first, in connection with the Allied bombing war against German civilian targets, and, secondly, in relation to the suffering of German refugees and expellees [Figures 8.2 and 8.3]. The publications of W.G. Sebald and Jörg Friedrich about the impact of aerial bombardment on German civilians were greeted in the German media as though a taboo had been broken at long last.[89] Friedrich's book in particular has described powerfully and in highly emotive terms the death of the German cities and the unbelievable suffering of the people living in these cities. Germans, it was alleged by several reviewers of his book, had somehow been not allowed to talk about their own suffering in the war. Literary historians, such as Volker Hage, or writers, such as Walter Kempowski, pointed out that books about the subject did exist after 1945 and that, if the public discourse was muted, this had much to do with the near-impossibility of narrating

[89] Lothar Kettenacker, ed., *Ein Volk von Opfern? Die neue Debatte um den Bombenkrieg 1940–1945* (Berlin, 2003).

Figure 8.2 Cologne cityscape, 1945, © Rheinisches Bildarchiv Köln. Photo: Karl Hugo Schmölz.

those experiences in book form. They were, however, often contained in personal family narratives, such as diaries or stories told at family gatherings.[90]

The public outcry that a taboo topic was being rediscovered was even more marked over the case of the refugees who fled from the approaching Soviet army and the expellees driven from their homes after 1945 in line with the Potsdam agreement. Ironically it was Günter Grass, the impeccable reunification critic, who kicked off this debate about German victimhood with the publication of a

90 Volker Hage, *Zeugen der Zerstörung: Die Literaten und der Luftkrieg* (Frankfurt/Main, 2003).

Figure 8.3 German refugee trek, 1945, © Bildarchiv Preussischer Kulturbesitz, Berlin. Photo: Vinzenz Engel.

novella entitled *Im Krebsgang* (Walking like a crab). It tells the story of the sinking of the German refugee ship *Wilhelm Gustloff* by a Soviet submarine in January 1945. It also recalls the story of the man after whom the ship was named. But most importantly the book is about the failure of the post-war generation of Germans to bear witness to German suffering in the war. It identifies an alleged taboo topic in German writing about the war and warns that such forgetfulness about German suffering will only haunt the younger generation of Germans and make them more vulnerable to right-wing extremist propaganda. 'History,' Grass formulates, 'more precisely, the history that we are stirring up, is a blocked toilet. We flush and flush, the shit still floats back up.'[91] If such blockage is to be overcome, German crimes and German suffering need to be seen together, according to Grass.

Grass's idea that German suffering represents a blank spot in the German memory of the Second World War is, however, a myth.[92] For the entire 1950s German victims of the war, especially the refugees and expellees, were commemorated far more prominently than the victims of German genocide and warfare. Streets in almost every town and city were named after the 'lost' regions and cities in the east. The *crème de la crème* of German historiography contributed to a multi-volume *Documentation of the Expulsion of Germans from East Central Europe*, which was financed by the government and published between 1954 and 1962. Innumerable memories of the 'lost *Heimat*' in the East were published. Some of the great names of German literature, journalism and history have written about their experience of fleeing from the advancing Red Army or

---

91 Günter Grass, *Im Krebsgang: eine Novelle* (Göttingen, 2002), p. 116.

92 Robert G. Moeller, 'Sinking Ships, the Lost *Heimat* and Broken Taboos: Günter Grass and the Politics of Memory in Contemporary Germany', *Contemporary European History*, 12 (2003), pp. 147–81.

being expelled from their homes: Walter Kempowski, Christa Wolf, Heiner Müller, Siegfried Lenz, Arno Schmidt, Dieter Forte, Leoni Ossowski, Marion Gräfin Dönhoff and Christian von Krockow are just some of the names which come to mind. TV and the cinema picked up the theme with a vengeance, and the very topic of Grass's novella, the sinking of the refugee ship *Wilhelm Gustloff* by a Soviet submarine in 1945 had already been the topic of a popular 1959 movie entitled *Night Fell over Gotenhafen.* Events sponsored by the expellees' organizations brought together hundreds of thousands of Germans in communities of remembrance of the 'lost East' every year. In the 1960s representatives of the refugees and expellees were among the most vociferous opponents of *Ostpolitik*, denouncing Brandt as a national traitor and cheering 'Brandt to the wall'. As *Ostpolitik* became the common sense of German foreign policy in the 1970s and 1980s, the expellees' organizations acquired a whiff of reactionary revanchism in many quarters. But the fate of German refugees and expellees was hardly forgotten even in this period.

Yet Grass undoubtedly hit a nerve in a Germany which spent much of the 1990s convincing itself that it was somehow moving towards a more 'normal' national identity. That normality entailed remembering the suffering of ordinary Germans. There is an uncanny resemblance of the contemporary debates to the ones in the 1950s, when German suffering was compared with and set off against German guilt. However, in contrast to the 1950s, many Germans supporting the memorialization of German suffering at the same time upheld the importance of remembering German guilt. They included many people on the left of the political spectrum. Thus, for example, the interior minister of the red-green government, Otto Schily, speaking at the 1999 meeting of the Association of Expellees (BdV), explicitly criticized the left for ignoring the crimes committed against Germans at the end of the Second World War. He subsequently became one of the main supporters of the idea, launched by the BdV's president, Erika Steinbach, of founding a documentation centre on the expulsions in Berlin. Since *Ostpolitik*, relations between the BdV and the left in the FRG had been virtually non-existent, but in 2003 Schily, a former civil rights lawyer with a record of defending left-wing terrorists in the 1970s, received the Wenzel Jaksch medal from the BdV. Other leading Social Democrats, including Peter Glotz, began supporting the idea of a documentation centre. Even Chancellor Schröder, who, following massive protests from within and without Germany, eventually declared himself against a documentation centre in Berlin at the present time, had come to celebrate the 50th anniversary of the expellees' charter in 2000. As for the planned centre, its future is uncertain. It could perhaps not be located in Berlin at all; there have been powerful voices arguing for such a centre to be located in Poland, which saw some of the greatest population movements between 1939 and 1946. Or the documentation centre might never come into existence. The minister in the chancellor's office responsible for culture and media, Christina Weiss, has argued compellingly that it would make more sense to network the many existing local initiatives in Europe commemorating the fate of refugees and expellees from diverse nations.[93]

[93] Christina Weiss, 'Niemand will vergessen', *Die Zeit*, 41 (2003).

It is impossible to deny that the decision of the Allies, reached at the Potsdam conference, to expatriate by means of force 12 to 15 million Germans from east-central Europe was a great crime. Hence some kind of initiative documenting the plight of the refugees would seem appropriate, especially given the continued topicality of refugees and expellees in the context of ongoing global and civil wars. However, as Götz Aly has pointed out, any such centre would have to document the vital link between the Holocaust and the expulsion of Germans, both of which were part and parcel of a wider history of enforced migration instigated by the Nazis in the Second World War.[94] In this way any simplistic and false comparisons between the fate of European Jewry and the fate of ethnic Germans from east-central Europe can be avoided. It will be one of the most difficult tasks for the contemporary memory culture in Germany to discuss, side by side, the contemporaneity of German suffering and German crimes. Walter Kempowski's massive collage entitled *Echolot* might indicate how this could be achieved. Thousands of pages in eight volumes contain largely autobiographical material, letters, family memorabilia, photographs, pasted together without comment, documenting 'the dailyness of life in war-time Germany'.[95] The reader is confronted with a cacophony of voices telling stories of loss and suffering from diverse perspectives. Just to give one example. Around the time the *Wilhelm Gustloff* sank and thousands of helpless German civilians drowned, close by, on the shores of Eastern Prussia, the death march of thousands of remaining inmates from the concentration camp Studthoff ended with their SS guards shooting them in the surf of the Baltic sea. Bringing these kinds of events together in the memorialization of the twentieth-century German past without fostering apologias for the unrivalled criminal energies of Nazi Germany will be the real challenge for the twenty-first century.

[94] Götz Aly, 'Europas Selbstzerstörung', *Süddeutsche Zeitung*, 24 July 2003.
[95] Peter Fritzsche, 'Walter Kempowski's Collection', *Central European History*, 35 (2002), pp. 257–67. See also www.kempowski.de

Conclusion: Reinventing Germany for the twenty-first century

The diverse reinventions of Germany after 1990 bore all the hallmarks of the old West German controversies about national history and national identity. National Socialism was still at the heart of many identity debates. Anti-Communism was, if anything, more vigorous than before. Constitutional patriotism, Westernization and Germany's role in international politics were heavily discussed, but the participants were rehearsing arguments which bore a strong resemblance to the ones put forward (often by the same people) a decade earlier. Overall the continuities between the Bonn and the Berlin republics have been considerable – not only in the area of national identity debates. Reinventing Germany in the 1990s has not ended with the triumph of a narrow nationalism, as some observers feared at the beginning of the decade. True, the emergence of an intellectual new right in the first half of the 1990s was worrying, as has been the rise of xenophobia, racist violence and antisemitism. Calls for Germany to return to a more independent power politics, attempts to rewrite the history of the FRG in a more negative way and the renaissance of a discourse of German victimhood have all raised serious questions about the future direction of the German nation state. Furthermore, West German elites often showed little concern for the sentiments of East Germans after 1990, riding roughshod over East German identities. Unsurprisingly, the gulf between the two halves of the reunified country has grown rather than diminished over the past decade.

But the ongoing reinvention of Germany after reunification gives also ground for hope. Official nationalism has been extremely modest and the political system has been extraordinarily stable. Germany is a democratic republic with one of the most liberal constitutional frameworks in Europe. The history of the old Federal Republic is seen by the vast majority of West Germans as a remarkable success story. East German regional identity will grow weaker in the medium term, as the memory of the GDR will grow more distant for a new generation of East Germans. The reunified Germany remains safely anchored in European and North Atlantic treaty organizations and has avoided all attempts at a renewed national *Sonderweg*. Anti-Western, antipluralist and antiparliamentary definitions of the nation – so popular in Germany before 1945 – have found few supporters after 1990. In dealing with the National Socialist past, despite many mistakes and shortcomings, Germans have been setting international standards for attempts to come to terms with dictatorial regimes.

This book's topic has been the ongoing, contested and open-ended construction, deconstruction and reconstruction of national identities in the German lands. The many threads of this story cannot be drawn together neatly, not least because they have been and continue to be woven together in different ways. The next pieces of knitwear are being produced as I am writing this last chapter, and I have tried to indicate its colours and textures as best as I can. However, many of the materials and weaving techniques used in the process have remained remarkably stable over the last centuries. Some of them we have encountered in almost every chapter of this book. Federal constructions of the nation, for example, have had a continued popularity in Germany – despite the attempts of the Nazi and Communist dictatorships to tone down their significance. *Heimat* could refer to locality, region and nation. In fact it frequently combined references to all three in a complex web of meaning in which the nation acquired its attractiveness through its close association with the narratives of *Heimat*. Territorially it has been notoriously difficult to define Germany. The nation state changed its geographical shape and meaning radically throughout the last two centuries, but the idea of *Heimat* remained popular in Germany even when many West Germans had become more sceptical of the nation in the 1970s and 1980s.

Inventions of Germany have also been highly gendered affairs throughout. Nations have regularly been imagined as families. Women were allocated important roles for the well-being of Germany: they had to bear and rear the next generation on whose shoulders the fortune of the nation was going to rest. Nations were symbolized by female figures, such as Germania. But women were not equal to men when it came to the affairs of the nation state. The male idea of 'separate spheres' for men and women reserved certain areas, such as politics, economics, war, and in general all public affairs of the state for men and banished women to the household and the family. The domestic virtues of Queen Luise of Prussia became a model for patriotic women well into the twentieth century. By contrast, the patriotic women who fought in the wars of liberty and on the barricades in 1848 were long excluded from the national pantheon on the grounds that their behaviour did not fit the gendered patterns of the national imagination. Men therefore often constructed the nation in ways which excluded women from citizenship. But women, as we have seen, claimed their own belonging to the nation as a means to demand greater participation in the affairs of the nation state. They refused to be mere objects of the national discourse, but participated strongly in inventions of the nation. Thus, for example, they constructed maternalism as national duty and built up mythologies of the superiority of the German housewife over housewives of other nations. They fought for national cohesion and against foreign influences in many of the nationalist mass organizations in Imperial Germany and beyond. The First World War formed a major watershed in incorporating women into the nation state and giving them crucial rights, including the vote. The comprehensive biologization of the nation under the Nazis sought to rout the discourse of emancipation. Women were rigorously excluded from the public sphere, but allocated an important place in the construction of the racial nation. After 1945 the Communist promises of emancipation produced important new opportunities for women but these were linked to the economic interests of the SED regime and did little to overcome traditional perceptions of gender roles. In the West the redomestication of women after 1945 was the most important strategy for re-empowering male definitions of the nation. It was only from the 1970s onwards that political emancipation was accompanied with measures which aimed at ending a whole string of discriminatory practices still directed at women.

Constructions of the nation relied heavily on the simultaneous construction of 'others' who were excluded from the nation. They could be 'foreigners', such as, in the German case, Slavs and the French. Under National Socialism the Slav 'other' was declared 'subhuman' and Slav populations were targeted either for extermination or for becoming slave labourers to the German master race. Even in the two German states after 1949, despite official rhetoric of international reconciliation and good neighbourly relations, we encountered strong sentiments against 'foreign' others, in particular guest workers, non-whites and asylum seekers. But the national 'other' could also come from within the German collective, and here our attention has been focussed on Jews and socialists in particular. The history of the Jews in nineteenth-century Germany is a success story of the gradual emancipation and integration into the German national community. On the eve of the First World War many Jews felt themselves entirely German, but the signs of a nasty subcurrent of antisemitism never vanished entirely. The Nazis' antisemitism ended in the attempt to murder European Jewry in its entirety. After 1945, the Holocaust would stand as a lasting chasm between the few remaining Jews in Germany and the rest of the nation's population.

Socialists had been dubbed 'fellows without a fatherland' by Bismarck in the 1870s and the period of persecution under the Anti-Socialist Laws left a lasting legacy of alienation from the nation which could only slowly be overcome in the *Kaiserreich*. However, socialists were rarely antinationalists, and, for the most part, championed democratic and participatory forms of national identity which still had the power, at certain times and places (e.g. the First World War) to deteriorate into ethnic nationalism and xenophobia. Their nationalization incorporated precisely those notions of a 'foreign' other which has been such a constitutive element of all national identity discourses.

The 'foreign' could, however, also be a model to emulate and to adapt. Cultural and political transfer was of major importance to the diverse inventions and reinventions of Germany throughout the nineteenth and twentieth centuries. The very idea of the modern nation was an import from the United States and France. The nineteenth century in particular saw heated debates about the applicability of the British constitutional model to German circumstances. Ultimately, as we have seen, the idea of the German 'special path' (*Sonderweg*) was an important ideological barrier against the progress of Western political and cultural ideas in the German lands. This only began to change in the FRG from the 1960s onwards. But, with the massive improvements in transport and communication which occurred throughout the last two centuries, the knowledge about 'foreign' models increased, as national governments strove to adopt what, now, is known as 'best practice'. Networks of experts, increasingly organized in a transnational way, sought to transfer what they regarded as 'best practice', so as to improve and strengthen 'their' particular nation state. Yet, as we have seen time and time again, what could be transferred and adapted depended crucially on the power relationships and material incentives which structured the national framework.

Religion had a major impact on the making and remaking of German identities. The Reformation of the sixteenth and the religious wars of the seventeenth centuries marked major watersheds for diverse constructions of Germanness. Many chapters in this book discuss the close links between Protestantism and nationalism from the late eighteenth century onwards. Catholics developed their own constructions of the nation, but, viewed from the Protestant perspective, Catholics had a dual loyalty to Rome and to the nation and were therefore at best unreliable patriots. The exclusion of Catholics from the nation culminated in the *Kulturkampf* in the 1860s. Its legacy could only slowly be overcome in Imperial Germany, and Catholic and Protestant constructions of the nation retained significant differences almost throughout the twentieth century. The foundation of the CDU after the Second World War marked an important point of departure for the integration of political Catholicism into the mainstream of German politics and society. With secularization impacting deeply on the two Germanies from the 1950s onwards, religious definitions of the nation became less important (especially in the GDR), but, as the debate about Turkey's entry into the EU has shown, Christian self-definitions still play an important role in keeping the Islamic 'other' before the gates of Europe at the beginning of the twenty-first century.

Finally, wars were crucial catalysts for many reinventions of Germany: the Thirty Years' War in the seventeenth century, the Seven Years' War in the eighteenth century, the Napoleonic wars and the Franco-Prussian war in the nineteenth century and the two world wars in the twentieth century. In modern warfare the mobilization of national sentiment was crucial to ensure maximum homogeneity and effort of those who had to fight the war. The Napoleonic wars gave German nationalism its strong anti-French direction, which was confirmed by the Franco-Prussian war. The latter brought about what the former had not been able to achieve: a unified German nation state along small-German, i.e. Prussian lines. The German nation had been created, in Bismarck's famous words, by 'blood and iron', and the idealization of the military in German society had much to do with the military's key role in bringing into existence the German nation. Prussian militarism became a byword for Germanness in many parts of Europe (and Germany) before 1914. The First World War brought a radicalization of the concept of the nation under the heading of the *Volksgemeinschaft*. The National Socialist racial nation was to have a lasting impact on national identity debates in Germany. Having been responsible for two world wars and genocide in the first half of the twentieth century, the Prussian Germany vanished for forty years. When the world was just getting used to two Germanies (and an independent Austria), the revolution of 1989 produced another unified Germany, which was, however, despite initial fears to the contrary, far removed from its Prussian past.

What, then, have been the patterns of development of the German national imagination from the late eighteenth century to the present time? Four major temporal watersheds in the ongoing construction of Germanness can be identified: around 1750, 1871, 1914 and the 1960s. Ideas about the German nation can be traced back a long way to medieval and early modern times. We have seen that some of these ideas had a remarkable continuity over several centuries, e.g. the enmity towards France as national 'other', the idea of the nation as family writ large, the idea of the warrior nation complete with the glorification of death for the fatherland and the *Reich* nation. Until the eighteenth century those who imagined themselves as part of the nation were tightly restricted in terms of numbers: nobility, clerics, highly educated intellectuals and city burghers. What happened between 1750 and 1850 was a qualitative sea change in the meaning of the word nation. It was now meant to incorporate theoretically all members of a given national community who were supposed to have equal rights and duties as citizens. The national idea promised inclusion and participation, but right from the beginning it was also always about exclusion. Thus, for example, national belonging defined citizenship, but the latter often excluded those without property and education, and, of course, women. The gendering of the national discourse and the divisions between a liberal and a democratic national discourse indicated that the national idea was about empowerment and limitations of empowerment.

Those who did much of the imagining in the eighteenth and early nineteenth centuries were members of the new middle classes who felt unrepresented in the traditional social order. The national idea was meant to overcome feudalism and legitimate the new bourgeois and capitalist order. Once again it was to empower those who felt that they should have more of a say over questions of politics and government. Unsurprisingly many liberal nationalists initially welcomed the French revolution of 1789, but their celebrations soon turned to despair. The universal Enlightenment values of liberty and national unity had been drowned in blood, it seemed, and the German nationalists' answer to the French revolution was a decisive turn towards history and culture. The search for a German nation was justified because of specifically German traditions of liberty rooted in the past, the language, the geography, the climate and the culture of the Germans. The wars of liberty against Napoleonic France boosted national sentiment – especially among the young, but the national movement was not yet a mass movement. In the 1800s its apostle, Friedrich Ludwig Jahn, would still have been regarded as a crank by respectable society in the German lands.

The minority who championed the national idea in the early nineteenth century had to come up against one key problem: the weakness of the central state. The Holy Roman Empire before 1806 and the German Confederation after 1815 were loose confederations of quasi-autonomous states with weak central institutions of government. In the post-Napoleonic Confederation state-building processes were strongest at the territorial level of the states rather than at the centre. German nationalists, unable to draw upon the resources of a strong central state, built civic associations in which they practised new forms of sociability and celebrated a new festival culture in the search for a stronger, more powerful and more liberal nation state. Their search for national symbols focussed on historical monuments, such as the Cologne dome and the Wartburg, and their desire for national heroes gave birth to the Luther and Schiller cults of the nineteenth century. The revolution of 1848 was their greatest opportunity to bring about a more liberal and more unified nation state. 1848 brought the lasting constitutionalization of politics in the German lands. It also brought claims for greater inclusivity from women, workers and Jews. But it failed to bring about a strong central state. Territorial definitions of Germany in and after the revolution remained as contested and vague as they had been before.

The majority of nationalists were 'greater German'. They hoped to incorporate the German-speaking parts of the Austrian-Hungarian empire into the future German state. Some North-German, in particular Prussian, liberal nationalists, however, thought a 'small-German' option more realistic. They construed a historical mission of Prussia to unite Germany and they could point to the commitment of the Habsburgs to the empire which was indeed difficult to square with the construction of a more unified German state. In the 'third Germany', the territories outside the Habsburg Empire and Prussia, many feared and rejected Prussian dominance. They were in favour of a process of unification which would respect the strong independence of the territorial states in the German Confederation. 1871 marked the victory of the 'small-Germans', although they had to make considerable concessions to the wishes of the 'third German' forces. Unity was achieved on the basis of three wars and its main architect was a well-known conservative Junker, Otto von Bismarck. In 1848 he had been the sworn enemy of liberal nationalist forces. But the revolution of 1848 also marked the point when conservatives realized that they ignored the mobilizing power of nationalism at their peril. Henceforth conservatives were to mould their own version of nationalism, which emphasized loyalty to dynastic principle and the feudal order. They appropriated the language of the nation for their own purposes. Bismarck came round to the opinion that it was better to put himself and Prussia at the helm of the national movement rather than oppose it outright. By doing this he hoped to shape the nation state in Prussia's image. Its economic and military might was, in any case, unparalleled elsewhere.

1871 therefore marked the second major watershed in the development of German nationalism. After 1871 the question of geography had been settled and nationalism was now being driven by the state and from within a strong civil society. Both complemented each other in their efforts to 'make Germans' in the *Kaiserreich*. Statism and antipluralism became the cornerstones of the emerging official construction of the nation. Notions of internal and external enemies were very important for these attempts to build the nation. The 'hereditary enemy' France, perfidious Albion and the Slav people as well as Jews, Catholics and Socialists were all regarded with suspicion and hostility. The internal enemies, far from being 'fellows without a fatherland', constructed their own versions of Germanness in which they negotiated their separateness from the official nationalism and sought alternative concepts of the nation which would allow them to be part of the national community. Social and democratic images of the nation were, for example, championed by the SPD who looked sceptically upon medieval *Reich* and emperor mythologies and the ongoing militarization of civilian society.

Above all, it was the economic success of the new Germany under Prussian leadership which facilitated its acceptance – especially in those regions which had not been too happy with Prussian dominance (and frequently Prussian occupation after 1866). The myth of the customs union as birthplace of German unity and German industrial might strengthened economic national identities in the *Kaiserreich*. But around the turn of the century the optimism of those predicting a glorious future for the new nation was paralleled by the pessimism and cultural despair of those who somehow felt unhappy with the prevalent ideas of modernity and progress. Germany became a Jekyll and Hyde nation: the dynamic, self-confident and optimistic side stood uneasily next to deep-seated cultural pessimism and self-doubts. The German elites' often aggressive search for the nation's 'place under the sun' in foreign and colonial policies was a sure sign of their uncertainty about Germany's status as a nation. The influx of Social Darwinist ideas contributed to the ethnicization of more traditional historical-cultural definitions of Germanness, although racial nationalism remained a marginal phenomenon in Imperial Germany. Particularist identities remained strong, and the national continued to be imagined through the idioms of the local and the regional. *Heimat* discourses negotiated the desires of the people with the demands of the new state. But, over more than forty years, and starting from relatively weak foundations, Imperial Germany was successful (certainly more successful than the other latecomer in nation-building, Italy) in its undertaking to 'make Germans' – despite its difficulties with developing binding national symbols and despite the ongoing contestedness of definitions of Germanness.

How successful Imperial Germany had been was impressively underlined by the Social Democrats' willingness to defend the *Reich* against separatist and foreign forces at the end of the First World War. The lost war, the revolution of 1918/19 leading to the setting up of a parliamentary republic, and the peace treaty of Versailles, which was perceived as a national humiliation by almost everyone in the German lands, marked the third major watershed in the national imagination. The complex mythologies of the First World War, the 'August experience', the 'ideas of 1914' and the 'community of the trenches' gave rise to the concept of the 'people's community' (*Volksgemeinschaft*). Racialized notions of the people's nation now rivalled and mingled with traditional statist ideas of Germany. The advocates of the *Volksgemeinschaft* ideal, in particular the representatives of the conservative revolution, positioned themselves in opposition to the republican nation. The latter's pluralist understanding of the nation and its interest politics made it deeply suspicious to those who preached the (racial) unity of the nation. Furthermore the republic was seen as the result of an unwanted revolution and it was made responsible for the loss of the war and the series of economic disasters which befell Germany in the inter-war period. Overall the national imagination in the Weimar Republic became deeply pillarized. Communist, republican and right-wing definitions of the nation were not without overlaps, but ultimately they were mutually exclusive. The right's success in capturing the wider national imagination contributed significantly to the rise of National Socialism.

The Nazis made the 'racial nation' into the key political religion of the Third Reich. They comprehensively biologized the nation and ruthlessly excluded and exterminated its alleged enemies, in particular the Jews. The Holocaust marked the moment when nineteenth-century dreams of a German-Jewish symbiosis were shattered. Race, war and struggle were of central importance to the Nazi imagination of the nation which left a deep impact on wider German society. Racial nationalism was not the preserve of the SS or a few mad and fanatic Nazis; racial nationalism entered the very pores of German society and influenced much everyday behaviour of Germans in the Third Reich. However, even during the darkest years of German nationalism, 'other Germanies' were being constructed by the opposition to Nazism – national-conservative, republican and Communist alternatives to the racial nation were put forward by those in exile and those opposing Nazism within Germany.

Their ideas were to have significant influence on the future shape of the two Germanies which were eventually to rise from the ashes of National Socialism as the result of the ensuing Cold War. The predominant national feeling in the West was self-pity. Coming to terms with German suffering in the war left hardly any room for the memory of the millions of German victims in that war. Germany itself was frequently imagined as victim of Hitler, as if the Nazis had nothing to do with German national history. Their racism was juxtaposed to an allegedly good German nationalism, represented, above all, by the national-conservative opposition to Hitler. The demonization of the dictator went hand in hand with the search for untainted national traditions. Complete silence about the National Socialist past was impossible after 1945, but West Germans were highly selective in their appropriation of that past.

National Socialism was widely interpreted as a totalitarian dictatorship – on a level with the Communist dictatorship in East Germany. Anti-Communism was in fact the most important ideological bridge between National Socialism and the post-war Federal Republic. If the national imagination was in need of a complete overhaul after 1945, at least West Germans could be reassured that their anti-Communism had been justified all along. Goebbels's tirades against 'Asian subhuman Bolshevism' still informed the extraordinary hostility against Communists in the early FRG. Unlike after the First World War, however, the Germans were not left to their own devices. The Allies, convinced of a deep-seated flaw in the German national character, initiated a variety of re-education programmes, which aimed at helping Germans to reimagine their nation in democratic and civil terms. Such Allied reinventions of Germany were widely rejected by Germans, but they were not without a longer-term impact. A new West German elite turned towards the project of Europe with a vengeance. They reinvented themselves as model Europeans in a bid to become accepted again in the wider community of nations. The repression of any signs of neo-Nazism combined with the 'economic miracle' were the prime conditions under which the medium-term Westernization of the FRG could be successful. Former Nazis were smoothly integrated into the democratic nation as long as they showed themselves willing converts to the new nation and its liberal-democratic ideals. The economic success of the FRG strengthened traditionally strong economic identities and helped along democratic learning processes.

Around the decade of the 1960s I would therefore locate the fourth (and to date final) important watershed in the national imagination. Over the post-war decades the German imagination had moved from firm anti-Western roots to staunch pro-Western sentiments. France, Britain and the USA were the most important political, economic and military partners of the FRG, and various cultural exchange programmes sought to cement the Western intellectual orientation of West Germany. Following *Ostpolitik*, the West German governments extended their hand of co-operation and dialogue to Eastern Europe seeking to overcome centuries of prejudice against the Slav people. The eventual absence of major external enemies went hand in hand with the commitment to democratizing all areas of society – something foregrounded by the Brandt government of 1969. Over the next two decades the Bismarckian Germany of 1871 was increasingly imagined as a failed nation. On the left demands for a postnational consciousness of West Germans prompted major debates about history and national identity in the 1980s. By 1989 the idea of reunification seemed at best a distant and unrealistic prospect for the long-term future.

The GDR seemed to have established itself as 'the second German state', and the idea of accepting the GDR citizenship became more and more popular. Some left liberals even demanded dropping the preamble of the Basic Law calling on all West German governments to seek, first and foremost, reunification of the fatherland. The relationship between the two German states seemed to have moved a long way from the harsh anti-Communism of the early 1950s. But, as the events in the autumn of 1989 were to demonstrate, the appearance of stability was hollow. The claims of the GDR to represent the 'better Germany' were not borne out by the perception of its people.

Initially the GDR appeared to make the more promising break with the National Socialist past. It denazified society more effectively and was more explicitly antifascist and anticapitalist. It self-consciously set about building an entirely different nation which was supposed to have learnt the lessons of the past. Yet the Communist national imagination always lacked democratic legitimacy. It could only establish itself with the help of the Soviet occupants and dictatorial means. From the 1950s onwards the Sovietization of its structures was considerable, but the cultural processes of Sovietization, in stark contrast to the Westernization of the FRG, went only skin-deep. The GDR eventually managed to come to an uneasy and tacit understanding with large sections of the population on the basis of a paternalist welfare state and the promises of steady and equal increases in prosperity. But endurance of the Communist regime was always more widespread than positive commitment to its values and ideals. The FRG remained the constant 'other' in the GDR's national imagination, especially in the economic sphere. The appeal of the 'golden West' to ordinary GDR citizens reflected the failure of Communist East Germany to satisfy their citizens as consumers.

By the early 1970s, under the impact of *Ostpolitik*, the illusory commitment of the Communist GDR to German reunification under Communist auspices eventually gave way to the idea of two emerging German nation states – one capitalist and one Communist. But the theory of the two Germanies remained unrealistic as long as the majority of the GDR citizens remained oriented towards West Germany. The 'socialist nation' could not hope to compete with its capitalist rival economically, and it continued to lack the democratic legitimacy that the parliamentary democracy in the West had. When the GDR eventually collapsed in 1989, the refusal of the USSR to back up its ally, economic failure and demands for democratization of the political sphere all played a major role. The nation only came into play, when the prospect of reunification brought the promise of a consumer revolution which the East Germans had watched for so long from the sidelines.

One of the biggest difficulties with the reunification process after 1990 was that West Germans had been far less concerned with the GDR than East Germans with the FRG. West Germans (often reluctantly) transferred massive amounts of money to help rebuild the East, but they also (often arrogantly) expected gratitude and demanded submission under the West German system. They rigorously exchanged the old GDR elites with West Germans in virtually all areas (with the exceptions of the police and the school teachers), with the result that many East Germans experienced reunification as humiliation. The perception of a reunification crisis contributed to the revival of the national discourse in the 1990s. The project of rethinking the nation took a variety of different forms: on the left many moved from postnationalism to the explicit endorsement of a Westernized nation. Liberal conservatives, by contrast, tended to denounce constitutional patriotism as 'bloodless' and demand the revival of more traditional forms of national identity. The return to the nation was preached most aggressively by the new right in the first half of the 1990s, but it failed to make an intellectual breakthrough. Extreme nationalism in Germany today remains the preserve of a neo-Nazi fringe which can draw on levels of xenophobia which are no higher in West Germany than in other West European societies.

At the beginning of the twenty-first century German soldiers are fighting wars again and acting as international peacekeepers in a variety of countries around the world. Over the second Iraq war, the German government, to much acclaim from within the German population, chose to oppose the Anglo-American alliance and sided with France to plead for more time and UN-backed action. Arguably Germany is in the process of developing a more proactive, interventionist and independent foreign policy, something that would have been difficult to imagine before 1990. And yet the reunified Germany remains firmly located in its alliance systems of the European Union and NATO. There are few signs of Germany wanting to flex its muscle either inside or outside these organizations. The discourse of good neighbourliness and partnership continues to be dominant in the country's foreign policy. The revival of totalitarian theories and of anti-Communism in some ways mark a return to the 1950s, but, of course, anti-Communism can no longer create an 'other' in the present, as there are no Communist regimes in Europe left. What anti-Communism has done very effectively is that it delegitimated the GDR and its elites. It was an important tool in restructuring the GDR, but it also contributed in a major way to the humiliation of tens of thousands of East Germans, something which continues to haunt domestic German politics today. The new discourse of Germany as a victim of the Second World War harked back to images of the 1950s, but, once again, this cannot be described as a straightforward return, as it now takes place through the prism of the period from the 1960s to the 1980s. During those decades substantial progress was made in working through the Nazi past, and many Germans today feel that it is justifiable to talk about German victims and German suffering without necessarily being accused of relativizing German guilt and crimes. The majority of Germans today fully accept the historical guilt of the Holocaust and the criminal energies of the

Nazi regime. And it is precisely because they recognize their special responsibility arising from these crimes that they feel that Germany can be a more self-confident nation again and talk about its own suffering and losses.

Whilst this is a soothing thought, and whilst Europe and the wider world has nothing to fear from Germany's democratic elites, it does raise the question whether talk about a renewed national normality is sensible. Not only will it always be problematic to talk about national normality in a post-Holocaust Germany; it also is an illusion that anything even remotely resembling national normality exists anywhere else in the world. I sincerely hope that this book will help towards a better understanding of why any such assumptions of normality are absurd when they concern such a context-dependent, complex and multifaceted concept as national identity. The many fundamental breaks and ruptures in the construction of Germany should remind us of the artificiality of all constructions of national traditions and histories.

Index